# Media Access

## Social and Psychological Dimensions of New Technology Use

# LEA's Communication Series

*Jennings Bryant/Dolf Zillmann, General Editors*

For a complete list of titles in LEA's Communication Series, please contact Lawrence Erlbaum Associates, Publishers, at www.erlbaum.com.

# Media Access

## Social and Psychological Dimensions of New Technology Use

Edited by

**ERIK P. BUCY**
*Indiana University, Bloomington*

**JOHN E. NEWHAGEN**
*University of Maryland, College Park*

**LEA**
**2004**

LAWRENCE ERLBAUM ASSOCIATES, PUBLISHERS
Mahwah, New Jersey
London

Lawrence Erlbaum Associates, Inc., Publishers
10 Industrial Avenue
Mahwah, NJ 07430

Cover design by Sean Sciarrone

**Library of Congress Cataloging-in-Publication Data**
Media access : social and psychological dimensions of new technology use/
edited by Erik P. Bucy and John E. Newhagen.
p. cm.
Includes bibliographical references and index.
ISBN 0-8058-4109-1—ISBN 0-8058-4110-5 (pbk.)
1. Mass media–Computer network resources.   2. Internet.   3. Mass media
and technology.   4. Mass media–Psychological aspects.   5. Mass media–Social
aspects.   I. Bucy, Erik P. 1963–   II. Newhagen, John E.

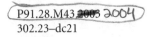
P91.28.M43 2003 2004
302.23–dc21                                          2003045400

Books published by Lawrence Erlbaum Associates are printed on
acid-free paper, and their bindings are chosen for strength and durability.

Printed in the United States of America
10  9  8  7  6  5  4  3  2  1

This book is dedicated to the memory of Steven H. Chaffee,
who taught us the importance of concept explication
and the disciplined use of words.

# Contents

# Preface:
# The New Thinking About
# Media Access

Relatively early in the Internet's widespread diffusion into society, it became clear that full access to new communication technologies implied more than network connectivity, hardware availability, and other technical considerations that were too frequently the focus of policy discussions. As Newhagen observed in a dialogue with Rafaeli (Newhagen & Rafaeli, 1996), "the Net engages users in cognitively effortful tasks and challenges them to be active" in ways mass media do not (p. 12). As such, it becomes important to ask what effect variable cognitive skills, such as the ability to process content or perform searches, have on the ability to exploit the Internet's potential. Equally important are the social and cultural factors that may constrain new technology adoption and use—particularly in disadvantaged communities. The problem of access, then, depends not only on the user's educational and economic background, but also on his or her social, cultural, and psychological characteristics.

The chapters of *Media Access: Social and Psychological Dimensions of New Technology Use* depart from popular understandings of new technology use by recognizing that a distinction can be made between having access to the Internet as a technology and being able to access the content that resides on it. The idea that physical access to a computer is sufficient to enable Internet use, however, seems to dominate the thinking of many policymakers looking for simple or immediate solutions. The Internet has taken hold as a major communications medium: An estimated 50% to 60% of all U.S. households are now connected (NTIA, 2002). Yet there are indications that adoption has reached a plateau, with some new users opting out of the cyberworld after a period of initial, frustrating use (see chapter 5, this volume). This seems odd because the conventional wisdom has it that once a new medium, such as television, gains general acceptance, the only important barrier to access is the cost of the physical apparatus. This view seemed valid through the 1980s and 1990s when personal computers cost several thousand dollars and monthly Internet access fees were introduced as an added expense. However, that economic barrier has been brought down with powerful computers now being sold at about the same price as a good television and a broadband Internet connection pegged at about the same price as a cable TV subscription. But the audience for online content is fickle. Despite its popularity, the Internet does not appear to be an economically self-sustaining medium in the sense that mass media such as television and newspapers are. We suspect this may have more to do with the user's ability to benefit from content than physical access to technology.

Perhaps more interesting than the *economic* issues associated with the Web's development and use is the *cognitive* cost of access to the user. Unlike traditional media, the Internet confronts the user with communication opportunities across a wide range of levels (e.g., interpersonal, group, organizational, mass) all at the same time—and frequently on the same screen (see chapter 3, this volume). Online, the user enters a *decision-intensive* environment. Even when the Internet is used as a mass medium, the experience differs significantly from old media because of the technical competence and literacy level required. Simply put, the Internet presents cognitive barriers that traditional mass media do not. Further confounding the problem, those barriers may be driven by factors within the user's social and cultural milieu.

## POLITICIZING THE DIGITAL DIVIDE

Without the requisite training and motivation, a significant portion of the population may get left behind—socially, economically, and perhaps politically—not because they lack interest in the Internet, but because they do not have the appropriate skills, information processing ability, or self-confidence necessary to hold their own in cyberspace. If research bears this out, then the digital divide—uneven access to new information technology based on education, income, gender, geography, and other demographic characteristics (NTIA, 1998)—may be much larger and persistent than originally anticipated. This argument becomes especially salient in light of important shifts in Internet access policy being pursued by the George W. Bush administration. The president has cited data showing Internet use among African Americans increasing at a faster pace than for Whites (Eunjung Cha, 2002). Bush seized on findings from two studies—a UCLA report showing a decreasing gap in online access when education is taken into account, and a government report showing the gap disappearing between urban and rural users—to reduce funding for two key programs addressing the problem. The targeted programs include the Education Department's Community Technology Centers program, which funds computer labs for after-school and adult education use, and the Commerce Department's Technology Opportunities Program, which assists local groups with the installation of computer networks (Eunjung Cha, 2002).

Critics of the move were quick to point out that neither study took a deeper look at the underlying causes for the digital divide, charging that important disparities in new technology use still exist and may be very difficult to eradicate. The work presented in this volume takes a similar tack. If the Internet is truly a new technology and not just an extension of mass media, then it stands to reason that the factors governing its use will also be unique. The chapters presented here call attention to a host of social, cultural, and psychological factors that may limit Internet use to a level well below the almost complete level of household saturation achieved by television. If such a plateau is reached, then the policy question concerning just what an acceptable level of Internet diffusion is has to be addressed. Say, for example, the diffusion curve breaks off at an asymptote that leaves 35% of the population behind as nonusers. The social and political ramifications could be considerable. At a political level, the quick fix for such a problem appears simple on its surface: Simply carpet-bomb those geographic and demographic regions found to be wanting with Internet-ready computers. However, as the chapters in this collection of original studies and essays point out, the barriers to access for that last group of nonusers are likely to be both subtle and stubborn.

Consequently, the contributors to *Media Access* are less concerned about access to technology per se than the skills and motivations necessary to derive meaning and value from the content conveyed by the technology. The three major sections of this book—on the psychological dimensions of media access, the social and cultural dimensions of media access, and media access to the public sphere—flow from this broadened notion of access.

## EXPANDING CONCEPTUALIZATIONS OF ACCESS

Reconceptualized as a multidimensional construct, media access has consequences at both the individual and social levels of analysis. At the individual level, cognitive access concerns the ability to effectively cope with and benefit from informational and technological complexity. Successful navigation and message processing may result in learning, knowledge gain, heightened efficacy, emotional satisfaction, and a multitude of other beneficial outcomes. Applied to different spheres of influence (e.g., economic, political, cultural), media access may enable those groups best positioned to benefit from technology to apply information and experiences gleaned from the mediated world to important aspects of their lives. At the top of the heap are the "digerati" (Brockman, 1996), members of a digital or cyber elite who are distinguished not so much by their financial position as by the technical and cognitive resources they wield to secure an advantageous position over members of the information underclass (see Adler, 1995). Lower in the techno-socio hierarchy are those who do not have the skills and motivation to effectively navigate complex information spaces and who may find the experience off-putting, abandon the enterprise altogether, or decide never to adopt. The prospect of a society bifurcated by information technology—one group running computers, the other largely oblivious to their influence—stands in sharp contrast to the very notion of an egalitarian, opportunity-filled society at the core of liberal democratic ideals.

At a social level, media access may be determined by factors within the user's community that delineate the relative importance and social value of new information and communication technologies. In this regard, citizens in highly developed regions enjoy a comparative advantage over people in underdeveloped and economically depressed areas. Yet, media access may still vary widely *within* a particular region or community (East Palo Alto, California, a depressed community in the heart of Silicon Valley, is a prime example). Over time, media access may thus prove to be a more vexing issue than discussions about the digital divide generally acknowledge because full access demands a level of know-how, technical competence, motivation, and cognitive ability that will be difficult for many citizens, even of advanced industrialized nations, to achieve.

Although the term *media access* is not new,[1] debates over information and communication technology use have received renewed attention because of the Internet. Advocates of cyber society, with growing frequency and force, have applauded the democratizing potential of the Internet, noting its capacity to facilitate civic discussion and online activism as well as foster community among, and distribute news and information to, a rapidly growing mass audience (e.g., Grossman, 1995; Hill & Hughes, 1998; Rheingold, 2000). The relative expertise and costs associated with using the Internet has led to a concern, however, about technological inequality and civic participation rates among digital haves and have-nots (van Dijk, 1999; Wilhelm, 2003). Rather than engendering broad democratic participation and equalizing information differences between citizens at opposite ends of the socioeconomic spectrum, the Internet, as with traditional mass media, may instead exacerbate existing knowledge disparities and further marginalize disadvantaged groups from the center of society.

Concern about a widening knowledge gap is not unique to online media and surfaced when other communication technologies were new (Tichenor, Donohue, & Olien, 1970). But the Internet raises questions about information benefits as well as the social, psychological, and technological hindrances to full media access. As more political and governmental functions become available online and as more economic, educational, and cultural processes become increasingly mediated by technology, issues of media access take on growing urgency. Indeed, the civic opportunities and technical challenges posed by digital convergence demand that citizens learn new skills and adapt to the changing information environment or risk being left behind. A small but illustrative example is the e-ticket method of booking airline reservations. When airlines discovered that issuing and handling paper tickets was their fourth largest expense, many began adding a $10 to $25 surcharge for that service. Travelers with Internet access can make reservations and check in electronically, avoiding the need for a travel agent or for standing in long lines at the airport. Some carriers even issue boarding passes using this technique. Although the fate of democratic society might not ride on the ability to book airline tickets online, if similar practices propagate, it is not hard to imagine how their cumulative impact may snowball into other, more important areas of social and political life. For instance, citizens cannot participate in e-democracy without Internet access (Wilhelm, 2003).

## MULTIDISCIPLINARY APPROACHES

*Media Access* is multidisciplinary in scope, representing the work of scholars across an array of fields, including journalism and mass communication, telecommunications, information studies, human-computer interaction, policy analysis, media sociology, and political science. The conceptual and methodological approaches are as varied as the contributors and encompass social explanations derived from large-scale survey data, cultural explanations derived from in-depth interviews and ethnographic methods, and psychological explanations inferred from experimental studies. The collection of studies gathered here stands apart from other recent books about information technology in that the contributors investigate questions not only about adoption but also about the processing of content. Indeed, the unique contribution of this book derives from the fact that it embraces a media perspective. Several of the contributors, including the editors, have media industry experience and their studies are to some degree informed by a content orientation. Notably, access to both traditional and new media receive due attention in the book.

Underlying the new thinking about access is the assumption that any complete model of media access should consider the interaction between social and psychological factors in information technology use. The contributors to this volume recognize this important fact and compare social and cognitive access to electronic media both *between* and *within* advantaged and disadvantaged groups, identifying factors associated with effectual use of information and communication technologies beyond demographic explanations and hardware solutions. Individual chapters develop expanded definitions and conceptual understandings of access to offer new perspectives on policy discussions, stimulate further research, and facilitate media participation among those being left behind.

## OVERVIEW OF THE BOOK

*Media Access* is organized into three main sections: psychological dimensions of media access; social and cultural dimensions of media access; and media access to the public sphere. In the introduction, we propose a conceptual framework for understanding the different dimensions of media access, unpacking the term into *technological access*, consisting of service provision and hardware considerations, and *content access*, consisting of social and cognitive considerations. While conceptualizing access as a technological problem is familiar, and subsidies for computer equipment a popular solution, the development and acquisition of new technologies alone will be unlikely to move everyone toward the information society's center (see also Wilhelm, 2003). Research must therefore begin to address questions concerning motivation to use new information and communication technologies as well as the user's ability to decipher meaning once a connection to the networked world has been established. The focus on making new technology cognitively accessible to a general, or mass, audience represents a departure from usability studies, which tend to research variables that affect navigational efficiency among existing computer users. Approaching the problem of access from a content perspective also represents a shift away from socio-demographic analyses common to digital divide research and emphasizes the importance of individual-level factors, such as cognitive sophistication and information processing ability, that aren't visibly apparent.

The chapters comprising the section on psychological dimensions of media access investigate questions pertaining to online content and computer avoidance, focusing on the psychological criteria of technology use and the role of education in facilitating cognitive access to new and traditional media. In an innovative experimental study of news processing, Grabe and Kamhawi examine the effect of media channel (television, newspapers, and the Web) and education level on recognition memory for, emotional responses to, and subjective evaluations of local news stories. They report that television, not newspapers or the Web, emerged as the most user-friendly medium, with the highest probability of providing cognitive access to news information. Their analysis reveals that low-education subjects—those with a high school education or less—found the Web versions of news stories significantly harder to understand than newspaper or television stories. Despite being *more* interested in the news than those subjects with a graduate education, the low-education group learned significantly *less* from the stories than graduate degree holders, and these differences in knowledge were most pronounced for news stories presented on the Web. These findings highlight the cognitive hurdles that the Internet presents to users of varying educational backgrounds in the effort to make sense of and derive meaning from online content.

The impact of online interactivity, a defining characteristic of the Web, is addressed in the chapter by Bucy. Interactive features, whether in the form of multimedia downloads, searchable archives, hyperlinks, or discussion forums, are assumed to enhance the audience's access to information while engaging users in processes that, in the words of one influential editor, "use technology to bring people closer to the news" (Brown, 2000, p. 26). At the same time, however, interactive features may exact a considerable cognitive and emotional cost by demanding more patience, expertise, and cognitive resources of the user, increasing the likelihood of confusion, frustration, and reduced memory for news. In an original experiment, Bucy examines the impact of media channel and interactivity level on user responses. Interestingly, he finds that, while interactive conditions were rated significantly more participatory, involving, and immediate than noninteractive conditions, interactive tasks also generated significantly more confusion, disorientation, and frustration than a noninteractive reading task. He refers to this dissonant set of results as the *interactivity paradox*. Although successful at bringing people closer to the news through features that invite involvement, online news operations are evidently leaving users who engage with interactive content somewhat confused. The negative consequences of too much interactivity are only infrequently recognized but have important implications for the development of new information technologies.

Given the frustration that use of computer technology seems to engender, the issue of avoidance comes to the fore. Despite the seemingly ubiquitous role computers play at work and home as a productivity tool and as a medium for information and entertainment, surveys by the Pew Internet & American Life Project indicate that a significant portion of the population harbors negative attitudes about them. Finn and Korukonda take up this question in their chapter on computer avoidance, examining the role that personality plays in attitudes toward the technology. They carry out a secondary analysis of a fascinating database generated at the University of North Carolina in the 1980s looking at computer usage. The data are unique because they were collected when personal computer use was just becoming widespread, a circumstance that allows the researchers to isolate prior experience as a factor in user satisfaction. The work explicates key personality factors that may affect computer avoidance, including agreeableness, conscientiousness, extraversion, openness to experience, and neuroticism. Agreeableness and conscientiousness appear to play a central role in mediating positive feelings about computer use. The examination of personality differences expands our view of factors affecting access beyond the list of the "usual suspects" such as income, education, gender, and geography. The work is especially interesting in the way it summarizes and modifies classic personality literature to accommodate the issue of computer use.

In a similar vein, Bessière and her colleagues explicate the concept of frustration as an important psychological dimension in explaining inhibitions to Internet use. The chapter makes a convincing case for how the research on barriers to access should be broadened beyond the demographic and economic constraints usually discussed. Although frustration has surfaced in a number of usage studies as an important hindrance (perhaps the *most important* hindrance) to Internet use, it has not been theoretically explicated as a concept. This work sets out to do just that and prepares the way for a research agenda geared toward identifying which user factors are unique to Internet use. Few viewers, by way of comparison, report abandoning television viewing because it is frustrating. As with the chapters by Bucy and by Grabe and Kamhawi, Bessière and her colleagues also open the door to bringing core psychological concepts such as emotion into the study of Internet use. Their explication entertains the possibility, for instance, that frustration may intensify into more primitive emotions such as anger or fear if the information-related task and its execution become too difficult. Such responses may be found to outweigh variables like prior computer experience if the goal of the frustrating encounter is sufficiently important and difficult to achieve.

In the second section, exploring social and cultural dimensions of media access, three teams of researchers compare social access to new technology among traditionally disadvantaged communities in such disparate regions of the United States as Texas, Georgia, and Michigan. Rojas and her associates consider the class dispositions and cultural assumptions that constrain the formation of techno-capital among six poor families in the largely Hispanic community of East Austin, Texas. In their case study of the LaGrange Public Internet Initiative in LaGrange, Georgia, Youtie and colleagues ask what happens when local government policy directly— and dramatically—reduces the economic and logistical costs of access to the user. From the HomeNet Too Project, Jackson and her team at Michigan State University report early findings of household Internet use among low-income families in East Lansing, Michigan. All three of these studies find racial and cultural factors to affect Internet use, even after the effects of income and education have been taken into account. The implication of these findings are important because they suggest that we will not be able to simply "educate" our way out of the digital divide. Rather, complex social and cultural factors will have to be addressed to fully incorporate these groups into the online world. Jackson and her colleagues' work also resonates with the Finn and Korukonda chapter in that it looks at the personality literature to identify factors that transcend demographic determinants of Internet usage.

The third section of the book pulls back another level of analysis to examine media access to the public sphere. McCrery and Newhagen reconceptualize the public sphere as a virtual space, looking at the variables of user efficacy and system technology. The survey data they examine compares a sample of randomly selected citizens to political elites, including members of Congress, their staff, and lobbyists. The study gains salience in the wake of the September 11th terrorist attacks because it looks at new media as a virtual alternative to the traditional public sphere located in open physical spaces. They find that highly efficacious private citizens, who share many of the traits of political elites who inhabit the halls of the traditional public sphere, may turn to talk radio as a civic forum. Hofstetter's chapter on the skills and motivations of interactive media participants reinforces the notion that citizens who have the skills to take part in public debate but are excluded from actual policy discussions are increasingly turning to political talk shows. He reconceptualizes political talk as a new technology. This perspective underlies the notion that what is "new" about new technology has as much to do with the way it is used as the physical form it takes.

Extending the usage theme, van Dijk performs a cross-national analysis of survey data from the United States and Europe to track persisting and increasing digital divides in new technology use, identifying what he calls "usage gaps" in access to digital democracy. He identifies four successive barriers to media access, which he suggests must be overcome for full inclusion into information and network societies. The first, which is psychological in nature, is the lack of any digital experience, caused by computer fear, a paucity of user interest, or a deliberate avoidance of the new technology. The second, which addresses material considerations, is the absence of computer or network connections. The third barrier to access involves digital skills, including the ability not only to operate computers and network connections but to search, select, and process information from a superabundance of sources. The lack of digital skills, van Dijk asserts, is not solely a user-centered problem (i.e., inadequate education) but may result from insufficiently user-friendly technology or inadequate social support. Fourthly, he expects usage opportunities to remain uneven for some time to come, where segments of the population systematically engage with and benefit from advanced information technology and more sophisticated applications and services, while other segments use only basic digital technologies for simple applications with a relatively large part of that use consisting of entertainment. Because of these barriers to access, he asserts, there is reason to believe that the digital divide will not be completely remedied through universal physical access to computer technology alone.

Closing out the section is a provocative essay by Shneiderman, which challenges the human-computer interaction community to empower every citizen by striving for digital interfaces with universal usability. The chapter presents a research agenda based on three challenges for attaining universal usability, which Shneiderman defines as a situation where more than 90% of all households are successful users of networked information and communication services at least once a week. The first challenge is attaining technology variety, which requires supporting access to a broad range of software, hardware, and network configurations. The second challenge is achieving user diversity, which involves accommodating users with varying skills, knowledge, age, gender, disabilities, literacy, culture, income, and so on. The third challenge is to reduce gaps in user knowledge, which involves bridging the chasm between what users know and what they need to know. Although this list might not be all-inclusive, it addresses important issues that are insufficiently funded by current initiatives. Universal usability is, to us, the crux of television's success as a mass medium; until networked computing achieves the broadcast media's ease of use, basic affordability, and intuitive appeal, we question whether the Internet can be a true medium of the masses. A final concluding chapter written by Lievrouw of UCLA's Department of Information Studies provides a synoptic overview of the media access approach while tying together common themes of the book.

## UNIQUE FEATURES

Taken as a whole, *Media Access* has several unique features:

- *Novel perspectives.* Each chapter explores issues relating to media access in a way that has not received much research attention, demonstrating new ways of addressing persistent questions. Grabe and Kamhawi, for example, employ education as a variable to show how questions of media access apply equally to new and traditional media. Finn and Korukonda identify key personality differences that may affect computer avoidance, an underutilized approach. Rojas and colleagues draw on the sociology of Pierre Bourdieu to identify a shared set of techno-dispositions that influence Internet use among a minority community in East Austin, Texas. And McCrery and Newhagen compare media and psychological determinants of access to the public sphere among a sample of everyday citizens with elected members of Congress, their staff, and lobbyists. These examples do not exhaust the novel perspectives found in the studies presented here.

- *Conceptual integration.* Each chapter addresses a vital aspect of media access and summarizes pertinent findings concerning it, weaving together results and developing analytical frameworks in a way that promises to provide much-needed integration. Different sections of the book are thematically integrated as well. The successive barriers to access outlined by van Dijk map onto the four dimensions of media access discussed in the introduction. Similarly, the causes and consequences of computer frustration and disorientation tie together the chapters by Bucy, Bessière and her colleagues, and Shneiderman. Questions about access to the public sphere interweave the chapters by McCrery and Newhagen, Hofstetter, van Dijk, and Shneiderman.

- *Multidisciplinary approaches.* The volume features a diverse array of conceptual and methodological approaches, demonstrating how questions of media access can be researched from a variety of perspectives. *Media Access* is truly multidisciplinary in scope, representing the work of scholars across a rich variety of fields, including journalism and mass communication, telecommunications, information studies, human-computer interaction, policy analysis, media sociology, and political science.

- *Shifting the policy and research agenda.* Owing to the diverse approaches employed, and the arguments and findings presented, this volume extends and redirects aspects of the digital divide debate while elaborating the "media access" approach to studying new technology use. The chapters present empirical findings that reveal complications associated with full access to new communication technologies and propose analytical frameworks for investigating media access in a manner that opens new avenues of scholarly investigation and policy consideration.

It is our hope that the collection of studies gathered here will demarcate a new area of research that brings sharper focus to questions loosely grouped under the umbrella of concerns related to the digital divide. Ideally, the media access approach may serve to inspire further investigations that illuminate the issues beyond the work presented here. Given the cross-disciplinary appeal of these studies, researchers, teachers, and policy thinkers across a broad range of fields should find this volume to be helpful in the effort to better understand and ameliorate the social disparities associated with uneven access to new technology.

## ACKNOWLEDGMENTS

As a final note, we would like to express our gratitude to series editor Jennings Bryant for encouraging the publication of this book. We also thank Linda Bathgate, our editor at Lawrence Erlbaum Associates, for recognizing the merit of this project and gracefully accommodating our requests for deadline extensions. The book also benefited from Debbie Ruel's expert guidance throughout the production process and Karin Wittig Bates' vital editorial assistance. Without their support, *Media Access* would still be an idea without tangible form. Lastly, each of the contributors deserves special praise for their timely submissions, for revising and refining their manuscripts with careful dispatch, and for making this volume a truly original collection of scholarly work.

— Erik P. Bucy
— John E. Newhagen

## ENDNOTE

[1] The term *media access* has been employed for some time to describe the openness of mass media organizations to incorporate the perspectives of various social and political groups—to provide, in the words of the Hutchins Commission on Freedom of the Press, "a representative picture of the constituent groups in society" as well as "full access to the day's intelligence" (see Siebert, Peterson, & Schramm, 1956, pp. 87–92). The meaning that this volume adopts was perhaps first espoused by Donohue, Olien, and Tichenor (1987), who used the term in a review article titled "Media Access and Knowledge Gaps" to describe how changing patterns of media organization and information distribution were affecting the dispersion of social power and influence (p. 87).

## REFERENCES

Adler, J. (1995, July 31). The rise of the overclass: How the new elite scrambled up the merit ladder—and wants to stay there any way it can. *Newsweek*, pp. 32–46.

Brockman, J. (1996). *Digerati: Encounters with the cyber elite.* San Francisco:HardWired.

Brown, M. (2000, October 2). Bringing people closer to the news. *Brandweek*, 26.

Donohue, G. A., Olien, C. N., & Tichenor, P. J. (1987). Media access and knowledge gaps. *Critical Studies in Mass Communication*, 4(1), 87–92.

Eunjung Cha, A. (2002, June 29). "Digital divide" less clear: As Internet use spreads, policy debated anew. *The Washington Post*, E1.

Grossman, L. K. (1995). *The electronic republic.* New York: Penguin Books.

Hill, K. A., & Hughes, J. E. (1998). *Cyberpolitics.* Lanham, MD: Rowman & Littlefield.

Newhagen, J. E., & Rafaeli, S. (1996). Why communication researchers should study the Internet: A dialogue. *Journal of Communication, 46*(1), 4–13.

NTIA (1998, July). *Falling through the Net II: New data on the digital divide.* National Telecommunication and Information Administration, U.S. Department of Commerce. Retrieved September 12, 2002, from http://www.ntia.doc.gov/ntiahome/net2/

NTIA (2002, February). *A nation online: How Americans are expanding their use of the Internet.* National Telecommunications and Information Administration, U.S. Department of Commerce. Retrieved September 12, 2002, from http://www.ntia.doc.gov/ntiahome/dn/index.html

Rheingold, H. (2000). *The virtual community: Homesteading on the electronic frontier* (Rev. ed.). Cambridge, MA: MIT Press.

Siebert, F. S., Peterson, T., & Schramm, W. (1956). *Four theories of the press.* Urbana: University of Illinois Press.

Tichenor, P. J., Donohue, G. A., & Olien, C. N. (1970). Mass media flow and differential growth in knowledge. *Public Opinion Quarterly, 34,* 159–170.

van Dijk, J. (1999). *The network society: Social aspects of new media.* London: Sage.

Wilhelm, A. G. (2003). Civic participation and technology inequality: The "killer application" is education. In D. M. Anderson & M. Cornfield (Eds.), *The civic Web: Online politics and democratic values* (pp. 113–128). Lanham, MD: Rowman & Littlefield.

# Introduction

# 1

# Routes to Media Access

JOHN E. NEWHAGEN
*University of Maryland, College Park*

ERIK P. BUCY
*Indiana University, Bloomington*

Politicians, civic leaders, and a host of other good-minded citizens agree that Internet access is good. Some go so far as to see access to the Internet as a key to the reinvigoration of democratic society (e.g., Rheingold, 2000).[1] Although the topic receives a great deal of public attention, discussions frequently omit the critical question, "Access to what?" One approach would reduce the issue of access to a simple discussion of power (Marx, 1867/1967). From that perspective, power resides in the hands of those controlling the means of production: land in an agrarian society, machines in an industrial society, and information in a postmodern society. If the Internet represents the enabling technology for the Information Age, then it follows that access to the Internet is a necessary condition for access to power. But is it sufficient? If the concept is limited to mean physical access to computer apparatus, the answer is "no." Access must be conceptualized in much broader human and technological terms.

The idea that physical access to a computer is sufficient to enable Internet use, however, seems to dominate the thinking of many policymakers looking for simple or immediate solutions. The idea of access as a social imperative usually manifests itself in television news spots featuring a local politician dedicating a new computer lab at a school or public library. But as the chapters in this volume demonstrate, these events may be no more than mere token gestures if the users of these machines do not possess the requisite skills, cognitive ability, and social motivation needed to enable full access to the content conveyed by the technology.

3

TABLE 1.1
Dimensions of Access Across Levels of Analysis

| | Dimensions of Access | |
| --- | --- | --- |
| Level of Analysis | Content | Technological |
| Individual | Cognitive | Physical |
| Aggregate | Social | System |

In any case, there seems to be a clear distinction between having access to the Internet as a technology and being able to access the content that resides on it. The first kind of access, technological, has two dimensions—physical access to a computer and access to the network itself—that we term *system access*. Once technological access is accomplished, the task shifts to content. *Content access* also has two dimensions—social and cognitive access.

Categorizing access in this manner is epistemologically parsimonious because it accommodates both aggregate and individual-level considerations. Table 1.1 shows the technological and content dimensions of access and their corresponding levels of analysis. On the technological side, physical access treats computers as individual nodes, whereas system access looks at the Internet in aggregation. On the content side, cognitive access addresses the individual user; social access considers aggregations of users. The category labeled "social" describing content aggregation points to an important difference between the Internet and previous mass media systems. In a mass media system, the inhabitants of this quadrant would be referred to as audience members. However, the idea of an audience as a passive grouping of content consumers (or "receivers" of broadcast messages) just does not describe the diversity of users who are online at a given point in time. Moreover, Internet users typically do not experience simultaneous exposure to the same message in the way that mass media audiences do.

## MEDIA ACCESS AS MEANING

The answer to the question "Access to what?" is meaning, and it involves more than the physical presence of information technology and an adequate connection to the communication system. It also requires the social motivation and cognitive ability necessary to fully apprehend the content conveyed by the technology. In virtually any communication system, meaning is embedded in content and is made up of information or data. Although the words *data* and *information* may be frequently interchanged in colloquial speech, there is a subtle but important difference between the two. Information is data structured in such a way as to have meaning. Digital data are represented by a stream of zeros and ones. Standing alone, these raw data have no meaning. Take a look at a data set from a public opinion poll and you will see a two-dimensional matrix of numbers that, in the absence of a data dictionary, look like a table of random numbers in the back of a statistics text. Data need structure to achieve the status of information, that is, to have meaning. Taborsky (1998) asserted that meaning is semiotic and specific to architectures she called *narratives*. Thus, information is data further organized into metanarratives, or stories. This process involves taking arbitrary signs, such as zeros and ones, and giving them symbolic meaning. In the opinion poll example, the zeros might signify males and ones females. With that knowledge, a story can be told about the gender balance of the study.

The problem of transforming data into information is not unique to the Internet—it is the central function of any communication system. Taborsky used the notion of narrative in a very general sense; DNA, for instance, is an information architecture that specifies a biological narrative. Engineers might think of narration as programming. Other architectures of meaning include natural language. Syntax can even be applied to the construction of visual images in a way that gives them narrative meaning—television producers and film makers practice this all the time when they employ such editing techniques as juxtaposition and shot sequencing.

The Internet stands out as a communication medium in its ability to provide the user with both verbal and nonverbal streams of information in a way that mass media do not. The verbal stream can take the form of either text on screen or spoken words. Nonverbal information can be visual or aural. At this writing, text is the dominant verbal form online. Some might argue that the only constraint limiting more extensive use of spoken words on the Internet is bandwidth. This problem will be solved, so the argument goes, as high-speed connections become more common in the workplace and at home. Yet despite gains in bandwidth capacity, text probably will continue to be the most effective representational system for narratives that are particularly information-dense. Sound is an effective vehicle for conveying meaning in the nonverbal stream, as with audio narration, natural sound, or music. But visual images are particularly effective in the transmission of information-dense nonverbal meaning. And the Internet is particularly good, and getting better at, the engineering task of displaying visual information. As bandwidth increases and screen resolution improves, image quality (important to both visuals and text on screen) will also improve. The Internet will likely remain, then, a medium dominated by text and image. This is not to dismiss the importance of sound or preclude the possibility that streaming audio may eventually displace other communication hardware, such as the radio receiver. But online, the user's primary focus will continue to center on images and text. As high-speed connections become more common, a growing number of users (and not just college students) may use their computer to download sound files or stream music in the background, while working at other tasks.

If information is power, then the answer to the question "Access to what?" is "a stream of words and images structured into narrative units called content." Generally, the closer information is to something concrete or "real," the easier it is to decode its meaning. In this sense television is considered "easy" because its meaning is derived from images that viewers may process without much textual literacy or advanced education (Reeves & Nass, 1996). On the other hand, print is considered "hard" because it is text-based and requires more mental effort to extract narrative meaning. The Internet is not unique in its ability to present both verbal and nonverbal meaning across modality—television and film have performed this feat for decades. What makes the Internet interesting is that it presents both text and images with enough resolution for the user to efficiently process, a claim other electronic media systems cannot make. Text can be presented on a television screen, but have you read much TV lately?[2]

If the meaning embedded in content was self-evident to all users, the physical presence of technology would be the only hindrance to access. But this is not the case. Consider the example of two Internet users. In the first instance, fast-forward not too far into the future and picture a football fan watching the Super Bowl on his Internet-TV. An ad featuring home-delivered pizza appears on the screen when the 2-minute warning sounds just before half time. This networked system features a touch-sensitive screen that allows the sports maven to order a pizza, promised to arrive at his door before the game resumes, by simply pressing his thumb onto the appropriate box on a menu.[3] In the second instance, imagine a hapless nature lover who builds her home on a rural wooded lot only to be infected by Lyme disease. It turns out that the disease, borne by deer ticks, can be very hard to diagnose. She first visits a doctor and complains of chronic fatigue, only to be falsely diagnosed as having a thyroid condition. Then her hearing goes bad, and another doctor wonders if she might have contracted syphilis. Finally, she ends up in the emergency room with a 103° fever and severe muscle pain. Blood tests are inconclusive, but one of the young internists asks her if she lives in the woods. When her condition stabilizes, she goes home, logs onto the Internet, and does a search on the key word "Lyme." After plowing through technical journal articles and even joining a listserv made up of the disease's victims, she learns the full spectrum of possible symptoms and appropriate tests. She returns to her doctor and demands a Western Blot blood test, which comes back positive. The proper diagnosis of her condition assures a swift recovery.

Of course, this comparison is not entirely fair; our football fan may only have seventh-grade reading skills, whereas the nature lover might have a master's degree in electrical engineering. Yet although both had access to the Internet, their experience was qualitatively different. The consequence of this disparity in usage may lead to what van Dijk (2000) identified as a "usage gap" between different segments of the population, where well-educated users make far greater use of advanced applications at work, home, and school settings than do the less educated who seek online amusement, game playing, and entertainment experiences. As computers continue to diffuse nationally and internationally, usage gaps are likely to grow, with differences between simple and advanced information uses among different socioeconomic groups increasing rather than decreasing (van Dijk, 2000).

## DIMENSIONS OF ACCESS

In Internet parlance, the answer to the question "Access to what?" is "content." The online industry's distinction between service providers and content providers implies two levels of access. A service provider is someone who connects the user's computer to the Internet. A content provider is someone who posts information on the Internet. The development of America Online's marketing philosophy is a good example of how this distinction emerged. As a service provider, AOL connects millions of users to the Internet by charging a monthly connect charge, but its management has always had a vision of controlling what their clients see and do once they get there. In the early days of the Web, AOL fashioned itself as a stand-alone network, hoping to work outside the publicly accessible Internet. As the Internet grew, it became clear that working outside the global network was no longer a viable strategy and the service gradually granted its users wider Internet access. But it did so begrudgingly; even today, some complain the service's browser is not up to snuff.

In recent years the company has articulated a role beyond that of mere service provider and has embraced the notion that the real money is in content. AOL's merger with Time Warner symbolizes this change of philosophy. But the dilemma posed by being both a service provider and content provider persists for the Internet's largest online service. In its advertising and promotion, AOL avidly promotes its ease of use, especially for novice users ("So easy to use, no wonder it's number one"), but this usability advantage applies mostly to e-mail and other chat features and avoids the thorny issue of content access. Perhaps AOL's top management did not hear the rallying cry of radical Internet politics: *information wants to be free.* Whereas Microsoft and AOL still aspire to be both service and content providers, a substantial portion of the market, made up of regional and local service providers, has no aspirations to provide content. The same is true for nonprofit providers, especially universities.

The distinction between providing access to media technology and making content accessible was not as pronounced in the high era of mass media. Because of their low literacy barrier, radio and television are (mostly) understood by all. Marshall McLuhan's (1964/1994) dictum—"The medium is the message"—resonated for the precise reason that the content of television seemed to follow its form, giving rise in McLuhan's view to new structures of feeling and thought. If television is an intuitive, emotionally involving, close-up medium, then it follows that the content will bear those characteristics, regardless of genre or program. Trying to make the distinction between medium and message does not make much sense with newspapers, either. Is a newspaper like *The Washington Post* a content provider or a service provider? True, it provides the service of running huge printing presses and managing an equally large distribution system to ensure that subscribers receive their daily newspaper. But it also maintains a large information-processing organization to generate the content that fills its pages.

The division of labor between service and content providers began to emerge as cable television matured, when it started making sense to think about the difference between delivering a signal to subscribers' homes as one function, and providing the content through that cable as another. Cable companies have tried their best to project themselves as content providers, an argument made easier to sustain by the fact that most of them until recently enjoyed regional monopolies. But direct broadcast television, with its inexpensive satellite dishes and growing number of high quality digital signals, has broken that monopoly and made many subscribers aware that they have content options independent of the technological delivery system. Some media economists fear that big media will come to dominate the Internet just as they have mass media, enclosing the online world with a costly commercial fence (McChesney, 1997). However, this may prove difficult if the Internet actually marks the divorce between service provision and content generation.

## Technological Access

Technological access addresses hardware and infrastructure considerations and has two dimensions, physical access to computers and access to the Internet as a system.

*Physical Access.*    Physical access entails actually being able to sit down in front of an Internet-ready computer. Arguments centering on the issue of physical access frequently point to the high cost of owning a multimedia computer as a barrier for economically disadvantaged groups (Schon, Sanyal, & Mitchell, 1999). One solution to this problem is to promote installation of public terminals in schools and libraries. However, that position is difficult to sustain given the decreasing cost of computers. For most of the past two decades, the cost of a good computer did not drop much below $2,000. It seemed as if the cost of a computer was pegged at that price. Although the per-unit cost of components such as memory chips or disk space fell, each succeeding generation of machine required more resources to be fully functional and the price remained relatively constant. The cost of computers finally plummeted in the late 1990s, when computer stores began to offer powerful machines to customers at no charge in exchange for signing a 3-year contract with an Internet service provider at the cost of about $400. Usually those contracts offered full Internet access for much less than the cost of cable television.

This drop in price brings the opportunity for access to home computing to a much broader segment of the population than previous economic realities allowed and lessens the need for public terminals. Those who forecasted that computers would never be affordable enough for the economic underclass are reminiscent of the skeptics in the 1960s who similarly predicted color television would remain so expensive it would always be a privilege of the wealthy. Large-scale surveys show that Internet use is becoming increasingly more pervasive, with Internet access above 50% nationwide (NTIA, 2002). A case can even be made that the cost of a computer is not an overwhelming obstacle in many (though not all) parts of the Developing World. A large portion of computer components are actually manufactured in Asia, and the technology is readily available, albeit primarily to the middle class, in Latin America as well.

*System Access.* System access does not get mentioned as much as it should. Laurel (1991) used the dramatic stage as a metaphor for the computer interface and made the point that the computer user, like the theater goer, is not aware of what is going on behind the scenes. Yet that is an important area where the Internet differs from other communication technologies, especially television.[4]

The distributed nature of Internet architecture technologically enables its interactivity, the single most important feature that distinguishes the new medium from earlier media systems. The architecture of the Internet in many ways reflects the neural networks that make up the brain. Cognitive psychologists Rumelhart and McClelland (1986) described human thought in terms of a network of interconnected nodes, where mental processes are distributed across the system and function in parallel. When one node is activated in the network, other nodes become active as well, according to the strength of their connection with the original node. An active group of nodes becomes a schema, which might be a memory or attitude. One of the revolutionary aspects of the neural net approach is the claim that meaning does not reside in individual nodes, but in the *connection strengths* between nodes. For instance, for most people the connection between the node for the color green would be very strong with the node for grass. At a system level, the connections between computers on the Internet looks like a neural network, where the strength of the nodes makes the difference in meaning. This again has to do with bandwidth, or the capacity and speed of a connection.

From the user's point of view, the issue of connection quality boils down to download times, which can range from annoyingly long to completely disabling. A bandwidth problem, download times really have to do with how close you are to the Internet backbone. Large research universities are the most likely to be a part of the backbone itself, but the increasing availability of high capacity fiber optic cable ties commercial enterprises to it as well. From a hardware standpoint, fiber optic cable has the most bandwidth, followed by coaxial cable and twisted-pair copper wire. Software engineering also enters into the picture, designing data compression techniques that have been responsible for increasing bandwidth to levels not imagined just a few years ago. The bandwidth of Internet connections is usually described in terms of line capacity, where T1 and T3 connections are the fastest and highest volume but usually are only employed by institutions. Telecommunications firms offer commercial and residential customers premium connections such as DSL or cable modems. Although an improvement over modem access, these commercially offered services are still peripheral to the system's backbone. In any event, the days of individual users logging on to the Internet via standard twisted-pair telephone line with a 56kb modem are not likely to last long. Already cable companies are upgrading their lines to fiber optic cable and are providing two-way connections with high speeds compared to what was available just a few years ago.

System access is really the level at which money talks, and corporate users have a distinct advantage over individual users. McChesney (1997) detailed how large commercial interests came to dominate radio and television by controlling the discussions that preceded government policymaking regulating the allocation of bandwidth. He extended his argument to the Internet, where he expected that, over time, hope for technological egalitarianism will fade into corporate dominance. Although there is reason to believe that the distributed nature of the Internet will make such predictions overly pessimistic, connection quality is one place where money does, and will continue to, make a big difference. This is not so much a problem for the individual user as it is for content providers on the server side. The problem is that not all nodes on the Internet are created equal. To the contrary, the basic communication model for the Internet is client–server, where the server has more power than the client. Despite some optimistic assessments (e.g., Oram, 2001), true peer-to-peer communication does not exist much on the Internet (and probably does not occur much in face-to-face communication, either). Servers have a distinct power advantage over users, and it costs money to maintain a connection to the Internet to establish a credible presence.

Discussions about system access inevitably must address how the server's technological superiority *as a node* translates into a social parity advantage. Setting up a server is really not that difficult. A standard personal computer can be configured with software to enable it to support all the activities needed for full server status. The ambitious undergraduate computer geek can convert his or her PC into a fully functional Web server by installing the Linux operating system and Apache server software for free.[5] The budding entrepreneur has only to pay Network Solutions a nominal fee for a domain name and address to be fully functional. Suppose our new Web master wants to publish an online newspaper. Will it have the same footing as, say, Washingtonpost.com? The answer is "yes"—until more than 20 users try to hit the site at one time and it crashes. The fact remains that those able to afford top-end computer hardware *and* pay for a high-speed connection are more empowered to establish sites capable of withstanding heavy traffic. Furthermore, whereas most see bandwidth solely as a problem that will eventually succumb to engineering solutions, differential costs such as DSL or high-speed modem charges for increased line capacity are not likely to disappear any time soon.

Bandwidth is particularly problematic for system access in the developing world where even governmental agencies can have difficulty establishing system access. Take the example of a branch of the Ministry of Agriculture in Brazil, which is attempting to develop a Web portal for field agents. As planned, the portal would host a full range of technical information and interactive services for agricultural agents throughout Brazil and, if successful, bear fairly heavy traffic. The technical problem the agency is dealing with does not concern server hardware capacity, which is relatively inexpensive. Indeed, the intranet at the headquarters site is just as robust as any such installation one might expect in the industrially developed world. The main bottleneck occurs with the ministry's satellite link to the Internet, which is limited to 60kb—a connection barely better than that available to the average home user in the United States. The intractable problem the ministry's developers have is really one of basic infrastructure—although upgrading servers might be an easy and inexpensive task, upgrading communication satellites is not.

This is not just a First World–Developing World problem. It can be a rural–urban problem as well, where high-speed connections are not readily available outside big cities. During the last decade, telecommunications companies in the United States spent considerable time and money laying fiber optic cable, but that enterprise has almost exclusively been limited to infrastructure either within or between large urban areas. Railroad companies stand to become big beneficiaries in the digital information revolution because many used their rights-of-way to bury high-capacity, fiber optic trunk lines. Real estate near railroad mainlines along the northeastern corridor of the United States is being eyed as prime ground for high-tech, information economy industrial parks simply because the fiber optic connection is so close. In the long run, system access may be a more chronic problem than physical access to computers, especially in areas where basic telecommunications infrastructure has lagged.

## Content Access

Content access concerns the motivation to use information technology and the ability to process meaning once the user is connected to a communication system. It also has two dimensions, social and cognitive access.

*Social Access.* As many chapters in this volume discuss, there are grave concerns among researchers and policymakers about a digital divide, where some social or demographic groups are systematically excluded from the information revolution. Early research showed typical Internet users to be predominantly young, White, middle-class males (NTIA, 1998). However, as new communication technology diffuses into society, the demographic base of users will continue to broaden. For instance, the percentage of women on the Internet has dramatically increased over the past decade and age appears to be playing less of a role. More recent research shows the strongest factor determining access is education (Nie & Erbring, 2000; NTIA, 2000, 2002).

Simply focusing on central demographic tendencies among disadvantaged social groups may not, however, allow us to fully understand the barriers to access at the societal level. It is important to remember that the theoretical level of analysis employed here is the group, and the description of a "typical" group member is a statistical aggregation; even while African Americans may lag behind in Internet use as a group, many are indeed wired. During the initial phase of research in this area, one important exercise might be to take a hard look at what statisticians call the *outliers*—those who do not fit the group pattern. Do African Americans and Hispanics who are wired fit the mainstream demographic pattern for Internet use? Demographic variables, such as race, are frequently confounded by other factors, such as education and income. The problem is how to unpack this set of important societal determinants. One way to address this area of concern is to ask the question: Would increasing education solve the access problem, or is it more deeply rooted?

One construct that offers some promise in the early going of media access research is efficacy. Efficacy has been researched in several contexts, notably by psychologists and political scientists. Two types of efficacy have been established—self and system—that correspond to individual and social outlooks. Self-efficacy is the sense of being able to cope with the social world (Bandura, 1997). Self-efficacy combines with system efficacy, a sense of how well the social system works, to generate individual motivation. The reason both self and system efficacy are important at the social level is that they can be group attributes. For instance, African Americans have lower system efficacy assessments for the American political system than Caucasians (Shingles, 1981).

If *self*-efficacy, an internally regulated state determined almost entirely by education, is an important constraint to Internet access, then society should be able to educate its way out of any disparity in Internet access between groups. On the other hand, *system* efficacy may be the driving force impeding access for some social groups. There is evidence, for instance, that Hispanic culture promotes the notion among young men that computers as a system are too complex for them to manage (see chapter 6, this volume). Notice the subtle but important difference between system and self efficacy. Here the culture is telling the individual that the Internet may be too complex, rather than the individual making a self-assessment. Although social class usually correlates with self-efficacy, there can be exceptions. For instance, during the Black Power movement of the late 1960s and early 1970s, blue-collar African Americans showed unusually high political self-efficacy, emphasizing poor system performance for their inability to advance economically and socially (Shingles, 1981). Bandura (1997) attributed this to the fact that low system efficacy can challenge the individual and actually increase self-efficacy toward goal attainment. If this is the case for Internet access, then one strategy might be to present the acquisition of computer skills as a challenge rather than a *fait accompli*.

In any case, cultural norms tend to be quite conservative and slow in changing. Thus, although a group might hope to educate itself out of a problem in a generation or so, that may not be an option if the problem resides within deeper rooted cultural norms.

***Cognitive Access.***    Cognitive access describes the psychological resources the user brings to the computer interface and addresses how individuals orient to the medium, process information, and engage in problem solving when using information and communication technologies.

Cognitive access differs from the study of human–computer interaction and usability studies in that it deals not only with efficient interface design and successful navigation in hypermedia environments but also the reception of meaning from content, whether from new or old media. A likely candidate for a research paradigm at the cognitive level is the information processing approach, which emanates from cognitive psychology (see Geiger & Newhagen, 1993). This approach represents a significant shift in levels of analysis in the study of media effects over the past 20 to 30 years. The very nature of mass-media architecture, delivering one message to a vast audience, lent itself to study from a sociological or sociopsychological perspective. However, as the search for opinion change and attitudinal effects stalled, researchers began to focus their efforts on cognitive and emotional outcomes of media use, such as attention, memory, liking, and learning, allowing the field to progress.

Applied to television, the information processing paradigm models a viewer with limited cognitive resources, faced with the challenge of making sense of a complex stream of visual and audio information in real time (Lang, 2000). It details cognitive heuristics, such as emotional cues, employed by viewers in that task (Bucy & Newhagen, 1999). This area of media research has focused primarily on processing the visual component of television rather than the verbal narrative. The Internet, on the other hand, displays both text and images in high resolution. Some Web developers, enamored with the bells and whistles of full motion video and high fidelity digital sound, see online text as transitional—an artifact of the Web's early development. However, as mentioned, a closer examination of Internet use leads to the conclusion that text will continue to be an important, if not dominant, component of Internet content. Because of its high level of abstraction as a representational system, text stands out as the best way to use a computer to communicate messages that are dense in information (Stephenson, 1999). Although the navigational component of Web pages may become more graphically oriented and user friendly, basic content will likely continue to be dominated by text.

The prospect of a medium that renders images and text with equal fidelity invites an examination of how the two modalities interact in the online environment in ways that they do not in mass media and adds another layer of complexity to the issue of cognitive access. The basic premise of the information processing perspective—that the user brings limited cognitive resources to the medium—stays in place for the Internet, but studying the simultaneous interaction of text and image suggests that a broader range of psychological processes will have to be considered than has been the case for traditional mass media.

Image processing is "natural" or automatic in the sense that mediated images correspond to an analogical system of communication, whereas words are almost wholly arbitrary and require a language system to have meaning. As Messaris and Abraham (2001) noted, "The relationship between most words and their meanings is purely a matter of social convention, whereas the relationship between images and their meanings is based on similarity or analogy" (p. 216). Visual recognition of objects does not seem to require prior familiarity with different representational styles or media, either. Because images "appear more natural, more closely linked to reality than words" (Messaris & Abraham, 2001, p. 217), cognitive access to mediated images is egalitarian; regardless of socioeconomic status, viewers all generally call the same psychological processes into play while viewing. Thus, on the morning of September 11, 2001, the images of the ill-fated jetliners plunging into the World Trade Center towers were processed in much the same way by all viewers who saw them, at least for the first few seconds of exposure. After initial exposure, individual differences in knowledge or literacy determined by such factors as education level and viewer sophistication may come into play (see chapter 2, this volume).

The extraction of meaning from textual information, on the other hand, requires the recognition and decoding of abstract symbols. Unlike the processing of images, text processing is not natural or automatic. It is a learned skill and varies widely between individuals. This fact makes the issue of access to textual content much more salient than it does for the processing of images. The low literacy barrier enjoyed by television (due to the medium's visual orientation) is not shared by the Web. This is true even for Web sites that are purely image-based because of the technological literacy required to access the online environment.

Given these constraints, the relationship between textual and visual content has important implications for the issue of content access. In the example given at the beginning of this chapter, for instance, the pizza selection screen accessed by the football maven was image-driven and required little skill, thus cognitive access was not much of an issue. On the other hand, the text and images dealing with medical information about Lyme disease used by the unfortunate nature lover were information-dense; thus, access to that content was limited by the cognitive skills the user brought to the interface. Although the example seems obvious, the issues underlying it are complex. Cognitive access to the Internet is more than an interface design issue. Granted, interface design driven by attention to human cognition can greatly enhance navigation (Shneiderman, 1998). However, the more complex or information-dense the content, the more that learned skills will become a factor— and the greater the chance for a "cognitive divide." Furthermore, it does not matter whether cognitive obstacles to access are real or imagined; either way they still impede access.

## THE TEMPORAL SEQUENCE OF ACCESS

The four dimensions of access discussed here—physical, system, social, and cognitive—exist, more or less, for all media technologies. The critical factor distinguishing Internet from mass media experiences concerns the way these dimensions are interrelated, both in terms of temporal sequence and linearity. Newhagen and Levy (1998) argued that the Internet stands apart from mass media due to its nonlinear architecture. Information flow in a mass-media system is linear, passing through an hourglass-shaped system of filters, gatekeepers, and value enhancers. The neck of the hourglass represents the place where data are converted into media content. This task is usually carried out by information professionals, such as journalists or entertainment producers. On the other hand, the Internet is made up of interconnected nodes that allow content formation to take place simultaneously and at locations distributed across the network. The idea of juxtaposing the linearity of mass media with the nonlinearity of the Internet has important implications for access.

### Access as a Linear Process

The one-way flow of information in a mass-media system encourages modeling access as a linear process. Figure 1.1 shows how this model generally sees technological access (indicated by the outer rings) as the first step, where users must acquire the system connections and physical hardware before progressing into the content access domain (indicated by the inner rings). With mass media such as newspapers, readers must have a hard copy to know what the journalists at *The Washington Post* are talking about; television viewers must have a receiver to watch this evening's lineup on NBC.[6] With the Internet, users similarly need a modem- or

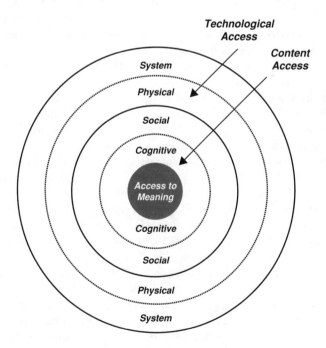

FIG 1.1.   Linear access to meaning.

ethernet-ready computer. As communication media converge, however, what "having a computer" means should be defined broadly so that discussions about access may embrace a range of different scenarios. Similarly, the scope of what is meant by "the Internet" should be defined as broadly as possible so that discussions about access may embrace as many scenarios as possible. Some prefer to use the term *matrix* in place of Internet because matrix is more inclusive (see December, 1996). In any case, it can generally be said that technological access is linear in the sense that the physical interface generator, usually a personal computer, must be present in order to access the content residing in the information system to which it is connected.

Once technological access is achieved, attention turns to the issue of content access. Here, the linear model generally places social access ahead of cognitive access, where individual characteristics such as education, gender, race, socioeconomic status, and cultural circumstances are viewed as determinants of cognitive access. Full media access can be achieved only after each level has been penetrated in turn. Thus, the policymaker concerned about African Americans being on the wrong side of the digital divide might sponsor a program to place computers in predominantly Black schools and offer Internet connections. This approach implies that the physical presence of the technology in the right place will enable access for the target group. This approach baits the issue of cognitive access but leaves for school officials the task of figuring out how to put the technology to gainful use after the public relations event celebrating the installation of the computers is over, the politicians have left, and the television camera lights have gone dim. Each successive level of access brings potential users closer to full media access, but proximity to content no more assures its sophisticated use and enjoyment than does being handed a book without the ability to read.

The inability of the linear model to deal with the issue of cognitive access calls the assumption of linearity into question. In the parlance of social science methodology, the model commits the ecological fallacy by using aggregate-level data to tell individual-level stories. Here, we have technological access ostensibly enabling content access. But let us not forget to do a follow-up visit to the fortunate high-technology high school after a few months to see how their computers are being used. If the machines are sitting in a pile in the corner gathering dust, the linear model must be deemed insufficient (see chapters 6–8, this volume).

The danger of the ecological fallacy rests in the fact that causes and effects may be convoluted (Langbein & Lichtman, 1978). Using data about *physical access* to tell stories about *cognitive access* jumps from the aggregate level to the individual level of analysis. Aggregate-level survey data may indicate that the *average* African American is on the wrong side of the digital divide, but the average is a statistical description of the group's central tendency and does not describe all group members. Many African Americans have the skills and resources necessary to manage the Internet and are very much on the *right* side of the digital divide. Thus, it seems that an equally plausible story about access can begin with cognitive issues first, then move to the social and technological dimensions. Here, the individual with the cognitive skills needed to make effective use of the Internet would likely enter into a social milieu where technological access is more likely. In this model, having the skills to manage the Internet enables social and technological access, not the other way around. If this is the case, then policymakers should sponsor programs that teach members of disadvantaged groups the analytical skills needed to survive in a world of computers, and let the rest of the problem take care of itself.

Another limitation of the linear model has to do with the assumption that content is preproduced and free standing. This opens the model to criticism from cultural scholars such as Carey (1992) and poses a major dilemma for the online industry, which distinguishes between service providers and content providers. It also goes against McLuhan's (1964/1994) insight that content follows the form of the medium through which it is transmitted. Content providers who use the linear model, which assumes pre-produced content is the motor for income generation, may be in real trouble. Implied by this linear process is the idea that content creation takes place somewhere behind the user interface and that exposure and enjoyment occur after development. If, however, the user is an active participant in content generation, as is the case with a growing number of interactive media, the content-as-income-generator model breaks down. Why would users pay for something they have a hand in creating? Remember the mantra of Internet radicals: *information wants to be free.* Here, free means at no monetary cost.

Landow (1992) suggested the nonlinearity of hypertext on the Internet provides an interesting test bed for the postmodern problem of meaning and content. His proposition can be extended to the issue of access.

## Media Access as a Nonlinear Process

The nonlinear model conceptualizes access as a process of content creation as well as acquisition. Here, some subtle but important distinctions need to be restated. Humans are surrounded by a vast and complex data ecology; data objects are the stuff of the physical world. The warming rays of the sun and the cold blast of the winter wind are data. Information is data given structure by humans through the use of an abstract symbol system such as language; access to that information is contingent on an understanding of that language. Content is information given meaning, or narrative structure. Information construction, then, is something that happens on the production side of communication technologies. In a mass-media system, it is something professionals such as journalists do. On the Internet, information resides on the server side of the client–server dyad. Content, on the other hand, can be generated by the client side of the interface; it is something that emerges when the user creates meaning from information. Thus, the fundamental difference between a linear mass-media system and the interactive Internet is that the locus of content creation can shift partly if not wholly from the sender (or server) side of the communication dyad to the receiver (or client) side.

Although assumptions about technological access may not change much in a nonlinear system, maintaining a clear distinction between social and cognitive access is not as straightforward. To begin with, the linear model never really addresses the process of cognitive access; conceptually, it seems like an artifact of social access. Survey data describing who surfs the Internet tell us that education, income, geographic location, and marital status are all statistically associated with physical access to computer technology (Bucy, 2000; NTIA, 1998, 2000, 2002; van Dijk, 2000). But sociodemographic markers, which serve as external indicators, do not specify the psychological processes involved in accessing, apprehending, and making gainful use of online content. The application of the information-processing paradigm has gone a long way toward explaining what happens cognitively during television viewing (see Lang, 2000). But mapping that paradigm to the Internet will require more than simply transferring the television-viewing model to computer use. Moreover, the information-processing perspective assumes that the basic psychological processes employed in television viewing are consistent across individuals. A viewer will orient to the screen when there is a loud noise or bright flash regardless of race, gender, or culture (Lang, 1990). The idea is that basic cognitive processes, such as attention and emotional reactions, are either hardwired in the brain, or represent such overlearned skills that their execution is automatic. Applying information-processing theory to the Internet calls this assumption into question on two counts.

First, social or cultural factors may play more of a role in basic psychological responses to media than currently believed. The facial expression of emotion, for instance, has been found to be remarkably constant across cultures (Ekman, 1982). Little work has been done, however, investigating the role emotion might play in the reception of media content by different social or cultural groups. There may be subtle differences in overlearned skills between cultural groups, for example, that only become apparent when the processing task becomes more complex. Information-processing studies of mass media have not yet looked at the possibility that race or culture might make a difference to variables such as memory and attention, although effects have been found for education (Grabe, Lang, Zhou, & Bolls, 2000; chapter 2, this volume) and age (Lang, Schwartz, & Snyder, 1999). The Internet, still far from a universally usable system, challenges users who have limited textual and technological literacy and who lack the social motivation to engage with the system in the first place. Chances are that the specific skills needed for cognitive access are learned in a specific cultural context. Interestingly, race persists as an important determinant of Internet use and awareness, especially for African Americans, even after controlling for the effects of income and education (Katz, Rice, & Aspden, 2001).

Second, the Internet's ability to present information-dense material, both textual and graphical, with comparable fidelity will require consideration of psychological processes employed by computer users that may differ from users of other electronic media. This again calls for closer examination of the social or cultural backdrop, where some groups may employ much different processing strategies than others. In summary, two things have to be considered as caveats to the assumption that cognitive access is invariant across users. First, cultural and social circumstances may affect basic psychological processes in ways not yet fully considered. Second, a wider range of psychological processes must be brought to bear in processing Internet content than is the case for other electronic media. Again, if cognitive access was consistent across individuals, then it would precede and determine social access.

If social or cultural barriers to new technology use do exist, then certain groups may be excluded from online opportunities entirely, regardless of access to computer hardware or telecommunications infrastructure. This is perhaps the clearest of all issues at a policy level. Liberal democracy works under the assumption that individual characteristics such as gender, race, and class should not impede access to economic opportunity and political empowerment. If the Internet represents the enabling technology in a society where information is power, then the implications of access in all its various manifestations are indeed serious.

Information and communication technologies have already become so pervasive in networked societies it is rapidly becoming impossible to function without at least brushing up against the Internet. Those who are simply outside the matrix of interconnected computers—the central nervous system and customer service interface of an increasing number of governmental and commercial services—are really noncitizens. The 1980s science fiction television drama *Max Headroom* depicted people outside the computer network as "blanks" because in a very literal sense, if they existed outside the network, they had no identity. In American society today, such a person could not have a Social Security number without entering into the governmental bureaucracy's vast computer network, thus excluding them from jobs with retirement and health benefits. They would not have access to credit, excluding them from bank accounts and credit cards, thus largely prohibiting them from owning any substantial property such as a car or house. Illegal immigrants are a good example of such noncitizens who are denied full access to the networked bureaucracy. This group, which substantially contributes to the economy, especially in the West, may be small but should not be overlooked by a society that takes pluralism seriously.

## Media Access as an Interactive Process

A final issue important to consider concerns the temporal sequence of access-related events. Granted, a user must have physical access to a computer before gaining system access to the Internet. However, the case is less clear for content access. Cognitive skills may constrain what can happen at a social or cultural level, but the previous discussion implies that social and psychological factors may be operating in tandem. Furthermore, if McLuhan's insight about the importance of technology to meaning can be carried over to the Internet, technological access and

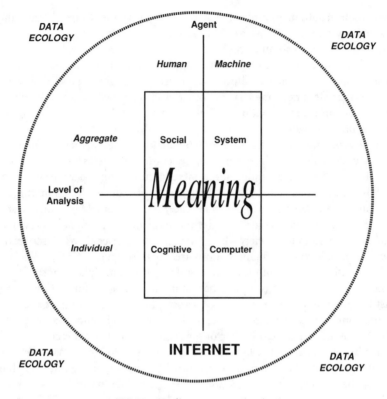

FIG 1.2.    Nonlinear access to meaning.

cognitive access may be interacting in a nonlinear fashion as part of the content creation process.

Problem solving in a postmodern Information Age is not as straightforward as was supposed in the Age of Enlightenment, where rational linear thought was elevated to the highest standard of meaning. The difference can be seen in Fig. 1.2, which models access as a nonlinear process where the user is positioned as an active agent in the creation of content. Here the user is immersed in a sea of information. So-called content providers have preprocessed the data using representational systems, such as language, into information called *messages*, just as they do in a mass-media system. These might be messages about the latest progress in the Middle East peace talks, or they may be messages about which stuffed animals are set for retirement in the Beanie Baby plush toy collection.[7] Depending on the user's background, these messages still may not contain meaning and ought not be confused with meaningful content. A user not versed in the historical complexity of the Middle East may process the message about the peace talks and understand it at a surface level, but not fully comprehend its broader meaning. Such comprehension is the result of both social and cognitive work done by the user on the message to render it meaningful.

In this model, information providers and users alike share in the process of content creation, which takes place in parallel and is distributed across the various levels of access. The model thus empowers the user in ways that a linear mass-media system does not. But it also implies an *active* user engaged in an effortful *intellectual* process. Thus, without remedy, the prospect of widening usage gaps may be truly bleak, suggesting a society where a small information elite, empowered with the social and cognitive skills to benefit from deep access to the Internet, gains an irreversible advantage over a large segment of the population excluded from meaningful access. What makes this process even more insidious is the fact that visible markers, such as race, culture, or gender, may not prove as useful as once assumed in identifying who has access and who does not. The research community should redouble its efforts to better understand and respond to the threats posed by uneven access to new technology from a content perspective, considering the importance of individual factors that are not visibly apparent.

## ENDNOTES

[1] Nevertheless, there are those who would constrain, control, or ban access to certain kinds of content, such as pornography, on the Internet. Some argue that access *per se* can be psychologically harmful, especially for the young. There is a sporadic but steady stream of articles in the popular press (e.g., Rosenstiel & Kovach, 1999) and in academic journals (e.g., Kraut, Patterson, Lundmark, Kiesler, Mukopadhyay, & Scherlis, 1998) critical of unrestricted access, sometimes going so far as to see intensive use as an addiction.

[2] This situation may change over time with the rollout of high definition television and Web TV technologies, but media behaviors will be slow to change.

[3] This technology is not so far-fetched. All the elements, including the touch-sensitive screen and system capable of capturing the user's home address, already exist. Similar prototype systems have been installed in some test markets.

[4] See Newhagen and Levy (1998) for a discussion of the possible impact of the Internet's distributed architecture on the mass communication process.

[5] The Linux operating system is a fully functional freeware version of the powerful UNIX operating system. It provides a counterpoint to the argument that the profit motive will dominate development on the Internet. The program was originally written by Linus Torvalds, a Norwegian graduate student, and distributed for free. Since then, programmers from around the world have enhanced and updated the program to make it one of the premiere versions of UNIX, the preferred operating system for a Web server. Linux is still available for free on the Web and stands as a potential competitor for Microsoft's Windows.

[6] This example obviously oversimplifies the process. Mass media are now available online and information from the newsroom of *The Washington Post* might reach consumers through other routes, such as opinion leaders who previously read the newspaper or portable communication devices. But the principle of the model still stands behind such variations.

[7] The apparent randomness of Web-based information also raises a normative issue of information value or importance. Social moralists might espouse the idea that "good" citizens should attend to

events in the Middle East more closely than they should recent retirements on the Beanie Baby Web site. However, from a strictly populist viewpoint, the fact that the Beanie Baby site (http://ty.com) has received billions of hits cannot be entirely ignored.

# REFERENCES

Bandura, A. (1997). *Self-efficacy: The exercise of control.* New York: W. H. Freeman and Company.

Bucy, E. P. (2000). Social access to the Internet. *Harvard International Journal of Press/Politics, 5*(1), 50–61.

Bucy, E. P., & Newhagen, J. E. (1999). The emotional appropriateness heuristic: Processing televised presidential reactions to the news. *Journal of Communication, 49*(4), 59–79.

Carey, J. W. (1992). *Communication as culture: Essays on media and society.* New York: Routledge.

December, J. (1996). Units of analysis for Internet communication. *Journal of Communication, 46*(1), 14–38.

Ekman, P. (1982). *Emotions in the human face.* Cambridge: Cambridge University Press.

Geiger, S., & Newhagen, J. E. (1993). Revealing the black box: An information processing approach to understanding media effects. *Journal of Communication, 43*(4), 42–50.

Grabe, M. E., Lang, A., Zhou, S., & Bolls, P. (2000). Cognitive access to negatively arousing news: An experimental investigation of the knowledge gap. *Communication Research, 27*(1), 3–26.

Katz, J. E., Rice, R. E., & Aspden, P. (2001). The Internet, 1995–2000: Access, civic involvement, and social interaction. *American Behavioral Scientist, 45*(3), 405–419.

Kraut, R., Patterson, M., Lundmark, V., Kiesler, S., Mukopadhyay, T., & Scherlis, W. (1998). Internet paradox: A social technology that reduces social involvement and psychological well-being? *American Psychologist, 53*(9), 1017–1031.

Landow, G. P. (1992). *Hypertext: The convergence of contemporary critical theory and technology.* Baltimore, MD: The Johns Hopkins Press.

Lang, A. (1990). Involuntary attention and physiological arousal evoked by structural features and emotional content in TV commercials. *Communication Research, 17*(3), 275–299.

Lang, A. (2000). The limited capacity model of mediated message processing. *Journal of Communication, 50*(1), 46–70.

Lang, A., Schwartz, N., & Snyder, J. F. (1999, August). *Slow down, you're moving too fast: Pacing, arousing content, and those aging boomers.* Paper presented to the Association for Education in Journalism and Mass Communication, Communication Theory and Methodology Division. New Orleans, LA.

Langbein, L. I., & Lichtman, A. (1978). *Ecological inference.* Beverly Hills, CA: Sage.

Laurel, B. (1991). *Computers as theatre.* New York: Addison-Wesley.

Marx, K. (1967). *Capital: A critical analysis of capitalist production.* New York: International Publishers. (Original work published 1867).

McChesney, R. W. (1997). *Corporate media and the threat to democracy.* New York: Seven Stories Press.

McLuhan, M. (1994). *Understanding media: The extensions of man.* Cambridge, MA: MIT Press. (Original work published 1964).

Messaris, P., & Abraham, L. (2001). The role of images in framing news stories. In S. D. Reese, O. H. Gandy, Jr., & A. E. Grant (Eds.), *Framing public life: Perspectives on media and our understanding of the social world* (pp. 215–226). Mahwah, NJ: Lawrence Erlbaum Associates.

Newhagen, J. E., & Levy, M. R. (1998). The future of journalism in a distributed communication architecture. In D. L. Borden & K. Harvey (Eds.), *The electronic grapevine: Rumor, reputation, and reporting in the new on-line environment* (pp. 9–21). Mahwah, NJ: Lawrence Erlbaum Associates.

Nie, N. H., & Erbring, L. (2000). *Internet and society: A preliminary report.* Retrieved September 30, 2000, from http://www.stanford.edu/group/siqss/Press_Release/Priliminary_Report-4-21.pdf

NTIA (1998, July). *Falling through the Net: Defining the digital divide.* National Telecommunications and Information Administration, U.S. Department of Commerce. Retrieved July 23, 2002, from http://www.ntia.doc.gov/ntiahome/fttn99/contents.html

NTIA, (2000, October). *Falling through the Net: Toward digital inclusion.* National Telecommunications and Information Administration, U.S. Department of Commerce. Retrieved July 23, 2002, from http://www.ntia.doc.gov/ntiahome/fttn00/contents00.html

NTIA (2002, February). *A nation online: How Americans are expanding their use of the Internet.* National Telecommunications and Information Administration, U.S. Department of Commerce. Retrieved July 23, 2002, from http://www.ntia.doc.gov/ntiahome/dn/index.html

Oram, A. (Ed.). (2001). *Peer-to-peer: Harnessing the power of disruptive technologies.* Sebastopol, CA: O'Reilly & Associates.

Reeves, B., & Nass, C. (1996). *The media equation: How people treat computers, television, and new media like real people and places.* New York: Cambridge University Press.

Rheingold, H. (2000). *The virtual community: Homesteading on the electronic frontier* (rev. ed.). Cambridge, MA: MIT Press.

Rosenstiel, T., & Kovach, B. (1999, February 28). And now . . . the unfiltered, unedited news. *The Washington Post,* B1.

Rumelhart, D., & McClelland, P. (1986). *Parallel distributed processing: Explorations in the microstructure of cognition.* Cambridge, MA: MIT Press.

Schon, D. A., Sanyal, B., & Mitchell, W. J. (Eds.). (1999). *High technology and low-income communities.* Cambridge, MA: MIT Press.

Shingles, R. (1981). Black consciousness and political participation: The missing link. *American Political Science Review, 75,* 76–91.

Shneiderman, B. (1998). *Designing the user interface: Strategies for effective human–computer interaction* (3rd ed.). Reading, MA: Addison-Wesley.

Stephenson, N. (1999). *In the beginning . . . was the command line.* New York: Avon Books.

Taborsky, E. (1998). *Architectonics of semiosis.* New York: St. Martin's.

van Dijk, J. (2000). Widening information gaps and policies of prevention. In K. L. Hacker & J. van Dijk (Eds.), *Digital democracy: Issues of theory & practice* (pp. 166–183). London: Sage.

# Psychological Dimensions
# of Media Access

# 2

# Cognitive Access to New and Traditional Media: Evidence from Different Strata of the Social Order

Maria Elizabeth Grabe
*Indiana University, Bloomington*

Rasha Kamhawi
*Ain Shams University, Cairo*

It is probably fair to argue that at this point, the majority of systematic research about the Internet is the result of aggregate-level, survey-type endeavors. These studies produced valuable information generally about who uses the Web, the regularity of usage, and the most popular uses of this medium. As the editors of this volume persuasively argue in the introductory chapter, more should be known about individual level processes and effects involved in the consumption of content through this new medium. But we depart from the editors' view that aggregate demographic variables are not as useful or important for Internet studies as they once were. In fact, the study reported here was designed to gather evidence not only at the aggregate and individual levels, but also at the intersection of these two dimensions.

To make the importance of this junction point between individual level processes and demography more concrete, let us take a hypothetical finding central to this book: Suppose low levels of cognitive access (as explicated in this book's opening chapter) to information on the Internet are randomly distributed among demographic groups in a society. It would be the work of neuroscientists and perhaps a small enclave of experimental psychologists to explain the phenomenon—perhaps in terms of particular differences in blood chemistry, information-processing aptitude, and, say, the emotional profile of individuals. Thus, if low cognitive access is randomly distributed in the U.S. population, it is likely to be studied and explained in a way similar to a condition such as attention deficit disorder. Yet, because of the growing body of survey findings, we are increasingly sure that Internet use is *not* randomly distributed across demographic groups (Norris, 2001; NTIA, 1998; Wilhem, 2000)—nor is cognitive access to the Internet. In fact, significant findings associated with demographic variables distinguish audience research on Internet effects. It is precisely because cognitive access to the Internet appears to be a demographically discriminatory phenomenon that this new medium is the subject of public debate and deserves the urgent and continued attention of scholars in mass communication and other fields. That said, variables traditionally associated with individual differences, such as emotion and cognition, might provide more nuanced insight into the aggregate findings for demographic inequity in Internet access.

The study reported here experimentally investigated the cognitive access and emotional responses of news consumers across demographic and media channel variables. Specifically, this study focused on education as a potential demographic influence on cognitive access. As we know from the knowledge gap literature, people at lower levels of the social hierarchy acquire information presented in the mass media less efficiently than those members of society who inhabit higher socioeconomic strata (see Gaziano, 1983, 1997, and Viswanath & Finnegan, 1996 for comprehensive reviews of the literature). In most studies, education level is used as the demographic indicator for socioeconomic status. Almost without exception, the knowledge gap has been studied at an aggregate level, using survey methodology, and employing an array of knowledge and memory tests.

The first study to experimentally test the knowledge gap linked the phenomenon to cognitive access and tested knowledge as the ability to encode information, as defined within the limited-capacity theory of information processing (Grabe, Lang, Zhou, & Bolls, 2000). The limited-capacity model provides a micro perspective on the process whereby individual subjects select, encode, store, and retrieve mediated matter. Yet the processing of a message is not seen as a distinctly linear procedure. New information often does not sequentially move through the selection, encoding, storage, and retrieval sequence. For example, encoded information might not be stored at all or already stored information might be used to support the encoding process (Lang, 2000, 2001).

At the heart of this cognitive course are the mechanisms whereby media consumers either automatically or deliberately allocate the limited available resources across messages and phases of information processing. Evidently, some messages or parts of messages enjoy resource allocation at the expense of other message components that are ignored or not digested very well. Controlled or deliberate allocation, as the concept implies, are under the control of the media consumer. Several factors may activate controlled resource allocation, including the goals, intentions, interests, and motivations of an audience member. Automatic allocation, on the other hand, is involuntarily triggered by characteristics of the message such as attention-grabbing production techniques or compelling message content. Motivation to attend to a message, or controlled processing, varies greatly from viewer to viewer as an individual difference, whereas the basic mechanics of automatic information processing are shared by most human biological systems. Thus, differences among viewers in terms of controlled information processing are largely explainable by varying levels of interest in the message; differences among viewers in terms of automatic processing are best explained by variance in aptitude to process information efficiently.

By activating automatic processing in subjects, the Grabe et al. (2000) study provided experimental evidence that adult subjects with lower levels of education (high school or less) have lower levels of cognitive access to television news than subjects with college degrees.[1] Although both groups paid equal levels of attention to the television news stories, the lower education group was significantly less effective in encoding information. More-educated viewers may remember more from the media than less-educated consumers because their thought processes and ability to make connections between related pieces of information are more elaborated (Park & Kosicki, 1995). Elaboration is important because it leads to a higher level of processing and an increase in the amount of information stored (Craik & Lockhart, 1972). Similarly, Chew and Palmer (1994), J. Robinson (1967), and Rogers (1976) argued that less-educated people may have less-developed cognitive abilities to select, store, and retrieve information, suggesting they may gain less knowledge from the same amount of information exposure than higher educated people. Because of these research findings, the first and second hypotheses are posed:

H1: Subjects with higher levels of education will have better recognition memory for news information than subjects with lower levels of education.

H2: Subjects with higher levels of education will report less difficulty in understanding news stories than subjects with lower levels of education.

As with the limited capacity theory, knowledge gap research approaches motivation as a prominent individual-level variable to explain information gain differences (see Gaziano, 1997; Viswanath & Finnegan, 1996). Motivation to attend to messages has been tested in relation to knowledge gain using variables such as viewer interest, involvement, concern, participation, and perceived message importance and credibility (Chew & Palmer, 1994; Ettema, Brown, & Luepker, 1983; Ettema & Kline, 1977; Fredin, Monnett, & Kosicki, 1994; Genova & Greenberg, 1979; Kwak, 1999; McLeod & Perse, 1994). Ettema and Kline (1977), as well as Ettema, Brown, and Luepker (1983), concluded that knowledge gaps exist in large part because of differing levels of interest in and use for information. They dismissed information-processing explanations for the knowledge gap by arguing that public affairs issues do not require highly developed processing abilities. Instead, they argued that public affairs issues are merely more relevant and useful to people in higher socioeconomic groups, which leads to the formation of knowledge gaps. The idea that people with lower levels of education are less motivated to acquire news suggests the third hypothesis:

> H3: Subjects with higher levels of education will rate news stories as more important, interesting, informative, believable, and objective, and have stronger emotional responses to news than subjects with lower levels of education.

The foregoing discussion highlighted how education level and motivation to gain information could be expected to explain some of the variance in cognitive access to news. This study also concerns medium or channel differences, in particular the potential of different media to advance or inhibit cognitive access. Channel, or news source studies, as they are sometimes called, have enjoyed considerable attention in mass communication research (e.g., Gunter, Furnham, & Gietson, 1994; J. Robinson & Levy, 1980; Stauffer, Frost, & Rybolt, 1987). Yet, viewed comprehensively, this body of findings appears somewhat inconclusive about the efficiency of different news channels in advancing an informed public. Contradictory findings can perhaps be explained as a function of inconsistent memory/knowledge measures, varying ecological validity of experimental stimuli, and differences in the data collection environment. The subject pools also vary across studies from undergraduate students to adult community members. In the study of news, it seems particularly important to use adult subjects because they are more likely than college undergraduates to be motivated and regular news consumers.

News channel research gained momentum when a number of survey studies began to document that media consumers did not seem to learn much from news, particularly television and radio news (Katz, Adoni, & Parness, 1977; Neuman, 1976; Wilson, 1994). For instance, at least two separate studies found that a few minutes after a newscast, about 50% of randomly selected survey participants could not recall a single news story (Neuman, 1976). Interestingly, the same type of survey research, asking people to recall news stories from newspapers they had just read, was never really done on print journalism. The research bias is to scrutinize television and radio for their efficiency in informing the public. Another series of survey studies linked people who cite television news as their primary source of news to lower levels of knowledge than those who primarily rely on print media for news (Becker & Whitney, 1981; Clarke & Fredin, 1979; M. Robinson, 1974; Wade & Schramm, 1969). Consequently, two popular explanations for television's inadequacy to enlighten citizens emerged: The videocentric nature of the medium discourages thorough processing (Patterson & McClure, 1976; Singer, 1980); and viewers pay less attention to television than to print media during exposure (Chaiken & Eagly, 1976; Levy, 1978). There were also investigations offering evidence that television was indeed not entirely inferior to print media in providing memorable information (Chaffee & Schleuder, 1986; Chaffee, Zhao, & Leshner, 1994; Culbertson & Stempel, 1986; Neuman, Just, & Crigler, 1992; Reese & Miller, 1981; Van Der Molen & Van Der Voort, 2000). These studies found that television could be a rich source of learning. At the same time, experimental work on news channel comparisons ensued. The studies by Gunter and associates are particularly emphatic in pegging television as the lesser channel for conveying important information to citizens (e.g., Furnham & Gunter, 1987; Gunter, 1987; Gunter, Furnham, & Gietson, 1994).

Facorro and DeFleur (1993) added the computer screen to the repertoire of information channels and found it to be almost as effective for learning as the printed word, with television the least effective medium tested. In channel comparisons across print and online news (Eveland & Dunwoody, 2000) and then print, television, and online news (Eveland, Seo, & Marton, 2001), support was found that print news is most effective, followed by online and television news. Research on information processing of Web news is limited but suggests superiority over television in memory tests. Although a small number of studies have offered evidence that television could, under certain circumstances, be as good as or better than newspapers in conveying memorable facts (Neuman, Just, & Crigler, 1992), the vast majority of research suggests otherwise (Facorro & De Fleur, 1993; Wilson, 1994) and forms the basis of the following hypotheses:

H4: Across all subjects, recognition memory for news information will be best for newspapers, followed by the Web, and then television.

H5: Across all subjects, newspaper stories will be perceived as less difficult to understand than Web-based and television stories.

Trusting the long line of media use studies (see, for example, the Pew Center archives) and McLuhan's (1964) pronouncement that "The medium is the message," news channels should produce variance in captivating consumers. In particular, as a cold and involving medium, most capable of directly conveying events in the social world, television news should be rated higher on importance, interest, informativeness, and believability compared to the same stories published in newspapers or on the Web. Moreover, television news should elicit stronger emotional responses than newspaper and news Web stories do. Hence, the following series of hypotheses regarding evaluative responses are posed:

H6: The content of television stories would be rated as more intense than newspaper or Web versions of the stories.

H7: Television stories would be rated as more important than newspaper or Web versions of the stories.

H8: Television stories would be rated as more emotionally captivating and inviting participation than newspaper or Web versions.

H9: Television stories would be rated as more informative and believable than newspaper or Web versions.

At the intersection of the two factors of concern in this study, education and media channel, stands the obvious question whether television, newspapers, and the Web might vary in their potential to facilitate and motivate cognitive access to news for audience members with different levels of education. Television has repeatedly been pointed out as the worst medium to convey information. At the same time, a number of knowledge gap studies produced evidence of television as the great equalizer of the knowledge gap (Galloway, 1977; Gantz, 1978; Neuman, 1976; Shinghi & Mody, 1976; Tichenor, Donohue, & Olien, 1970; Torsvik, 1972). Other knowledge gap study findings showed television's inability to rectify information inequities across socioeconomic strata. In fact, a number of knowledge gap studies have contradicted the notion that television viewing eliminates the knowledge gap (Gandy & El Waylly, 1985; Griffin, 1990; Gunter, 1987; Horstmann, 1991; McLeod & Perse, 1994; Simmons & Garda, 1982). Overall, it is perhaps most accurate to describe investigations of television's capacity to create a more evenly informed citizenry as inconclusive. The flurry of optimism about television's potential to serve democracy aside, information-processing literature has demonstrated that television news viewing is not a simple cognitive task. The cognitive system is burdened with processing multiple audiovisual channels (voice, ambient sound, visual material) in a social environment crowded with distraction (Drew & Grimes, 1987; Graber, 1990; Newhagen, 1998).

The uncertainty about the interaction of channel and education variables begs for experimental investigation. Evidence exists on how viewers with varying levels of education respond to a single medium. Understanding the comparative effectiveness of different media to inform and captivate audience members with different levels of education seems imperative.

Knowledge gap research confirms that people on the lower socioeconomic strata tend to depend more on television than print media for information (Bogart, 1981; McLeod & Perse, 1994). Yet people in higher and lower education groups do not obtain information from television news with the same efficiency (Grabe et al., 2000; Stauffer, Frost, & Rybolt, 1978). A possible explanation is that the educational processes that develop specific reading and writing skills may enhance the general ability to process visual and aural information (Park & Kosicki, 1995). Given the absence of research findings to ground hypotheses, the following two research questions are proposed:

RQ1: Are there interaction effects across education level and channels for dependent measures of motivation?
RQ2: Are there interaction effects for education level and media channels for recognition memory?

## METHOD

To investigate these questions, this experiment employed a mixed 3 (channel) × 2 (education) × 4 (message) × 3 (order of presentation) factorial design. The between-subjects factors were education and order of presentation. There were two levels of education, higher and lower. Subjects with lower levels had a high school education or less; those in the higher education group had graduate degrees. They either completed a PhD or were enrolled in a doctoral program. Each subject was randomly assigned to one of three presentation orders where the order of channels was counterbalanced. The within-subjects variables were: channel (television, newspaper, and World Wide Web) and message, represented by the four different news stories that each subject was exposed to in each channel (television, newspaper, and World Wide Web).

### Stimuli

The stimuli for this experiment consisted of 12 news stories, each packaged in all three channels (television, newspaper, Web). Each subject was exposed to all 12 stories but in different combinations of television, newspaper, and the Web. Thus, every subject responded to 12 stories—four presented in each of the three channels.

Stories were selected from a larger sample of news coverage in the *Philadelphia Inquirer* newspaper, the paper's Web site, and the ABC television news affiliate in Philadelphia (WPVI), during the weekdays of April 10 to the 14, 1999. Stimuli were pulled from the Philadelphia news market to reduce the likelihood that subjects in a Midwestern city had already been exposed to the stimuli. Stories with a distinct local angle were chosen.

Twenty stories were covered in all three media during the 5-day period chosen for stimuli selection. A manipulation check was performed to select stories eliciting the same level of emotion across channel versions. The final selection of stories was based on similarity of information, arousal, and length across channels. The twelve selected stories where about the arraignment of a suspected serial killer, a bus driver charged with assaulting students, a child stalker on the loose, inoculation against bacterial meningitis at a school, a motorist fined for using a cellular phone while driving, the mayor's new crime initiative, a local drug company's plunging stock, pollution of a creek, an infant swing recall, a highway expansion, an energy company's decision not to move its headquarters out of the city, and plans to expand a commuter rail service.

The television stories featured the full range of broadcast news formats, including voice-over (VO) and voice-over sound on tape (VO/SOT) stories, as well as packages.[2] Stories ranged from 26 to 150 seconds in duration. The average length of the stories was 65 seconds. Their corresponding newspaper versions also varied in length ranging from news in brief (±230 words) to major stories (±600 words).[3] To ensure comparability, the Web stories were taken from the newspaper's Web site.[4]

One goal of this study was to preserve the ecological validity of the stimuli as far as possible. Often in channel studies, television stories are transcribed for the print or online version. Although this approach offers a high level of experimental control, the claim of studying news channel differences is contrived. The styles of writing and the packaging of information differ substantially between media channels. To extract a portion from one channel to validly represent another channel is ecologically erroneous. The decision was therefore made to sacrifice some level of experimental control within this study in favor of ecological validity. No changes were made to either the newspaper or television versions of the stories. Subjects read the newspaper stories from the original newspapers but were instructed not to read continuations for two stories located elsewhere in the paper. This was done to keep the amount of information equal across channels. Television stories were transferred to videotape in three orders of presentation. No changes were made to them. The online stories were minimally edited for length to control for volume of information across the three channels. Moreover, the name of the *Philadelphia Inquirer* was removed from the index page to avoid association between the newspaper and the online conditions.

## Dependent Variables

Viewed as one of the important catalysts of information processing, recognition memory was used to assess the encoding process (Lang & Basil, 1998; Lang, Dhillon, & Dong, 1995; Newhagen & Reeves, 1992). Because encoding is a requirement for subsequent information processing phases, it is used here as an early indicator of cognitive access. Twenty-four forced multiple-choice questions measured recognition memory. There were two questions for each story, each with five options and one correct answer.

Subjects' emotional reactions to the stories were measured using SAM (Self-Assessment Mannequin). This picture scale has been used to measure valence, arousal, and dominance responses to media fare. It includes five boxed-in images of a gender-neutral human figure for each emotion. Subjects were instructed to mark on or between the five images yielding a nine-point scale for each dimension of emotion. The SAM valence scale has five facial expressions ranging from a smile to a frown. The SAM scale for arousal depicts emotional states ranging from drowsiness to extreme excitement. The dominance dimension measures feelings that incrementally vary from unempowerment, represented by a miniature-sized mannequin figure, to a sense of empowerment depicted by a mannequin filling the box around it.

Similarly, nine-point semantic differential scales were used to record other evaluative responses. These measures were anchored by bipolar concepts and assessed the importance of the information to the larger community where the news broke and to the subject personally, how engaging, informative, believable, objective, interesting, and easy to understand stories were, and how pressing the issues reported in the stories were, as well as the perceived intensity with which people featured in the news were involved in the issues.[5]

## Subjects

Subjects consisted of 42 people, equally divided by gender and education, and selected on specific media consumption behavior. At a minimum, subjects attended to each of the three media at least once a week.[6] Around 83% of subjects were between 30 and 49.[7] Three subjects were minorities (two African American and one Asian). No undergraduate students participated in the experiment. Subjects were recruited through e-mail solicitation and posted flyers at community centers.

## Procedure

Data were collected over a month period in August 2001. Subjects were randomly assigned to a stimulus order at the beginning of each session. The room where the experiment was conducted looked like a furnished living room. Two upholstered sofas, a coffee table, and a television and videotape player on a stand comprised the television viewing area. This is also where subjects read the newspaper stories. I-Mac computer terminals, on the other side of the room, were used to access the online stories.

Subjects were greeted at the door by the experimenter, seated on the sofa, and offered a soft drink. They were asked to make themselves as comfortable as possible and encouraged to take their shoes off or to put their feet on the coffee table if they wished to do so. They first read and signed the consent form[8] and were briefed about the general procedure of the study. The emotion and semantic differential scales were explained and subjects were given the chance to ask questions. Two subjects, belonging to the same education group, were scheduled to participate at a time. The experimenters collected data from one subject at a time if the second one failed to show up. The experimenter stayed in the room during the experiment to coordinate exposure to the three channels. At times when the subjects were recording their responses the experimenter was seated at a table, at a comfortable distance from the subject, and stayed engaged in reading.

After attending to each story, subjects paused to respond to the battery of evaluative measures. After all the stories had been read or viewed, subjects provided demographic information and then watched a short segment from the television sitcom, *Friends,* which served as a short-term memory distracter. They were asked to identify the theme of the segment. Subjects were then handed randomly ordered multiple-choice questions. Subjects were thanked, given a $15 monetary reward for participating, and asked not to discuss the study with anybody to prevent contamination of other potential subjects.

## RESULTS

### Education

In line with the knowledge gap literature, Hypotheses 1 and 2 tested cognitive access to news across education groups. The predictions were that the lower education group would have poorer recognition memory and also perceive the news as harder to understand than the higher education group. Although there were no significant differences between the two groups in how understandable the stories were $F(1, 42) = 1.57$, $p < .210$, their recognition memory for news story facts varied significantly. The main effect $F(1, 42) = 8.43$, $p < .001$ for education on recognition memory reveals that the low education group was not as accurate in recognizing information in a multiple choice test as the high education group. Table 2.1 summarizes the results of all ANOVA tests for education level.

The third hypothesis predicted that subjects in the higher education group would report higher levels of motivation to gain information from the news. This hypothesis predicted the highest scores for those with graduate education across all evaluative measures, including the importance of news events, emotional responses to stories, and evaluations of all three media channels' credibility. Although Table 2.1 shows several main effects for education, the means are not all in the predicted direction. In fact, it appears that the low education group was generally more impressed by the importance of news events than subjects with higher education. Subjects with lower levels of education also rated how intensely *people* in the news

TABLE 2.1
Main Effects for Education

| Variable | Lower Education Group M | Higher Education Group M | p |
| --- | --- | --- | --- |
| Recognition memory | 4.96 | 18.00 | 0.001 |
| Hard to understand | 2.66 | 2.88 | 0.210 |
| Intensity of involvement | 7.07 | 6.28 | 0.001 |
| Magnitude of problem | 6.73 | 6.20 | 0.008 |
| Importance for community | 7.62 | 7.27 | 0.010 |
| Personal importance | 4.94 | 4.27 | 0.005 |
| Interesting | 6.01 | 5.58 | 0.016 |
| Arousal | 4.70 | 7.78 | 0.652 |
| Dominance | 6.05 | 5.86 | 0.340 |
| Valence (positive) | 3.92 | 4.43 | 0.001 |
| Informative | 6.77 | 6.03 | 0.001 |
| Objective | 5.35 | 5.74 | 0.039 |
| Believable | 7.58 | 7.32 | 0.045 |

*Note:* All means based on nine-point scale except recognition memory that indicates mean scores on a maximum of 24. With dominance, a lower score means more empowerment.

were involved in issues $F(1, 42) = 16.07$, $p < .001$ and how pressing *issues* and *problems* in news reports were $F(1, 42) = 7.12$, $p < .008$ significantly higher than the higher education group. Ratings of the perceived importance of news for the community at large $F(1, 42) = 5.93$, $p < .01$ and for the subjects individually $F(1, 42) = 7.90$, $p < .005$ also produced significant main effects in the opposite direction than predicted. Less-education subjects rated the importance of news for them personally and for the communities where the news events happened higher than subjects with more education. Subjects with lower levels of education also found news generally to be more interesting than those with graduate education $F(1, 42) = 5.80$, $p < .01$.

At the same time, the high education group did not appear to be emotionally more captivated by news than the low education group. Of the three measures for emotional involvement, only one, valence, produced a significant main effect for education $F(1, 42) = 14.83$, $p < .001$. The group with higher levels of education produced an overall close-to-neutral rating ($M = 4.43$ on a 9-point scale) for the valence measure, whereas the low education group showed a negatively valenced ($M = 3.93$) response to the news stories. This might indicate more emotional stability in the high education group when consuming news. On the other hand, although not statistically significant, the means for arousal and dominance (the two other dimensions of emotion) were in the predicted direction.

The education factor also produced significant main effects for the three measures of news reliability. Contrary to prediction, though, subjects with lower levels of education rated news stories as significantly more informative $F(1, 42) = 20.04$, $p < .001$ and believable $F(1, 42) = 4.03$, $p < .045$ than subjects with higher levels of education. At the same time, as predicted, subjects with higher levels of education evaluated the news stories overall as more objective than the lower education group $F(1, 42) = 4.30$, $p < .038$.

## Channel

Hypothesis 4 predicted that recognition memory would be best for newspaper stories, followed by the Web and television. The main effect for channel on the multiple-choice scores approached significance $F(2, 42) = 2.43$, $p < .08$. Yet, television stories were remembered best ($M = 17.58$, $SD = 0.61$), followed by Web versions ($M = 16.20$, $SD = 0.66$) and newspaper stories ($M = 15.78$, $SD = 0.61$). Following a similar pattern, news on the Web ($M = 3.18$, $SD = 2.12$) was rated as significantly harder to understand than the same stories covered in the *Philadelphia Inquirer* newspaper ($M = 2.73$, $SD = 1.86$) and on the ABC-TV affiliate newscast ($M = 2.42$, $SD = 1.63$) $F(2, 42) = 6.60$, $p < .001$. Contrary to the predictions of Hypotheses 4 and 5, across all subjects, newspaper versions of stories were not perceived as aiding understandability as much as TV and Web versions. In fact, the Web emerged as the most user-unfriendly, and newspapers were associated with the lowest levels of cognitive access. Television, on the other hand, was rated not only as presenting news in the most understandable manner but also as the best catalyst for cognitive access based on recognition memory measures.

The results for the evaluative measures generally produced support of McLuhan's (1964) notion of television as a highly involving medium. First, Hypothesis 6 predicted that television would have greater potential to intensify content aspects of news stories than the two text-based channels employed in this study, newspaper and the Web. To test this prediction, two items probing subject evaluations of (a) how intense people featured in stories were engaged in news issues, and (b) the magnitude of issues presented in stories, were used. The main effect for channel on evaluations of how engaged people in the stories were was not significant $F(2, 42) = .31$, $p < .74$. The main effect for the other item, subject perceptions of the magnitude of issues, approached significance $F(2, 42) = 1.70$, $p < .18$, and the means were in the predicated direction. Issues in television versions of stories were perceived as more serious ($M = 6.71$, $SD = 2.20$) than either Web ($M = 6.40$, $SD = 2.13$) or newspaper ($M = 6.27$, $SD = 2.26$) versions of the stories.

Second, Hypothesis 7 predicted that television news stories would be rated as more important than the Web and newspaper versions. The potential of the different media to render importance to news events was investigated by asking subjects to rate the importance of each story to the members of the community where the news event occurred and to them personally. Both items produced insignificant main effects: $F(2, 42) = .38$, $p < .68$ and $F(2, 42) = .31$, $p < .73$, respectively.

Third, Hypothesis 8 predicted that television would be rated as the most emotionally captivating, followed by the Web and then newspapers. The results generally supported this hypothesis. Four scaled items were used to test this prediction. The SAM scale for emotional arousal produced no significant differences between channels, $F(2, 42) = .26$, $p < .77$. Yet, there was a significant main effect for the SAM valence measure $F(2, 42) = 8.03$, $p < .001$. Stories that appeared on television news ($M = 4.54$, $SD = 1.63$) elicited significantly higher levels of positive emotion than Web ($M = 4.07$, $SD = 1.36$) and newspaper ($M = 3.91$, $SD = 1.34$) versions. The main effect for the SAM dominance scale was also significant $F(2, 42) = 2.93$, $p < .05$ and in the predicted direction. Subjects reported that they were more empowered and encouraged to take action by what they saw in the television news stories ($M = 5.63$, $SD = 2.31$) than what they read on the Web ($M = 6.05$, $SD = 2.15$) or in newspapers ($M = 6.21$, $SD = 2.20$).[9] The main effect for channel on ratings of how interesting the stories were was also significant $F(2, 42) = 2.89$, $p < .05$—again in the predicted direction. Indeed, television stories ($M = 6.09$, $SD = 1.88$) were rated significantly more interesting than Web ($M = 5.71$, $SD = 2.12$) or newspaper versions ($M = 5.59$, $SD = 1.80$).

Finally, Hypothesis 9 predicted that television news would be perceived as more reliable than newspapers or online news. Of the three scaled measures used to test this proposition (informative, believable, objective[10]), none produced significant main effects for channel.

## Channel by Education Interaction

Research questions 1 and 2 queried about possible interaction effects across education level and news channel for motivation and cognitive access variables. Although there is not enough research evidence to pose specific hypotheses, it is not unreasonable to expect that subjects with lower levels of education might respond overall more favorably to television stories, whereas the high education group might show an overall preference for and competence in using text-based media. In the interaction test, about one third of the dependent variables produced significant or near significant factorial relationships in the expected direction.

First, of the emotional response series, the SAM dominance scale produced a near significant interaction $F(2, 42) = 1.72$, $p < .170$ (see Fig. 2.1). The low education group is associated with lower ratings of empowerment (emotional dominance) for text-based media (newspaper and Web) than for television. By contrast, the higher education group showed less variance in their reported empowerment across media.

Second, two measures regarding the perceived reliability and usability of the different news channels produced notable interactions (see Figs. 2.2 and 2.3). Subjects in the lower education group rated newspapers lower on objectivity than television and the Web, whereas the higher education group provided a high objectivity rating for newspapers. This interaction approached significance $F(2, 42) = 1.91$, $p < .140$. Finally, there was a significant channel by education interaction for ratings of perceived difficulty to understand the news stories $F(2, 42) = 17.91$, $p < .008$. As shown in Fig. 2.3, the low education group found

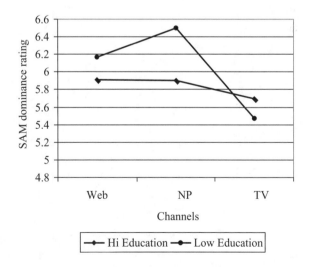

FIG 2.1.  Interaction for channel by education level on SAM dominance scale.

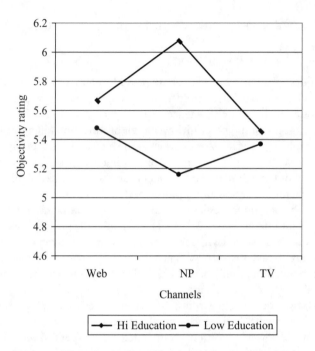

FIG 2.2.   Interaction for channel by education level on objectivity.

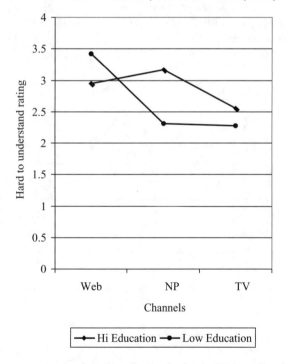

FIG 2.3.   Interaction for channel by education level on evaluations of how hard it was to understand news stories.

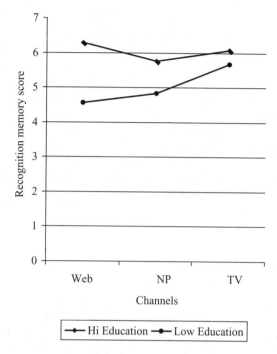

FIG 2.4.    Interaction for channel and education level on recognition memory.

the Web versions of stories significantly harder to understand than newspaper or television stories. In comparison, the high education group rated newspaper stories as the most difficult to understand.

Third, these results show that people with different levels of education have different skills in encoding information presented in different media channels. The recognition memory test produced a near significant interaction effect $F(2, 42) = 2.67$, $p < .070$. In fact, as Fig. 2.4 indicates, the knowledge gap is most pronounced for Web stories, least obvious when news is offered in the television format.

## DISCUSSION

This study found little evidence to support survey research claims that people with lower levels of education are less motivated than those with higher levels of education to be captivated by news stories. To the contrary, it appears that the subjects in the low education group were more interested in the news than those with graduate education. It is therefore unlikely that the lower education group deliberately withheld information-processing resources over which they had control due to lack of motivation. At the same time, although not statistically significant, subjects with lower levels of education reported less arousal and empowerment in response to the news stories than the high education group. This finding supports earlier research that showed significantly lower levels of self-reported and phys- iological arousal associated with news viewing by subjects in a lower education category (Grabe et al., 2000). The results reported here provide more evidence that people with lower levels of education are less efficient in allocating uncon- trolled resources to information processing. The results also seem to confirm that subjects with lower levels of education have lower aptitude as encoders of news information. In that sense, this study joins the large body of research that offers evidence of a knowledge gap between people on higher and lower levels of the social hierarchy. What stands out about the reported findings is that the automatic, not controlled, allocation of resources appears to be the specific area in which people with lower levels of education are unequally equipped for information processing.

This study also provides important insight into news channel differences. Con- trary to what most channel studies have reported, television, not newspapers, emerged as the most user-friendly medium with the highest probability of pro- viding cognitive access to news information. There might be several reasons why the study reported here departs from existing findings that link print media to efficient information processing. One specific methodological difference concerns the nature of experimental stimuli. The most common way in which stimuli have been prepared for channel studies is to take television stories as is, to remove video to represent the radio versions, to type up the television news scripts for the print versions, and to post that text on a server for the online versions. This method of creating stimuli certainly enhances experimental control. At the same time, eco- logical validity is sacrificed to the point where stimuli do not resemble the distinct media channels and external validity is fatally compromised.

Radio, television, newspapers, and perhaps to a lesser degree the online envi- ronment, have distinct styles of packaging news information.[11] Most distinctly, television employs a narrative or chronological style of storytelling and blends am- bient sound, reporter voice recounting of events, sound bites from interviewees, and direct address to camera with the video channel. Oftentimes, images and am- bient sound alone tell portions of the story. In sharp contrast, the inverted pyramid style of newspaper reporting promotes summary writing in which the bottom line is offered up front and details unfold in later paragraphs. Radio and the Web also have their irreconcilable channel peculiarities. When researchers use one medium to spin off stimuli for another, they are not testing channel differences. In this study, the researchers chose to sacrifice some experimental control to preserve the integrity of channel characteristics and boost ecological validity. In the end, this might explain why some findings contradict existing research. Importantly, what was measured here was arguably a more reliable snapshot of what news consumers encounter and process when they attend to mass media in their daily lives than the controlled but contrived stimuli representations often used in "channel" studies.

From this study it is possible to conclude that television provides the easiest access to information, particularly to subjects in the lower education group, and that it has the potential, under certain circumstances, to repair some of the knowledge disparity between people at higher and lower levels of the social order. What is also clear from the education by channel interactions is that the Web can be expected to widen the knowledge gap because of cognitive access (measured here as encoding of information) inequities between those with lower and higher levels of education.


# ENDNOTES

[1] Automatic processing was activated using negatively compelling visual content. Moreover, recognition memory tests have been shown to be effective in measuring the encoding phase and was employed in the Grabe et al. (2000) study.

[2] In voice-over stories a news anchor reads the script while video or graphic depictions appear on the screen so that the anchor is heard, not seen. In such stories interviews and reporters are not present in voice or in appearance. A VO/SOT (voice-over sound on tape) is a story similar to the voice-over but in this case there is typically one interview and no reporter present. A package is a story in which the anchor reads an introduction on camera and then a reporter appears in voice narration and often in a stand-up address to the camera. In other words, it is an independent report compiled and narrated by the reporter. Often more than one interview is included.

[3] Four of the story continuations on subsequent pages were not included to keep the stories between channels corresponding in size and amount of information.

[4] The online stories on the television station and newspaper sites were similar in format. Graphics, pictures, audio, and video were absent. Only 3 of the 12 stories selected were available on the television station's Web site, whereas the newspaper's Web site carried 10 of the 12 stories. The newspaper Web stories were identical to the ones published in the newspaper. The two missing Web stories were therefore created based on newspaper stories.

[5] Story-specific questions were designed for the last two evaluative measures of intensity.

[6] Around 56% were online once a week, 17% were online two to three times a week, and 27% were online more than 4 times a week. In newspaper consumption, 29% read a newspaper once a week, 29% did so 2 to 3 times a week, and 42% reported that they read a newspaper more than 4 times a week. Exposure to some form of television news occurred once a week for 60.3% of subjects, 2 to 3 times a week for 24.3% of subjects, and more than 4 times a week for 15.4% of subjects.

[7] About 14% were below 30, and 2% were above 49.

[8] They were assured that their comments would be anonymous.

[9] A lower mean indicates more empowered, whereas a higher mean suggests ratings of powerlessness and reluctance to take action.

[10] Informative: $F(2, 42) = 1.82$, $p = .16$
Believable: $F(2, 42) = 1.93$, $p = .39$
Objective: $F(2, 42) = 1.90$, $p = .65$

[11] Although national news sources such as msnbc.com and nyt.com are good examples of multimedia Web sites, local news Web sites, such as the one used in this study, still mirror their print versions closely.

# REFERENCES

Becker, L., & Whitney, C. (1981). The effects of media dependencies on audience assessment assessments of government. *Communication Research, 2,* 167–188.

Bogart, L. (1981). *Press and the public: Who reads what, when, where and why in American newspapers.* Hillsdale, NJ: Lawrence Erlbaum Associates.

Chaffee, S., & Schleuder, J. (1986). Measurement and effects of attention to media news. *Human Communication Research, 13*(1), 76–107.

Chaffee, S., Zhao, X., & Leshner, G. (1994). Political knowledge and the campaign media of 1992. *Communication Research, 21*(3), 305–324.

Chaiken, S., & Eagly, A. (1976). Communication modality as a determinant of message persuasiveness and message comprehensibility. *Journal of Personality and Social Psychology, 3*(4), 605–614.

Chew, F., & Palmer, S. (1994). Interest, the knowledge gap and television programming. *Journal of Broadcasting & Electronic Media, 38*(3), 271–287.

Clarke, P., & Fredin, E. (1979). Newspapers, television and political reasoning. *Public Opinion Quarterly, 40,* 337–348.

Craik, F., & Lockhart, R. (1972). Levels of processing: A framework for memory research. *Journal of Verbal Learning and Verbal Behavior, 11,* 671–684.

Culbertson, H., & Stempel G., III (1986). How media use and reliance affect knowledge level. *Communication Research, 13,* 579–602.

Drew, D., & Grimes, T. (1987). Audio-visual redundancy and TV news recall. *Communication Research, 14,* 452–462.

Ettema, J., Brown, J., & Luepker, R, (1983). Knowledge gap effects in a health information campaign. *Public Opinion Quarterly, 47,* 516–527.

Ettema, J., & Kline, F. (1977). Deficits, differences and ceilings: Contingent conditions for understanding the knowledge gap. *Communication Research, 4,* 179–202.

Eveland, W. P., & Dunwoody, S. (2000, June). *A test of competing hypotheses about the impact of the World Wide Web versus traditional print media on learning.* Paper presented at the annual meeting of the International Communication Association, Acapulco, Mexico.

Eveland, W. P., Seo, M., & Marton, K. (2001). *Learning from the news in campaign 2000: An experimental comparison of TV news, newspapers, and online news.* Paper presented at the annual meeting of the Association for Education in Journalism and Mass Communication, Washington, DC.

Facorro, L., & DeFleur, M. (1993). A cross-cultural analysis on how well audiences remember news stories from newspapers, computer, television and radio sources. *Journalism Quarterly, 70*(3), 585–601.

Fredin, E., Monnett, T., & Kosicki, G. (1994). Knowledge gaps, social locators and media schemata: Gaps, reverse gaps and gaps of disaffection. *Journalism Quarterly, 71*(1), 176–190.

Furnham, A., & Gunter, B. (1987). Sex, presentation mode and memory for violent and nonviolent news. *Journal of Educational Television, 11,* 99–105.

Galloway, J. (1977). The analysis and significance of communication effects gaps. *Communication Research, 4*(4), 363–386.

Gandy, O., & ElWaylly, M. (1985). The knowledge gap and foreign affairs: The Palestinian-Israeli conflict. *Journalism Quarterly, 62,* 777–783

Gantz, W. (1978). How uses and gratifications affect recall of television news. *Journalism Quarterly, 55,* 664–672.

Gaziano, C. (1983). The knowledge gap: An analytical review of media effects. *Communication Research, 10,* 447–486.

Gaziano, C. (1997). Forecast 2000: Widening knowledge gaps. *Journalism & Mass Communication Quarterly, 74*(2), 237–264.

Genova, B., & Greenberg, B. (1979). Interests in news and the knowledge gap. *Public Opinion Quarterly, 43*(1), 79–91.

Grabe, M. E., Lang, A., Zhou, S., & Bolls, P. (2000). Cognitive access to negatively arousing news: An experimental investigation of the knowledge gap. *Communication Research, 27*(1), 3–26.

Graber, D. A. (1990). Seeing is remembering: How visuals contribute to learning from television news. *Journal of Communication, 40*(3), 134–155.

Griffin, R. (1990). Energy in the eighties: Education, communication and the knowledge gap. *Journalism Quarterly, 67,* 554–566.

Gunter, B. (1987). *Poor reception: Misunderstanding and forgetting broadcast news.* Hillsdale, NJ: Lawrence Erlbaum Associates.

Gunter, B., Furnham, A., & Gietson, G. (1994). Memory for the news as a function of the channel of communication. *Human Learning, 3,* 265–271.

Horstmann, R. (1991). Knowledge gaps revisited: Secondary analyses from German. *European Journals of Communication, 6,* 77–93.

Katz, E., Adoni, H., & Parness, P. (1977). Remembering the news: What the picture adds to recall. *Journalism Quarterly, 54,* 231–239.

Kwak, N. (1999). Revisiting the knowledge gap hypothesis: Education, motivation and media use. *Communication Research, 26*(4), 385–413.

Lang, A. (2000). The limited capacity model of mediated message processing. *Journal of Communication, 50*(1), 46–70.

Lang, A. (2001). The limited capacity theory of mediated message processing. *Journal of Communication, 501,* 46–70

Lang, A., & Basil, M. (1998). What do secondary task reaction times measure anyway? In M. Roloff (Ed.), *Communication Yearbook, 21* (pp. 443–470). Beverly Hills: Sage.

Lang, A., Dhillon, K., & Dong, Q. (1995). The effects of emotional arousal and valence on television viewers' cognitive capacity and memory. *Journal of Broadcasting & Electronic Media, 39,* 313–327.

Levy, M. (1978). "Television news uses: a cross national comparison. *Journalism Quarterly, 53,* 334–337.

McLeod, D., & Perse, E. M. (1994). Direct and indirect effects of socioeconomic status on public affairs knowledge. *Journalism Quarterly, 71,* 433–442.

McLuhan, M. (1964). *Understanding media: The extensions of man.* New York: McGraw-Hill.

Neuman, W. R. (1976). Patterns of recall among television news viewers. *Public Opinion Quarterly, 40,* 115–123.

Neuman, W. R., Just, M., & Crigler, A. (1992). *Common knowledge: News and the construction of political meaning.* Chicago: University of Chicago Press.

Newhagen, J. E. (1998). TV images that induce anger, fear, and disgust: Effects on approach-avoidance and memory. *Journal of Broadcasting & Electronic Media, 42*(2), 265–276.

Newhagen, J. E., & Reeves, B. (1992). This evening's bad news: Effects of compelling negative television news images on memory. *Journal of Communication, 42,* 25–41.

Norris, P. (2001). *Digital divide: Civic engagement, information poverty, and the Internet worldwide.* New York: Cambridge University Press.

NTIA (1998, July). *Falling through the Net: Defining the digital divide.* National Telecommunications and Information Administration, U.S. Department of Commerce. Retrieved July 23, 2002, from http://www.ntia.doc.gov/ntiahome/fttn99/contents.html

Park, E., & Kosicki, G. M. (1995). Presidential support during the Iran-Contra affair: People's reasoning process and media influence. *Communication Research, 22*(2), 207–236.

Patterson, T., & McClure, R. (1976). *The unseeing eye.* New York: Putnam.

Pew Research Center for the People and the Press. (2002, September). *Homepage.* Retrieved September 24, 2002, from http://www.people-press.org/

Reese, S., & Miller, M. (1981). Political attitude holding and structure: The effects of newspaper and television news. *Communication Research, 8*(2), 167–188.

Robinson, J. (1967). *Public information about world affairs.* Ann Arbor, MI: Survey Research Center.

Robinson, J., & Levy, M. (1980). *The main source: Learning from television news.* Beverly Hills: Sage.

Robinson, M. (1974). The impact of the televised Watergate hearings. *Journal of Communication, 24,* 17–30.

Rogers, E. M. (1976). Communication and national development: The passing of the dominant paradigm. *Communication Research, 3,* 213–240.

Shinghi, P., & Mody, B. (1976). The communication effects gap: A field experiment on television and agricultural ignorance in India. *Communication Research, 3,* 171–190.

Simmons, R. E., & Garda, E. C. (1982). Dogmatism and the "knowledge gap" among Brazilian mass media users. *Gazette, 30,* 121–133.

Singer, J. (1980). The power and limitations of television: A cognitive-affective analysis. In P. Tannenbaum (Ed.), *The entertainment functions of television* (pp. 31–65). Hillsdale, NJ: Lawrence Erlbaum Associates.

Stauffer, J., Frost, R., & Rybolt, W. (1987). Recall and learning from broadcast news: Is print better? *Journal of Broadcasting, 25*(3), 253–262.

Tichenor, P. J., Donohue, G., & Olien, C. (1970). Mass media flow and differential growth in knowledge. *Public Opinion Quarterly, 34,* 159–70.

Torsvik, P. (1972). Television and information. *Scandinavian Political Studies, 7,* 215–234.

Van Der Molen, J., & Van Der Voort, T. (2000). The impact of television, print and audio on children's recall of the news: A study of three alternative explanations for the dual coding hypothesis. *Human Communication Research, 26*(1), 3–26.

Viswanath, K., & Finnegan, J. (1996). The knowledge gap hypothesis: Twenty-five years later. *Communication Yearbook, 19,* 187–227.

Wade, S., & Schramm, W. (1969). The mass media as sources of public affairs, science, and health knowledge. *Public Opinion Quarterly, 33,* 197–209.

Wilhem, A. G. (2000). *Democracy in the digital age: Challenges to political life in cyberspace.* New York: Routledge.

Wilson, E. (1994). The effect of medium on loss of information. *Journalism Quarterly, 51,* 111–115.

# 3

# The Interactivity Paradox: Closer to the News but Confused

ERIK P. BUCY

*Indiana University, Bloomington*

The rise of the World Wide Web as a mass medium has attracted considerable research attention on the growth (Pew Research Center, 2000, 2002), credibility (Bucy, 2003a; Flanagin & Metzger, 2000; Johnson & Kaye, 1998, 2000), and form of online news sources (Barnhurst, 2002; Bucy, 2003b) as well as the changing role of the journalist in a networked communication system (Newhagen & Levy, 1998). A key feature distinguishing online news from the printed or broadcast version is the interactivity, or reciprocal communication, that the Internet makes possible. Interactive features on news sites, whether in the form of multimedia downloads, searchable archives, hyperlinks, or discussion forums, are assumed to enhance the audience's access to information while engaging users in processes that, in the words of one influential editor, "use technology to bring people closer to the news" (Brown, 2000, p. 26). At the same time, however, interactive features may exact a considerable cognitive and emotional cost by demanding more patience, expertise, and cognitive resources of the user, increasing the likelihood of confusion, frustration, and reduced memory for news (Sundar, 2000). As news organizations continue to experiment with new methods of digital storytelling, the rise of interactive news and information raises an important question that media research has not adequately addressed: What happens on an emotional level when users are placed in the online news environment and engage with interactive content?

Contrary to some early, optimistic assumptions about interactive communication (see Rafaeli, 1988), not all interactivity is associated with positive outcomes. Recent research examining the processing and perception of online news found that audio and video downloads, a form of content interactivity (Massey & Levy, 1999), hinder memory and contribute to negative perceptions of the Web site overall as well as the quality of news content (Sundar, 2000). Audio downloads, in particular, have a negative impact on perceived coherence, an effect that becomes more pronounced when pictures are present. By demanding more of the user, namely more navigational effort and computer literacy, audio and video downloads ostensibly increase the cognitive overhead or amount of required metalevel decision making, causing confusion (Sundar, 2000). The resulting experience of disorientation, a common problem in hypermedia environments (Conklin, 1987; Thuring, Hannemann, & Haake, 1995), may then elicit negative evaluations. At the same time, ironically, a majority of participants in the study cited audio and video downloads as the best part of the site. In a political context, interactive conditions (operationalized as embedded hyperlinks, branching structures, and e-mail) have been associated with positive candidate assessments, especially among politically apathetic subjects (Sundar, Hesser, Kalyanaraman, & Brown, 1998). But too much interactivity can have harmful effects, owing in part to the extra demands placed on the user: whereas moderate levels of Web site interactivity can contribute to a political candidate's appeal, higher levels call for greater user involvement and can detract from it (Sundar, Kalyanaraman, & Brown, 2003).

A consistent finding in current research, as well as in studies of hypertext from the pre-Web era, is the disorientation that users experience when navigating unfamiliar, vast, or complex information spaces. In a benchmark review of hypertext systems, Conklin (1987) defined the disorientation problem as "having to know (1) where you are in the network and (2) how to get to some other place that you know (or think) exists in the network" (p. 38). Unlike linear mass media, hypermedia offers the user more degrees of freedom or dimensions in which to freely move and hence magnifies the potential for losing one's place and increases the difficulty in finding desired information. Indeed, Conklin (1987) noted that as hypermedia documents grow more complex, "it becomes distressingly easy for a user to become lost or disoriented" (p. 19). Although Conklin made this observation in relation to stand-alone hypertext systems, a recent study examining information processing of the "Why Files" science Web site (http://whyfiles.org) seems to validate his point in cyberspace. The study found that users spend a substantial proportion of their cognitive effort—up to 39%—simply orienting to the content and structure of the site, and that this effort comes at the expense of elaborative processing important for integrating information into memory (Eveland & Dunwoody, 2000).

Studies on disorientation generally focus on the impact that feeling lost in cyberspace has on task performance, whether learning, navigational efficiency, document size estimation, or other instrumental outcomes (see, for example, Elms & Woods, 1985; Eveland & Dunwoody, 2001; McDonald & Stevenson, 1996; Tripp & Roby, 1990). Although important for goal-oriented uses of hypermedia systems, this focus on performance overlooks the impact of emotional responses to new communication technologies that may determine continued use beyond specific, short-lived information needs. As a mass medium, the World Wide Web may evoke a range of responses in users, both cognitive and affective (Perse & Ferguson, 2000), and in the long run, a sense of medium satisfaction may take precedence over task efficiency. Even for sites that are primarily informational in nature, cognitive outcomes such as information gain or learning are not the only important effects. A substantial component of audience responses to the news, whether electronic or print, involves emotion. Indeed, Reeves and Nass (1996) asserted that, "media experiences are *emotional* experiences . . . there is virtually no type of content and no form of presentation that is *in*capable of causing changes in emotions" (p. 136). Fundamentally, the feeling of being disoriented in a complex information and navigational space is a negatively valenced affective response to a cognitive problem.

Summarizing a decade's worth of research on navigation in hypertext, McDonald and Stevenson (1996) noted "a growing consensus among researchers in the area that disorientation is hypertext's major limiting factor" (p. 62). This chapter examines the disorientation that users may experience in response to major newspaper and television news sites on the World Wide Web. The study uses as its point of departure the observation that disorientation in hypermedia environments is not merely a nuisance problem but a potentially serious issue affecting cognitive access to online content. To assess the degree of disorientation experienced in the context of Net news, a repeated measures experiment was conducted in the weeks before and after the 2000 presidential election. Study participants were placed in both interactive and noninteractive conditions on major news Web sites and answered questions that addressed the emotional and evaluative consequences of online content—an understudied aspect of user experiences with Internet technology. Beyond the hypermedia literature on disorientation, the study was conceptually grounded in the *media access* approach to new technology research, summarized next.

## THE *MEDIA ACCESS* APPROACH

As discussed by Newhagen and Bucy in chapter 1, the media access approach departs from common understandings of new technology use by recognizing that a distinction can be made between having access to the Internet as a *technology* and being able to access the *content* that resides on it. Whereas issues of technological access may be explained by infrastructure availability that enables *system access* to network connections or socioeconomic status that enables *physical access* to the latest computer technology, access to online content is influenced by an array of cultural conditions that occur within the family and community (*social access*) and psychological constraints that operate within the individual (*cognitive access*). Sociocultural factors affecting content access might take the form of technodispositions within families and communities that encourage or discourage computer use (see Rojas, Straubhaar, Roychowdhury, & Okur, chapter 6, this volume) or such life circumstances as marital status or family structure (Bucy, 2000). But even if system, physical, and social access requirements are met, users are empowered to make full use of new communication technology only to the extent they are cognitively able. As a consequence, any complete model of access must consider the cognitive skills and psychological resources that individual users bring to the media interface.

Although the cognitive barriers to hypermedia access have been known for some time, much research attention and policy discussion about the Internet remains focused on physical access to information technology and demographic trends among online adopters (Katz, Rice, & Aspden, 2001; NTIA, 1998, 2000, 2002). The motivations, abilities, and psychological responses of individual users—dimensions of cognitive access that help predict profitable use of new media—have thus far received only sporadic research attention (e.g., Katz & Aspden, 1997a, 1997b) and almost no policy discussion. Unlike traditional media, the Net confronts the user with communication opportunities at a wide range of levels (e.g., interpersonal, group, organizational, mass) all at the same time—and frequently on the same screen (see December, 1997). Online, the user enters a cognitively demanding environment marked by many different and at times contrasting configurations of communication (Morris & Ogan, 1996), where even the motivation to learn may not be sufficient to guarantee actual information gain (Eveland & Dunwoody, 2001). What seems certain, however, is that regardless of knowledge or expertise level, the various demands and requirements of information interfaces will produce affective responses in users.

Consistent with the literature on disorientation, emotional and evaluative responses to online content are conceptualized in this study as an important precursor to effectual content access. Frijda (1988) defined emotion as an action state produced by a mismatch between an organism's goals and some internal or environmental stimulus. During Web browsing or hypermedia searching, emotions may be evoked by content that is novel, compelling, or surprising as well as navigation that is difficult or unsuccessful. Importantly, emotions are often described as occurring in behavioral hiatus, "specifically, when actions are delayed or inhibited" (Lang, Bradley, & Cuthbert, 1997, p. 99). Thus, the challenges associated with knowing where you are in the network, finding needed information, downloading files and updates, or working with new applications endemic to the online environment should evoke a range of emotional responses in users. On encountering complex navigational spaces, users (depending on expertise level) may experience a sense of mastery or disorientation, confidence or uncertainty, satisfaction or frustration, either in conjunction with cognitive outcomes like knowledge gain or as a primary response to complexity.

Emotional responses to media technology are cognitively consequential and may in fact augment or interfere with information processing. As the television effects literature has shown, emotional responses to the news may temper message processing and assessments of medium satisfaction in significant ways (see Bucy & Newhagen, 1999; Lang, 2000; Reeves & Nass, 1996). In a study on the effects of negative compelling images in the news, Newhagen and Reeves (1992) found that footage of war, disaster, and civil mayhem on the evening news retroactively inhibited memory for material that preceded them, while proactively enhancing memory for material that followed. Studies of political information processing have also demonstrated how emotional evaluations of novelty and threat, which heighten awareness and increase anxiety levels, serve to engage attention and facilitate rational calculation important for democratic decision making (Marcus, Neuman, & MacKuen, 2000). Disorientation seems to have a mostly negative cognitive impact. Indeed, hypermedia research has found that as disorientation increases, learning is likely to suffer (Beasley & Waugh, 1995; Tripp & Roby, 1990). Beyond negative impacts on learning, Eveland and Dunwoody (2001) observed that, if a Web site "is too complex and produces disorientation, it might discourage individuals from ever returning or from seeking information [there] in the future" (p. 57).

## THE INTERNET AS A COMPLEX COMMUNICATION SYSTEM

For the mass audience accustomed to televisual media and other one-way platforms, the complexity of the Web should not be underestimated. Despite several generations of graphical user interfaces and a decade of growth and development, the Web still does not enjoy television's low literacy barrier, ease of use, or basic affordability (given the cost of a state-of-the-art multimedia computer). The interconnected, software-dependent quality of networked communication technology makes the Web strikingly different from broadcast media, such as conventional radio and television. Beyond selecting a station or program, broadcast media minimize the amount of expertise and number of decisions users must make to fully access content; decision making is instead frontloaded onto content producers, who rely on storytelling techniques, or a compelling narrative in the case of news, to captivate and hold the viewer's or listener's attention. Once the story is constructed, audiences can derive satisfaction simply by watching or hearing the story unfold transparently through the receiver. The Web provides this opportunity only after successfully navigating the software interface. In the case of a broadcast medium such as television, which does not place such software demands on users,[1] neither textual nor technical literacy is a precondition of enjoyment.

Online, the user enters a qualitatively different media environment with a considerably higher cognitive (and emotional) barrier to entry than broadcast media. Once physical access is achieved and the interface is all that separates the user from the plethora of content that resides on the Web, a myriad of choices arise. On a news and information site, one possible choice is the decision to customize the way information is presented. With customization, however, the resulting complexity multiplies. An occasional Web user, for instance, may establish a personal portal page and set his or her preferences for local items of interest and national news.

On the screen, the following links could appear, as they did on February 16, 2001 when this example was drawn from the Microsoft Network's home page:

Today on MSN:
US strikes Iraq | Movies: top critic picks | Compare city rent costs | How to win over your in-laws | Find hottest local spots to take a date | Survivor II: Who should have been dumped? | 360 sprint: new Lexus | Hannibal book, 20% off | Stargaze on your PC | Balance money and love | Watch J. Lo at work | Save 10% on your next car rental | Is an ounce of pot really legal in 10 states?

The first thing that stands out about these links is their utter lack of coherence. This curious collection of non sequiturs presents a "news" index of sorts but one focused more on individual concerns and consumer suggestions than information with broader social relevance. The list beckons the user to click through the confusion to pursue at least one link in greater detail. But the random presentation raises the question of whether this hodgepodge of choices and communication levels facilitates or hinders access to the content that resides on the site. Are users comfortable with interfaces that feature such bewildering variety and mixed levels of analyses? The random juxtaposition of unrelated hyperlinks raises the *cognitive overhead* problem identified by Conklin (1987) in relation to hypertext. As the number of choices about which links to follow and which links to leave alone increases, so does the amount of metalevel decision making required of the user. The additional effort and concentration necessary to contemplate and follow several trails at the same time may provide some diversion for users accustomed to multitasking but also interferes with information integration and retention (Eveland & Dunwoody, 2001; Mayer, Moreno, Boire, & Vagge, 1999).

Ironically, one brings this complexity on oneself by customizing one's information preferences, which the MSN site allows.[2] But does enabling such disparate juxtapositioning of information together on the same screen really represent a form of user empowerment and control, as the "Personalize My MSN" option implies? If the desired end result is learning, then the answer is probably no. In fact, hypermedia structures that offer increased user control have been found to heighten cognitive load (Oliver, 1996)—the amount of mental effort required to locate information and understand how it fits within a larger information source (Eveland & Dunwoody, 2001). As research conducted from a limited capacity perspective has found, a person's ability to process information is finite and easily overloaded by the amount of information available in the environment (Lang, 2000). On exposure, if a message or piece of information is not selected for further processing, it may be overwritten by new information and lost—the likely outcome of scanning and navigating through a haphazard index of links. Beyond information loss, if the interface becomes too complex or confusing, the user may experience disorientation and begin to feel "lost in space" (Conklin, 1987).

Now, contrast this presentation with a traditional mass medium. Imagine the front page, above-the-fold section of almost any newspaper, from small town courier to major metropolitan daily, giving equal emphasis to a similar array of items from the news, sports, business, metro, lifestyles, and classifieds sections—all on the same page! No print editor would think of presenting the news this way to readers.[3] Online, could it be that content providers do not understand the filtered, categorized, and hierarchically structured nature of mass media, or is a portal site like MSN driven as much by advertising considerations as information provision? Assuming the presentation is revenue driven and represents a sort of scattershot or fishing expedition approach to attracting the user's interest, the resulting lack of information structuring can be seen as a byproduct of a design process that implicitly assumes online audiences welcome and benefit from confusing presentations. Beyond layout, there are important channel differences that distinguish new from traditional media.

## Media Channel

Demographic studies of the traditional news audience have consistently documented younger users' preference for electronic media over print media, which in the pre-Internet era translated into a preference for television over newspapers. With the rise of the World Wide Web, both forms of old media are hastily refashioning themselves to appear more like hypermedia (Bolter & Grusin, 1999). In an effort to attract the interest of a younger demographic, whose disposable income draws advertisers, some news organizations are turning to younger talent and shorter stories with flashy graphics. Sometimes this strategy succeeds in building an audience, as when CNN overhauled the look and feel of its "Headline News" program in the summer of 2001. Although critics panned the program's busy format and editorial policy of no longer covering stories primarily for their news value but also for their appeal to younger viewers, the show's ratings experienced a 104% increase among 18- to 34-year-olds (Aberman, 2002).

The same tactics are now embraced by print media, as planned changes to *Rolling Stone* magazine illustrate. After experiencing a steady decline in ad revenue, the storied counterculture magazine with a history of publishing epic political narratives, soul-searching rock star interviews, and literary journalism has opted for a front-to-back-cover makeover. To reestablish its salience in the digital era, the magazine's publisher has hired a managing editor from the racy world of British men's magazines and announced that the publication would become more visually oriented (Carr, 2002)—a necessity recognized 20 years ago by the newspaper chain Gannett with the launch of *USA Today*. A newspaper report of the *Rolling Stone* makeover noted that:

> In a world saturated with media choices, many editors have concluded that the words in magazines are often beside the point, as some of the more successful publications like *Maxim* communicate visually with funny charts, outrageous photos, and articles that are increasingly little more than captions on pictures (Carr, 2002).

Old media are also adjusting to the new reality of online media by committing substantial resources to their Net news operations and have become the dominant sources of news online (Jupiter Media Metrix, 2002). A 2-year analysis of the home pages of major newspaper and TV network affiliate news sites in the top 40 U.S. media markets found some notable differences between print and broadcast approaches to online news in terms of visual appeal, information accessibility, and interactivity (Bucy, 2003b). Television sites in both 1998 and 2000 featured more graphic elements, especially photographs, than newspaper pages, whereas newspaper pages carried more story summaries and text. Within station sites, home pages incorporated much more content-driven interactivity (multimedia), such as clickable graphics, audio and video feeds, online polls, and searchable databases, than opportunities for interpersonal communication, including bulletin boards, chat rooms, and feedback forms. Newspaper sites, although criticized early in the Web's development for being pseudointeractive and smug (Katz, 1994), featured more interpersonal communication features than the network affiliate sites in both years of the analysis, but roughly the same amount of content interactivity. The mere presence of reader forums and e-mail links to editorial staff is no guarantee of media responsiveness, however.[4]

The analysis also identified differences in the ways Net news operations were making information accessible in the online environment through personalization features and customization options. For both years, newspaper sites featured more page elements that enhanced usability and information accessibility, such as site maps, lists of frequently asked questions (FAQ), news story summaries, and the ability to modify information delivery or display, than network affiliate sites. NBC affiliate sites, which rivaled newspapers for the presence of usability items in the 2000 data, were a notable exception (Bucy, 2003b). Overall, Net news sites were found to be increasing in sophistication and interactivity over time, with a rise in the number of elements that make content readily available, easily digested, and personally tailored. Besides informational content, the appeal of Net news to *young* Web users may depend on its participatory depth. Interestingly, online newspapers have assumed a commanding lead in most local markets over network affiliate sites, attracting more than 10% of the adult audience (Jordan, 2001).

Surveys of Internet use report that education and age are among the most important demographic factors facilitating or inhibiting Internet access (Bucy, 2000; Lenhart, 2000). Age emerges as an important factor in examining emotional and evaluative responses to online content because different age groups report different gratifications obtained from Internet use. College students, in particular, utilize the Internet and World Wide Web primarily as a form of entertainment and social connection and only secondarily as a source of news and information (Howard, Rainie, & Jones, 2001; Perse & Ferguson, 2000). This contrasts with older users' more utilitarian interest in the Web as a source of business or health-related information. Older users, specifically aging baby boomers and senior citizens, are also the most resistant age group to adopt or even express an interest in the Internet as a mass medium (Lenhart, 2000). A Pew Research Center (2000) study on the impact of Internet news on the broadcast news audience found that although younger users do not express as much interest in keeping up with the news as older users, they do enjoy having access to a variety of information sources. Older Americans, who have a greater affinity for the news, often feel overwhelmed by the increasingly crowded media landscape, the report noted.

An experimental study of media credibility comparing student and adult Internet users found younger users, with an average age of 20, to be more favorable toward and less critical of network television news sites than older users, with an average age of 49 (Bucy, 2003a). Spending time in the online environment at network news sites performing either a reading or interactive task also enhanced younger users' evaluations of Net news credibility compared to a control group without any media exposure. The finding that Web use leads to positive credibility assessments among younger users suggests that mere exposure produces favorable evaluations of online news content, at least for network television sites. Although this result may hold in relation to a control group, in a within-subjects study design where all subjects are required to spend some time online, the influence of media channel and online activity should become more apparent. The greater visual orientation of TV news sites and the general preference of younger audiences for television over newspapers suggests a main effect for media channel on emotional and evaluative responses:

H1: Young Web users will respond to television news sites more favorably than to newspaper sites.

## Interactivity

Beyond their traditional media ties, one of the primary ways in which newspaper and TV news sites may differ is in their degree of interactivity, or as Steuer (1995) defined the term in relation to new media, "the extent to which users can participate in modifying the form and content of a mediated environment in real time" (p. 46). The different types of interactivity that may occur online have been categorized by researchers into two general dimensions. The first, more common, type is content or *user-to-system* interactivity, which involves the control that news consumers exercise over the selection and presentation of editorial content, whether story text, audiovisuals, multimedia, or other aspects of the interface (Bucy, Lang, Potter, & Grabe, 1999; Massey & Levy, 1999; McMillan, 2002). Unlike linear mass media, the online environment allows users to more fully interact with the content and medium itself by navigating via hyperlinks, participating in online polls and surveys, downloading information, calling up streaming media, searching archives, customizing information delivery, and making electronic purchases, all "without ever directly communicating with another person" (Stromer-Galley, 2000, p. 118).

The second, less common type of interactivity that may occur on news sites is interpersonal or *user-to-user* interactivity, involving person-to-person conversations mediated by communication technology. Dominick (1983) recognized such "machine-assisted interpersonal communication" at the dawn of the personal computer era. Such computer-mediated communication includes both synchronous (real-time) and asynchronous (delayed) exchanges, whether in the form of e-mail (and its various permutations such as Instant Messenger), chat room discussions, message boards, user forums, Internet telephony and videoconferencing (e.g., Net-Meeting), and, on entertainment sites, distributed game playing or multiplayer role-playing adventures. Stromer-Galley (2000) drew a similar distinction between media and human interaction on political Web pages. On news sites, political pages, and Web pages generally, content interactivity is far more prevalent than interpersonal interactivity (Bucy, 2003b; Bucy et al., 1999; Massey & Levy, 1999; Stromer-Galley, 2000), a function of the additional costs associated with managing potentially volatile, real-time discussions in cyberspace and responding to a high volume of audience communications electronically, as well as the loss of control that content providers risk when opening their sites to public discussion, feedback, and criticism. Both types of interactivity may be facilitated by the same Web site, depending on the features offered.[5]

As mechanisms of engagement, interactive features may be responsible for giving Net news sites their "stickiness," or continuing appeal, which online sources are increasingly expected to have. The association of interactivity with increased acceptance of and satisfaction with media experiences leads to the prediction that:

> H2: Web users will evaluate interactive conditions more favorably than noninteractive conditions; specifically, they will rate interactive conditions to be more participatory, involving, and immediate than noninteractive conditions.

At the same time, interactive processes have the potential to make a communication event more effortful and to confuse or overload the user with technical demands, unclear navigational requirements, or an undesired recursive information flow. A minimal amount of interpersonal or content interactivity may be desirable for some users (here, the adult user who uses America Online to check his e-mail every few days comes to mind), whereas intense two-way communication may serve as the norm for others (think of the teenager with five simultaneous instant messenger sessions open on her screen at the same time). To the extent that media preferences and digital skills vary between individuals, complex interactive environments are likely to be poorly calibrated with the "average" user's orientations. Indeed, the hypermedia literature suggests that content and domain expertise moderate the effects of hypermedia use (Eveland & Dunwoody, 2001). Mismatches between user expectations and abilities with interface demands should produce an adverse reaction if the demands are unwelcomed, unfamiliar, or beyond the user's skill level. This should especially be true if there is a time limitation on task completion and the user feels somewhat rushed.

Rather than enhancing learning and other performance-related outcomes, as the interactivity and user control literatures suggest (e.g. Milheim & Martin, 1991; Rafaeli, 1988), hypermedia systems may instead increase cognitive load and produce disorientation among users, particularly those with little experience or content familiarity (Eveland & Dunwoody, 2001). Unlike the preproduced narratives and storytelling characteristic of traditional mass media, hypermedia environments place an additional burden on users in that they require "a certain overhead of metalevel decision making, an overhead that is absent [with linear mass media] when the author has already made many of these choices for you" (Conklin, 1987, p. 40). Interestingly, neither prior Web experience nor the amount of time spent online reduces the proportion of processing devoted to this metalevel decision making, or orientation (Eveland & Dunwoody, 2000).[6] Finding and maintaining one's bearings is a persistent problem in cyberspace. The additional cognitive effort necessitated by hypermedia and the potential for disorientation associated with interactive environments suggests a third hypothesis:

H3: Performing a series of interactive tasks will generate more confusion and disorientation on Net news sites than performing a noninteractive reading task.

In addition to independent, or main, effects of media channel and Web site interactivity on emotional and evaluative responses to online content, the interaction between the two factors should impact user responses in significant ways. Based on the foregoing discussion, it can be predicted that:

H4: Television news sites in the interactive condition will elicit the most favorable responses from young Web users and newspaper sites in the noninteractive condition the least.

## METHOD

To test these hypotheses, this experimental study uses a 2 (media channel) × 2 (interactivity level) within-subjects factorial design. The first factor, media channel, has two levels: national newspaper and network television news sites. The second factor, Web site interactivity, is a task-based variable with 2 levels: interactive and noninteractive (reading only). A total of 74 undergraduate students enrolled in communications courses at a large Midwestern university participated in the study, which took place in the weeks before and after the 2000 presidential election from late October to mid-November. A majority of subjects (56.8%, $n = 42$) participated in the study before election day and the remaining number (43.2%, $n = 32$) after. The study was completed before the final results of the 2000 election were known, so the uncertainty over who would be president was consistent throughout.

Subjects ranged in age from 18 to 30 ($M = 20$) and received extra credit for their participation in the study. There was roughly an equal number of male ($n = 35$)

and female ($n = 39$) participants. Most subjects were Caucasian (90.5%, $n = 67$); the remaining subjects were either Asian, African American, or Hispanic. Overall Web use was high, as might be expected with a student subject pool. More than four in five (86.5%) reported daily Web use; the mean number of days spent online per week was 6.77. Use of the Web for political information was much less intense. Almost half the subjects (47.4%) reported going online for political news 1 to 3 days per week ($M = 1.91$ days). Traditional media use was moderate. On average, subjects relied on newspapers ($M = 3.38$) and local television news ($M = 3.35$) less than they used the Internet, but more than cable TV ($M = 2.34$) or network news ($M = 2.12$). Indicative of their cohort group, subjects were avid viewers of late-night talk shows, with 54.1% reporting 3 to 5 days of viewing per week ($M = 2.82$ out of 5 weekdays).

## Procedure

At the beginning of the study, subjects completed a preexperiment questionnaire asking about their media use, political attitudes, demographics, and efficacy. They were then randomly assigned to one of four stimulus orders that required them to alternately visit an existing network TV news (ABC, CBS, or NBC) and national newspaper (*New York Times, Washington Post,* or *USA Today*) Web site. To maximize ecological validity, subjects were assigned to visit actual news sites on the World Wide Web rather than a researcher-designed mock news page.[7] On the sites, subjects performed either an interactive task or noninteractive, reading task, guided by a set of printed instructions. The interactive task instructed subjects to engage in three online activities, including voting in a poll of the day, viewing a slide show of their favorite candidate, e-mailing the news organization about their election coverage, or a similar activity. The noninteractive reading task asked subjects to read the lead story on the news home page, plus two other stories of interest. The intent of these tasks was not to saturate subjects with political information for a delayed memory test but to immerse them in a directed way in the online news environment long enough to cultivate meaningful impressions of the site. As a distractor activity, subjects also visited the campaign site of either leading candidate, George W. Bush or Al Gore, and watched a television network news story about the presidential debates.

After spending 5 minutes on each site, subjects completed a series of emotional and evaluative measures assessing their affective reactions to and evaluative perceptions of their online experience. Affective reactions were measured in two ways. First, subjects completed a series of 5-point scales (where $1 = $ *not at all* and $5 = $ *very*) for the following discrete emotions: overwhelmed, frustrated, interested, confused, discouraged, impatient, confident, disoriented, bored, and irritated. These feeling states generally correspond to the items comprising the nonlinear media disorientation assessment scale developed by Beasley and Waugh (1995). Next, a series of 20 evaluative measures were presented to ascertain user perceptions of the site's informativeness, credibility, organization, and responsiveness.[8] Although many of the measures used in the study were negative, and hence intended to capture the adverse side of online experience, there were several neutral or positive items (e.g., interested, confident, useful, relevant, responsive), allowing a fuller emotional and evaluative picture to come into focus. Moreover, subjects had the option of circling "not at all" on each of the negative items to nullify their relevance if warranted.

## Manipulation Check

To verify that subjects perceived the interactive conditions as intended, a 5-point interactivity measure (1 = not at all, 5 = very) was included in the evaluative scales as a manipulation check. Analysis of variance revealed a strong main effect for the interactivity manipulation $F(1, 144) = 21.75$, $p < .0001$. Subjects perceived the online activities associated with the interactive condition to be significantly more interactive ($M = 3.62$, $SD = .98$) than the noninteractive reading task ($M = 2.86$, $SD = 1.04$), even though they both took place in a hypermediated environment. Thus, the experimental manipulation was experienced as intended.

## RESULTS

Repeated measures analysis of variance (ANOVA) was used to analyze differences between mean scores for emotional and evaluative responses using the mainframe version of BMDP 2V. Figure 3.1 shows a main effect for media channel on the degree of interest and boredom generated by the two different types of Net

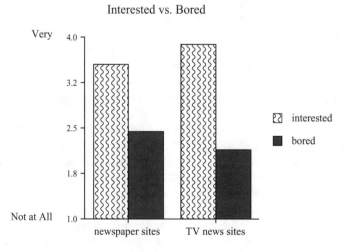

FIG 3.1. Main effect for media channel.

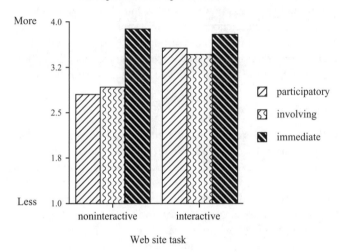

FIG 3.2.    Main effect for interactivity level.

news sites. Overall, subjects were more interested than bored by the sites. Between channels, however, TV news sites generated significantly more interest ($M = 3.88$, $SD = .83$) than newspaper sites ($M = 3.56$, $SD = .99$), $F(1, 144) = 4.39$, $p < .05$. They also provoked the least amount of boredom ($M = 2.12$, $SD = .93$ compared to $M = 2.44$, $SD = 1.11$ for newspaper sites), although the differences only approached significance, $F(1, 144) = 2.85$, $p < .10$. Another indication that young users respond more favorably to television sites was born out by the credibility ratings. Subjects rated TV news sites to be significantly more credible ($M = 4.11$, $SD = .75$) than newspaper sites ($M = 3.86$, $SD = .80$), $F(1, 144) = 3.99$, $p < .05$. Together, these results support Hypothesis 1, that young Web users will respond to TV news sites more favorably than to newspaper sites.

Figure 3.2 shows a main effect for interactivity level on perceptions of Net news responsiveness. As predicted, subjects perceived interactive conditions to be significantly more participatory ($M = 3.60$, $SD = 1.10$) and involving ($M = 3.48$, $SD = .91$) than noninteractive conditions ($M$s = 2.83 and 2.97, $SD$s = 1.02 and .98), $F$s$(1, 144) = 20.30$ and $11.45$, $p$s $< .001$, respectively. The ratings for immediate, although slightly higher than the other measures, did not significantly differ by condition ($M$s = 3.81 and 3.90, $SD$s = .94 and .88), $F(1, 144) = .37$, n.s. Interestingly, subjects perceived the noninteractive reading task to be as immediate as the online activities associated with the interactive condition. Nevertheless, the findings for participatory and involving support Hypothesis 2, that Web users will evaluate interactive conditions more favorably than noninteractive conditions.

Next, analysis of variance was performed on the disorientation and Web site organization measures to assess whether the interactive tasks generated more

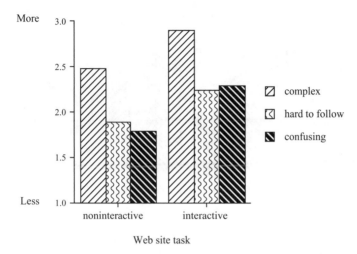

FIG 3.3.   Main effect for interactivity level.

confusion and disorientation than the noninteractive reading task. Figure 3.3 shows a main effect for perceptions of Web site organization. As predicted, Net news sites in the interactive condition were regarded as significantly more complex ($M = 2.90$, $SD = 1.13$), hard to follow ($M = 2.22$, $SD = 1.15$), and confusing ($M = 2.28$, $SD = 1.26$) than sites associated with the noninteractive reading task ($Ms = 2.46$, 1.88, and 1.78, $SDs = 1.12$, .94, and .94), $Fs(1, 144) = 4.98$, 3.73, and 7.58, $ps < .05$, respectively.

Figure 3.4 shows a main effect for three disorientation measures. In response to the online activities associated with the interactive condition, subjects reported that they felt more frustrated ($M = 2.05$, $SD = 1.18$), confused ($M = 2.25$, $SD = 1.20$), and disoriented ($M = 2.01$, $SD = 1.11$) than they did in response to the noninteractive reading task ($Ms = 1.78$, 1.77, and 1.70, $SDs = .89$, .95, and .74), $Fs(1,144) = 2.90$, 8.43, and 4.53, $ps < .10$, .01, and .05, respectively. Results for the other emotion terms associated with disorientation, including overwhelmed, discouraged, and confident, were not significant. Figure 3.5 shows an interaction for media channel and interactivity level on self-reported disorientation. Interactive newspaper sites caused subjects to feel more disoriented ($M = 2.20$, $SD = 1.11$) than the other conditions, noninteractive newspaper sites the least ($M = 1.57$, $SD = 1.84$), $F(1, 144) = 4.07$, $p < .05$. Overall, the findings for the disorientation and Web site organization measures support Hypothesis 3, that interactive tasks will generate more confusion and disorientation than the noninteractive condition. Table 3.1 summarizes the main effects findings for the interactivity factor.

The fourth hypothesis predicted an interaction between media channel and interactivity level, namely that TV news sites in the interactive condition would

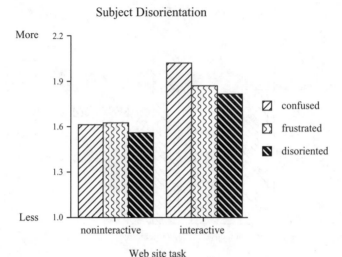

FIG 3.4.   Main effect for interactivity level.

receive the most favorable evaluations and noninteractive newspaper sites the least. Among the remaining evaluative items, there were significant interactions for informative, $F(1, 144) = 3.96$, $p < .05$, credible, $F(1, 144) = 3.99$, $p < .05$, and relevant, $F(1, 144) = 5.42$, $p < .05$. Consistent with the prediction, interactive TV news sites were evaluated as the most informative, credible, and relevant of any

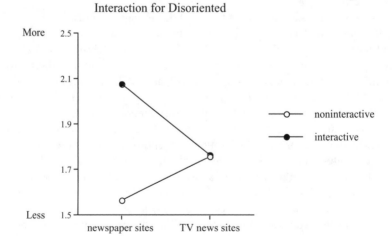

FIG 3.5.   Interaction for media channel and interactivity level.

TABLE 3.1
Main Effects for Interactivity Level

| Responsiveness Measures | Interactive Condition | Reading Task | df | F | p |
|---|---|---|---|---|---|
| | Interactivity Level | | | | |
| Participatory | 3.60 (1.10) | 2.83 (1.02) | 144 | 20.30 | .0001 |
| Involving | 3.48 (.91) | 2.97 (.98) | 144 | 11.45 | .001 |
| Immediate | 3.81 (.94) | 3.90 (.88) | 144 | .37 | n.s. |
| Organization Measures | | | | | |
| Complex | 2.90 (1.13) | 2.46 (1.12) | 144 | 4.98 | .05 |
| Hard to Follow | 2.22 (1.15) | 1.88 (.94) | 144 | 3.73 | .05 |
| Confusing | 2.28 (1.26) | 1.78 (.94) | 144 | 7.58 | .01 |
| Disorientation Measures | | | | | |
| Frustrated | 2.05 (1.18) | 1.78 (.89) | 144 | 2.90 | .10 |
| Confused | 2.25 (1.20) | 1.77 (.95) | 144 | 8.43 | .01 |
| Disoriented | 2.01 (1.11) | 1.70 (.74) | 144 | 4.53 | .05 |

Note: Mean ratings reported. For each item, 1 = not at all, 5 = very. Standard deviations appear in parentheses.

condition ($Ms = 4.37, 4.23, 4.35, SDs = .77, .69, .64$). However, as indicated by Fig. 3.6 through Fig. 3.8, noninteractive newspaper sites did not receive the brunt of negative evaluations; rather, the lowest evaluations were dispersed among the various conditions. These results partially support Hypothesis 4—although interactive TV sites did elicit the most favorable evaluative responses, noninteractive newspaper sites were not universally disliked.

## DISCUSSION

A large component of any human adaptation to novel situations and environments is emotional (Plutchik, 1980), and yet most empirical research on new technology use has ignored the direct affective experience of users. Working from the media access perspective outlined in the introduction to this volume, this study employed emotional and evaluative measures in a factorial experiment to address this deficit,

Perceptions of Informativeness

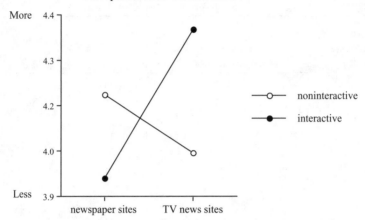

FIG 3.6.    Interaction for media channel and interactivity level.

manipulating the level of interactivity and type of news site that subjects experienced. As predicted, student subjects responded more favorably to television sites
than to newspaper sites, and evaluated interactive conditions more favorably than
noninteractive conditions. Of the four different treatment combinations, television sites in the interactive condition were rated the most credible, informative,
and relevant. Perhaps the most interesting finding is that, although interactive
conditions were rated significantly more participatory, involving, and immediate

Perceptions of Credibility

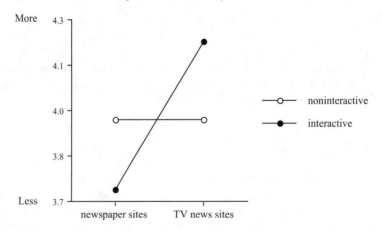

FIG 3.7.    Interaction for media channel and interactivity level.

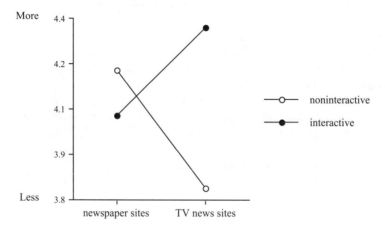

FIG 3.8.    Interaction for media channel and interactivity level.

than noninteractive conditions, interactive tasks also generated significantly more confusion, disorientation, and frustration than the reading task (albeit at fairly low levels). This dissonant set of results is referred to as the *interactivity paradox.* Subjects evidently enjoyed news site interactivity and the active involvement that it entailed more than reading electronic text, but this form of online participation produced a certain amount of disorientation, exacting a cognitive and emotional cost. Although successful at bringing people closer to the news through features that invite involvement, online news operations are evidently leaving users who engage with interactive content somewhat confused. Other discordant experimental findings—that multimedia downloads hinder memory and contribute to negative evaluations, yet are regarded as the best part of the site by users (Sundar, 2000)—corroborate this view.

The negative emotional impact of interactivity found in this study adds to a nascent literature beginning to document the downside of demanding too much of the media audience. Interactive processes generally have been thought to enhance user experiences with digital media, including increased motivation, acceptance, satisfaction, and learning, as well as more thoughtful engagement with the task at hand (see Rafaeli, 1988). However, both the disorientation literature cited earlier and more recent empirical research involving interactive media call these early findings and assumptions into question. A recent study of interactive movie viewing, for example, found that viewers with lower cognitive capacity feel more entertained and evaluate a film more positively when they watch *without* any interactivity, or choice over story direction, than with (Vorderer, Knobloch, & Schramm, 2001). Viewers with greater cognitive capacity, by contrast, evaluated the same movie more positively when they watched interactively.

Looking past the hyperbole and wishful thinking associated with interactive media, the finding that interactivity does not contribute uniformly, or linearly (Sundar, Kalyanaraman, & Brown, 2003), to positive impressions of user experiences with new technology should not be surprising. Information processing and behavioral performance models in psychology have long noted the relationship between overstimulation and decreased cognitive and behavioral performance. As Hebb (1949, p. 199) observed with his inverted-U curve of arousal, increasing levels of stimulation are beneficial up to a point, but then once an optimal level is attained, performance suffers. Moreover, in an interactive environment such as the Web, the role of the user is that of active information seeker, requiring online media audiences to perform their own story and feature selection, or gatekeeping (Sundar & Nass, 2001); this, too, may exact a certain amount of cognitive overhead. Education and cognitive skills may moderate the effects of placing increased demands on users, giving an advantage to more sophisticated audience members (Vorderer, Knobloch, & Schramm, 2001), but, as this study found in relation to online news, there may be emotional fallout from asking too much of even practiced Internet users.

Further research on the effects of interactivity should keep the skill level and cognitive abilities of the audience in mind. If, as Vorderer, Knobloch, and Schramm (2001) predicted, the future of interactive media will be successful only with that portion of the general audience with the cognitive skills necessary to benefit from information complexity, then news organizations and other mass media content providers may want to intentionally limit the amount of online interactivity they provide. Alternately, interactive features may be assigned to certain areas of Net news sites designated for advanced users. This option, of course, raises questions about unequal cognitive access to information important to informed citizenship, in favor of cyber elites. Unlike mass media, which are particularly good at packaging the news in ways suitable for a general audience (Grabe, Zhou, Lang, & Bolls, 2000), hypermedia reveal their content through a software shroud that users must learn to navigate their way around. Whereas experts may desire total freedom in navigating through information spaces, that does not preclude them from feeling some disorientation when encountering interactive content. Novices, on the other hand, may become completely lost or disoriented (Gygi, 1990). In any event, successful hypermedia navigation is a learned analytical strategy (Liebscher & Marchionini, 1991); television viewing is not. Online, the novice's need for structure may trump the expert's need for flexibility.

Although not large in an absolute sense, the mean values for disoriented, confused, and frustrated reveal the potential for disorientation effects inherent in interactive media. On a psychological level, the action state implied by negatively valenced orienting emotions associated with bewilderment is, first, to stop activity and, second, to explore or search (Plutchik, 1980). A third impulse to action judged to exist in the presence of such orienting emotions—Plutchik (1980, p. 357) included in his list vacillating, puzzled, uncertain, bewildered, confused, perplexed, ambivalent, and surprised—is to withdraw or get away. Within hypermedia environments, this action tendency may manifest as aversive behavior when inexperienced users feel overwhelmed or simply not up to the task. Indeed, in a separate study of Net news credibility involving a similar interactivity manipulation, several older adult subjects refused to participate in the online component once they realized the effort and expertise required to perform the tasks (Bucy, 2003a). The aversive action tendency suggested by disorientation, whether actually experienced or merely anticipated, stands in stark contrast to the approach impulse implied by more positively valenced orienting emotions such as curious, amazed, or wondering, which are associated with the urge to welcome or be with (Plutchik, 1980). This may explain why some hypertext researchers (e.g., Mayes, Kibby, & Anderson, 1990) contend that mild levels of disorientation in discovery learning systems, where making wrong turns is a necessary part of the process, can be desirable. When positively valenced, orienting emotional responses can aid in understanding.

Despite arguments for mild disorientation and the early skepticism of literary critics like Landow (1990), the feeling of being disoriented or potentially overwhelmed in hyperspace may impair full access to online content and even prevent some less skilled or efficacious users from even attempting an interactive session. A potential confound in the experimental design of this study was the written instructions that guided subjects through their online tasks. The instructions were, by necessity, longer and more complex for interactive conditions than they were for the noninteractive reading task.[9] Even though all the relevant pages for the study were bookmarked in the Internet Explorer Web browser, part of the confusion and frustration felt by subjects may have derived from using these instruction sheets to guide their online experience. Future study designs should minimize the amount of written instruction provided to subjects, incorporating simple-to-read, hotlinked directions into the design of the computer interface itself. To better understand user experiences with interactive media in the online environment, follow-up studies should also examine the influence of individual differences, such as computer expertise and Internet efficacy (see, for example, Eastin & LaRose, 2000) on cognitive and emotional outcomes. The interactivity paradox suggested by the results of this study leads to the conclusion that the major problem of earlier hypertext systems, namely how to effectively manage complexity and not overwhelm users with vast amounts of information (Gygi, 1990), now appears to apply to news sites on the World Wide Web.

## ACKNOWLEDGMENTS

An earlier version of this chapter was presented at the IAMCR/ICA Symposium on the Digital Divide at the University of Texas, Austin, November 2001. This research was supported by a Grant-in-Aid of Research from the Office of Research and the University Graduate School, Indiana University, Bloomington. The author expresses his gratitude to Kimberly S. Gregson for her assistance with data collection and input.

## ENDNOTES

[1] New technologies with increasingly intricate channel selection and programming interfaces, such as digital cable, WebTV, personal video recorders, and satellite systems, are beginning to change this basic fact of television, but broadcast TV remains the simple-to-use system it always has been.

[2] The site's "Personalize My MSN" feature also allows registered users to change their color scheme and page layout, or order of content presentation. Nonregistered users (those without a Microsoft Passport) are not allowed to alter the content, layout, or color scheme.

[3] McLuhan (1953/1995), 50 years ago, commented on the seeming random presentation of different news items on the pages of newspapers and magazines, which he said lacked coherence: "Each item lives in its own kind of space totally discontinuous from all other items. A particularly vigorous item will sprout a headline and provide a kind of aura or theme for surrounding items...the news page tends to cubism and surrealism [so] that every page of newspapers and magazines, like every section of our cities, is a jungle of multiple, simultaneous perspectives" (p. 310). But print media do adhere to thematic coverage patterns by section, which portal pages on the Web at this point in time do not closely follow.

[4] Katz (1994), for instance, charged that, "Online papers pretend to be seeking and absorbing feedback, but actually offer the illusion of interactivity without the reality, the pretense of democratic discussion without yielding a drop of power. The papers seem careful about reading and responding to their e-mail, but in the same pro forma way they thank readers for writing letters. They dangle the notion that they are now really listening, but that's mostly just a tease–the media equivalent of the politically correct pose" (p. 54).

[5] In addition to *user-to-user* interaction, McMillan (2002) distinguished between two types of media interaction, *user-to-system* and *user-to-documents*. Although the former addresses the interaction between people and the computer or new media system itself, the latter involves the "perceived interaction with content creators and actual creation of content" (p. 169).

[6] In their study examining information processing on the Web using think-aloud protocols, Eveland and Dunwoody (2000) defined orientation as "expressed attempts to understand the content and structure of the information space, often taking the form of a rhetorical question or a prediction about content or structure" (p. 229). Disorientation was operationalized as statements indicating misunderstanding, unintended navigation, or uncertainty over how to proceed, such as "Oops, that's not what I meant to do," "I have no idea how to get the information that I want," and "Why did that take me back?" (p. 232).

[7] As the news sites were subject to frequent updating, this required periodic revision of the instructions to adjust for expired links and other changes. The instructions were written in such a way to minimize the need for revision. The noninteractive conditions merely asked subjects to read the lead story on the home page, plus two other stories that were of interest, whereas the interactive conditions required that subjects engage with special interactive features on the sites. As these features are costly to develop, news organizations have a vested interest in keeping them for a length of time as a consistent fixture of the pages. Revisions to the instructions were therefore limited for the most part to relinking features that had been moved to another part of the site.

[8] Evaluative measures were grouped into four categories, with five scaled items each for informativeness (in-depth, useful, informative, relevant, trustworthy); credibility (believable, reliable, fair,

accurate, credible); organization (hard to follow, confusing, usable, complex, difficult); and responsiveness (responsive, interactive, participatory, involving, immediate). Reliability analysis performed on these groupings separately for newspaper and television network news sites confirmed their conceptual coherence, overall Cronbach's alpha for informativeness = .81, credibility = .85, organization = .68, and responsiveness = .79.

[9] The instructions for the interactive conditions asked subjects to perform various online activities. The instructions for the interactive version of the ABC News home page were as follows:

**First, visit the ABC News home page (as bookmarked)**

Spend 5 minutes on this site and do the following activities:

1. Scroll up and down the page to get an overall sense of the coverage.
   • http://abcnews.go.com

Then, submit a vote in Sam Donaldson's poll of the day (right-hand side, towards bottom). Be sure to look at the results.

Now, click on the Politics link (left-hand side, towards the top) and go to the politics page.

2. On the Politics page, click on Candidate Profiles (right-hand side, towards the top, under ABC 2000 vote) and select either George W. Bush OR Ralph Nader.

Click on the Issues tab, select an issue, and read about it.

   • http://abcnews.go.com/sections/politics

Close the Candidate Profile window.

3. Lastly, go to the ABC News feedback page from the Favorites menu (open the Web Study folder / ABC News folder / Feedback Page)

E-mail ABC about their Web site.

Use your own name and e-mail address or this one if you wish to remain anonymous: "icrlab" and "icrlab@hotmail.com"

At the end of 5 minutes, complete the 2-page TV News Site questionnaire.

---

By contrast, the instructions for the noninteractive reading version of the ABC News site were shorter and more straightforward:

**Next, visit the ABC News Politics page**

   • http://abcnews.go.com/sections/politics

Scroll up and down the page to get an overall sense of the page. In the next 5 minutes, please do the following:

1. Select one of the main stories on the page and read the full story. While reading the story, do not click on outside links or leave the page. Also, do not listen to or view any multimedia.
2. Second, read another story on the page that interests you. Again, stay with the story and avoid multimedia.
3. If you have extra time, read a third political story that appeals to you. Stay with the story and avoid multimedia.

At the end of 5 minutes, complete the 2-page TV News Site questionnaire.

# REFERENCES

Aberman, S. (2002, March 12). Seeking the fountain of youth. *OnlineNewsHour Extra*. Retrieved June 13, 2002, from http://www.pbs.org/newshour/extra/features/jan-june02/youthnews.html

Barnhurst, K. (2002). News geography and monopoly: The form of reports on U.S. newspaper Internet sites. *Journalism Studies, 3*(4)477–490.

Beasley, R. E., & Waugh, M. L. (1995). Cognitive mapping architectures and hypermedia disorientation: An empirical study. *Journal of Educational Multimedia and Hypermedia, 4*(2/3), 239–255.

Bolter, J. D., & Grusin, R. (1999). *Remediation: Understanding new media*. Cambridge, MA: MIT Press.

Brown, M. (2000, October 2). Bringing people closer to the news. *Brandweek*, 26.

Bucy, E. P. (2000). Social access to the Internet. *Harvard International Journal of Press/Politics, 5*(1), 50–61.

Bucy, E. P. (2003a). *Media credibility reconsidered: Synergy effects between on-air and online news. Journalism of Mass Communication Quarterly, 80*(2), 247–264.

Bucy, E. P. (2003b, April). *Second generation Net news: Interactivity and information accessibility in the online environment*. Top paper presented at the annual meeting of the Broadcast Education Association, Communication Technology Division, Las Vegas, NV.

Bucy, E. P., Lang, A., Potter, R., & Grabe, M. E. (1999). Formal features of cyberspace: Relationships between Web page complexity and site traffic. *Journal of the American Society for Information Science, 50*(13), 1246–1256.

Bucy, E. P., & Newhagen, J. E. (1999). The emotional appropriateness heuristic: Processing televised presidential reactions to the news. *Journal of Communication, 49*(4), 59–79.

Carr, D. (2002, June 13). *Rolling Stone*, struggling for readers, names Briton as editor. *The New York Times*. Retrieved June 13, 2002, from http://www.nytimes.com/2002/06/13/business/media

Conklin, J. (1987, September). Hypertext: An introduction and survey. *IEEE Computer*, 17–41.

December, J. (1997). *The World Wide Web unleashed*. Indianapolis: Sams.net Publishing.

Dominick, J. R. (1983). *The dynamics of mass communication*. Reading, MA: Addison-Wesley.

Eastin, M. S., & LaRose, R. (2000). Internet self-efficacy and the psychology of the digital divide. *Journal of Computer Mediated Communication, 6*(1). Retrieved July 23, 2002, from http://www.ascusc.org/jcmc/vol6/issue1/eastin.html

Elms, W. C., & Woods, D. D. (1985). Getting lost: A case study in interface design. *Proceedings of the Human Factors Society 29th Annual Meeting* (pp. 927–931). Santa Monica, CA: Human Factors Society.

Eveland, W. P. Jr., & Dunwoody, S. (2000). Examining information processing on the World Wide Web using think aloud protocols. *Media Psychology, 2*, 219–244.

Eveland, W. P. Jr., & Dunwoody, S. (2001). User control and structural isomorphism or disorientation and cognitive load? Learning from the Web versus print. *Communication Research, 28*(1), 48–78.

Flanagin, A. J., & Metzger, M. J. (2000). Perceptions of Internet information credibility. *Journalism & Mass Communication Quarterly, 77*(3), 515–540.

Frijda, N. (1988). The laws of emotion. *American Psychologist, 43*(5), 349–358.

Grabe, M. E., Zhou, S., Lang, A., & Bolls, P. D. (2000). Packaging television news: The effects of tabloid on information processing and evaluative responses. *Journal of Broadcasting & Electronic Media. 44*(4), 581–598.

Gygi, K. (1990). Recognizing the symptoms of hypertext . . . and what to do about it. In B. Laurel (Ed.), *The art of human–computer interface design* (pp. 279–287). Reading, MA: Addison-Wesley.

Hebb, D. O. (1949). *The organization of behavior*. New York: John Wiley & Sons.

Howard, P. E. N., Rainie, L., & Jones, S. (2001). Days and nights on the Internet: The impact of a diffusing technology. *American Behavioral Scientist, 45*(3), 383–404.

Johnson, T. J., & Kaye, B. K. (1998). Cruising is believing?: Comparing Internet and traditional sources on media credibility measures. *Journalism & Mass Communication Quarterly, 75*(2), 325–340.

Johnson, T. J., & Kaye, B. K. (2000). Using is believing: The influence of reliance on the credibility of online political information among politically interested Internet users. *Journalism & Mass Communication Quarterly, 77*(4), 865–879.

Jordan, R. (2001, February 21). TV network affiliates coming alive in battle for local Web audience; some beat daily newspapers. *The Media Audit.* Retrieved September 3, 2001, from http://www.themediaaudit.com/tv_aff.htm

Jupiter Media Metrix. (2002, March 14). *Olympics have positive impact on news channels and spawn debut of new Web sites. February 2002 Internet ratings.* Retrieved June 14, 2002, from http://www.jmm.com/xp/jmm/press/2002/pr_031402.xml

Katz, J. (1994, September). Online or not, newspapers suck. *Wired,* 50–58.

Katz, J. E., & Aspden, P. (1997a). Motivations for and barriers to Internet usage: Results of a national public opinion survey. *Internet Research: Electronic Networking Applications and Policy, 7*(3), 170–188.

Katz, J. E., & Aspden, P. (1997b). Motives, hurdles, and dropouts: Who is on and off the Internet and why. *Communications of the ACM, 40*(4), 97–102.

Katz, J. E., Rice, R. E., & Aspden, P. (2001). The Internet, 1995–2000: Access, civic involvement, and social interaction. *American Behavioral Scientist, 45*(3), 405–419.

Landow, G. P. (1990). Popular fallacies about hypertext. In D. H. Jonassen & H. Mandl (Eds.), *Designing hypermedia for learning* (pp. 39–59). New York: Springer-Verlag.

Lang, A. (2000). The limited capacity model of mediated message processing. *Journal of Communication. 50*(1), 46–70.

Lang, P. J., Bradley, M. M., & Cuthbert, B. N. (1997). Motivated attention: Affect, activation, and action. In P. J. Lang, R. F. Simons, & M. T. Balaban (Eds.), *Attention and orienting: Sensory and motivational processes* (pp. 97–135). Mahwah, NJ: Lawrence Erlbaum Associates.

Lenhart, A. (2000, September 21). *Who's not online: 57% of those without Internet access say they do not plan to log on.* Washington, DC: Pew Internet & American Life Project. Retrieved July 23, 2002, from http://www.pewinternet.org/reports/toc.asp?Report=21

Liebscher, P., & Marchionini, G. (1991). Performance in electronic encyclopedias: Implications for adaptive systems. In J. M. Griffiths (Ed.), *Proceedings of the American Society for Information Science annual meeting, Vol. 28* (pp. 39–48). Medford, NJ: Learned Information Inc.

Marcus, G. E., Neuman, W. R., & MacKuen, M. (2000). *Affective intelligence and political judgment.* Chicago: University of Chicago Press.

Massey, B. L., & Levy, M. R. (1999). Interactivity, online journalism, and English-language Web newspapers in Asia. *Journalism & Mass Communication Quarterly, 76*(1), 138–151.

Mayer, R. E., Moreno, R., Boire, M., & Vagge, S. (1999). Maximizing constructivist learning from multimedia communications by minimizing cognitive load. *Journal of Educational Psychology, 91,* 638–643.

Mayes, T., Kibby, M., & Anderson, T. (1990). Learning about learning from hypertext. In D. H. Jonassen & H. Mandl (Eds.), *Designing hypermedia for learning* (pp. 227–250). New York: Springer-Verlag.

McDonald, S., & Stevenson, R. J. (1996). Disorientation in hypertext: The effects of three text structures on navigation performance. *Applied Ergonomics, 27*(1), 61–68.

McLuhan, M. (1995). Culture without literacy. In E. McLuhan & R. Zingrone (Eds.), *Essential McLuhan* (pp. 302–311). New York: Basic Books. (Original work published 1953)

McMillan, S. J. (2002). Exploring models of interactivity from multiple research traditions: Users, documents, and systems. In L. A. Lievrouw & S. Livingstone (Eds.), *Handbook of new media* (pp. 163–182). Thousand Oaks, CA: Sage.

Milheim, W. D., & Martin, B. L. (1991). Theoretical bases for the use of learner control: Three different perspectives. *Journal of Computer-Based Instruction, 18,* 99–105.

Morris, M., & Ogan, C. (1996). The Internet as mass medium. *Journal of Communication, 46*(1), 39–50.

Newhagen, J. E., & Levy, M. R. (1998). The future of journalism in a distributed communication architecture. In D. L. Borden & K. Harvey (Eds.), *The electronic grapevine: Rumor, reputation, and reporting in the new on–line environment* (pp. 9–21). Mahwah, NJ: Lawrence Erlbaum Associates.

Newhagen, J. E., & Reeves, B. (1992). This evening's bad news: Effects of compelling negative television news images on memory. *Journal of Communication, 42*(2), 25–41.

NTIA (1998, July). *Falling through the Net: Defining the digital divide.* National Telecommunications and Information Administration, U.S. Department of Commerce. Retrieved July 23, 2002, from http://www.ntia.doc.gov/ntiahome/fttn99/contents.html

NTIA, (2000, October). *Falling through the Net: Toward digital inclusion.* National Telecommunications and Information Administration, U.S. Department of Commerce. Retrieved July 23, 2002, from http://www.ntia.doc.gov/ntiahome/fttn00/contents00.html

NTIA (2002, February). *A nation online: How Americans are expanding their use of the Internet.* National Telecommunications and Information Administration, U.S. Department of Commerce. Retrieved July 23, 2002, from http://www.ntia.doc.gov/ntiahome/dn/index.html

Oliver, R. (1996). Measuring users' performance with interactive information systems. *Journal of Computer Assisted Learning, 12,* 89–102.

Perse, E. M., & Ferguson, D. A. (2000). The benefits and costs of Web surfing. *Communication Quarterly, 48*(4), 343–359.

Pew Research Center for the People and the Press (2000, June 11). *Internet sapping broadcast news audience.* Retrieved July 23, 2000, from http://people-press.org/reports/display.php3?ReportID=36

Pew Research Center for the People and the Press (2002, June 9). *Public's news habits little changed by September 11.* Retrieved July 23, 2002, from http://people-press.org/reports/display.php3?ReportID=156

Plutchik, R. (1980). *Emotion: A psychoevolutionary synthesis.* New York: Harper & Row.

Rafaeli, S. (1988). Interactivity: From new media to communication. In R. Hawkins, J. Wiemann, & S. Pingree (Eds.), *Advancing communication science: Merging mass and interpersonal processes* (pp. 110–134). Newbury Park, CA: Sage.

Reeves, B., & Nass, C. (1996). *The media equation: How people treat computers, television, and new media like real people and places.* New York: Cambridge University Press.

Steuer, J. (1995). Defining virtual reality: Dimensions determining telepresence. In F. Biocca & M. R. Levy (Eds.), *Communication in the age of virtual reality* (pp. 33–56). Hillsdale, NJ: Lawrence Erlbaum Associates.

Stromer-Galley, J. (2000). Online interaction and why candidates avoid it. *Journal of Communication, 50*(4), 111–132.

Sundar, S. S. (2000). Multimedia effects on processing and perception of online news: A study of picture, audio, and video downloads. *Journalism & Mass Communication Quarterly, 77*(3), 480–499.

Sundar, S. S., Hesser, K. M., Kalyanaraman, S., & Brown, J. (1998, July). *The effect of Web site interactivity on political persuasion.* Paper presented at the 21st General Assembly and Scientific Conference of the International Association for Media and Communication Research, Glasgow, UK.

Sundar, S. S., Kalyanaraman, S., & Brown, J. (2003). Explicating Web site interactivity: Impression-formation effects in political campaign sites. *Communication Research, 30*(1), 30–59.

Sundar, S. S., & Nass, C. (2001). Conceptualizing sources in online news. *Journal of Communication, 51*(1), 52–72.

Thuring, M., Hannemann, J., & Haake, J. M. (1995). Hypermedia and cognition: Designing for comprehension. *Communications of the ACM, 38*(8), 57–66.

Tripp, S. D., & Roby, W. (1990). Orientation and disorientation in a hypertext lexicon. *Journal of Computer-Based Instruction, 17*(4), 120–124.

Vorderer, P., Knobloch, S., & Schramm, H. (2001). Does entertainment suffer from interactivity? The impact of watching an interactive TV movie on viewers' experience of entertainment. *Media Psychology, 3*(4), 343–363.

# 4

# Avoiding Computers: Does Personality Play a Role?

SETH FINN
*Robert Morris University*

APPA RAO KORUKONDA
*Bloomsburg University of Pennsylvania*

## INTRODUCTION

In the fall of 2000, a Pew Internet & American Life Project telephone survey of 2,503 adults reported that that 59% of Americans over the age of 18 were connected to the Internet (Lenhart, 2000). Most readers considered this statistic just another indication of the phenomenal growth of the Internet as a communication medium over the previous decade. But the Pew survey went on to question the 41% of the sample who were non-users about their future Internet plans. Here the results were equally surprising. Whereas 41% of those who reported they were not yet online said they would either definitely or probably go online, the largest share of respondents not yet online, 57%, said they would definitely or probably not go on the Internet. A majority of those who lacked any plans to go online turned out to be 60 years of age or older. And yet, even among the youngest age group surveyed, 18 to 39 years old, 14% fell into the definitely not or probably will not categories. This reluctance to use the Internet among younger Americans implies that advancing age and unfamiliarity with new technology is not a sufficient explanation of why individuals avoid the Internet. Despite the ubiquitous role computers play at work and home as a productivity tool and a medium for information and entertainment, a significant portion of the population seems to harbor negative attitudes about them. Thus, studying the sources of such negative feelings about computer technology has become a vital area of social research.

## The Technology Acceptance Model Paradigm

The question of what motivates individuals to avoid computer use has been of critical importance to the field of information systems (IS) research as organizations try to design computer systems that will win user acceptance. To a great extent, IS researchers were guided over the past decade by what was labeled the *technology acceptance model* (TAM, Davis, 1989), which itself is a specific application of Fishbein and Ajzen's (1975) theory of reasoned action. In their general model of behavior derived from attitudes, Fishbein and Ajzen asserted that behavioral intention (BI) is a function of an individual's attitudes toward the contemplated behavior (A) and his or her perceptions of what other important people think of the behavior, which are grouped in a construct referred to as the *subjective norm* (SN). In Fishbein and Ajzen's characteristic mathematical notation, $BI = A + SN$.

Davis' TAM model (see Fig. 4.1) refined Fishbein and Ajzen's concepts for an information systems environment by positing two specific attitudes—perceived usefulness (U) and perceived ease of use (E)—that are always components of the individual's attitude toward using an available technology. At the same time, Davis discounted the subjective norm (SN) construct due to the difficulty of "disentangling the direct effects of SN on behavioral intention from the indirect effects" that individuals unavoidably factor into their preexisting attitudes about an intended behavior (Davis, Bagozzi, & Warshaw, 1989, p. 986).

Instead, subjective norms along with other supposedly indirect influences on behavioral intentions were collapsed into a single category of antecedent factors known as *external variables,* the left-most component in Davis' TAM model.

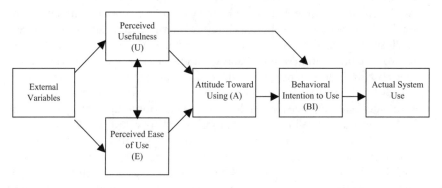

FIG 4.1.   Davis' TAM Model.

The diffusion of the TAM model among IS researchers is testimony to its success in focusing attention on the problem of why end-users refuse to use available systems. The application of the model has achieved paradigmatic status. Studies using the TAM model range from e-commerce to telemedicine to conventional small office computer networks. No one can fault the TAM model in an organizational setting where, as Davis et al. (1989) explained, "We are particularly interested in how well we can explain and predict future user behavior from simple measures taken after a very brief period of interaction with a system" (p. 983). However, as the schematic diagram makes evident, the existence of any preexisting barriers to computer use are relegated to the catch-all category of external variables. Yet it is just those preexisting variables that require consideration when one reads a statistic that 14% of all 18- to 39-year-olds have no intention of going online. Although they can certainly be questioned about preexisting attitudes, one must wonder: What is it about human nature or social origins that mediate positive or negative responses to computer technology? And once we sit an individual in front of a computer, what internal traits guide his or her visceral response?

## A Uses and Gratifications Approach to Computer Technology Research

Of course, information systems researchers do not have a monopoly on studying new technology. Mass communication researchers have consistently focused on the social impact of new technologies as large-scale industries evolved to exploit the commercial possibilities of film, radio, television, cable, and now the Internet. More than 50 years ago, Herzog (1944) literally invented the uses and gratifications paradigm as a logical approach when she began backtracking the process to better understand women's motivations for listening to the radio. She did this in an attempt to develop a more valid description of radio's effects on women soap opera listeners. It is interesting to note that 30 years later, just about the time Fishbein and Ajzen were codifying their model of attitude change and behavioral intent, Katz, Blumler, and Gurevitch (1974) were reviving the uses and gratifications paradigm. And then a generation later, in an issue of the *Journal of Communication* devoted to the Internet, Newhagen and Rafaeli (1996) suggested resurrecting the uses and gratifications paradigm to orient future Internet research. Rafaeli characterized the uses and gratifications approach as especially appropriate for spotlighting the motivations that drive people to take part in the Internet. Offering his own set of motivational factors that guide Net use, he asked, "What are the relative weights of prurience, curiosity, profit seeking, sociability?" (Newhagen & Rafaeli, 1996, p. 10). Those were their Big Four. We will soon introduce the Big Five.

## The Uses and Gratifications Paradigm

Mapping behaviors that involve computer and Internet use onto the uses and gratifications model, by the latest count, has generated nearly a dozen studies correlating

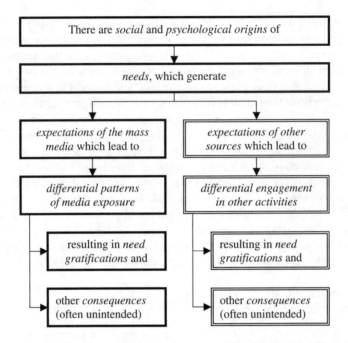

FIG 4.2.    The elements of a uses and gratifications model (McQuail & Windahl, 1993).

media use motives and types of Internet and computer use since 1998 (see LaRose, Mastro, & Eastin, 2001, for a review and critique). However, uses and gratifications researchers, like their IS counterparts, have generally ignored antecedent conditions, such as personality, in their investigations. This is particularly evident when we look at Katz et al.'s (1974) often quoted précis, which characterized the uses and gratifications paradigm as an approach that traces:

> (1) the social and psychological origins of (2) needs, which generate (3) expectations of (4) the mass media or other sources, which lead to (5) differential patterns of media exposure (or engagement in other activities), resulting in (6) need gratifications and (7) other consequences, perhaps mostly unintended ones. (p. 20)

McQuail and Windahl (1993) were the first to transform this verbal précis into a graphical model; however, Finn, (1997) subsequently revised their version to emphasize the non-media opportunities for gratification that Katz et al. (1974) built into their psycho-social framework (see Fig. 4.2). In Finn's (1997) rendition communication media represent just one set of alternatives for achieving gratification. A competing pathway always exists. This formulation is especially appropriate in modeling computer use since computers can be envisioned as either a new medium or a distinct pathway to gratification, a dualism we explore in developing hypotheses about avoiding computer use.

Since the publication of Katz et al.'s (1974) précis, their framework has promoted considerable research and refinement in regard to the relationship between expectations and need gratifications, but not in regard to antecedent conditions. For example, Palmgreen, Wenner, and Rosengren (1985) presented a much more elaborate model after observing that the predictive power of the paradigm could be enhanced by operationally differentiating between gratifications sought and gratifications obtained. And, most recently, LaRose et al. (2001) persuasively argued for a reformulation that integrates essential components of social-cognitive theory, such as self-regulation (Bandura, 1991) and self-efficacy (Bandura, 1997) into the traditional model. Interestingly, IS researchers have also employed social-cognition theory to untangle the social norms conundrum posed by TAM (Compeau & Higgins, 1995; Compeau, Higgins, & Huff, 1999; Morris & Turner, 2001; Venkatesh & Davis, 1996; Venkatesh & Morris, 2000).

All these innovations, however, have occurred in the expectations-exposure-effects components of the model, for the most part ignoring the most stable characteristics of the user, the social and psychological origins that are generalized into a set of needs. A major problem for uses and gratifications researchers in the past has been where to begin a study of salient psychological factors, given the breadth of research into individual differences. However, the relatively recent convergence among personality theorists on a five-factor model (Digman, 1989, 1990) suggests an important place to start. The current list of stable and reliably measured basic personality traits has been pared down to just five—extraversion, neuroticism, openness to experience, agreeableness, and conscientiousness—and in a competing list to as few as three—extraversion, neuroticism, and psychoticism (Eysenck, 1991).

Costa and McCrae (1988), who have both led the theoretical conceptualization of the five-factor model and developed a popular instrument for measuring the five signal traits, neatly characterized these personality dimensions as follows:

> Individuals high in Neuroticism worry about others' opinions of them, are defensive, and guarded, and want care and sympathy; those high in Extraversion have needs for social contact, attention, and fun. Open individuals appreciate variety, intellectual stimulation, and aesthetic experiences, and are adventurous and unconventional. Individuals who score high on Agreeableness are neither domineering nor argumentative; they enjoy helping people and tend to be self-effacing and apologetic. Finally, those who score high on Conscientiousness value organization and accomplishment, and are persistent, careful, and deliberate. (p. 261)

## Designing a Secondary Analysis of Archival Data

It is the development of this consensus about what constitutes a global set of personality traits and the opportunity to examine their influence on attitudes toward computer use that prompted the research project reported in this chapter. In this study we exploit a rich set of archival data gathered by the Institute for Research in Social Science between 1985 and 1988 to explore personality factors that may be linked to computer use (Odum Institute for Research in Social Science, 1988). The entire archive represents data collected over 5 academic years, beginning in the fall of 1983 when the Institute annually enlisted a random sample of 96 University of North Carolina undergraduates to spend 60 to 90 minutes per week for 20 weeks answering survey questionnaires via computer terminals. The project, known as the Computer Administered Panel Survey (CAPS), was the brainchild of then IRSS director Bibb Latané (1989), who believed that the efficiency of social science research would be substantially enhanced if systems of data collection and archiving were fully automated and made available online. The range of the archive is monumental, but for the purposes of this study, the most important are measures of personality that can be connected to the feelings of students about their participation during a weekly CAPS exit interview. In addition, the archival data set supplies a broad range of background variables that permits us to control for differences in family social class and human capital, thereby attending to the social origins component of the uses and gratifications model.

Despite the breadth of measures available in the CAPS archive, embarking on a study of personality traits and feelings about computer use can truly be a trip into uncharted waters. The use of a comprehensive set of personality dimensions as predictors of media exposure (Finn, 1997; Weaver, 1991; Weaver, Walker, McCord, & Bellamy, 1996) and computer attitudes (Hudiburg, 1999) is a relatively recent and rare phenomenon. Some convergence of the two domains is in order. Certainly, computer use and media use are analogous to the extent that both involve electronic technology used to store and convey information. Furthermore, one can argue that human–computer interaction, especially when one is responding to a set of verbal questions presented on a video screen, is an extreme form of asynchronous interpersonal communication. By that we mean that all computer users are in fact communicating across time and space with the corporate authors of the computer program they have selected. The corporate authors, who "write" first, must nevertheless have prepared a set of further statements with utmost regard to the total realm of responses their future correspondents may employ. But in regard to only one of the big five personality traits—openness to experience—might one argue that a finding from a media study may be replicated by analogy in a computer use study. The point is, however, to start somewhere. Therefore, we propose the hypothesis that openness to experience enhances appreciation for the novelty of CAPS content and its format. This assertion is based on previous findings about the connection between openness to experience and a preference for viewing film, a medium characterized by novel content, rather than TV, which carries conventional programming (Finn, 1997).

In direct contrast to similarities that may exist between media and computer use, participation in the CAPS project also represented a commitment to completing a series of assigned tasks that made this activity motivationally different from voluntary mass media use (participants were paid $5 dollars per session). Accordingly, it is reasonable to speculate that the two personality dimensions, agreeableness and conscientiousness, which relate to power relations on one hand and dedication and discipline on the other, may, in these work-like circumstances, play a more influential role than they do in voluntary media exposure. Willingness to submit to someone else's demands, as indicated by agreeableness, or push ahead to finish an assignment, as indicated by conscientiousness, could well moderate negative feelings about the activities completed. Therefore, we hypothesized that as agreeableness and conscientiousness increase, so too would positive feelings about the CAPS project.

A final factor in the development of our hypotheses were the findings from the sole empirical study we could find that related computer use to the Big Five personality dimensions. An investigation of the connection between the Big Five and computer stress documented some limited forms of influence of neuroticism, extraversion, and openness on computer use (Hudiburg, 1999). Although analysis of questionnaire data revealed no direct relationship between computer stress and any of the Big Five factors except openness, Hudiburg used regression analysis to demonstrate that both neuroticism and extraversion generate moderating effects on anxiety ratings that correlate with his computer hassles scale. As he described the effect, extraversion "acts as a variable that would 'immunize' one against the effects of computer hassles as a stressor, whereas Neuroticism would exacerbate symptoms" (p. 478). This finding points toward a negative relationship between neuroticism and computer attitudes and a positive relationship between extraversion and computer attitudes.

The one positive correlation Hudiburg (1999) reported between openness and his computer hassles scale is at first counterintuitive because as argued earlier, openness should moderate whatever negative impact is associated with new experience. In this case, though, a closer look at the operationalization of Hudiburg's (1995) computer hassle scale revealed that it confounds the variety of experience with the total severity of the hassles experienced. That is, hassle scores increase in direct proportion to the breadth of the individual's experience, even if the hassles experienced are only "somewhat severe." High hassle scores can reflect extensive experience rather than high severity and vice versa, thereby creating the conditions for a positive relationship between openness to experience and increased hassle in using computers.

In view of such factors, we began our secondary analysis with a set of general hypotheses based more on extensions of previous theorizing about the Big Five personality variables than actual empirical findings. Intuition, common sense, and previous experience studying personality traits led us to the following two groupings: (a) conscientiousness, agreeableness, openness to experience, and extraversion would be positively related to positive feelings about participation in CAPS whereas (b) neuroticism would exhibit an inverse relationship to positive feelings about participation.

## Analytical Issues

The analysis itself was conducted with four additional design considerations. As already intimated, the uses and gratifications model gives equal theoretical weight to social as well as psychological origins of needs. To assure that we were not dismissing such social origins, we included measures of family social status, father's education and occupational status, and mother's education and occupational status. Given the relatively homogeneous composition of the undergraduate population at the University of North Carolina at Chapel Hill, we did not expect differences in family status and human capital to materially affect the results, but controlling for such variation was an implicit requirement of the uses and gratifications model.

On the other hand, the substantial literature devoted to sex differences in regard to exposure to and attitudes toward math, science, and computers (Chen, 1986, 1987; Colley, Gale, & Harris, 1994; Flake, 1991; Venkatesh & Morris, 2000; Williams, Ogletree, Woodburn, & Raffeld, 1993) made it evident that sex was, in fact, a surrogate for divergent socialization processes, which could have an impact on student responses to CAPS participation. Indeed, much gender-focused research has been oriented toward seeing whether "expectations" about computers can be altered, so that important educational goals can be met without threat to fundamental psychological needs, such as maintaining or heightening self-esteem. Thus, the analysis included provisions to document differences in personality dimensions, social status, and CAPS feeling scores for male and female students.

Third, we were not satisfied to look just at the correlations between personality traits and individuals' feeling scores on a week-to-week basis. We expected personality traits to be most pronounced during the first sessions of the year. However, in contrast to the conventional view that attitudes are precursors of behavioral intention, we were well aware of the possibility that these students' experiences—that is, the behaviors they performed—would impact their attitudes (Kelman, 1972). Researchers employing social-cognitive theory have been particularly focused on how this self-reflective capability influences expectations (Compeau et al., 1999; LaRose et al., 2001). Thus, we anticipated that in a very short time, the influence of personality traits on feelings about CAPS could be overwhelmed by direct personal experience, reflecting changes in perceived usefulness and ease of use (Venkatesh & Davis, 2000). Accordingly, we decided to examine correlations between personality and changes in feeling about CAPS from the first week to the second, third, and fourth rather than to compute correlations with the raw weekly scores alone. Those weekly scores were eventually subsumed in semester-long averages.

Finally, although there was essentially no remedy to this concern, we anticipated that the use of archival data from the mid-1980s would generate skepticism about the relevance of the students' experience. Computers are clearly more versatile machines than they were then and the range of activities that students might engage in would be qualitatively different. Putting aside for the moment the value of the available data about each student in conjunction with full documentation of his or her participation in a year-long computer project, it would be virtually impossible these days to assemble a sample of students with such limited computer experience as these individuals had when they began their participation in the CAPS project. In that way, this study mimics the special opportunities afforded communication researchers who were able to investigate the impact of television on communities where it was late in arriving, such as Williams' (1986) study of children in "NOTEL," an isolated community in western Canada, and Parker's (1963) study of adults in various small towns in Illinois. The impact of personality traits might be more readily apparent in this mid-1980s sample precisely because the participants' previous computer experience was not so great as to overwhelm the psychological origins of their reactions.

## METHODOLOGY

Data for this study were collected during the academic years 1985–1986, 1986–1987, and 1987–1988, using the Computer Administered Panel Survey (CAPS) facility at the Odum Institute for Research in Social Science (IRSS) at the University of North Carolina at Chapel Hill. The facility employed approximately 100 undergraduates each academic year who agreed to spend 60 to 90 minutes per week for 20 weeks responding to computer-administered questionnaires and experimental tasks. For their effort, they received $5 per session plus various bonuses designed to maintain their year-long commitment to the research project.

A three-stage procedure was used to select a sample that, aside from gender, was demographically representative of the undergraduate student body. Each year a random sample of undergraduates, stratified to select an equal number of males and females, was drawn from the records of the university registrar. Interested students were then invited to sign up for the project. The final sample was then randomly selected from the pool of applicants who provided informed consent. Although the three annual samples represented three overlapping student populations, in only one case did a respondent participate for more than 1 academic year. That female student was apparently part of the random sample in both her freshman and junior years. Demographic characteristics of each year's sample were very similar to each other as well as the undergraduate student body over those 3 years. The vast majority of students were from in-state homes and graduated in the top 10% of their high school classes. Age, racial composition, and SAT scores also matched the known parameters of the undergraduate population.

### Measures of Psychological Origins

Five dimensions of personality were measured using the NEO Personality Inventory developed by Costa and McCrae (1989). Participants responded to 180 randomly ordered statements presented in 5-point Likert format, ranging from 0 for strong disagreement to 4 for agreement. Eighty-four of the 180 questions were recoded for reverse polarity.

Forty-eight statements were devoted to each of three dimensions, neuroticism, extraversion, and openness. The neuroticism scale statements attempted to assess such qualities as anxiety, hostility, depression, self-consciousness, impulsiveness, and vulnerability. The extraversion scale statements related to warmth, gregariousness, assertiveness, activity, excitement-seeking, and upbeat emotions. Finally, the openness scale evaluated dispositions toward fantasy and aesthetics as well as diverse feelings, actions, ideas, and values.

The agreeableness and conscientiousness scales were based on responses to 18 statements each. Statements typical of the conscientiousness scale were "I try to do jobs carefully, so they won't have to be done again" and "I like to keep everything in its place so I know just where it is." Statements typical of the agreeableness scale included "I believe that most people are well-intentioned" and "Starving masses in foreign countries leave me pretty cold," the latter requiring inverse scoring.

Computer presentation of this instrument permitted some innovations in its administration that have been used to selectively eliminate suspect students from the sample. The 180-question survey was routinely administered in four segments with an extra question at the end of each asking students, in the same 5-point Likert format, if they had honestly answered the items. Students whose average response was less than "I agree" on the four segments were eliminated from the correlational analysis. Time spent on each of the four segments was also recorded, and low honesty scores were often matched with short response times, although not always so.

## Measures of Social Origins

An extensive background questionnaire, developed by CAPS personnel and administered to all participants at their first CAPS session, provided five useful measures of social origins. The most global measure was a subjective estimate of their family's social status in the community where they grew up. Students were presented with a 7-point scale marked at the ends with 1 for low status and 7 for high status. In addition, there was a closed-ended question asking the level of each parent's education, which offered a seven-point scale from 1 for eighth grade or less to 7 for PhD.

Finally, there were separate questions asking for the father's and the mother's occupational status after respondents viewed a 100-point scale that listed a number of familiar occupations with representative values next to them—for example, 2 for physician, 11 for lawyer or dentist, 22 for civil engineer, 31 for building contractor, continuing down to 88 for garbage collector. These ratings were compared with responses to separate open-ended questions asking how the students' mothers and fathers were employed. Fewer than a dozen responses were judged inadvertent errors, such as a high school graduate mother who did not work outside the home receiving a maximum employment status rating of 0, or excessively inflated, such as a state trooper with a partial college education rated by his daughter as having an employment status higher than a physician.

## Measures of Feelings about CAPS

After students completed the final task of each of their 20 sessions, they were routinely prompted about their feelings. On a scale of 0 to 100, they were asked how they generally felt at that moment and in a follow-up question specifically how they felt about participating in the CAPS project. They were also given an opportunity to record up to six lines of personal comments. In this study, the feelings about CAPS responses were used to generate six measures: the Session #1 Score, the Sessions #2, #3, and #4 Change Scores, and the Semester #1 and the Semester #2 Mean Scores. The Session #1 Scores are the students' initial responses to CAPS participation on the scale from 0 to 100. The Session #2, #3, and #4 Change Scores were computed by subtracting the raw score from each of those sessions from the Session #1 Score, thereby giving priority to their initial encounter with CAPS as a baseline for week-to-week changes. Finally, the semester mean scores were the average of all CAPS feeling scores recorded each semester. Because administratively it took time to recruit the CAPS volunteers at the beginning of each academic year, only 8 sessions took place in the fall semester whereas 12 were scheduled for the spring semester.

## RESULTS

Aggregating the IRSS archival data for 3 years yielded 270 respondents whose records included all five measures of social status and human capital, 286 respondents who had completed the entire NEO Personality Inventory, and 262 respondents whose records provided sufficient data to compute the six measures of CAPS feelings used in the multivariate analysis. Given that the administrators of the CAPS project attempted to maintain a sample of 96 students throughout the academic year, there is obvious evidence of sample mortality although the biases that resulted would not seem to be systematic, with one exception. The NEO Personality Inventory is administered at a single session in the middle of the spring semester. However, only 250 of those students were members of the panel for Session #1 in the fall semester, and of the approximately 12 students a year who dropped out of the study before the NEO-PI was administered, a disproportionate number may have had negative feelings about CAPS.

## Social Origins

Table 4.1 reports the measures of social origins. The students on average perceived their families to be relatively high in social status in their home communities ($M = 5.28$). Father's reported education level approached a college degree ($M = 4.71$); average mother's education was closer to the rating of some college or community college ($M = 4.38$). The average occupational status of fathers was

TABLE 4.1
Mean Scores: Social Origins Indicators with Differences by Gender

| Sociological Origins | Male ($n > 126$) | Female ($n > 130$) | Overall Mean ($n > 256$) | sd | F-Statistic ($df = 1, > 254$) |
|---|---|---|---|---|---|
| Family Social Status | 5.36 | 5.21 | 5.28 | 1.01 | 1.43 |
| Father's Education | 4.86 | 4.56 | 4.71 | 1.33 | 3.54 |
| Mother's Education | 4.41 | 4.34 | 4.38 | 1.08 | 0.37 |
| Father's Occupational Status | 25.73 | 31.68 | 28.74 | 16.81 | 8.48** |
| Mother's Occupational Status | 42.34 | 41.43 | 41.88 | 18.19 | 0.16 |

Note: ** $p < .01$

judged to be slightly higher than that of a building contractor ($M = 28.74$), whereas the mothers' average ($M = 41.88$) was equivalent to an electrician or county agricultural agent. The one-way analysis of variance revealed one significant difference between male and female students. Female students appeared to come from families in which the fathers' occupational status was lower than in the families of male students.

## NEO Personality Traits

Univariate statistics from the 180-question NEO-PI instrument, as well as a comparison of male and female mean scores, are presented in Table 4.2. Overall, they appear reasonable for a representative sample of undergraduates from a selective state university campus. The mean score for neuroticism was 90.17 ($sd = 19.20$), for extraversion, 117.04 ($sd = 17.21$), for openness, 116.82 ($sd = 17.07$), for agreeableness, 45.36 ($sd = 6.82$), and for conscientiousness, 46.74 ($sd = 9.31$). With only one exception, both the means and standard deviations were within one point of the scores reported by Costa and McCrae (1989, p. 4) as typical of 17- to 20-year old college students. The mean score for openness for the CAPS participants was about 5 points lower than for Costa and McCrae's sample of 526 college students. The NEO scores are also distinguished by three statistically significant

TABLE 4.2
Mean Scores: NEO Personality Inventory with Differences by Gender

| Psychological Origins | Male ($n = 139$) | Female ($n = 141$) | Overall Mean ($n = 280$) | sd | F-Statistic ($df = 1, 278$) |
|---|---|---|---|---|---|
| Neuroticism | 84.54 | 95.72 | 90.17 | 19.20 | 25.82*** |
| Extraversion | 116.15 | 117.91 | 117.04 | 17.21 | 0.729 |
| Openness | 114.12 | 119.49 | 116.82 | 17.07 | 7.09** |
| Agreeableness | 44.43 | 46.28 | 45.36 | 6.82 | 5.23* |
| Conscientious | 47.18 | 46.30 | 46.74 | 9.31 | 0.62 |

Note: * $p < .05$, ** $p < .01$, *** $p < .001$

TABLE 4.3

CAPS Participation Feelings with Differences by Gender

| Feelings about CAPS Participation | Male ($n > 131$) | Female ($n > 131$) | Overall Mean ($n > 262$) | sd | F-Statistic ($df = 1, > 260$) |
|---|---|---|---|---|---|
| Session #1 | 75.61 | 80.49 | 78.04 | 15.98 | 6.27** |
| Session #2 Change | 2.23 | 0.34 | 1.28 | 14.99 | 1.04 |
| Session #3 Change | 0.27 | −0.55 | −0.14 | 15.67 | 3.54 |
| Session #4 Change | −1.85 | −1.31 | −1.58 | 15.52 | 0.78 |
| Mean for Semester #1 Sessions | 72.77 | 76.51 | 74.64 | 15.21 | 4.08* |
| Mean for Semester #2 Sessions | 67.33 | 68.55 | 67.95 | 18.18 | 0.31 |

Note: * $p < .05$, ** $p < .01$.

differences in means between the female and male subsamples. The female subsample scored higher most notably on neuroticism, $F(1, 278) = 2.82$, $p = .001$, followed by openness, $F(1, 278) = 7.09$, $p = .004$, and agreeableness, $F(1, 278) = 5.23$, $p = .02$.

## Feelings about CAPS

Aside from the generally positive ratings evidenced by the CAPS Feeling measures, they reveal an overall decline in feelings over the course of the academic year (see Table 4.3). The mean for Session #1 is 78.04, which increases by 1.28 points at Session #2, but then falls after Session #3 and Session #4, portending the overall decline in positive feeling revealed by the two semester mean scores. Female participants report statistically significant higher mean feeling scores for the first session, $F(1, 261) = 6.27$, $p = .01$, and for the first semester overall as well, $F(1, 264) = 4.08$, $p = .04$.

## Personality Dimensions and Feelings about CAPS Participation

Fifth order partial correlations were computed to complete the statistical analysis in a framework that approximates the uses and gratifications model (see Fig. 4.2). Family social status, mother's educational level and occupational status, and father's educational level and occupational status were designated social origins control variables to test the strength of relationships between the NEO measures, selected as global measures of the students' psychological origins, and the students' subsequent indications of feelings about participating in CAPS at the outset and throughout the academic year.

Table 4.4 presents the results of this multivariate analysis. Statistically significant partial correlation coefficients, as well as those approaching significance, are presented for the entire sample and the male and female subsamples. Listwise deletions

TABLE 4.4
Partial Correlations: NEO-PI Scores and CAPS Participation Feelings

| Feelings About CAPS | | Neuroticism | Extraversion | Openness | Agreeableness | Conscientiousness |
|---|---|---|---|---|---|---|
| | All | n.s. | n.s. | n.s. | .21*** | n.s. |
| Session #1 | Males | −.15 | n.s. | −.15 | .27*** | n.s. |
| Score | Females | n.s. | .17* | .19* | .13 | n.s. |
| | All | n.s. | .11 | n.s. | −.13* | .23*** |
| Session #2 | Males | n.s. | n.s. | .27** | n.s. | n.s. |
| Difference | Females | n.s. | .13 | n.s. | −.14 | .24** |
| | All | n.s. | n.s. | n.s. | n.s. | .12* |
| Session #3 | Males | .14 | .17* | n.s. | n.s. | n.s. |
| Difference | Females | n.s. | .13 | n.s. | n.s. | .23** |
| | All | n.s. | n.s. | n.s. | n.s. | n.s. |
| Session #4 | Males | n.s. | n.s. | n.s. | n.s. | n.s. |
| Difference | Females | n.s. | n.s. | n.s. | n.s. | n.s. |
| | All | n.s. | .14* | n.s. | .24*** | .11 |
| Semester #1 | Males | −.18* | n.s. | n.s. | .30** | n.s. |
| Mean Score | Females | n.s. | .23** | .18* | .17* | .22* |
| | All | −.12* | n.s. | n.s. | .26*** | .11 |
| Semester #2 | Males | n.s. | n.s. | n.s. | .31*** | n.s. |
| Mean Score | Females | −.17* | n.s. | .20* | .28** | .13 |

*Note:* One-tailed, fifth-order partial correlations, controlled for family social status, father's educa-tion and occupational status, and mother's education and occupational status. Sample $n = 210$; male subsample $n = 100$; female subsample $n = 110$.

Only coefficients with $p < .10$ are reported: * $p < .05$, ** $p < .01$, *** $p < .001$. All other coefficients are denoted as nonsignificant (n.s.).

and the implementation of a validity check for the NEO-PI scores reduced the total sample size to 210, comprised of 100 male and 110 female students. As expected, the most frequently occurring relationships are revealed by correlations beween positive feelings for CAPS and the personality dimensions of agreeableness and conscientiousness. Agreeableness is an especially strong correlate for the male sub-sample in response to CAPS Session #1 and then recurs for both sexes in regard to the averaged weekly CAPS feeling scores for Semesters #1 and #2. By contrast, conscientiousness appears to play an important role as a motivating factor only for the female subsample, especially in the second and third weeks of their CAPS par-ticipation. This female-only result is apparent once more when conscientiousness is correlated with the Semesters #1 CAPS feeling score. However, the relationship only approaches statistical significance for Semester #2.

Among the other surprising results in Table 4.4 is a recurring relationship, es-pecially among female students, between extraversion and positive feelings about CAPS during the first weeks of the academic year and Semester #1 overall. Some-what similar is the relationship between openness and positive feelings for CAPS, which is exhibited for the female subsample during Session #1 and reveals itself again in regard to females' mean feeling scores for each semester. By contrast, the expected inverse relationship between neuroticism and positive feelings toward CAPS does not fully emerge until Semester #2, by which time it is no longer evident in the male subsample. Finally, by Session #4, as we anticipated, the connections between personality and changes in weekly feeling scores dissipate, presumably because attitudes are shaped increasingly by reflections on direct experience.

## DISCUSSION

In *Reason in Human Affairs,* Nobel prize-winner Herbert Simon (1983) reminded us that "we live in what might be called a nearly empty world—one in which there are millions of variables that in principle could affect each other but that most of the time don't" (p. 20). Simon's intent was to emphasize how short-term and bounded are the decision-making processes that guide human behavior. For any social scientist, his was a sobering observation on two accounts. First, it reminded us of the high degree of variability in human behavior that naturally arises because individuals make up their minds based on only a few factors that have seized their attention at any particular moment. Second, it underscored the difficulty of identifying, from among an unending list of potential factors, those that recur frequently or powerfully enough to create a perceptible impact. As Simon explained, "In gravitational theory everything is pulling at everything else, but some things pull harder than others, either because they're bigger or because they're closer" (p. 20).

This test of the uses and gratifications model is premised on the theoretical assumption that social and psychological origins effect sufficient gravitational pull on human thinking about computer technology to have a systematic impact on attitudes. Judging from results of the data analysis, there is sufficient statistical evidence to support the claim that variations in personality traits and gender are linked to diverse attitudes about computers, but if these are "bigger" variables (in Simon's terms), they may not be precise enough to account for more than very modest amounts of variance in individual attitudes. The situation is complicated further by the specifics of the CAPS enterprise and the probable self-selection of individuals who thought they would like to work with computers as respondents for an extensive social science interviewing project. Thus, the initial positive disposition of the participants may have led to a sample with less variability in their attitudes than the student population from which they were drawn. As noted in the methodology section, sample mortality would have also reduced variability and skewed the sample toward more positive views, in as much as students who felt negatively about their CAPS experience had ample time to drop out of the study before the NEO-PI was administered in the spring.

Nevertheless, the data analysis revealed correlations between personality traits and feelings about CAPS in the directions hypothesized. Agreeableness and conscientiousness, which are conspicuous by their absence as influences on media exposure, appear to play the central role in mediating positive feelings about computer use. It is particularly interesting to trace the sex differences exhibited in Table 4.4. In the early weeks, it appears that agreeableness moderates the male students' responses to CAPS participation, whereas conscientiousness is more closely associated with the female students' feelings. Such subtle differences suggest divergent strategies in acclimating individuals to computer technology, although in the long run agreeableness seems to be the dominant factor for both males and females. One caveat is in order, however. We do not know to what degree agreeableness may have influenced how students responded to the wrap-up questionnaires. Students who scored high on the trait may naturally rate CAPS participation highly as well, and students who scored low on the trait may not be as inclined to respond to the demand characteristics of the task.

By far, the most surprising results were the positive correlations between extraversion and positive feelings about CAPS. This finding is counterintuitive to popular notions of the compulsive, emotionally intensive, and socially inept computer hacker. In this regard, the relative weakness of any apparent relationship between neuroticism and positive computer attitudes also points out the inappropriateness of this iconic image in any environment where computer technology has been made widely available. It is difficult to pinpoint what aspect of the CAPS experience may be at the center of this result, but the content of CAPS questionnaires themselves, which frequently focused on personal information about the respondent or evaluations of other people, experiences, and ideas, may have contributed to positive feelings about participation.

Also noteworthy among the results are the relationships exhibited between openness to experience and positive feelings about CAPS. Here some speculation may be in order about the sex-based implications of the results for the first two sessions. Female openness scores are correlated with positive feelings at their first exposure, whereas male students exhibit an uncharacteristic negative response that turns positive at the second session. Could it be that the female students, less experienced in using computers, are accepting or not accepting of the new technology at first introduction based on their openness to experience? The male students, however, who are open to experience are, in fact, more savvy about computer technology and faintly disappointed by this initial experience. On returning for the second session, however, those who are more open to experience have decided to make the best of the situation, and therefore, in comparison with their first week scores, their second week scores are now positive.

There is good reason to be skeptical of such fine-grained post hoc analysis of partial correlation coefficients. And for that reason, we have refrained from extending our analysis to include the six facet scores that can be computed for the neuroticism, extraversion, and openness dimensions. Instead, we invite you to challenge our interpretations with your own analysis of either the facet scores or other personality variables, such as state–trait anxiety or sensation-seeking measures, which are among dozens of relevant variables for this sample, all of which are available online from the IRSS data archive (www2.irss.unc.edu/irss/home.asp). Our intention is to look next at the verbatim comments that participants typed into the record at the end of each session as the best source of data for analyzing the factors that motivated them or discouraged them in their use of computer technology. Of course, as the data are public, you may beat us to them. But having many competing groups study the CAPS project may be the best way to enhance the validity and usefulness of everyone's findings.

## REFERENCES

Bandura, A. (1991). Social-cognitive theory of self-regulation. *Organizational Behavior and Human Decision Processes, 50,* 248–287.

Bandura, A. (1997). *Self-efficacy: The exercise of control.* New York: Freeman.

Chen, M. (1986). Gender and computers: The beneficial effects of experience on attitudes. *Journal of Educational Computing Research, 2,* 265–282.

Chen, M. (1987). Gender differences in adolescents' uses of and attitudes toward computers. In Margaret L. McLaughlin (Ed.), *Communication yearbook 10* (pp. 200–216). Newbury Park, CA: Sage.

Colley, A. M., Gale, M. T., & Harris, T. A. (1994). Effects of gender role identity and experience on computer attitude components. *Journal of Educational Computing Research, 10,* 129–137.

Compeau, D., & Higgins, C. (1995). Computer self-efficacy: Development of a measure and initial test. *MIS Quarterly, 19,* 189–211.

Compeau, D., Higgins, C., & Huff, S. (1999). Social cognitive theory and individual reactions to computing technology: A longitudinal study. *MIS Quarterly, 23,* 145–158.

Costa, P. T. Jr., & McCrae, R. R. (1988). From catalog to classification: Murray's needs and the five-factor model. *Journal of Personality and Social Psychology, 55,* 258–265.

Costa, P. T. Jr., & McCrae, R. R. (1989). *NEO-PI/FFI manual supplement.* Odessa, FL: Psychological Assessment Resources.

Davis, F. D. (1989). Perceived usefulness, perceived ease of use, and user acceptance of information technology. *MIS Quarterly, 13*(3), 319–340.

Davis, F. D., Bagozzi, P., & Warshaw, P. R. (1989). User acceptance of computer technology: A comparison of two theoretical models. *Management Science, 35,* 982–1003.

Digman, J. M. (1989). Five robust traits: Development, stability, and utility. *Journal of Personality, 57,* 195–214.

Digman, J. M. (1990). Personality structure: Emergence of the five-factor model. *Annual Review of Psychology, 41,* 417–440.

Eysenck, H. J. (1991). Dimensions of personality: 16, 5, or 3?—Criteria for a taxonomic paradigm. *Personality and Individual Differences, 12,* 773–790.

Finn, S. (1997). Origins of media exposure: Linking personality traits to TV, radio, print and film use. *Communication Research, 24,* 507–529.

Fishbein, M., & Ajzen, I. (1975). *Belief, attitude, intention and behavior: An introduction to theory and research.* Reading, MA: Addison-Wesley.

Flake, W. L. (1991). Influence of gender, dogmatism, and risk-taking propensity upon attitudes toward information from computers. *Computers in Human Behavior, 7,* 227–235.

Herzog, H. (1944). What do we really know about daytime serial listeners? In P. F. Lazarsfeld & F. N. Stanton (Eds.), *Radio research 1942–43* (pp. 3–33). New York: Duell, Sloan, & Pearce.

Hudiburg, R. A. (1995). Psychology of computer use: XXXIV. The computer hassles scale, subscales, norms, and reliability. *Psychological Reports, 77,* 779–782.

Hudiburg, R. A. (1999). Preliminary investigation of computer stress and the big five personality factors. *Psychological Reports, 85,* 473–480.

Katz, E., Blumler, J. G., & Gurevitch, M. (1974). Utilization of mass communication by the individual. In J. G. Blumler & E. Katz (Eds.), *The uses of mass communications: Current perspectives on gratifications research* (pp. 19–32). Beverly Hills, CA: Sage.

Kelman, H. C. (1972). Processes of opinion change. In W. L. Schramm & D. F. Roberts (Eds.), *The process and effects of mass communication* (pp. 399–425). Chicago: University of Illinois Press.

LaRose, R., Mastro, D., & Eastin, M. S. (2001). Understanding Internet use: A social-cognitive approach to uses and gratifications. *Social Science Computer Review, 19,* 395–413.

Latané, B. (1989). Social psychology and how to revitalize it. In M. R. Leary (Ed.), *The state of social psychology: Issues, themes, and controversies* (pp. 1–12). Newbury Park, CA: Sage.

Lenhart, A. (2000). *Who's not online: 57% of those without Internet access say they do not plan to log on.* Washington, DC: Pew Internet and American Life. Available: http://www.pewinternet.org/reports/pdfs/Pew_Those_Not_Online_Report.pdf.

McQuail, D., & Windahl, S. (1993). *Communication models for the study of mass communications.* London: Longman.

Morris, M. G., & Turner, J. M. (2001). Assessing users' subjective quality of experience with the World Wide Web: An exploratory examination of temporal changes in technology acceptance. *International Journal of Human–Computer Studies, 54,* 877–901.

Newhagen, J. E., & Rafaeli, S. (1996). Why communication researchers should study the Internet: A dialogue. *Journal of Communication, 46*(1), 4–13.

Palmgreen, P., Wenner, L., & Rosengren, K. (1985). Uses and gratifications research: The past ten years. In K. Rosengren, L. Wenner, & P. Palmgreen (Eds.), *Media gratifications research* (pp. 11–37). Beverly Hills, CA: Sage.

Parker, E. B. (1963). The effects of television on public library circulation. *Public Opinion Quarterly, 27,* 578–589.

Simon, H. A. (1983). *Reason in human affairs.* Stanford, CA: Stanford University Press.

Odum Institute for Research in Social Science (1988). *Computer administered panel survey (CAPS)* [Computer file]. Chapel Hill: Institute for Research in Social Science [Producer and Distributor]. Modules (BACKG2, NEO, WRAPUP). Available: http://www2.irss.unc.edu/irss/home.asp.

Venkatesh, V., & Davis, F. D. (1996). A model of the antecedents of perceived ease of use: Development and test. *Decision Sciences, 27,* 451–481.

Venkatesh, V. & Davis, F. D. (2000). A theoretical extension of the technology acceptance model: Four longitudinal field studies. *Management Science, 46,* 186–204.

Venkatesh, V., & Morris, M. G. (2000). Why don't men ever stop to ask for directions? Gender, social influence, and their role in technology acceptance and usage behavior. *MIS Quarterly, 24,* 115–139.

Weaver, J. B. (1991). Exploring the links between personality and media preferences. *Personality and Individual Differences, 12,* 1293–1299.

Weaver, J. B., Walker, J. R., McCord, L. L., & Bellamy, R. V (1996). Exploring the links between personality and television remote control device use. *Personality and Individual Differences, 20,* 483–489.

Williams, S. W., Ogletree, S. M., Woodburn, W., & Raffeld, P. (1993). Gender roles, computer attitudes, and dyadic computer interaction performance in college students. *Sex Roles, 29,* 515–525.

Williams, T. M. (1986). *The impact of television.* New York: Academic Press.

# 5

# Social and Psychological Influences on Computer User Frustration

KATHERINE BESSIÈRE
*Carnegie Mellon University*

IRINA CEAPARU
*University of Maryland, College Park*

JONATHAN LAZAR
*Towson University*

JOHN ROBINSON
BEN SHNEIDERMAN
*University of Maryland, College Park*

Every computer user encounters problems with technology. Frustration is a common theme with information technology. Frustration tends to be the result when, for example, a computer application crashes with no warning, taking the last 30 minutes of work with it. As technology rapidly advances, users must deal with the ensuing error messages that invariably result, as well as the gap in knowledge that users face when a new technology or software emerges. We believe that user frustration is a significant issue that has consequences and implications in many areas. For instance, many policymakers discuss the digital divide, which is the growing gap between those who have access to computers and networks and those who do not. But even if universal access to technology is attained, users will still struggle with the technology. Even with up-to-date hardware and software, sufficient training and documentation, and tech support, users may find computers difficult to use (Kraut, Scherlis, Mukhopadhyay, Manning, & Kiesler, 1996). This is unfortunate, because the use of well-designed, easy-to-use software, along with sufficient support and training, can make a measurable impact on people's lives. A good example of using technological resources to improve the economic situations and overall lives of people is the community networking and software project developed at MIT for the residents of Camfield Estates, a low-income housing community in Roxbury, MA (Pinkett, 2002; see also chapters 6–8, this volume).

Certainly, computers should be designed in ways that make the user experience more pleasant for everyone, including users of various ages, cultural backgrounds, and economic situations, which is known as *universal usability* (Shneiderman, 2000). But although universal usability is the end goal for technology, it is important to first examine the root causes of user frustration from a social psychological point of view. It is possible that there are other techniques, aside from improved computer design, that could impact or lessen user frustration.

This chapter examines the factors that influence the experience of frustration in computer usage. This chapter has three goals: to examine the research literature on human frustration, to place the frustration research in the context of human-computer interaction, and to present a new model of user frustration with technology. Individuals' prior experiences, psychological characteristics, level of computer experience, and social system can all affect how they deal with frustrations with their computers. In addition, factors such as the importance of the task that was interrupted, the frequency of occurrence (of both same and different frustrations), and the amount of time or work lost as a result of the problem, can affect the experience of frustration. The existing psychological literature on frustration provides a foundation for the examination of the frustration process in computer use. In addition, literature on computer attitudes and anxiety has relevance to the topic of frustration. Examining the factors correlated with frustration helps to elucidate the nature of the frustration experience as regards computer use. Based on this published research, a technology frustration model is presented. Based on the technology frustration model, the implications for numerous stakeholders, including users, managers, software designers, and policymakers, are discussed.

## FRUSTRATION

A review of the psychological literature reveals diverse definitions of frustration. Freud introduced frustration as a concept with external and internal aspects and related it to goal attainment. Frustration occurs when there is an inhibiting condition that interferes with or stops the realization of a goal. All action has a purpose or goal, whether explicit or implicit, and any interruption to the completion of an action or task can cause frustration. For Freud, frustration included both external barriers to goal attainment and internal obstacles blocking satisfaction (Freud, 1921/1961). This conception of frustration as a duality is continued in the analysis of frustration as both cause and effect (Britt & Janus, 1940). As a cause, frustration is an external event, acting as a stimulus to an individual and eliciting an emotional reaction. The emotional response, in this case, is the effect—the individual is aroused by this external cause—and a response is often directed toward the environment.

Frustration can be defined as "an interference with the occurrence of an insti-gated goal-response at its proper time in the behavior sequence" (Dollard, Doob, Miller, Mowrer, & Sears, 1939). Because an instigated goal response entails only that the goal be anticipated, frustration is due to the expectation and anticipation of a goal, not the actual attainment of the goal (Berkowitz, 1978). If the goal is un-fulfilled, frustration is experienced because satisfaction was not achieved and the hopes of attaining the goal were suddenly destroyed. The thwarting or hindrance, terms often used synonymously with frustration, is not limited to the actual activity in progress, but relates to what the individual is expecting (Mowrer, 1938a).

Frustrations, in all of these cases, are aversive events (Ferster, 1957) and have as their main defining feature the element of a barrier or obstruction. This bar-rier can take the form of an actual barrier, or an imaginary one such as the re-sponse to anticipated punishment or injury (Mowrer, 1938b). A frustrating situa-tion, then, is defined as any "in which an obstacle—physical, social, conceptual or environmental—prevents the satisfaction of a desire" (Barker, 1938). These blocks to goal attainment may be both internal and external (Shorkey & Crocker, 1981), similar to the duality proposed by Freud. Internal blocks consist of deficiencies within the individual such as a lack of knowledge, skill, or physical ability. External blocks could include the physical environment, social or legal barriers such as laws or mores, or the behavior of other people.

## Factors Affecting Level of Frustration

The level of frustration experienced by an individual clearly can differ, depending on the circumstances surrounding the frustrating experience and the individual. One major factor in goal formation and achievement is goal commitment, which refers to the determination to try for and persist in the achievement of a goal (Campion & Lord, 1982). Research on goal theory indicates that goal commitment has a strong relationship to performance and is related to two factors: the importance of the task or outcome and the belief that the goal can be accomplished (Locke & Latham, 2002). Individuals will have a high commitment to a goal when the goal is important to them and they believe that the goal can be attained (Locke, 1996). How important the goal is to the individual, in addition to the strength of the desire to obtain the goal (Dollard et al., 1939), will affect the level of goal commitment as well as the strength of the subsequent reaction to the interruption. Self-efficacy, the belief in one's personal capabilities, can also affect goal commitment (Locke & Latham, 1990) in that the belief about how well a task can be performed when it involves setbacks, obstacles, or failures may affect how committed individuals are to that goal (Bandura, 1986). Judgments of efficacy are related to the amount of effort expended, how long they persist at the task, and resiliency in the case of failure or setback (Bandura, 1986, 1997b). Self-efficacy affects emotional states as well; how much stress or depression people experience when in difficult situations is dependent on how well they think they can cope with the situation (Bandura, 1997a). The level of frustration that people experience, therefore, would be affected by how important the goal was to them, as well as how confident they are in their abilities. "Because goal-directed behavior involves valued, purposeful action, failure to attain goals may therefore result in highly charged emotional outcomes" (Lincecum, 2000), including, we believe, frustration.

Cultural factors may also play a role in the level of frustration experienced by individuals when coming across obstacles to their path of action. Social learning theory (Bandura, 1973) states that "rather than frustration generating an aggressive drive, aversive treatment produces a general state of emotional arousal that can facilitate a variety of behaviors, depending on the types of responses the person has learned for coping with stress and their relative effectiveness" (p. 53). The community and culture in which they are raised constrains the behavior of individuals, and their reactions and acceptable responses to frustrating situations are constrained as well. Hochschild (1979) and Ekman (1982) put forth two concepts associated with the way that emotions are governed by society: feeling rules and display rules. Feeling rules (emotion norms) regulate what kinds of feelings are appropriate and how intense or broad they are, as well as long they can last. Display rules (expression norms) regulate how these internal feelings can be displayed externally in terms of emotional behaviors.

According to symbolic interactionist theory, emotions are caused by the arousal of individuals due to environmental events combined with specific sociocultural factors (Schachter & Singer, 1962). Mowrer (1938b) suggested that human frustration is linked to two major aspects of culture: the transmission of useful techniques and skills across generations, and the perpetuation and enforcement of the regulations and codes that govern social conduct. Ways of coping with frustration are therefore learned from the society and are governed and constrained by the laws of a society. This can contribute to the level of frustration tolerance that individuals have, which is also affected by their prior experience and self-efficacy related to specific tasks.

According to Freud (1921), it is not simply the nature of the frustrating incident that determines how people will react to the incident. Rather, there is an interplay between the situation and the psychological characteristics of individuals. The level of maturity of the individual also plays a part (Barker, Dembo, & Lewin, 1965) in the reactions to frustration. With maturity, there is an increase in (a) the variety of responses to a situation employed by individuals, (b) the control of the environment, and (c) their ability to employ problem-solving behavior and plan steps to obtain the goal. It would appear that learning, which is culturally determined, is a major factor in developing socially acceptable responses to frustration.

One final factor that may affect the force of the frustration is the severity of the interruption and the degree of interference with goal attainment (Dollard et al., 1939). All obstructions are not equally frustrating; the severity and unexpectedness of the block will also factor into the strength of the response. In addition, if individuals perceive that the thwarting was justified by socially acceptable rules, as opposed to being arbitrary, the frustration response may be minimized (Baron, 1977). This may be due to the lowering of expectations because of extra information available to the individual. As stated earlier, it is the anticipation of success that affects frustration and not the actual achievement of the goal. Therefore, if individuals expect to be thwarted or have a low expectation of success, frustration may be minimized.

## Responses to Frustration

The responses to frustration by individuals can be either adaptive or maladaptive (Shorkey & Crocker, 1981). Adaptive responses are constructive and are implemented to solve the problem that is blocking goal attainment. They may include preemptive efforts to avoid the block or, once the block is encountered, problem-solving strategies to overcome or circumvent the problem. Freud (1921) listed two types of adaptive responses: transforming stress into active energy and reapplying this energy toward the original goal, and identifying and pursuing alternative goals. Maladaptive responses, on the other hand, are characterized by a lack of constructive problem solving and often make the frustrating experience worse by creating additional problems. These maladaptive responses may be further categorized into objective (aggression, regression, withdrawal, fixation, resignation) and subjective (extrapunitive, intropunitive, impunitive) responses (Britt & Janus, 1940).

*Aggression.* Early research on aggression suggested that aggression is the natural, unlearned reaction to frustration (Dollard et al., 1939; Mowrer, 1938b). Other reactions to frustration occur as a result of the conditioning process achieved through cultural and societal restrictions. The Frustration–Aggression Hypothesis (Dollard et al., 1939) stated that aggression is a consequence of frustration with two propositions: aggressive behavior presupposes the existence of frustration, and every frustration leads to aggression. However, subsequent research has shown that aggression is not the only resultant reaction to frustration, a fact attributed to prior learning experiences (Bandura, 1973; Miller, 1941). Through experience, individuals learn other, possibly more culturally acceptable, ways to react to frustration, which in turn inhibit the aggressive tendency. Subsequently, the Frustration–Aggression Hypothesis was revamped with a hierarchy of responses influenced by prior learning.

*Regression.* Barker, Dembo, and Lewin (1965) hypothesized that regression, defined as immature behavior, is the major response to frustration. Aggression, according to this theory, is simply one type of regressive behavior. As individuals mature, they develop a greater variety of responses as they are able to control their environment more and learn problem-solving skills. Learning is the key factor to developing these socially acceptable responses.

*Withdrawal.* Also known as regression, withdrawal here refers to a flight re-action in the face of adversity. Withdrawal is a learned reaction as well; social conditioning, previous experience, or the anticipation of pain or punishment causes the individual to withdraw from the situation and thus reduce the state of tension caused by the frustration (White, 1929).

*Fixation.* The repetition of courses of action that were once effective can occur either when this course of action was once successful in the past or because of a lack of skill or knowledge resulting in a low problem-solving ability. Here, the ability to develop new ways of responding to situations is impaired. When severe frustration is encountered, Maier (1961) hypothesized that fixation occurs completely and people become "frozen" in a course of action and lose awareness of the external world.

*Resignation.* Also known as inertia or apathy, this occurs when individuals lose all motivation to pursue goal-directed activity and is characterized by a complete loss of hope.

*Extrapunitive/Intropunitive/Impunitive.* These three subjective responses were defined by Rosenzweig (1935) as responses to frustration. The extrapunitive response occurs when individuals get angry at something external such as people, objects, or circumstances, and blame the problem on an external source. Intropunitive responses occur when individuals attribute blame to themselves, and feel guilt or remorse about the situation. Impunitive reactions occur when individuals try to avoid blame or gloss over the situation and try to reconcile the situation or make excuses for the problem.

## Computer Anxiety

The reactions of people to computers have also been studied extensively, particularly attitudes toward the computer (Loyd & Gressard, 1984; Nash & Moroz, 1997), computer anxiety (Cambre & Cook, 1985; Cohen & Waugh, 1989; Glass & Knight, 1988; Maurer, 1994; Raub, 1981; Torkzadeh & Angulo, 1992), and computer self-efficacy (Brosnan, 1998; Compeau & Higgins, 1995; Meier, 1985; Murphy, Coover, & Owen, 1989). Each of these variables, combined with the factors listed earlier, can affect how frustrated individuals will become when they encounter a problem while using a computer. The number of times a problem has occurred before can affect their perception of the locus of control and, therefore, influence their reaction as well. This may be related to anxiety; people with low computer self-efficacy may be more anxious (Brosnan, 1998; Meier, 1985) and more likely to view the computer suspiciously and react with great frustration when something occurs, especially when they have run into it before. Different levels of anxiety will affect performance when something unforeseen or unknown occurs, causing anxious people to become more anxious (Brosnan, 1998). On the other hand, the level of experience may temper this if the prior experience increases computer self-efficacy (Gilroy & Desai, 1986) by lowering anxiety and reducing frustration when a problem occurs. The perceived ability to fix problems on the computer, as well as the desire to do so, may also affect levels of frustration. If problems are seen as challenges rather than problems, they may not be as frustrating, which is most likely directly related to level of prior experience as well as computer self-efficacy.

## Computing Frustration Model

There are many situations that can cause frustration in users. For instance, a software application may crash, an error message may be unclear, or an interface can be confusing (Preece, Rogers, & Sharp, 2002). If the computer interface does not provide sufficient information for the user, the user can be confused as to the current status of the system and the appropriate next steps (Preece, Rogers, & Sharp, 2002). When any of these things happen, users can lose work and waste time. A recent news report described users getting so frustrated with computers that they hit and broke their machines, and in some cases, even assaulted their coworkers (BBC, 2002). The question is, what specific aspects of the situation or the individual lead to feelings of frustration? Based on the frustration literature, goal-attainment theory, and the literature on computer attitudes and anxiety, we propose a Computing Frustration Model (see Fig. 5.1).

Frustration theory indicates that it is the interruption of a goal or task that causes individuals to become frustrated. There are various factors that can then subsequently affect the level of frustration experienced. These fall into two categories: incident-specific factors, and individual-level factors.

*Incident Specific Factors.* The incident-specific factors that affect the level of frustration experienced by end-users include the level of goal commitment, the severity of the interruption, and the strength of the desire to obtain the goal. These are factors caused by the specific details of the incident, and these differ from incident to incident. For instance, if the user did not feel that it was especially important to complete the task, the result might be a low level of frustration. However, if the task was very important and there was a large amount of time lost trying to achieve the goal, the user might experience a high level of frustration.

Goal theory tells us that experience, self-efficacy, and the importance of the goal all affect the commitment to the goal or task. When the goal interruption occurs, the level of goal commitment will directly affect the amount of frustration experienced by individuals. Severity of interruption can be thought of as a combination of the time it takes to fix the problem and the time lost due to the problem. The strength of desire for the goal is also affiliated with how important the goal is, so importance is also used here as a proxy for strength of desire. These incident-specific factors, which influence the level of frustration, are harder to control because they are unpredictable, as many of the causes of user frustration are also unpredictable.

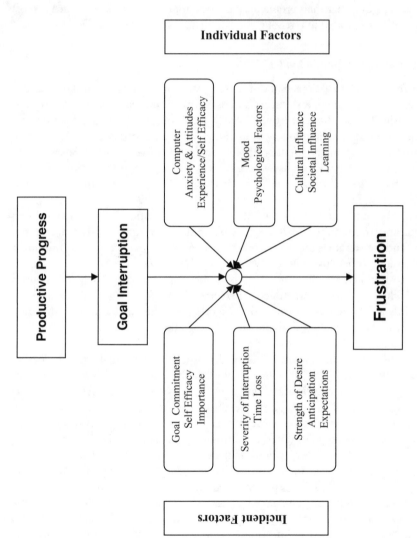

FIG 5.1.   Computing frustration model.

The individual-level factors, discussed next, are more predictable and are therefore easier to address.

*Individual Level Factors.* Individual-level factors affecting the strength of frustration include computer experience variables, mood and other psychological factors, and the cultural and societal influences on the individual. These individual-level factors influence the level of frustration, regardless of the specifics of the frustrating incident. For instance, satisfaction with life, how often users get upset over things, and general mood, can all affect the level of frustration, regardless of the specific cause of the frustration. Computer anxiety (i.e., how users feel about computer technology), as well as self-efficacy (i.e., how confident users feel in their ability to succeed), can also influence the level of frustration. Computer variables are separated into computer experience/self-efficacy and computer anxiety/attitudes. Finally, computer experience (factors such as years of computer use, and hours of computer use per week) can influence the level of frustration. A newer user may become more easily frustrated than an experienced user. These individual-level factors of user frustration are easier to address than incident-specific factors. For instance, to improve self-efficacy and lower computer anxiety, users may be offered training and other forms of support, such as documentation or a help desk. New training techniques might be developed specifically to address user frustration, to prepare users in advance for situations that might be frustrating.

## CONCLUSION

Based on the published literature and our technology frustration model, we can begin to understand the basis of user frustration, with the ultimate goal of reducing the amount of frustration that users face with computers. Frustrating incidents are very problematic for users, who can waste large amounts of time trying to rectify these incidents. Preliminary research on user frustration has found that nearly 30% to 45% of the time spent on the computer is wasted, due to frustrating situations (Ceaparu, Lazar, Bessière, Robinson, & Shneiderman, 2002). Some of the most frustrating incidents reported by users include error messages, dropped/refused network connections, application freezes, and long download times (Ceaparu et al., 2002). The technology frustration model can highlight some of the actions that the various stakeholders (such as users, developers, and managers) can take toward the goal of lessening user frustration.

### For Users

Although it is hard for users to predict in advance the various incident-specific factors (such as level of goal commitment and time loss) that cause frustration, it seems that the individual-level factors that lead to frustration are easier to predict and account for. For instance, if self-efficacy is one of the major individual-level influences on frustration, then it is possible that comprehensive support for users can lessen the effects of frustration. For instance, support can come in the form of documentation (manuals), training, or a call center. It is possible that this support will improve users' confidence and perception that they can successfully respond to the frustrating situation. Although ideally the employer should be responsible for providing such support, if the employer fails to do so, it might be helpful for the user to acquire training or documentation, which will possibly increase the user's self-efficacy, thereby lowering his or her level of frustration when dealing with troubling computer incidents.

## For Developers

Software developers can do much to lessen the effects of frustration. Much of what causes user frustration with computers is due to poor or confusing design of the interface. For example, if one of the incident-level factors that influence frustration is the severity of interruption and the time loss, then good interface design, through error messages, can lessen the time loss and lower the resulting frustration. When encountering an error situation, a clearly worded error message would allow the user to have (a) an understanding of what occurred, and (b) an understanding of how to respond appropriately to the error situation (Shneiderman, 1997). If users have a clear understanding of what occurred and how to respond, then they may be able to exit the error sequence quickly and return to their previous task goals with only a minimal amount of time lost. If users cannot exit an error sequence quickly, this can lead to other more serious errors, increasing the severity of the interruption (Carroll & Carrithers, 1984)–and, therefore, increasing the frustration. A good error message can speed along this process, helping users limit the amount of time lost, and limiting the severity of the interruption, possibly reducing levels of frustration. Other sources of user frustration, such as incompatible file formats and indecipherable menus, can also be alleviated by developers.

## For Managers

Managers in workplaces want their employees to succeed with their computer tasks. Ideally, the employees' computer tasks will help support the mission of the organization, and will therefore be important to the managers. To lessen the frustration, it might be helpful for managers to provide support to the users, to assist them in responding to the frustrating incidents. This user support may come in the form of a help line, tech support, training, and/or system documentation. This support may assist with the individual-level components of frustration (from the technology frustration model) by making users more confident in their ability to solve a frustrating situation and by providing the information they need to work around blocks to goal attainment.

For managers, the individual-level components of frustration are easier to address than the incident-level components of frustration (again, from the technology frustration model). For instance, on the incident-level, managers have no control over the time loss due to frustrating technology. In addition, another component of incident-level frustration is the importance of the task. To lower the level of user frustration, theoretically, the managers could lower the level of importance of the tasks. However, it is unlikely that managers would lower the level of task importance by telling the employees that the tasks are really not that important after all! Therefore, it appears that managers could positively affect the individual-level components of frustration, but it is unlikely that they could easily improve the incident-level components of frustration.

If users, managers, and developers work together, it is possible to lower the levels of user frustration. The user of the future should not be forced to deal with systems that leave them frustrated and unable to reach their task goals.

## ACKNOWLEDGMENTS

We appreciate partial support from National Science Foundation Grant for Information Technology Research (#0086143), *Understanding the Social Impact of the Internet: A Multifaceted Multidisciplinary Approach.* We appreciate the devoted efforts of Professor Shirley Anne Becker, formerly of the Florida Institute of Technology, and her students Ali Al-Badi and Madhan Thirukonda, in preparing the Web site for data entry, and Kent McKay of Adonix Systems for help in transferring and converting the system for use at the University of Maryland. We also thank Cheryl Schroeder-Thomas for comments on an earlier draft.

## REFERENCES

Bandura, A. (1973). *Aggression: A social learning analysis.* Englewood Cliffs, NJ: Prentice-Hall.
Bandura, A. (1986). *Social foundation of thought and action: A social-cognitive theory.* Englewood Cliffs, NJ: Prentice Hall.
Bandura, A. (1997a). Self-efficacy. *Harvard Mental Health Letter, 13*(9), 4–6.
Bandura, A. (1997b). *Self-efficacy: The exercise of control.* New York: Freeman.
Barker, R. (1938). The effect of frustration upon cognitive ability. *Character and Personality, 7,* 145–150.
Barker, R., Dembo, T., & Lewin, K. (1965). Frustration and regression: An experiment with young children. In R. Lawson (Ed.), *Frustration: The development of a scientific concept.* New York: MacMillan.
Baron, R. A. (1977). *Human aggression.* New York: Plenum.
Berkowitz, L. (1978). Whatever happened to the frustration-aggression hypothesis? *American Behavioral Scientist, 21*(5), 691–708.
British Broadcasting Company. (2002). Web rage hits the Internet. Retrieved February 20, 2002 from http://news.bbc.co.uk/hi/english/sci/tech/newsid_1829000/1829944.stm
Britt, S. H., & Janus, S. Q. (1940). Criteria of frustration. *Psychological Review, 47*(6), 451–469.
Brosnan, M. J. (1998). The impact of computer anxiety and self-efficacy upon performance. *Journal of Computer Assisted Learning, 14,* 223–234.

Cambre, M. A., & Cook, D. L. (1985). Computer anxiety: Definition, measurement, and correlates. *Journal of Educational Computing Research, 1*(1), 37–54.

Campion, M., & Lord, R. (1982). A control systems conceptualization of the goal-setting and changing process. *Organizational Behavior and Human Performance, 30,* 265–287.

Carroll, J. M., & Carrithers, C. (1984). Training wheels in a user interface. *Communications of the ACM, 17*(8), 800–806.

Ceaparu, I., Lazar, J., Bessière, K., Robinson, J., & Shneiderman, B. (2002, May 12). *Determining causes and severity of end-user frustration.* Human-Computer Interaction Laboratory, University of Maryland. College Park, MD. Technical Report. Retrieved online, from ftp://ftp.cs.umd.edu/pub/hcil/Reports-Abstracts-Bibliography/2002-11html/2002-11.pdf.

Cohen, B. A., & Waugh, G. W. (1989). Assessing computer anxiety. *Psychological Reports, 65*(1), 735–738.

Compeau, D. R., & Higgins, C. A. (1995). Computer self-efficacy: Development of a measure and initial test. *MIS Quarterly, 19,* 189–211.

Dollard, J., Doob, L. W., Miller, N. E., Mowrer, O. H., & Sears, R. R. (1939). *Frustration and aggression.* New Haven: Yale University Press.

Ekman, P. (Ed.). (1982). *Emotion in the human face* (2nd ed.). Cambridge: Cambridge University Press.

Ferster, C. B. (1957). The function of aggression and the regulation of aggressive drive. *Psychological Review, 71,* 257–272.

Freud, S. (1961). Types of onset and neurosis. In J. Strachey (Ed.), *The standard edition of the complete psychological works of Sigmund Freud* (Vol. 12, pp. 227–230). London: Hogarth Press. (Original work published 1921)

Gilroy, F., & Desai, H. (1986). Computer anxiety: Sex, race, and age. *International Journal of Man–Machine Studies, 25*(1), 711–719.

Glass, C. R., & Knight, L. A. (1988). Cognitive factors in computer anxiety. *Cognitive Therapy and Research, 12*(4), 351–366.

Hochschild, A. R. (1979). Emotion work, feeling rules, and social structure. *American Journal of Sociology, 85,* 551–575.

Kraut, R., Scherlis, W., Mukhopadhyay, T., Manning, J., & Kiesler, S. (1996). The HomeNet field trial of residential Internet services. *Communications of the ACM, 39,* 55–65.

Lincecum, L. (2000). *The effects of software disruption on goal commitment, task self-efficacy, computer self-efficacy, and test performance in a computer-based instructional task.* Unpublished doctoral dissertation, Texas Tech University, Lubbock, TX.

Locke, E. A. (1996). Motivation through conscious goal setting. *Applied Preventative Psychology, 5,* 117–124.

Locke, E. A., & Latham, G. P. (1990). *A theory of goal setting and task performance.* Englewood Cliffs, NJ: Prentice Hall.

Locke, E. A., & Latham, G. P. (2002). *Building a practically useful theory of goal setting and task motivation: A 35-year odyssey.* Unpublished manuscript.

Loyd, B. H., & Gressard, C. (1984). The effects of sex, age, and computer experience on computer attitudes. *AEDS Journal, 18*(2), 67–77.

Maier, N. R. F. (1961). *Frustration: The study of behavior without a goal.* Ann Arbor: University of Michigan Press.

Maurer, M. M. (1994). Computer anxiety correlates and what they tell us. *Computers in Human Behavior, 10*(3), 369–376.

Meier, S. (1985). Computer aversion. *Computers in Human Behavior, 1*(1), 171–179.

Miller, N. E. (1941). The frustration–aggression hypothesis. *Psychological Review, 48,* 337–342.

Mowrer, O. H. (1938a). Preparatory set (expectancy)—A determinant in motivation and learning. *Psychological Review, 45,* 62–91.

Mowrer, O. H. (1938b). Some research implications of the frustration concept as related to social and educational problems. *Character and Personality, 7,* 129–135.

Murphy, C., Coover, D., & Owen, S. (1989). Development and validation of the computer self-efficacy scale. *Educational and Psychological Measurement, 49*, 893–899.

Nash, J. B., & Moroz, P. A. (1997). An examination of the factor structures of the computer attitude scale. *Journal of Educational Computing Research, 17*(4), 341–356.

Pinkett, R. (2002). Camfield Estates-MIT creating community connections project: High technology in a low-to-moderate income community. In J. Lazar (Ed.), *Managing IT/community partnerships in the 21st century* (pp. 221–246). Hershey, PA: Idea Group Publishing.

Preece, J., Rogers, Y., & Sharp, H. (2002). *Interaction design: Beyond human–computer interaction.* New York: John Wiley & Sons.

Raub, A. (1981). *Correlates of computer anxiety in college students.* Unpublished doctoral dissertation, University of Pennsylvania.

Rosenzweig, S. (1935). Tests of frustration. *American Journal of Orthopsychiatry, 5*, 395–403.

Schachter, S., & Singer, J. (1962). Cognitive, social, and physiological determinants of emotional state. *Psychological Review, 69*, 379–399.

Shneiderman, B. (1997). Designing the user interface: Strategies for effective human-computer interaction (3rd ed.). Boston, MA: Addison-Wesley.

Shneiderman, B. (2000). Universal usability: Pushing human-computer interaction research to empower every citizen. *Communications of the ACM, 43*(5), 84–91.

Shorkey, C. T., & Crocker, S. B. (1981). Frustration theory: A source of unifying concepts for generalist practice. *Social Work, 26*(5), 374–379.

Torkzadeh, G., & Angulo, I. E. (1992). The concepts and correlates of computer anxiety. *Behavior and Information Technology, 11*(1), 99–108.

White, W. A. (1929). The frustration theory of consciousness: Mind as energy. *Psychoanalytical Review, 16*, 143–162.

PART

# III

# Social and Cultural Dimensions of Media Access

# 6

# Communities, Cultural Capital, and the Digital Divide

VIVIANA ROJAS
*University of Texas, San Antonio*

JOSEPH STRAUBHAAR
DEBASMITA ROYCHOWDHURY
OZLEM OKUR
*University of Texas, Austin*

Much of the debate about the digital divide has centered on the question of who has access to computers and the Internet. A series of studies by the National Telecommunications and Information Administration (NTIA, 1995, 1999, 2000, 2002) revealed that those in low-income, low-education, minority-racial, and rural-location groups have unequal access to the new technologies. The most recent NTIA (2002) report indicated that the gaps in access are narrowing. However, this chapter argues that a number of fundamental aspects of the digital divide persist, above and beyond access issues. It examines continuing gaps that underlie the digital divide from a case study of Austin, Texas. A highly wired city, Austin reveals the social and cultural barriers that remain in place when most conventional remedies, such as public access centers, Internet-connected schools and libraries, and computer training programs, become fairly widely available.

This chapter seeks to understand the social construction of information technology in the lives of working-class and poor Hispanics and African Americans in East Austin. We examine the economic and social causes for why many families in disadvantaged communities do not have, do not use, or do not seek access to new technologies. Among other factors, these causes include class, ethnicity, age, geographic location, and gender-role constraints. The analysis focuses on the sources of cultural capital these families employ as they decide whether and how to make use of technology in their lives. These forms of cultural capital contribute to "technodispositions" about information and communication technologies (ICTs). A central question throughout the research is whether lower class, minority youths and their parents are forming a more durable and consistent class pattern (or *habitus*) toward ICTs than commonly assumed. Interviews with a group of twelve teenagers, their parents, and, in some cases their siblings, were structured to answer this question and constituted the main elements in gathering the data.

## MINORITIES AND TECHNOLOGICAL LAG

The NTIA studies found that despite the general growth in information access, the technology gap between Caucasians and ethnic minorities was, in fact, widening. Several demographic variables, including income, education level, race, age, and household make-up, were associated with gaps in access to and use of new information and communication technologies. Caucasians are still more likely to have access to the Internet from home than African Americans or Hispanics regardless of geographic location (NTIA, 2000). Moreover, the gap between African Americans and Latinos on the one hand, and Whites and Asian Americans on the other, widens at the lowest or poorest levels (NTIA, 2000). It seems that the high tide of the Information Age does not raise all boats equally. Although more than 40% of American households owned a computer at the end of 1998, there are fault lines in the Information Age that continue to separate Whites, Asians/Pacific Islanders, those with higher incomes and educational level, African Americans, Hispanics, and those in rural areas or central cities (Benton Foundation, 1998; Tomás Rivera Policy Institute, 2002).

Researchers have addressed the intersection of ICTs, race, gender, and class in diverse ways. Drawing on Bourdieu's concept of cultural capital, Reza (1998) illustrated that education was the main anticipated factor in access to and use of home computers, which also mediated the transition from lower class to higher socioeconomic class status. Although gaps in access to computers and the Internet between certain demographic groups remain striking, some reports indicate that they are narrowing (NTIA, 2000), particularly in the case of Hispanics. As a consequence, some commentators argue that when computers become cheap enough and free Internet service providers are available, the digital divide will, by definition, no longer be a problem (Cato Institute, 2000; Heritage Foundation, 2000).

A recent study of the digital divide in the state of Texas showed that access has improved in recent years (Strover & Straubhaar, 2000). A statewide telephone sample of 800 adults fielded in April 2000 found that a majority of Texans had both computer and Internet access. More people lower down the income scale now have access than was earlier the case, reflecting the pattern found in the 2000

NTIA report. However, the gap between African Americans and Latinos on the one hand, and Whites and Asian Americans on the other, still widens significantly at the lowest or poorest levels, that is, below an annual household income of $30,000.

A report by the Pew Internet & American Life Project (2000) suggested that Internet penetration may be reaching social limits in the case of groups that do not regard ICTs as advantageous to their lives. The Pew study highlighted older Americans, but earlier studies by the Tomás Rivera Policy Institute also indicated that many Hispanic families were ambivalent about the Internet (Wilhelm, 1998). A Kaiser Family Foundation report (1999) asserted that children who live or attend school in lower income communities spend more time with most types of media than children in wealthier neighborhoods, but are significantly less likely to use computers. Largely due to income differences, children from minority groups have substantially less access to computers outside of school. Racial disparities in computer use among 2- to 7-year-olds who are not yet in school are particularly pronounced, with Caucasian youngsters about twice as likely as African American or Hispanic children to use a computer.

## INEQUALITIES AND THE SOCIOLOGY OF PIERRE BOURDIEU

So far this discussion of the digital divide has taken a structural point of view. Many analyses point to income as the key issue in access, which leads many to assume that when computers and Internet access become cheap enough for all income levels can afford them, then lower income consumers will, as a matter of course, adopt and use them. However, both the national NTIA research and the recent Texas study showed that, particularly within lower income populations, ethnicity is still related to less frequent use of the Internet. Economic structures related to class are crucial in limiting access to media, but culture, as indicated by ethnic differences, remains important (Mosco, 1996; NTIA, 1999; Strover & Straubhaar, 2000).

Bourdieu (1980, 1984, 1993a) introduced the concepts of *habitus, field,* and *capital* to elaborate the continuity, regularity, and regulated transformation of social action that solely structural explanations fail to account for, such as technology use by individuals and groups. He described habitus as a set of dispositions that create "durable" and "transposable" practices and perceptions over a long process of social inculcation. The similarity of dispositions and practices experienced by members of the same social class constitutes class habitus for Bourdieu (Johnson, 1993). Such shared orientations help explain why groups acquire and hold dispositions against the use of certain technologies like networked computers, even when those technologies become accessible and receive favorable publicity in the media.

These kinds of dispositions seem specific to groups defined by more than just economic class. Bourdieu highlighted that it is the *interrelationship* between different pertinent properties (sex, age, capital, ethnicity, education, etc.) that constitutes a social class, rather than a collection of properties or the property itself.

Both this theory and prior empirical work on the digital divide seem to suggest that combinations of interrelated factors or characteristics should be analyzed— notably, economic capital, cultural capital, ethnicity, age, and gender—to understand something as subtle as a disposition toward a technology (Hoffman & Novak, 1998; Schement, 1998). When these dispositions are held by a number of people in the same class circumstances, we can speak of a *class habitus* toward technology.

Bourdieu's theoretical framework, also known as the theory of practice or theory of symbolic power (Brubaker, 1993; Garnham, 1986), is based on distinctions among several kinds of capital, notably economic, cultural, and social. Cultural capital, which is separate and relatively autonomous from economic capital, is defined as the possession of certain cultural competencies, bodies of cultural knowledge that provide for distinguished modes of cultural consumption (Bourdieu, 1984). Just as economic relations that express the networks of power are quantified as economic capital, the cultural relations that express different levels of learned and empowering potentialities constitute cultural capital.

Cultural capital is distributed differentially throughout society and is accumulated and transferred from generation to generation, just like economic capital. Bourdieu (1986) argued that in modern societies, the accumulation of cultural capital requires a long-term investment of time and education. Although they are not reducible to each other, economic and cultural capital are convertible (Johnson, 1993).

Bourdieu discussed *social capital* as resources encapsulated in sets of social relations. The concept specifically refers to:

> the aggregate of the actual or potential resources which are linked to possession of a durable network of more or less institutionalized relationships of mutual acquaintance and recognition—or, in other words, to membership in a group—which provides each of its members with the backing of the collectivity-owned capital, a "credential" which entitles them to credit, in the various senses of the word. (Bourdieu, 1986, pp. 248–249)

Social and cultural capital are employed in the reproduction of social stratification, particularly the restricted possibilities that individuals have for change.

Although the literature on social capital strongly emphasizes its positive consequences, the network of associations social capital embodies can have negative effects as well (Portes, 1998). There is a sociological bias "to see good things emerging out of sociability; bad things are more commonly associated with the behavior of *homo economicus*. However, the same mechanisms appropriable by individuals and groups as social capital can have other, less desirable consequences" (Portes, 1998, p. 15). Portes labeled this *negative social capital*. Social capital within youth gangs, for example, may lead to connections and networks that enable "success" in what would be considered criminal behavior.

Bourdieu and Wacquant (1992) used the term *field* to account for the concrete social situations within which agents operate, accumulating and using different forms of capital. A field is defined primarily in terms of the particular form of capital present and secondarily through the relations developed around it as agents struggle to acquire and/or maintain that capital (p. 99). Fields, whether economic, political, cultural, technological, or educational, are hierarchically organized and relatively autonomous but structurally homologous with each other. The economic and educational fields, for instance, are related to each other in the sense that people with economic capital also tend to acquire educational capital, and vice versa.

In this scheme, individuals (as agents) act in the different social fields with the capital they have accumulated and used—knowledge, financial resources, social connections, etc.—in the course of their life trajectory. Bourdieu and Wacquant (1992) used the analogy of a game to explain why people participate or invest in a system of objective forces (field of forces) in which people compete or struggle for resources, including access to jobs (p. 17). The gaps in access to and use of new information technologies (or technofield) is part of this process where people make specific investments according to their class habitus. That habitus implies a certain knowledge and recognition of the stakes in the field and generates the strategies of action with which people participate (Bourdieu, 1993b).

## AUSTIN AS A WIRED CASE STUDY

Austin should present a best-case scenario for narrowing the digital divide. This dynamic southwestern city has a thriving information economy, which tends to pull people toward technologically oriented education as well as training for the new jobs the sector creates. Austin media seem to report constantly about that economy, those new jobs, and what is required for them. Austin has a number of innovative training programs, such as the Capital Area Training Foundation and other organizations like Austin Free-Net, working very hard to make public access to information and communication technologies a reality in libraries, community centers, and housing developments.

However, in Austin, Hispanics and African Americans face more than a digital divide; they face ethnic, gender, income, and neighborhood divides, too. In a city with a dynamic information economy, with strong educational institutions and Internet access in most homes, there is an ever-widening wealth gap that affects working-class residents. Two out of three private sector jobs created in the 1990s paid wages below the city's average. Those jobs, such as construction and domestic services, drew heavily on minority migrants from rural areas and from Mexico. One third of the Austin work force must get by on a weekly income of $350 or less (Holstein, 2000). That is particularly true of the minority populations concentrated in East Austin.

The internal stratification and inequities within Austin are on display in the public schools. Whereas the Austin Independent School District (AISD) has a number of excellent high schools, Johnston High in East Austin is routinely portrayed in newspaper accounts as a neglected and troubled school. Johnston is considered one of 13 "low-performing" schools in the AISD, according to recent standardized test scores (Kurtz & McEntee, 2000). With 1,774 students (in 1999–2000), it had the highest dropout rate among the AISD's 10 regular high schools, as well as the highest teen pregnancy rate and one of the highest proportions of low-income students. The three zip code areas that feed into the school have the highest teen pregnancy rates in Austin, and inside the school, "one out of 20 Johnston High school students is either a parent or has a child on the way" (Kurtz & McEntee, 2000, A1–A14). Nearly half of Johnston students live in poverty and most of the students work full time. According to data from the Texas Education Agency, 47% of the students are eligible for free or reduced-priced lunch as compared to 31% in the District's other high schools (Kurtz & McEntee, 2000). The student body at Johnston is diverse; nearly two thirds of the high school's students are Hispanic, 20% are African American, and 17% Anglo.

Most of the Caucasian students at Johnston attend the Liberal Arts Academy. The Liberal Arts Academy (constituting 15% of Johnston's total students) is an AISD-wide magnet school that draws more affluent and competitive students from throughout the district. Although the Liberal Arts Academy draws students from Johnston's own district to its enriched curriculum, giving some students opportunities they would not otherwise have, its presence on campus also masks some problems in the rest of the school. In 1999–2000, only 241 of 1,774 total Johnston students were seniors, and in 1999 only 25 regular (non-Liberal Arts Academy) students took the SAT college entrance exam. At Johnston, a combination of student apathy, difficult home situations, absence of a strong parental support network, and long bus rides keep student participation in extracurricular activities low—a factor that some feel contributes to low self-esteem at the school (Kurtz & McEntee, 2000, p. A1). Johnston's principal, Al Mindiz-Melton, predicted that it would take 5 to 8 years to change what he saw as Johnston's "culture of resignation" (Kurtz & McEntee, 2000, p. A16).

The situation at the school illustrates Bourdieu's class ethos, in which youths have subjective hopes that might clash with perceived objective chances. Some of the students interviewed for this project also saw resignation in their teachers. They complained that instructors at Johnston did not use the full class period to teach and allowed students to make up work or sleep in classes. If students did not see their teachers as motivated, some teachers cited "institutional neglect" from the school district as a principal cause of the school's decline. Teachers complained that the district was not dedicating enough resources to the school or investing adequately in either the personnel or equipment necessary to provide students with a quality education. A 2-year delay in school renovations at Johnston had temporarily housed the library in a gym, which many at the school considered a case of neglect or even abandonment on part of the school district administration (Kurtz & McEntee, 2000, p. A14).

Except perhaps for the Liberal Arts Academy program, Johnston High does not operate as a catalyst for changing the social constraints faced by poor and minority teens in their pursuit of an education that will enable them to overcome economic and technological barriers. Poor schools in the United States in general do not have the ratio of computers per student that can assure even minimum access to new technology. A 1998 Benton Foundation report asserted that despite considerable progress, schools in low-income communities had fewer computers and modems than schools serving wealthier districts (p. 7). According to the report, *Computers and Classrooms: The Status of Technology in U.S. Schools,* a study by the Educational Testing Service (1997), minority and poor students had significantly less access to computers in their classes than more affluent children. Schools with minority enrollment greater than 90% had a student-to-computer ratio of 17 to 1, compared to the national average of 10 to 1.

Johnston High in particular, has consistently had among the worst computer access statistics in the Austin Independent School District (S. Hershey, former technology coordinator Johnston High school, personal communication with J. Straubhaar, September 15, 2001). At the time of the study, Johnston only had six accessible computers in a temporary library in the girls' gym, plus computers in about half of the classrooms for teachers' use. More computers were sitting in boxes awaiting the conclusion of a construction project that had been dragging out for over a year. In the face of such a high-tech handicap, a question arises: If teens do not acquire cultural capital about technology at home and do not receive it as social capital from peers or relatives, how can they successfully compete in school and later in the labor market? Bourdieu and Passeron (1977) explained this by arguing that education is not the great social equalizer we assume it to be. School instead can be a place that *reproduces* and *perpetuates* the class inequalities already existent in society (Wacquant, 1996, p. 154).

## METHOD

This chapter is based on interviews with 12 Austin families during fall 1999, spring 2000, and into the summer months of 2000. Initial contact with the respondents was established through collaboration with administrators and teachers at Johnston High. During the fall of 1999, the parents of 12 students in a ninth-grade algebra class allowed their children to participate in, and agreed themselves to be interviewed for, a study exploring how ethnic minorities perceive the role of technology in their lives. There were nine Hispanic families, two African American families, and one Caucasian/Anglo family in the study. Interviews were carried out during the study by a group of 21 students, both undergraduate and graduate, enrolled in a research seminar on the digital divide in the College of Communication at the University of Texas.

Several research questions guided the study (the topic guide of suggested interview questions appears in the appendix):

- How do parents and teenagers in disadvantaged communities perceive the importance of information and communication technologies in their lives?
- What attitudes do parents and teenagers in disadvantaged communities have toward computers and the Internet?
- What cultural capital about technology (or technocapital) do these parents transfer to their children?
- What technocapital are these children receiving from school and other sources?

For this project, it seemed important to understand how people make sense of what they hear and see about computers and the Internet, while also probing the origin of the cultural capital they employ when deciding whether to make use of these technologies. To that end, this research relied on semistructured interviews. At least two hour-long interviews were conducted with each respondent. The first interview was a sort of grand-tour interview of each person's life history, intended to get a sense of how they saw themselves and illuminate what for them was most important. The second focused more specifically on each respondent's interest in information technologies, the sorts of information that the respondents saw as useful or relevant to their lives, and where they tended to go for that information. Interviewers had a topic guide of suggested questions but were trained to let the respondents speak from their own points of view with as little prompting as possible. Care for developing nonexploitative relationships during the interview process was taken throughout the research. Interviewers were sensitized to be responsive and open, reflexive about their own roles as well as class position and racial/ethnic orientation.

This interview-based research was intended to be inductive in the sense of letting participants speak for themselves without an *a priori* superimposition of theory. Still, the project began by assuming that family trajectories, life experiences, and social structures help to form cultural capital, which in turn affects perceptions and use of new information and communication technologies. On completion of the interview phase of the research, a team of several graduate students and the principal investigator elaborated the analytical constructs of technodisposition and technocapital, relating some of Bourdieu's core concepts more closely to the study's central concerns.

## Technodisposition and Technocapital

As mentioned, Bourdieu introduced the concept of habitus to describe the dispositions that create durable and transposable practices and perceptions over a long process of social inculcation. In our case, we identify a coherent, shared set of "technodispositions" that reflect the "technocapital" held by minority groups in the Information Age. In the case of East Austin, the "technofield" is the site, or structured space, where struggles over media access are enacted by appropriating resources. These resources in part consist of technocapital, a specific form of cultural capital encompassing the acquired knowledge, skills, and dispositions to use information technologies (personal computers plus the Internet) in ways that are considered personally empowering or useful.

In the analysis, we examined respondents' technodispositions, which interact in a reciprocal, complex relationship with technocapital. For example, accumulation of cultural capital about computers may lead to the formation of technocapital, which in turn affects one's disposition toward the use of technology. However, if alternative social and cultural influences communicate that computer use is not socially relevant or desirable, then an individual's technodisposition may direct him or her away from computer use. Both technodispositions and technocapital operate within a specific technofield of human endeavor.

For the purposes of this study, technodispositions are delineated by such indicators as social practices, perceptions and attitudes, technical education, awareness of technology, desire for information, job requirements, social relations, community interactions, and geographic location. Social practices include an individual's and family's history of technology use, especially the Internet and other ICTs, as well as patterns of mass media consumption (e.g., radio, television, film).[1] Perceptions and attitudes are operationalized as respondents' thoughts about ICTs and how they are perceived as a component of individual, family, and community life. Education incorporates formal/institutional education as well as less formal technology training and vocational studies. Technological awareness refers to the understanding among community members about the potential value of ICTs for economic mobility. Desire for information involves the relevance of various kinds of information and related use of ICTs to conduct searches in everyday life. Individuals' dispositions toward technology are affected by job requirements and workplace propensities toward ICTs. Social interactions within the community and community organizations themselves, with their capacity to foster an environment encouraging ICT use, may also affect peoples' technodispositions. Finally, the geographical location of the place itself, East Austin, structures the interplay of agency with technology through its infrastructure and basic resources as a site of struggle over media access.

*Technocapital,* a product of technodispositions, provides certain competencies and resources to negotiate within the technofield. As a structured space, the technofield is analyzed as an arena where human agency is enacted in relation to other social forces—political, economic, social, cultural, and so forth. Techno-competencies, the acquired skills for and knowledge about ICTs, are shaped by the interplay between technocapital on one hand and the other forms of capital (social, economic, cultural, symbolic) on the other. In East Austin, the logic of the technofield is contingent upon the interaction between individual technocompetencies and such social factors as attitudes toward information technologies, minority status, the emergence of Austin as a technopolis (and its attendant need for information workers), local income scarcity, and spotty educational and living standards in different parts of the city. Sources of cultural capital include education, family traditions, and other social resources. Sources of social capital include extended family ties, respondents' immigration history, perceived social mobility, community relations and neighborhood interactions, and peer groups. Finally, economic capital is comprised of occupation, income, family size, and geographic location. The interactions between these fields of power are analyzed to bring to light the concept of *technocapital*, crucial for reconceptualizing the digital divide in a way that goes beyond physical access to information and computer technology.

## Interview Analysis

To illustrate the complexity of the various forces at play in the formation of technocapital, consider the example of a Hispanic mother and her ninth-grade son interviewed for this study. The boy has watched his mother work her way up from welfare to Wal-Mart clerk to secretary. She is very proud of having her own office space, desk, and computer. She sees herself as upwardly mobile and wants to get her son involved in information technology work. Indeed, she would like to focus him on technology as a life endeavor. But she must overcome prevailing attitudes about minorities and technology in East Austin. She is irritated that counselors at Johnston High suggested to her son that he think about going into refrigerator repair, instead of more academic courses.

The son likes drawing but had trouble getting into art courses at the high school. He seems to want to be an architect, but does not realize that drafting and design work is now computer-aided. Nor does he have any adult male role models who use information technology at work or during their off-hours. He has little exposure to computers at school, except as a tool for word processing. In a focus group for this study, he heard his friends tell him computers and the Internet are for geeks. (One boy asked, in the discussion, as an aside, "Who would want to be one of those computer geeks?" The same classmate specifically noted in another aside during the group discussion that a billboard for a local Internet service provider, which exhorted passersby to call "1-800-BE-A-GEEK," was off-putting.)

If we think about his case in sociological terms, this minority teen is receiving conflicting pieces of both cultural and social capital. On the one hand, his mother is pushing him toward acquiring technocapital and encouraging a positive disposition toward information technology. On the other hand, his school counselor, friends, adult male role models, and, to some degree, the media (at least commercial messages) seem to be either directly or indirectly telling him to be negatively disposed. (A parallel study of popular radio stations in Austin in 1999 found that Black and Hispanic-oriented stations carried significantly fewer advertisements for computers, software, or Internet services than did Anglo or general population oriented stations (Rupertus, Straubhaar, & LaPastina, 2001).

As L. J. Smith, an adult education teacher in a neighboring, largely Black and Hispanic high school, said "Most of our potential students see computers as women's work" (interview with L. J. Smith by Zeynep Tufekcioglu, February 2001, conducted as part of an evaluation of the Austin Community Technology Training Center). The message to minority boys seems clear: these technologies are not really for them. These sources of cultural and social capital, especially school, friends, and adult male role models, frame technology in terms of class, ethnicity, and gender. They tell them what a working-class male Hispanic or Black teenager is *supposed* to be interested in.

Looking at the patterns and consistencies among the other families, we continue to see a complex trend in which family resources, class economic habitus, and associated life trajectories form a set of boundaries that place limits on the formation of positive technodispositions. Within those bounds, ethnicity seems to powerfully affect different sources of capital that might form technocapital. Among both the older and younger age groups, ethnicity seems to frame how gender is constructed. These constructions of masculine and feminine roles then affect choices among possible sources of cultural and social capital that influence orientations toward technology.

## Parents' Life Trajectories and Cultural Capital

Among the nine Hispanic families interviewed for this research, all but one were of Mexican heritage, either first-, second-, or third-generation immigrants. The one exception was a mother of Puerto Rican descent. The five poorest families spoke Spanish at home. But even though they were fluent in their native tongue, they all recognized difficulties in reading and writing in Spanish. One mother in our group of respondents was functionally illiterate; she did not write or read either Spanish or English. Only three parents had earned a high school diploma; none held a college degree.

For the Hispanic parents, there was a significant difference between first-, second-, and third-generation status. Most first-generation immigrants' described their life in this country as one of bare survival and commented how their own parents had little or no schooling. Most recalled poverty and deprivation and in some cases indicated they started working as farm labor or in service work as children. These parents now work as various skilled laborers—as a baker, truck driver, carpenter, school janitor, Wal-Mart merchandise stocker, and clothes hanger at a dry cleaner's. On average they spent considerably more than a regular full-time shift outside the home while at work and had irregular work hours; some of them also worked weekends. The second- or third-generation Hispanic parents tended to have more education as well as better-paying jobs with regular hours.

Of the two African American mothers interviewed, one was very poor and had been on and off welfare; the other was working class, with a fairly steady job. The one Caucasian, non-Hispanic parent interviewed was a recently divorced woman, a computer professional who ordinarily would be considered middle class. Her residence in the low-income Johnston High School district was anomalous, a result of temporary poverty due to the divorce. Most of the parents had married young—during or before their 20s. Five of the couples had been married for around 20 years; one mother remarried twice but several were divorced or single.

Understanding the parents' and teens' dispositions toward technology requires an appreciation of family dynamics. Like conventional socialization theory, which considers the family to be the key agency of cultural transmission, Bourdieu's conceptual scheme regards the family to be the "primary habitus" (Murdock, 1989). The family has "a set of generalized schemes of thought, perception, appreciation and action" through which people think about and respond to the social world (Murdock, 1989, p. 93). Consistent with Bourdieu's idea that a person's class location structures his or her cultural consumption, it can be argued that families structure the cultural preferences of their members and contribute to the formation of a class ethos.

## Minority Teens and the Education Field

Poor and working-class families share a class habitus in the sense that they adjust to their social position "either because they feel 'made' for jobs that are 'made' for them [...] or because they adjust their aspirations to their objective chances" (Bourdieu, 1984, p. 110). This process of adjustment and conformity can be analyzed through the concept of class ethos, which designates a "system of implicit and deeply internalized values which, among other things, helps to define attitudes toward cultural capital and educational institutions" (Bourdieu, cited in Swartz, 1977, p. 32). Bourdieu used this concept to show how parents' educational background affects their children's academic performance. The structures that shape the material world of the parents, and their perception of it, also shape the habitus of their children. This conceptualization of reproduction in part explains why some teenagers and their siblings are at risk of dropping out of school. Bourdieu asserted that whether or not youth stay in school depends appreciably on their perceptions of the probability that people of their social class will succeed academically (Bourdieu & Passeron, 1977; Swartz, 1977).

In our study of disadvantaged teens, education was a highly regarded commodity, key to almost all the families interviewed. In several cases, families have sacrificed their goal of returning to their country of origin (in most cases, Mexico) to assure their children's stability in school. All the parents interviewed wanted their children to graduate from high school. For several, their immediate concern was to keep their children from dropping out of school. However, with regard to higher education, only two students among the poorest six families clearly stated their goal was to continue on to college, and only one of the mothers said she was committed to helping her kids do so. Desire to attend college was clearer among the three families slightly higher on the socioeconomic scale (lower middle class). Part of the class habitus that limits most of these families is the perception that high school, rather than college, is the culmination of a formal education. Indeed, the teens we interviewed tended to reflect the educational aspirations that their parents had for them.

Our respondents' opinions varied from relative satisfaction to significant dislike for their neighborhoods and schools, leading some to express concerns about the unequal opportunities between East and West Austin. Johnston High School, in particular, seemed to represent downward social mobility, especially when several of the teens compared Johnston to previous schools they had attended. A couple of parents interviewed from the lower middle class Hispanic neighborhood of Dove Springs were upset that their children were being bused to Johnston.[2] As they reviewed their life histories, the fact that several of the teens had changed schools so much inside and outside of Austin constituted a source of familial regret and discontent.

## Parents and New Information Technologies

Parents we interviewed, especially the immigrant families from Mexico, recognized that they themselves lacked access to the newest communication technologies in their youth, such as radio, telephone, and television. Therefore, their technodispositions tended to be conservative. Today, the parents expressed that they possess most of the latest consumer technologies, including media and communication devices such as cell phones, VCRs, stereos, cordless telephones with caller ID, and video games, as well as household appliances like microwave ovens, washers, and dryers. In most of our respondents' households, there also were one or two cars. But despite all this investment in media and technology, there were very few computers.

Four families out of the twelve we interviewed did own a computer. The temporarily poor, divorced computer professional had two. And two of the second-generation Hispanic families had machines. One was set up specifically to support the family business; the other was purchased by the family's eldest son. He had finished high school 2 years earlier and recently bought himself a used computer mainly for graphic arts, hoping to establish a small business in the near future. One African American father said he owned a computer and had shown his son how to access and search the Internet with it, but due to a divorce his son lived with his mother.

Half of the parents we interviewed did not have access to a computer at home or work, nor did they know how to use one. Among the half dozen who did understand the technology, one said he had used a computer more than 20 years ago when he "punched cards in the Air Force." Another parent had taken a course in word processing more than 10 years earlier. A third parent said she was allowed to enter some numbers into a spreadsheet program at work, although only while being supervised; two of the other parents were employed as secretaries, and the sixth used a computer to do the books for the family business.

Only a few of the parents knew how to surf the Net, although several more were aware of the Internet's existence. Three of the mothers we interviewed had begun to access the World Wide Web at work and were thinking about bringing an Internet connection into their homes. Several parents were also aware (mainly through the news) of the possible negative consequences of the Internet for teenagers, especially access to pornography. Two mothers were aware of the Internet only because of a subplot in the Mexican telenovela, *Tres Mujeres,* broadcast by Univision in prime time during December 1999.

## Teenagers and New Information Technologies

Comments from the teenaged respondents reflected a wider use of media technologies than their parents. Their usage ranged from radio and television to stereos, VCRs, cellular phones, pagers, and CD players. The use of multiple media technologies illustrates these teens' capacity to comprehend and appropriate ICTs (excepting computers) in everyday life. Their media savvy constituted an integral part of their technocompetencies; however, their technology use was largely entertainment oriented. The interviews revealed that most of our teenaged respondents were avid video game players. Some of the teens suggested that video games stimulated their interest in new media technology and noted that they enjoyed playing various fighting and racing games such as Jet Moto, Grand Cruiser, and Street Fighter. The gradual progression from game consoles like Atari and Nintendo to Playstation reflects a positive disposition toward technology nurtured by the quest for entertainment. In contrast, other teens clearly expressed a dislike of video games and reported that traditional forms of media, namely television soap operas and music, appealed more to them in everyday life.

## Technocapital

Most of our teenage respondents said their awareness about the Internet and computers arose from their social networks, including relatives and classmates. Commenting on the limited appeal of Internet ads on television, they pointed out the commercials' seeming irrelevance and inability to make a strong impression on them. Family and friends serve as important mediating resources for our respondents' computer competencies. They not only provide computer access but also convey positive dispositions for and familiarity with computer literacy. Immediate family played a particularly supportive role for several of our respondents. Family encouragement for "getting out" from under their disadvantaged status reinforced the need for education and technological knowledge for social and economic mobility. Within the realm of extended family, aunts and uncles provided the base for many of our respondents' initial interactions with computers and the Internet. However, the relatives who knew most about computers were women, which limited their impact as role models for the teenage boys. Several of the boys, as in the example cited at the beginning of this chapter, learned about computers from their mothers and aunts, but did not see their "pink collar" jobs as something they would aspire to themselves.

Throughout our interviews, there was an exception that tended to prove the rule about gender typing of technology. The African American boy whose divorced father introduced him to the Internet described an intense interest in computers, a predilection he has had since early childhood. This teen, somewhat studious compared to his peers, used the Internet to research assignments and play solitaire; he also enjoyed communicating with his cousins, aunts, and uncles by e-mail. Dedicated to his studies, he wanted to enroll in summer school to learn algebra so that he could take geometry and other math courses the following year. His goal was to attend college, and he already had his sights on the University of Texas. He envisioned typical Internet users as "nerds," but did not mind being called a nerd. Facing down peer pressure, he would rather pursue an education than wind up on the street or in a juvenile detention center, where many of his friends have already landed.

Friends also provided much of the discursive and practical space for the introduction and interplay of new technologies in these teens' everyday lives. While few of our families owned a computer or maintained an Internet connection at home, most of our respondents were friends with someone whose parents did. Indeed, many had played computer games or had accessed the Internet at friends' houses. However, they did not really consider this indirect access to technology as their own.

At times, our interviews showed that peers can have a negative influence on technocapital. Several boys in particular brought up the fact that their friends did not find computers or the Internet socially acceptable (i.e., "cool"). During an initial group discussion about the project, held in the algebra classroom at Johnston High, the African American boy previously mentioned, a fan of computers as well as video games, began to get rather excited at the prospect of learning more about computers. On seeing his response, two other boys in the class stared at him pointedly, as if to say, "Don't get too excited about this, you are not supposed to like this stuff." Feeling this peer-group disapproval, our teen immediately stopped talking and kept to himself; the other two boys declined to be involved any further in the study, as if to make it clear where they stood. Although the naysayers could not dampen our teen's enthusiasm for computers, they could keep him from expressing his interest in public.

The institutional framework of school likely constitutes the most important arena in which teenage respondents interact and negotiate with restrictions and resources to develop a repertoire of technological competencies. This repertoire is built through such mechanisms as computer classes that teach basic skills and research assignments that give students the opportunity to apply their knowledge— and learn more on their own. While providing basic instruction in computing and word processing, many computer classes have acquired a "boring" connotation because they focus too heavily on typing skills. For a few of the respondents, the impression that computers were dull had been formed in middle school, where keyboarding was taught on simple machines with monochrome monitors. Some of the male respondents also implied that labels such as "keyboarding" gendered these classes—and computer use generally—as "something girls do."

Computer and Internet exposure generally occurred in the fifth grade. Given little or no prior experience, many of our teens' first encounters with information technology proved frustrating. One female respondent told us that she "hated it so much that I didn't understand it. So I just don't even mess with it no more . . . like the Internet, you gotta go www- this and that. And I was trying to get into it, but it's so confusing I left it alone." Even so, at the time of the initial interview at Johnston, she still expressed interest in taking a computer class at school. Unfortunately, we learned during a follow-up interview that a counselor had barred her from the course because she had insufficient prior knowledge of computers.

In addition to these social and experiential obstacles, the physical arrangement of computer and Internet access at Johnston High was also problematic. The school district had allowed a construction project, which closed the regular library, to drag on for 2 years. As a result, the library, ordinarily the point of online access, was "temporarily" housed in a gym with very limited computer network connections. Computers intended for networked labs were sitting around in boxes awaiting the completion of construction. Furthermore, the time scheduled for open Internet access came mostly during lunch, which conflicted with our respondents' desire to spend free time with friends. Observed one: "For some people, before school and lunch time is the only time to hang out with their friends . . . I will have something that I need to look up on the Internet but I want to spend lunch with my friends. They need to make a study hall." Another teen who used school computers to access the Internet said he logged on when he wanted to find information about cars and sports; he also looked up rap, hip-hop, and free-style music online. The idea for tracking music online was the result of cross-promotion efforts on television and CD covers that, he said, have the "www thing on it." After (and sometimes before) school, most of our teenage respondents held regular part-time jobs, which limited their Internet use at places off-campus, such as public libraries or community centers.

## Technodispositions

Although only four of the parents in our group said they worked directly with computers, the parents overall realized the importance of the technology for their children's future and seemed willing to acquire their own machine sometime soon. Issues of class and socioeconomic status were raised by one respondent, a Mexican American mother who perceived the new technology to be for "rich and educated people" and not for minority consumers like herself living on a modest income.

Understandings of the Internet reflected respondents' practical encounters with the technology at school and home. From an educational standpoint, the teens perceived the Internet as an efficient tool for researching school projects, whereas for entertainment purposes they regarded it as a medium for following their favorite sports teams and television shows. E-mail and online shopping were also recognized by some of our respondents as relevant ways of using the Internet. Almost all acknowledged computers as important, in one way or another. Commented one female respondent: "That's what's going to be it pretty soon, nothing but technology. You're either gonna stay with it or get lost. If you learn about it now, it can help you now and in the future [to get a] better job—if you know how to mess with a computer."

However, the idea that the teens we interviewed would use computers in their daily lives seemed somewhat remote, something they envision for the distant future, particularly the boys. In response to a question about the technology, one male teen commented that "computers are for working people... or for people who have nothing else to do." Information technology may become important and personally relevant for this teen when he is older, but for the time being computers do not catch his attention. Although he could access the Internet at the branch public library near his house, he has never been curious enough to go. Perhaps, he told us, he would be attracted to the Internet if more of the content was posted in Spanish.

Although rhetoric of the Information Age permeated almost all of the interviews, few of the students had much actual experience with the technology of the Internet. Even without this experience, the connection between computer skills and upward mobility was something our respondents discursively acknowledged. These technodispositions are reproduced into practice by way of family encouragement, incentives from school and, in some cases, motivations from friends. However, as noted before, peers were also discouraging of computer use, particularly for the male students we interviewed. These teens do not see information technology as occupying a central part, or any part, of their life. This feeling is enhanced in East Austin by the structural arrangements at school and public libraries where time restrictions and lack of guidance contribute to an unsuccessful experience with the technology. This experience is reflected by one student's first memory of computers from the sixth grade when she would see computer terminals at the school library; she never got the chance to use one that year because of the number of people in line. Asked about public access centers, several students and one parent specifically said they did not feel comfortable with public libraries, that they were too controlled and institutional.

## CONCLUSION

The most immediate boundary that prevented the poorest of these teens from acquiring technocapital or a positive technodisposition was economic class and the formation of a demotivating class habitus that reinforced their social standing, as theorists like Bourdieu and Mosco have suggested. In fact, among the poor and working-class families we interviewed, there appeared to be a homogeneity of dispositions associated with their social position as posed by Bourdieu in *Distinction* (1984). Lack of access to a quality education due to neighborhood location, the necessity of sustaining a large family on little income, the fact of having a recent immigration history, and the inability of the parents to progress beyond low-paid, unskilled jobs all contributed to the class habitus of the poorest families we interviewed. Deferring their own dreams, many of the parents perceived they had no option *but* to work as unskilled, manual laborers so their children could perhaps achieve a different position in the social hierarchy.

In the six poorest families we interviewed, computers and Internet access were considered far too expensive for personal adoption; few relatives or friends could afford it either. Furthermore, the cultural capital related to technology (techno-capital) that the parents were able to transfer to their children was minimal or nonexistent—most were barely aware of the new information and communication technologies. These teenagers had little or no knowledge of how computers and the Internet worked, even in the case of those exposed to computers in middle school. Although they recognized a connection between computers and the Internet, they were not able to specify or articulate the relationship. None of these teenagers perceived computers to be of immediate relevance to their lives; despite receiving extra credit for completing school assignments on a word processor, they refused to access the technology at community centers or libraries. Interestingly, even the poorest teens were familiar with household electronics such as VCRs, stereos, microwaves, cordless telephones, caller ID, and so forth. Furthermore, all had video games in their homes. Yet, they remained intimidated by computers. None knew the difference, for example, between an IBM-compatible PC and an Apple Macintosh brand computer. All of our teen respondents had friends who accessed the Web for information about their favorite personalities and activities—music, wrestling, sports, and celebrities—but they did not make the connection that they, too, could as easily have access to this information if they only visited the community center or library.

Social networks and social capital do not really compensate for this lack of economic and cultural capital in the immediate family. All of the teenagers interviewed for this project knew at least one person or family member who owned a computer. But they did not consider that access their own. Public access does not necessarily solve the problem, either. The connection between libraries and the Web lifestyle is not established; libraries are just a place to study or get books. For our respondents, a connection existed between libraries, *silence*, and books. Public libraries are viewed as unfriendly places where people make you be quiet.

Schools could perhaps introduce new cultural capital for these poorest teenagers, but as Bourdieu and Passeron (1977) predicted, the high school experience tends to reproduce or reinforce the class habitus and social dispositions that children receive from their parents. Regarding the long-term relevance of information technology, our respondents vaguely recognized that it *might* be useful to know how to use a computer at some point in their lives but reckon they have time to learn; at least for now, computing is not something they want to invest the effort in.

In the working-class families (annual incomes of at least $30,000), greater resources gave parents more possibilities of obtaining computer and Internet access as well as greater cultural capital to work with. Several working-class parents had exposure to computers at work and some were considering them for home. These parents are more likely to have and to pass on cultural capital and technodispositions favorable to computing and Internet use. Indeed, several working moms were thinking about how to transfer what they were learning at work to their children at home. Within this group, though, parent and child gender matters, as does social capital from neighbors, friends, and peers about technology. Whereas an African American father could effectively encourage his son to defy peer pressure and pursue his interest in computers, even at the risk of being labeled a "geek," an Hispanic mother we interviewed had a much harder time overcoming her son's peer influences and lack of a male role model to encourage him to develop computer literacy in the face of this demotivational pressure.

In the social relationships between parents, teens, relatives, neighbors, and peer groups, a complex interplay transpires between class, ethnicity, and gender. The teenagers are trying to sort out what the future holds, a future partially determined by their family class habitus and the limitations of their own restricted agency. However, these teens are also strongly influenced by other adult role models as well as their peers. We found that the social capital imparted from both of these sources can have a harmful effect on the development of technodispositions. Relatives and neighbors can facilitate online access for some disadvantaged teens, but at the same time may reinforce negative dispositions toward the use of technology. This is particularly true when gender types, which are often shaped and nuanced by ethnic identity, come into play. What is considered appropriate for a working-class Hispanic boy to do, for example, almost certainly does not involve the "woman's work" of "keyboarding" in front of a "boring" computer monitor.

In this chapter we have documented what Bourdieu and Passeron (1997) called reproduction of inequalities within a school system a publicly sanctioned process that does not socially *level* the students. However, Bourdieu (1977), in the *Outline of a Theory of Practice*, perceived a possibility of change in the tension between agency and structure. This "restricted/constrained freedom" (p. 13) for change comes from the individual who manages to apply strategies (practices) that do not contain the regulatory traces of the structure. Where is the likelihood of an exit from poverty for these kids? This is where Bourdieu is criticized as a determinist, for he maintains there is no exit. Actors, however, are cultural agents. They not only reproduce a class habitus, they creatively use it. With regard to the liberating promise of information technology, we wonder whether empowerment is imparted on different levels; on one level is the family and the "innovator" within the family, on another level are peer groups, and on another level is the institutional context of the school. Despite some ominous warning signs, we remain optimistic and see the potential for positive influence exerted by both extended family and peer groups, as well as from institutional promotion free of gender or racial bias. Such considerations should be the subject of further work.

## ENDNOTES

[1] For Bourdieu, practices are the strategies agents use to play in different fields, such as the technofield. Perception, awareness, and desires form part of the habitus that is a cognitive and motivational structure. Starting from simple indicators, we build a definition of *technodisposition*, which inasmuch as it is widely shared across the group, constitutes a class habitus.

[2] Such protests were frequent enough that children from this neighborhood were reassigned the following year to another high school, Crockett, which is predominantly Caucasian and working class.

## REFERENCES

Benton Foundation (1998). *Losing ground bit by bit: Low-income communities in the Information Age.* Retrieved January 29, 2002, from http://www.benton.org/Library/Low-Income/

Bourdieu, P. (1977). *Outline of a theory of practice.* Cambridge: Cambridge University Press.

Bourdieu, P. (1980). *The logic of practice* (Richard Nice, trans.). Stanford, CA: Stanford University Press.

Bourdieu, P. (1984). *Distinction: A social critique of the judgment of taste.* Cambridge, MA: Harvard University Press.

Bourdieu, P. (1986). The forms of capital. In J. G. Richardson (Ed.) *Handbook of theory and research for the sociology of education* (pp. 241–258). Westport, CT: Greenwood Press.

Bourdieu, P. (1990). *In other words: Toward a reflexive sociology.* Stanford, CA: Stanford University Press.

Bourdieu, P. (1993a). *The field of cultural production.* New York: Columbia University Press.

Bourdieu, P. (1993b). *Sociology in question.* London: Sage.

Bourdieu, P., & Passeron, J. C. (1977). *Reproduction: In education, society and culture.* Beverly Hills: Sage.

Bourdieu, P., & Wacquant, L. (1992). *An invitation to reflexive sociology.* Chicago: The University of Chicago Press.

Brubaker, R. (1993). Social theory as habitus. In C. Calhoun, E. LiPuma, & M. Postone (Eds.), *Bourdieu: Critical perspectives* (pp. 212–234). Cambridge: Polity Press.

Cato Institute. (2000, June 16). *Digital divide? What digital divide?* Retrieved December 10, 2001, from http://www.cato.org/dailys/06-16-00.html. Washington, DC.

Educational Testing Service (1997, May). *Computers and classrooms: The status of technology in U.S. schools.* Retrieved January 23, 2002, from http://www.ets.org/research/pic/pir.html.

Garnham, N. (1986). Extended review: Bourdieu's *Distinction. Sociological Review, 34*(2), 423–433.

Heritage Foundation (2000, April 20). *How free computers are filling the digital divide.* Retrieved December 10, 2001, from http: //www.heritage.org/library/backgrounder/bg1361.html.

Hoffman, D. L., & Novak, T. P. (1998, February 2). *Bridging the digital divide: The impact of race on computer access and Internet use.* Retrieved March 21, 2002, from http://elab.vanderbilt.edu/research/papers/html/manuscripts/race/science.html.

Holstein, W. (2000, February 21). A tale of two Austins: How one boomtown is coping with the growing wealth gap. *U.S. News & World Report.* Retrieved March 21, 2002 from http://www.usnews.com/utils/search.

Johnson, R. (1993). Editor's introduction. In P. Bourdieu, *The field of cultural production* (pp. 1–25). New York: Columbia University Press.

Kaiser Family Foundation. (1999, November 15). *Kids & media @ the new millennium.* Retrieved December 10, 2001, from http://www.kff.org/content/1999/1535/.

Kurtz, M., & McEntee, R. (2000, January 23). Hard times at Johnston. *Austin American-Statesman,* A1, A14–16.

Mosco, V. (1996). *The political economy of communication.* Thousand Oaks, CA: Sage.

Murdock, G. (1989). Class stratification and cultural consumption: Some motifs in the work of Pierre Bourdieu. In F. Coalter (Ed.), *Freedom and constraint: The paradoxes of leisure: Ten years of the Leisure Studies Association* (pp. 90–101). London: Comedia/Routledge.

NTIA (1995, July). *Falling through the Net: A survey of the "have nots" in rural and urban America.* National Telecommunication and Information Administration, U.S. Department of Commerce. Retrieved January 23, 2002, from http://www.ntia.doc.gov/ntiahome/fallingthru.html.

NTIA (1999, July). *Falling through the net: Defining the digital divide.* National Telecommunication and Information Administration, U.S. Department of Commerce. Retrieved August 7, 2000, from http://www.ntia.doc.gov/ntiahome/fttn99/contents.html.

NTIA, (2000, October). *Falling through the Net: Toward digital inclusion.* National Telecommunication and Information Administration, U.S. Department of Commerce. Retrieved March 12, 2002, from http://www.ntia.doc.gov/ntiahome/fttn00/contents00.html.

NTIA (2002, February). *A nation online: How Americans are expanding their use of the Internet.* National Telecommunication and Information Administration, U.S. Department of Commerce. Retrieved March 21, from http://www.ntia.doc.gov/ntiahome/dn/index.html.

Pew Internet & American Life Project. (2000, September 21). *Who's not online.* Retrieved March 15, 2002, from http://www.pewinternet.org/reports/index.asp.

Portes, A. (1998). Social capital: Its origins and applications in modern sociology. *Annual Review of Sociology, 24*, 1–24.

Reza, N. (1998). Social origins, social statuses and home computer access and use. *Canadian Journal of Sociology, 23*(4), 427–450.

Rupertus, J., Straubhaar, J., & LaPastina, A. (2001, May). *This Internet is NOT for you: Mismarketing the Internet to minorities.* Paper presented at the annual meeting of the International Communication Association, Washington, DC.

Schement, J. R. (1998). Thorough Americans: Minorities and the new media. In A. Korzick (Ed.), *Investing in diversity: Advancing opportunities for minorities and the media* (pp. 51–84). Washington, DC: Aspen Institute.

Strover, S., & Straubhaar, J. (May 2000). *E-government services and computer and Internet use in Texas.* Telecommunications and Information Policy Institute, University of Texas. Retrieved December 10, 2001, from http://www.utexas.edu/research/ti2e/tipi/resources/reports/full.htm.

Swartz, D. (1977). Pierre Bourdieu: The cultural transmission of social inequality. *Harvard Educational Review, 47*(4), 545–555.

Tomás Rivera Policy Institute (2002). *Latinos and the information technology: The promise and the challenge.* Retrieved March, 21, 2002, from http://www.trpi.org/PDF/Latinos%20and%20IT.pdf.

Wacquant, L. (1996). Reading Bourdieu's "capital." *International Journal of Contemporary Sociology, 33*(2), 151–170.

Wilhelm, A. G. (1998). *Closing the digital divide: Enhancing Hispanic participation in the Information Age.* Claremont, CA: Tomás Rivera Policy Institute.

# APPENDIX

## Interview Protocol

**General Questions** (recommended initial interview questions for adults and children)

- Tell me about yourself?
- Where are you from?

- How long have you lived in Austin? Why did you move here?
- Where did you live before?

- What direction do you see yourself going in the future?
- What direction do you see your family going in the future?
- What would you most like to do when you are about 20?

- If you could change anything in your life right now, what would it be?
- What kind of information do you need for your life right now?
- How are you different from your Mom (or Dad) in where you go for information you need?

- How do people in your family get the information they need?
- How do you get (your) information?
- Who or what supports you in seeking information?
- What do you teach your family about how to get the information they need?

- What are some memories you have about technology from when you were growing up?
- What kind of technology is important to you?
- Do you feel that technology benefits you?

- What things caught your attention the most when you arrived in the United States (for immigrants)?

- How do you like Johnston High School for your children?

**Media Use Questions**

- Do you watch TV? What kind of shows do you watch?
- Do you play video games? What kinds? Why do you like them?
- Do you like radio? What about it do you like best?
- If you had a computer, would you play on it?
- Of TV, radio, video games, computers, and stuff like that, which do you like most?

- What kinds of stuff are cool to you?
- What technologies are cool?
- What kinds of things would you most like to have?

- Have you ever heard of the Information Superhighway?
- What does the Information Superhighway mean to you?

- When did you first hear about computers?
- What is your earliest/first memory of a computer?

- Who are computers for?
- Who is the Internet for?
- How do you feel toward computers?
- Do you get the feeling that computers are for people like you?
- Do you get the feeling that the Internet is for people like you?

- Do you need a computer?
- Do you need the Internet?

- Would your friends think having a computer was cool?
- What do you need to use the Internet?
- What do you think of the Internet?

- What comes to mind when you see someone using the Internet?
- How do you see yourself in relation to the Internet?
- Do you think the Internet is/would be useful to you?
- Do you consider the Internet a vital part of your everyday life? If yes, why and how so?

- How do you keep in touch with relatives out of town (like in Mexico)?
- Would the Internet help you get ahead?
- Do you have any interest in using computers/the Internet?

- Do you see the Internet as a useful source of information?
- What kinds of information do you need from the Internet?
- Does the Internet help everybody?

**Follow-up Questions for the Second Interview**

- Do you have a computer at home?
- How old were you when you first had a computer in your home (when you first saw one)?

**Internet-Specific Questions**

- Have you seen ads about the Internet?
- What did they tell you about it?
- How did they make you think about it?
- Did they make you want to use it?

- If you needed to use the Internet, where would you go?
- How has your family encouraged or discouraged your involvement with the Internet?
- Is the Internet available easily enough for people in your community?

## Questions If Participants Know About the Internet

- Where did you hear about the Internet?
- What kind of things can people do with the Internet?
- Do people in your family use the Internet?

## Questions If Participants Have Used the Internet

- Where do you (or would you) get access to the Internet?
- What do you like on the Internet?
- What do you personally like most on the Internet?
- Why do you not want to use the Internet?
- When you see an ad for the Internet, what are the images usually shown?

## Culturally Specific Questions

- Would you use the Internet more often if it were in Spanish?
- Rank how important different technologies are to you according to how often you use them (phone, computer, etc.)
- How do minorities use the Internet? Do they want to take advantage of what it can deliver or not?
- Is the Internet important to your culture?

# 7

# Reducing Barriers to Access via Public Information Infrastructure: The LaGrange Public Internet Initiative

JAN YOUTIE
*Georgia Tech Economic Development Institute*

PHILIP SHAPIRA
*Georgia Institute of Technology*

GREG LAUDEMAN
*Georgia Tech Economic Development Institute*

Much contemporary discussion concerning information technology policy focuses on concerns about a growing disparity or "digital divide" between users and nonusers of new information technologies, and the differential rate of adoption of information technology along socioeconomic lines. The U.S. National Telecommunications and Information Administration charted this divide in five reports (NTIA, 1995, 1998, 1999, 2000, 2002). The first four identified clear demarcations between urban and rural, rich and poor, white and minority, male and female, and high and low education. Although recent studies found a trend toward broader diffusion of Internet access (Horrigan & Rainie, 2002; NTIA, 2002), there remain issues of whether Internet access translates into social access (Bucy, 2000), and whether the technology is being used in a "transactional arena" or a "home digiplex." With the emergence of the Internet as an important new communication medium, raising all citizens to the ranks of those able to access and benefit from information technology (IT) has emerged as an explicit social and policy objective (Anderson, Bikson, Law, & Mitchell, 1995).

Often, efforts to bridge the digital divide are like modern permutations of historical efforts to provide universal telephone service, focusing primarily on reducing the cost of access. Such programs effectively transform telecommunications and computing into a public good: Use by one does not diminish the good or exclude others from using it. Public provision of Internet access is based on the rationale that broader social benefits will emerge when the technology is ubiquitously available. Conceptual discussions of virtual community (Castells, 1989; Levy, 1997; Mitchell, 1995; Teilhard de Chardin, 1964) and examinations of online communities (Baker, 1997; Cohill & Kavanaugh, 1997; Dutton, Blumler, & Kramer, 1987; Guthrie & Dutton, 1992; Rheingold, 2000; Schuler, 1996) suggest that information infrastructure supports not only communication and information sharing but also deep and meaningful social interaction. Thus the Internet becomes a platform for more equitable economic opportunity and renewed democratic participation. But it is far from clear these benefits are inherent in the use of IT. There is a counterargument that the Internet increases social fragmentation and undermines social institutions (Stoll, 1995), and supports the political status quo (Margolis & Resnick, 2000).

These divergent views are reflected in the empirical literature. Internet usage has been shown to be associated with loss of contact with social environment and increased time spent at work (Nie & Erbring, 2000), and with increased feelings of loneliness, decreased social circle, and decreased communication with household members (Kraut et al., 1998). The attitude–use relationship can apparently go the other direction, as well. In a study of IT use by nongovernmental organizations in Latin America, Gomez (1998) noted that attitudes toward the formal instantiations of technology—service providers and virtual communities—had a mitigating effect on its application to civic processes. In a study relating attitude regarding the Internet to usage, Anandarajan, Simmers, and Igbaria (1998) found, not surprisingly, attitudes toward the usefulness of the Internet to be positively correlated with use, but also with productivity and job satisfaction. Similar results were reported by Baker (1997), who found that students who did not have access to the Internet had little interest in it, whereas those who did have access felt that it supported their academic work and improved their professional opportunities.

On the other hand, recent research by the Pew Internet Project (2000) indicated that the majority of Internet users—particularly women—find that e-mail has increased their connection and communications with family members and friends. In their study of one of the most widely noted "wired cities," Blacksburg, Virginia, Kavanaugh and Patterson (2001) found that Internet use supported dense and broad communication and improved access to information. These capabilities translated into greater civic participation for those "poised to participate," but

Kavanaugh and Patterson also found evidence of a bifurcation that increased the distinction between the involved and the uninvolved. Similarly, Riedel, Dresel, Wagoner, Sullivan, and Borgida (1998) conducted a longitudinal research project to examine social capital accumulation, equity issues, and civic participation impacts resulting from the GrandNet electronic network in a rural part of Minnesota. Results indicated that citizens with more resources had higher rates of technology adoption than did those with fewer social resources.

A critical difference between universal service and the digital divide is that the communications technologies of yesteryear were less complex and skill-intensive than modern telecommunications and computing. The costs of using IT include not only monetary costs but also soft costs associated with getting the technology to work correctly and learning to use it (Kiesler, Zdaniuk, Lundmark, & Kraut, 2000). Consider that few people paid for classes in how to use a telephone, but a multitude have invested in computer and Internet classes. It has been shown that ability to use a computer effectively, and willingness to pursue those skills, are profoundly impacted by computer anxiety, especially for those groups associated with the digital divide (Brosnan, 1998; Caputi, 2000; Ellis & Allaire, 1999; Hemby, 1998). Thus the digital divide does not just result from the emergence of a new means of communication—as was the case for universal telephone service—but also from the structure and form of the technology.

One means of reducing the soft costs associated with the Internet is to make it less complex, to "dumb it down," making it more like traditional media such as television. Insights into such an approach may be gleaned from efforts to "smarten up" television. Considerations of pre-Internet interactive media—including interactive TV and videotext—focused on the system as a new venue for consumers (Dupagne, 1990; Olander & Sepstrup, 1987; Russo, 1987). But even at that time there was empirical evidence that this approach was flawed (George, 1987; Sepstrup & Mayer, 1988), that ease of use, usage-related skills, and gratifications resulting from use were critical factors in adoption (Cowles, 1989; Kuhlman & Balderjahn, 1989), all factors that were only superficially addressed by pre-Internet interactive media. Theoretical perspectives also suggested the need for interactive media to reach a critical mass of usage before it could be viable (Fullerton & Allen, 1989; Markus, 1990). The same themes were being sounded in post-Internet considerations of interactive media. Even commentators who suggest interactive media must be more flexible, user-centric, and simply more reliable doggedly insist that it will be like television (Masi, 1997; Miles, 1997). It has been argued that even though interactive media is constructed as a new form of communication, its structure and form are inevitably shaped by the culture of television. The fundamental problem with this approach is that at least two important functions of TV viewing, watching for recreation and viewing experience as a common social reference—"mood elevation" and "social grease" in Lee and Lee's (1995) terms—are arguably diminished by interactivity.

Schwartz (1995, 9) concluded his consideration of interactive TV with a solid "no thanks":

> I just want to plop down on the sofa, turn on the entertainment, tune out my higher brain functions, and exercise my constitutional right to stare vacantly at the tube, resting assured that interactive television is still little more than an oxymoron.

Just because the technology is readily available does not mean it will be used; attitudes toward technology, social context, and user perceptions can function as barriers as much as direct monetary costs (see chapters 1 and 6, this volume). Taken together, the literature mentioned suggests that a truly public information infrastructure doesn't just meet the economic definition of being nondiminishable and nonexclusionary in consumption; it must be simple to use and culturally comprehensible. But the literature also suggests that such a system might be counterproductive: Why bridge the digital divide if it simply creates a population of digital couch potatoes? The hypothetical justification for publicly provisioning information infrastructure is to realize gains in marketable skills and in enhanced social interactions that result from access. As yet there have been few opportunities for robust tests of the effects of public policies to accelerate the take-up of information technologies, particularly community-level initiatives to publicly provide access to targeted social and economic groups or peripheral localities.

This chapter examines the early adoption effects of the availability of information technology infrastructure by focusing on the LaGrange Internet Television (LITV) service, the public information utility of LaGrange, Georgia. LaGrange is arguably the first traditional city to create a truly public information utility. It is truly public in that the barrier to entry is very low—no computer or technical skills are required—and it is available to any city resident. Similar programs have been implemented in suburbs or in planned communities (Gurstein, 2000; Hampton & Wellman, 1999), but these systems are public only for the narrow socioeconomic group that chooses to and can live in a wired suburb, in part to have access to the system. In large cities, advanced technology wired buildings are now being built for residents, but again these are mostly up-market, which restricts them to higher income social groups. In contrast, LaGrange, with a population of just under 26,000, is a rather typical small rural city, with most residents of moderate means who, as yet, are seemingly being bypassed by the new information economy. The city specifically created this initiative to overcome the effects of the digital divide and barriers to online adoption.

## TELECOMMUNICATIONS AND THE CITY OF LAGRANGE

LaGrange offers a unique opportunity to test community information technology impacts based on its socioeconomic and population stability, status as a rural

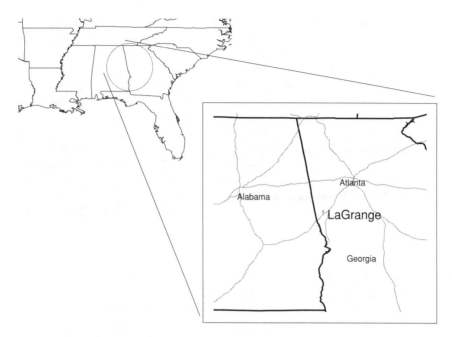

FIG 7.1. Location of LaGrange, Georgia, in the southeastern United States.

city, and recent city-wide introduction of the LITV service. The county seat of rural Troup County, LaGrange was incorporated as a city in 1828. It is located near the Alabama border about 60 miles southwest of downtown Atlanta (see Fig. 7.1). Until the 1970s, the textile industry composed 70% of LaGrange's employment base. However, textile employment has been steadily declining and, over the last three decades, LaGrange has undertaken a concerted effort to diversify its economy. The city established an economic development authority; invested more than $100 million in water, sewer, roads, schools, and hospital infrastructure; and built an industrial park. Since the 1970s, the population of LaGrange has varied little.

Many other small rural communities have taken similar steps. But in the 1990s, LaGrange began to do something different. In an effort to develop an information-intensive sector to complement its manufacturing and distribution industries, the city appointed a telecommunications committee, which identified elements of the local telecommunications infrastructure that were not state-of-the-art for attracting information-intensive businesses. The city then hired an engineering firm in 1992 to validate telecommunications infrastructure needs and suggest an implementation process. In 1993, LaGrange city leaders entered negotiations with the local telephone company, but the company did not respond to the city's expectations for its local telecommunications infrastructure, arguing that it could not justify the investment. LaGrange then decided to deploy its own telecommunications infrastructure based on its experience as a full-service city that operates its own electricity, natural gas, sanitation, and water and sewer utilities. Between 1993 and 1995, the city hung a 4-mile ring of dark fiber cable on its existing electric poles, and leased it to a carrier that deployed a long-distance point of presence in the city. Eventually, the local telephone company deployed a remote digital switch in LaGrange. The city began operating its own telecommunications service in 1997, primarily serving businesses and institutions, when it obtained certification from the Georgia Public Service Commission (Read & Youtie, 1996; Youtie, 2000).

For residential customers, LaGrange established a public-private joint venture in 1998 with Charter Communications, which was purchasing the local cable system to provide broadband cable service. The city financed and built a hybrid fiber coax network and leased back to the cable operator some of the capacity for video entertainment. Overall, some $11 million was spent by the city to upgrade its communications infrastructure.

The telecommunications committee, deactivated once the city took over operation of telecommunications services, was reestablished in late 1999 as the LaGrange Information Technology Telecommunications Task Force. With the formation of the task force, the city began to recognize that it needed to address factors beyond telecommunications infrastructure and focus on the broader aspects required of the community for information preparedness—education, social awareness, and attitudinal barriers. In recognition of the city's history of strategic activities in the telecommunications area, LaGrange won the World Teleport Association's Intelligent City of the Year award in 2000.

Through the efforts of the development authority and the city, LaGrange has attracted some 35 new industries to the area, and the percentage of employees in the textile industry has dropped to 10%. However, these new industries have had difficulty finding skilled workers in the local labor pool with the information skills now required in all types of jobs. LaGrange officials suggested that a telemarketing firm employing 100 workers closed its LaGrange facility because it was unable to fill positions. LaGrange relied on programs at the local technical institute to upgrade worker skills. However, the city has a smaller percentage of high school and college graduates than the state average. Likewise, per capita income and employment growth are below the state average, and unemployment rates are higher than the state average.

## Reducing the Costs of Access to the User

To improve information preparedness, LaGrange announced in March 2000 that it would provide broadband Internet access and a Web terminal free of charge to any resident, making the city arguably the first locale to create a truly public information utility in the context of a traditional community. The LaGrange Internet TV system acts as a terminal server that allows users to access e-mail and the World Wide Web through a cable television set-top box and wireless keyboard. Connection speeds approximate 150kbps, with a fast system response time (due to the service's terminal–host architecture rather than a client–server configuration). The terminal–host system is provided by WorldGate Service, and the set-top boxes are Motorola DCT2000s and DCT5000s. The city purchases all equipment and services through an arrangement with Charter Communications.

Although LITV is not a full implementation of computer-enabled Internet access, its configuration bears more resemblance to a personal computer (PC) than to interactive television systems. For example, the infrared keyboard used in LITV is almost identical to a laptop layout, whereas other devices use a traditional television remote. LITV also interfaces directly to the Internet without a cumbersome menu system. The city of LaGrange has developed custom content tailored both to the system's distinctive screen standards and local user interests, so its pages do not have the awkward feel that users get when accessing the Internet via the more limited television-based Internet systems.

On the other hand, the LITV system has some key differences from a PC. Notably, it is integrated with cable television, so users can look up Web sites cross-promoted on TV with the click of a button. Given its terminal–host architecture, the system lacks advanced features and has no local intelligence. The LITV system functions as an "information appliance" (rather than a computer), consistent with the frequently expressed perspective that Internet access will evolve through multiple, easy-to-use, single-purpose devices rather than the all-purpose PC (see Norman, 1999). The city chose this particular technology in part because it was less complex to use than a personal computer and thus had lower entry barriers for current computer nonusers.

When a household signs up for the service, a city employee installs all the necessary equipment free of charge. The only requirement is that the household must have basic cable television service. In LaGrange, the cable system is municipally owned and basic service costs $8.95 a month. All of LaGrange's 11,000 households are reached by the city's cable system and, of these, about 9,000 households already subscribe to cable service, meaning that they face no extra charge to obtain the LITV service. In low-income circumstances where a household expresses a desire for Internet access but cannot afford the basic cable fee, the city reduces or waives the monthly charge. In the spring of 2000, the city committed to providing online Internet access to interested LITV users without additional charge for at least 2 years.[1] The LITV service was activated in the fall of 2000, and was reconsidered and approved for continuance by the city council in late summer 2001.

LITV's managers report that the technology itself has not presented major problems to new users. After installing the equipment, LITV technicians briefly show new users how to get online, similar to a digital cable subscription walk-through. If the technician finds that the existing cable connection is not adequate for Internet access, the city's cable company rewires the house for free.

With infrastructure and end-user devices established, the city's attention turned to content. The city contracted for the creation of a 20-minute training program that runs continuously on cable, allowing the user to simultaneously interact with the Internet. There also are periodic programs about the LITV service on the local TV station and training programs at a senior center. In addition, the city created a Web portal to facilitate user access to local content (see http://www.lagrange-ga.org/homepage.cfm). The portal contains online education exercises to promote basic Internet access skills, including keyboarding, and a gateway that provides LITV users with easy access to a variety of educational and local government services. The portal also offers online community Web pages through an arrangement with a local Internet start-up featuring message boards, a community calendar and newsletter, and classified ads. Local neighborhood groups, church congregations, civic associations, and other service organizations have set up neighborhood pages after receiving training from the city to administer these sites. To facilitate online shopping, the portal has a local business directory. Information about city services, including utilities, fire, police, and economic development, can also be found on the portal site.

LaGrange has promoted the LITV service using a multipronged strategy, entailing (a) four rounds of mailings (one to all city residents, one to all residents with school-age children, and two to churches in low-income neighborhoods); (b) placing notices on the door of every house in the city; (c) a telemarketing campaign; (d) a month of daily local newspaper advertisements; (e) five months of local television announcements; (f) efforts to work with school officials to increase student awareness of the service; and, (g) rallies in public housing communities that featured an appearance by Georgia Senator Max Cleland. Students at a local college also planned a special marketing campaign aimed at neighborhoods with a high proportion of lower income and African American residents. Selected city staff also canvassed households door-to-door in lower income neighborhoods.

As of August 2000, the city reported that it had installed systems in about 1,500 households, with some turnover occurring as people moved or gave back their LITV set-top boxes. By September 2001, the number of households with installed systems had jumped to 4,377, an almost 40 percent city-wide penetration rate. The estimated costs for the initiative include $300,000 in annual operating expenses and $120,000 in fixed capital improvements. The city, in turn, receives about $200,000 in annual revenues from Charter Communications for installing set-top boxes in LITV user households.

## Policymakers' Goals and Expectations

The city announced five goals for the LaGrange Internet Television Initiative: (a) improve citizen computer skills, ability to access Internet information, and e-mail-based communication proficiency and comfort; (b) complement school programs; (c) develop a citywide intranet for job and other postings; (d) increase interchange between residents and city officials; and, (e) develop local e-commerce. These formal goals reflect the stated objectives of the program. Nevertheless, personal interviews with key stakeholders and city policymakers uncovered a diverse range of hopes and aims underlying the establishment of LITV.

The city's economic development and special projects manager described LITV as part of a 30-plus-year effort to move the local economy off of a textile footing to a more diverse manufacturing economy and now onto a knowledge-based economy. He commented that LaGrange was competing with cities around the globe for business relocations; to be attractive to technology firms, the local economy *needed* a more skilled workforce. LITV would help introduce local working-age adults to information technology, providing them with keyboarding skills valued by local industry and businesses that might relocate to the city. Eventually, the hope was, LITV users might upgrade to personal computer use. To this economic development officer, LaGrange's survival in the knowledge economy hinged on initiatives such as LITV.

A member of the city's Information Technology Telecommunications Task Force also saw LITV's roots in the city's 30-plus-year legacy of trying to diversify the local economic base. The task force sought to respond to demands from local businesses for better voice and data communications capabilities to support their adoption of information technology and productivity initiatives. At the same time, this task force member acknowledged that the city's existing labor force, consisting of a fair number of workers lacking even a high school diploma, realistically limited the city's long-term economic goals. Although LITV offers affordable access to new information technology, he observed that use of the system was not universal. Reasons why some citizens did not take up the LITV system included apprehensions about the technology involved (mainly among the city's minority population), concerns about the system displacing television, and frustrations with the device's limitations (mainly among experienced computer users). This task force member's focus was on the local school system and the challenges of integrating LITV into a curriculum where not everyone in the system had the same access to it.

The city manager, Tom Hall, who oversees the city's other utilities, was concerned about deregulation's impacts on revenues from electric utility service. Because the city did not levy property tax, 40 percent of municipal budget revenues came from its electric utility business. He saw the city's telecommunications services in general, including LITV, as a way to supplement potentially declining utility revenues by helping to complete a package of city services that could eventually be attractive to citizens on a cost basis. The city manager also expressed a desire to transform and change the lives of local citizens. Nevertheless, the fiscally conservative approach inherent in LaGrange's telecommunications policy—leaseback arrangements and partnerships with Charter rather than overbuilding it and becoming a competing cable TV provider as has been done by other Georgia cities—was influenced by the city manager's attention to revenue considerations. The city's arrangements with Charter Communications—as well as WorldGate Services and Motorola—wound up not requiring an extensive outlay of funds. The service provider discounted its service to the city, and the cable company, as mentioned, pays the city to install the set-top boxes in user households.

LaGrange's mayor, Jeff Lukken, articulated a vision that defined the city's place in the knowledge economy. He came up with the big ideas about giving everyone in the city free Internet access, despite initial concerns from the financially focused city manager, and argued for the establishment of Web sites for every neighborhood in the city.

The Chamber of Commerce president, Jane Fryer, emphasized the image-building, marketing, and visibility impacts of LITV. She found LITV to be an asset in promoting the city to industrial prospects interested in locating a facility in LaGrange. Industries were impressed by the initiative and believed it to be indicative of a local government with foresight and vision. She hoped that LITV would enable LaGrange to attract more types of technology-based industry and business.

A representative of a major national company that has distribution facilities located in LaGrange believed that LITV might have an impact on new employees' ability to more easily and quickly use computer-based applications such as in-house training programs on CDs. However, this firm was not directly incorporating LITV into its training or operating activities. The company had adopted information technology in many operating areas, but still located in the city for the most part because of the area's traditional workforce. When describing labor concerns, the employer emphasized his need for finding enough workers with basic skills, such as the ability to operate a forklift, rather than fluency with information technology.

In summary, LITV was seen by these stakeholders and policymakers as more than a vehicle for addressing digital divide concerns about differential access to new technology. Various voices with a stake in LITV's outcome hoped that it would generate additional revenue, help market the city to companies in need of new facilities, enhance the computer skills of working-age adults, and transform the city's economy from a manufacturing base to knowledge-based industries.

On closer inspection, LITV stakeholders raised contradictory expectations. Policymakers saw LITV as raising workforce proficiencies to attract industry, whereas the industry representative, while recognizing the value of LITV to expose working-age adults to information technology, emphasized the ongoing need for basic skills. Some policymakers stressed existing revenue impacts from LITV, whereas others articulated a vision for the city in the global economy. And despite LITV's potential to help ameliorate digital divide concerns, the IT task force member felt that some disadvantaged groups might not want to take up the service over fears about the technology or reluctance to interfere with their television use.

## HOUSEHOLD EXPECTATIONS AND USE: RESULTS
## OF A BASELINE SURVEY

Did users without PCs or Internet access take up LITV with an expectation that it would help them cross the digital divide? This section analyzes household responses from a baseline survey of users designed by the authors for the city. The one-page survey included questions about household composition and demographics, prior experience with PCs and other technologies (e.g., faxes, cell phones, VCRs), as well as expectations about LITV. The city used this survey as part of its LITV installation process. Service installers employed by the LaGrange city government administered the survey at the point of installation. In cases where the installers could not gather the data, the city's customer service representatives fielded the user survey by telephone. Most of the surveys were completed in September and October 2000. Baseline responses were obtained from 1,352 user households. The results were analyzed statistically and supplemented with selected interviews of LITV users.

There are slightly more women than men in LITV households. Nearly nine out of ten households participating in the LITV baseline survey have females and 75% include males. Adults aged 31 to 60 comprise the largest LITV user group, 58% of LITV households; younger adults aged 18 to 30 are found in 39% of LITV households, followed by seniors older than 60, who can be found in just 17% of LITV households. School-age children can be found in one third of the households, and 16% of the households have children younger than age 5. Twenty-seven percent of LITV households are composed of a single individual who is, on average, senior and female. Another 30% are two-person households. By education, high school graduates compose 39% of households, persons with some college can be found in 26% of households, and those with at least college degrees are included in 31% of households. Among households providing income information ($n = 886$), middle-income households ($25,000 to $50,000) compose 44% of LITV households. One third have annual household incomes below $25,000, and 23% earn more than $50,000.

### Access to Computers and the Internet

Survey results suggest that LaGrange lagged somewhat behind the rest of the country in both PC adoption and Internet access. Forty-three percent of LaGrange households had a PC at home prior to the LITV service. This percentage was somewhat below national figures from the survey conducted in August 2000 by the U.S. Department of Commerce for its most recent *Falling Through the Net* study (NTIA, 2000). That survey reported 50% of rural households with PCs at home, and 47% of Georgia households with home PCs. Among LITV PC households, access to Internet applications was higher than indicated in the U.S. Department of Commerce survey. More than 60% of LITV PC households in LaGrange reported

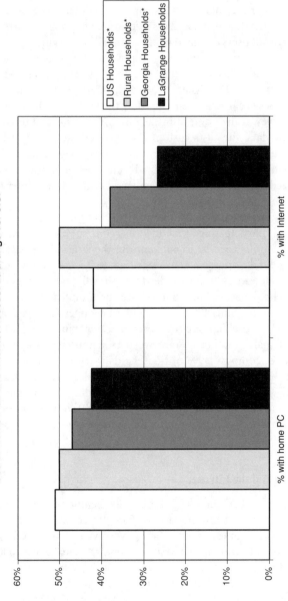

**Use of Home PCs and Internet Access: LaGrange vs. U.S.**

Legend:
☐ US Households*
☐ Rural Households*
▨ Georgia Households*
■ LaGrange Households

% with home PC

% with Internet

FIG 7.2.  Use of home PCs and Internet access: LaGrange, Georgia (2001) compared with the United States and the state of Georgia (2000). Source: National Telecommunications and Information Administration, 2000 (data for US All Households, US Rural Households, and Georgia Households); Analysis of City of LaGrange Survey of LITV Households, 2001 (LaGrange Households).

having access to Internet applications such as e-mail, Web sites, and online shopping. This percentage is higher than U.S. Department of Commerce survey figures of 50% for rural areas and 38% for Georgia (see Fig 7.2).

On the other hand, the LITV initiative did reach an additional segment of households without access to PCs. Examining households without access to PCs can be best described in terms of a "venn diagram" of overlapping circles of users (see Fig 7.3). Nearly three out of ten LITV users had access to computers both at home and at work. Another 14% had access to PCs only at home. An additional 20% had access to PCs only at work, but not at home. But a full 37% lacked access to a PC either at home or at work prior to the introduction of LITV. Households that composed this 37% were more apt to have income below $25,000, include seniors over age 60, include persons without some college education, and be a single-person household. These households had the classic digital divide demographics (see Fig 7.4). Nevertheless, just focusing on households without any prior PC access without incorporating the additional 20% with "work only" access can understate the impact of LITV. If these two segments are added together, LITV provided new at-home access to more than half the households surveyed.

Nearly six in ten LITV households with PCs used them for e-mail, Internet/Web surfing, word processing, and games. The latter two applications, of course, typically do not require Internet access. E-mail and Internet/Web surfing were slightly more common among households with seniors. Spreadsheets (used by one third of PC households) and online shopping (used by 30% of PC households), as well as word processing, were especially prominent among households with young

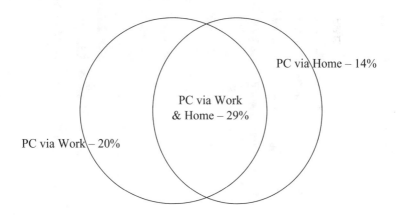

No PC via Work or Home – 37%

FIG 7.3.    Prior access to personal computers by LaGrange LITV users, 2001 (Source: Analysis of City of LaGrange Survey of LITV Households, 2001).

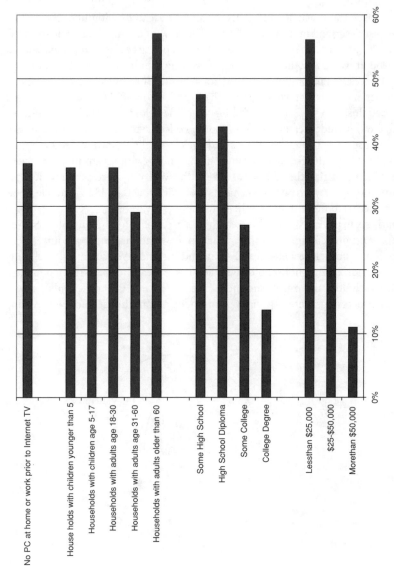

FIG 7.4.  LaGrange LITV users, household characteristics, 2001 (Source: Analysis of City of LaGrange Survey of LITV Households, 2001).

children. Games predominated among households with children ages 5 to 17. Education and income level played particularly significant roles in that households with highly educated and high-earning members were consistently more likely than other households to use all applications except games.

Households taking up the LITV service were not strangers to other information technologies. Nearly eight in ten households had VCRs. Cable television, prior to LITV service, was in 66% of the LITV households, which meant that more than 450 households subscribed to cable to obtain the LITV service. More than half the households had a cellular telephone, although fewer than 20% had a second phone line. And video game stations were in use in one third of LITV households, mostly those with children.

### Reasons for Adopting LaGrange Internet Television

At the time that this baseline survey was conducted, the impacts on user experiences and skills could not be assessed. To the extent that reasons for signing up for LITV foretell interest in skill acquisition, LITV households were asked about their motivations for adopting interactive television (see Fig 7.5). Communication via e-mail or chat rooms was the most popular explanation for obtaining LITV, cited by users in 53% of households. Entertainment was mentioned by users in 50% of LITV households, followed by educational development (45%) and obtaining specialized information (42%).

Seniors were most interested in communication (61%) and least interested in skill improvement (19%). Education was also a prominent factor among households with adults age 18 to 30—these households had the highest percentage of households signing up for LITV for educational reasons (probably for their own education) of any of the age groups. Communication, education, and entertainment were the top three reasons for signing up for LITV among working age adults in the 31 to 60 age range; however, what distinguished these householders was that a higher percentage of them were interested in being able to access information than were any other age group. Not surprisingly, educational development was the primary concern for households with children. Nearly 64% of households with school-age children picked education development as a reason for taking up LITV.

## INSIGHTS FROM EXPLORATORY INTERVIEWS

To supplement the initial survey, we conducted several exploratory interviews to understand why people took up the service, how they use it, and what they have gained from it. For these interviews, we selected a diverse mix of users of varying age, ethnicity, income, and computer experience. Interviews were conducted mainly in respondents' homes. The interviews were structured to explore the following issues: how LITV was used in the household, especially e-mail and Web usage; how users

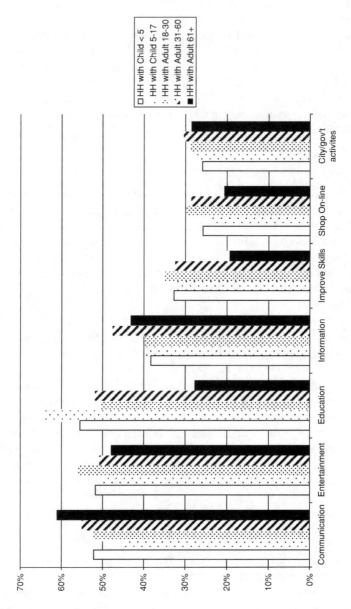

FIG 7.5. Reasons for obtaining LITV, LaGrange households (HH) using LITV, 2001 (Source: Analysis of City of LaGrange Survey of LITV Households, 2001).

learned about LITV and what led them to sign up for it; the nature of user reactions to LITV; user awareness and access of city-generated content; and, benefits received as a result of using LITV. The responses of seven LITV users to the new system are summarized next.

Our first interview was with a teenage African American male living in public housing. Relatively experienced with PCs, the Internet, and video games, he took up the service because it was free and because he did not have a working computer at home. LITV was installed on the television in his bedroom. He relies on the system for information-searching significantly more than for communicating with others by e-mail. Specifically, he uses LITV to search for jobs, peruse police reports, and play video games. Skilled at information retrieval, he once won a local radio program's trivia game contest by using the system. From reading the local *LaGrange Daily News* online, he learned about programs and scholarship opportunities at the local technical college and has now enrolled in a degree program.

Our second interview was with a Caucasian woman in her late 60s who had no prior computer experience and lives alone. She signed up for the service after hearing about it through her volunteer work with an organization that supports local business. Intrigued by the Internet, she thought that LITV would be a less complicated way of exploring the online world than having to use a PC. The service is installed on the main TV in her living room. Instead of the phone, she now uses e-mail frequently to communicate with friends around the world. She also consults Web sites to find information about vacations and recreational activities after she has made initial arrangements by phone. She reads the *LaGrange Daily News* online and has tried to use the city's community links site, but has experienced technical difficulties.

Our third set of interviews was with the director and headmaster of a faith-based school for lower income children. Despite the city's efforts to encourage the school to adopt the interactive television service, the school has just one working LITV unit. Neither the director nor the headmaster use LITV themselves, but nearly all the students have LITV at home. Students reportedly use the system to research school assignments, but make little use of e-mail. Benefits from Internet use, according to the school officials we interviewed, include improved technology skills and an enlivened classroom environment. Both officials felt that LITV made it easier for their students to gain experience with information technology by reducing the costs and apprehension associated with access to the online world.

Our fourth interview was with a retired teacher who lives alone. Having virtually no PC experience, she took up LITV because it seemed less complicated than a personal computer, because it was free, and because she thought it could help her conduct genealogical research. LITV is located on her main television. She uses e-mail in place of long-distance phone calls to reduce communications costs. But she does not do much Web surfing or online genealogical research, despite her best intentions. She likes the service, but now wishes it had more capabilities.

Our fifth interview was with a working father in a family of four who, in his role as breadwinner, works two jobs. Computer savvy, he uses a PC at work and owns a home computer as well. Attracted to LITV because it was free, he installed the service on all three of his household television sets. As a consequence, everyone in his family uses LITV. He sends e-mail through the system to supplement his discussions with business associates, professional colleagues, friends, and family, but still relies on the phone for the majority of his communications. He also accesses the Internet through LITV to search for information, but does not visit the city's Web page. Although he acknowledges that his family spends more time online as a result of having interactive television, he dislikes the limited function keyboard and would not use the service if he had to pay for it.

Our sixth interview was with an African American single mother who works in a low-level administrative position. Prior to LITV, she used a computer only minimally in her position. The decision to take up LITV was not an easy one, given her doubts about the service truly being free and a few initial problems getting the service to work. She uses LITV to e-mail friends and neighbors in the city, communicate with a niece who works nights, and reduce communication costs with a son who attends college out of town. LITV has helped her find directions to stores and other locations. She also uses it to get information about television shows and read book reviews, which informs her library visits. She was not aware of features on the city Web site. Her grandchildren are avid users of LITV, and one "goes for the keyboard first thing" when he comes to visit. She and her grandson used LITV to find educational software for a persistent problem he was having with math. She now uses the Internet in her job and has convinced family and friends to adopt the service.

Our seventh interview was with a retired teacher whose husband found a job in LaGrange through LITV. She initially took up the service to learn about the Internet and keep in touch with friends and family. She uses LITV to support her hobbies and read newsletters. She also exchanges e-mail with family in other countries, as well as with neighbors locally, so the system saves her money. When they visit, her grandchildren are ardent users of LITV. The only city-generated content used by this interviewee was the TV channel that demonstrates how to set up the service.

In summary, these interviews suggest that LITV's free availability and installation was a significant factor in user decisions to adopt the service. In a few cases, the users we interviewed would not have had Internet access without LITV. Another important motivation was computer anxiety, as discussed earlier. A few LITV adopters we talked to said they gave the service a try because they were curious about the Internet but were apprehensive about computer technology; this may be a generational issue, as most of these users were seniors. These motivations suggest that the LITV initiative is reaching some individuals who would not normally have Internet access because they do not own, or know how to operate, a personal computer.

Overall, users described general rather than specific benefits resulting from LITV. In the interviews, users mentioned improved online searching skills or more frequent use of the Internet as a result of LITV. Respondents generally valued the quick information access the system provided, but even those who had never used a computer complained that the LITV keyboard was limited. Despite their computer anxiety, they expressed a desire for a system with more technical capabilities.

Several users emphasized the appeal of e-mail over the system, especially for communicating with family and friends who lived out of town and overseas. Interestingly, in none of our interviews did LITV users report making online purchases. A few actually went out of their way to use traditional means of making reservations, although they employed the system to locate directions or learn about hotel amenities, using it to supplement the actual transaction.

The interactive TV system also made meaningful information acquisition possible. The college-bound teen we interviewed said he learned about educational programs at the local technical college, along with scholarship offerings, and decided to enroll in classes. Another respondent helped her grandchild find educational software to address a troubling math problem. Beyond educational benefits, other LITV users found value in the system by locating online sources that allowed them to explore and expand their interests. The husband of a retired teacher we interviewed used LITV to find a job. Such examples may proliferate as users gain more experience with the service.

Despite the city's efforts to develop local content, the LaGrange Web site was not widely consulted among the users we interviewed. One subject mentioned she tried to access the community links page but ran into technical problems. Another talked about using the instructional channel to set up her system. No references were made to contacting local officials by e-mail or using LITV to learn about other city services. Contrary to conventional wisdom about the need to have local information to attract users, these exploratory interviews do not show initial value to local content in a small-town setting, although the city's content efforts have not yet been fully developed.

## CONCLUSIONS

The findings reported in this chapter represent an early summary of the effects and implications of LaGrange's LITV initiative. Further controlled surveys and additional user and stakeholder interviews are planned as part of a longer study. What can we say at this point about the city's efforts to bridge the digital divide by offering the LITV service as a free public information infrastructure? With the caveat that what we present are initial findings, LaGrange's personal computer and Internet penetration rates were not significantly different from national figures, which could lead some to question whether there was a significant need for an intensive program to overcome the digital divide. If the city's telecommunications initiative is to be viewed as a success, we would certainly expect, after some further time has elapsed, that LaGrange's computer and Internet penetration rates would exceed comparable national rates (based on US Census Bureau data as discussed earlier). More than 60% of LITV households already had access to personal computers at home, work, or both. A significant minority of LITV households, 44%, were educated and affluent enough to purchase computers and use the Internet without the need for government support. Indeed, the city's economic development director said, "We expected that with the service offered free of charge, we would have big interest in communities where people had been unable to afford Internet service" (Holsendolph, 2001). Likewise, many LITV households previously had experience with other information technologies such as VCRs and cellular telephones.

One interpretation of these findings is that LITV may not have as much potential to address a perceived or real digital divide in LaGrange as the city had hoped. Households already exposed to information technology—and presumably already aware of its productive and beneficial uses—made up most of early LITV customers. Information technology adoption is more about understanding the value of technology than about cost. Even free access to the Internet is not enough to motivate many nonusers to take up the interactive television service, in part, as one of our interviews suggested, because of suspicions that the service was not really free. This finding is consistent with Kavanaugh and Patterson's (2001) studies of the Blacksburg Electronic Village and Riedel, Dresel, Wagoner, Sullivan, and Borgida's (1998) GrandNet study.

Of course, not all policy stakeholders saw LITV solely as a way to bridge the digital divide, and some had expectations for LITV that went beyond digital divide outcomes. The city manager saw LITV as part of a package of municipal telecommunications service offerings to residents and businesses that would augment city revenues. Several stakeholders viewed LITV as a way to generate new economic development opportunities in existing manufacturing industries and by attracting new high-tech firms. The city sought to market its image as a player in the information economy by promoting its World Teleport Association award and through press releases about LITV. Quite possibly, these external goals and expectations may have influenced the service's local rollout and resulting outcomes. For example, more effort may have initially been placed on press releases to outside audiences than on marketing to prospective nonusers within the city, although external promotion may have also generated local interest in LITV.

That said, the LITV service did reach a segment of its target population without prior exposure to personal computers. Although this group did not constitute a majority of the service's users, at 37 percent it is a significant minority, with LITV bringing Internet access to nearly 750 LaGrange households that previously had no such access from home or work. These households without prior personal computer experience reflected classic digital divide demographics—lower education, lower incomes, and older ages. Not surprisingly, in most of our interviews, users mentioned the importance of not having to pay for LITV in their decision to adopt the service.

Some of the LaGrange residents we interviewed with sufficient means to purchase a computer said they had not bothered out of a concern about the technology's complexity (admittedly, these residents were seniors who share a generational lack of computer exposure). Given the difficulty of convincing households with no prior PC experience to adopt an Internet access service, city policymakers' beliefs that LITV would be perceived as a less complicated way to get residents to use information technology appear correct.

In an increasingly information-driven economy, LITV is seen by several stakeholders as having important implications for the city's long-term survival. Survey respondents reported signing up for the service generally for reasons that related to enhanced electronic communications and information acquisition skills. More than half of all LITV households reported signing up for the service to communicate via e-mail or chat room. Forty-two percent of all households, and nearly half of households with working-age adults (age 30 to 60), expressed a desire to obtain specialized information (e.g., health-related or work-related information) through the service's Internet connection. There was an educational component in motivations for taking up LITV as well, as two in three households with school-age children reported signing up for the service to assist educational development. Whether skill improvement will translate into improved economic well-being remains to be seen. The subjects we interviewed showed signs of movement in this direction with reports of new jobs or expanded opportunities from enrolling in postsecondary educational programs.

At the same time, the service has not made many inroads in furthering local connections or increasing interaction with the city. Government services were not prominent among the reasons respondents gave for adopting the service; in just 28% of LITV households did users specify this motivation. Although LaGrange sought to develop a "virtual town mall" to help build e-commerce within the community, users in only 27% of LITV households said they expected to shop online. Interviews also confirmed that some users found it difficult to access the city's online community Web sites, even if some did regularly read the online version of the local newspaper. As a result of having free access to the system, users appeared to communicate more with people outside the city, and perhaps around the globe, than locally. LaGrange may find more local connections as the technical difficulties with its community Web sites are addressed, more local content is placed on these sites, and users find them more substantive and valuable. However, the ability of increased Internet access through the LITV system to introduce nonlocal influences on citizens' communications, information, and transaction patterns cannot be denied.

Overall, LaGrange's early efforts to deliver Internet access through the user-friendly medium of television could be judged as a success in reaching a segment of the population without previous information technology experience. Whether at the local, regional, or national level, telecommunications policies that emphasize widespread low cost or free provision should recognize that most beneficiaries might be those who already have the technology. Resolving the digital divide is not just a matter of delivering affordable, ubiquitous technology; it is also a matter of overcoming perceptual, attitudinal, and social barriers that prevent users from fully recognizing the technology's value.


## ACKNOWLEDGMENT

This chapter draws on early results from a longer-term research project, Impacts of Public Information Infrastructure Access. This project has received research sponsorship from the National Science Foundation (Award SES-0095191). For more information on the project, see http://www.cherry.gatech.edu/lagrange. The authors also gratefully acknowledge the cooperation of officials and residents of LaGrange, Georgia. The interpretations and judgments reported in the chapter are those of the authors and should not be ascribed to the National Science Foundation or the city of LaGrange.


## ENDNOTES

[1] The interactive television service is also offered to most cable subscribers in Troup County who live outside LaGrange city limits, but not free of charge as is the case in the city.


## REFERENCES

Anandarajan, M., Simmers, C., & Igbaria, M. (1998). An exploratory investigation of the antecedents and impact of Internet usage: An individual perspective. *Proceedings of the 31st Hawaii International Conference on System Sciences, 4,* 22–30.

Anderson, R. H., Bikson, T. K., Law, S. A., & Mitchell, B. M. (1995). *Universal access to e-mail: Feasibility and societal implications.* Santa Monica, CA: RAND.

Baker, S. (1997). Access and attitudes regarding online services among socioculturally diverse college students. *POTLATCH NECC '97 National Educational Computing Conference Proceedings* (pp. 417–424).

Brosnan, M. J. (1998). The impact of computer anxiety and self-efficacy upon performance. *Journal of Computer Assisted Learning, 14*(3), 223–235.

Bucy, E. P. (2000). Social access to the Internet. *Harvard International Journal of Press/Politics, 5*(1), 50–62.

Caputi, P. (2000). Cognitive interference in computer anxiety. *Behaviour & Information Technology, 20*(4), 265–274.

Castells, M. (1989). *The informational city: information technology, economic restructuring, and the urban-regional process.* New York: Blackwell.

Cohill, A. M. & Kavanaugh, A. L. (Eds.). (1997). *Community networks: Lessons from Blacksburg.* Virginia. Boston: Artech House.

Cowles, D. (1989). Consumer perceptions of interactive media. *Journal of Broadcasting & Electronic Media,* Winter 1989, *33*(1), 83–90.

Dupagne, M. (1990). French and US videotex: Prospects for the electronic directory Service. *Telecommunications Policy, 14*(6), 489–505.

Dutton, W. H., Blumler J. G., & Kramer K. L. (1987). Continuity and change in conceptions of the wired city. In W. H. Dutton, J. G. Blumler, & K. L. Kramer (Eds.), *Wired cities: Shaping the future of communications* (pp. 3–26). Boston: G. K. Hall & Co.

Ellis, R. D., & Allaire, J. C. (1999). Modeling computer interest in older adults: The role of age, education, computer knowledge, and computer anxiety. *Human Factors, 41*(3), 345–56.

Fullerton, H. S., & Allen, D. (1989). Rejoinder: Microeconomic theory and critical mass. *Telecommunications Policy, 13*(2), 167–170.

George, R. J. (1987). In-home electronic shopping: Disappointing past, uncertain future. *The Journal of Consumer Marketing, 4*(4), 47–57.

Gomez, R. (1998). The nostalgia of virtual community: A study of computer-mediated communications use in Colombian non-governmental organizations. *Information Technology & People, 11*(3), 217–234.

Gurstein, M. (2000). *Community informatics: Enabling communities with information and communications technologies.* Hershey, PA: Idea Group Publishing.

Guthrie, K. K., & Dutton, W. H. (1992). The politics of citizen access technology: The development of public information utilities in four cities. *Policy Studies Journal, 20*(4), 574–597.

Hampton, K. N., & Wellman, B. (1999). Netville online and offline. *American Behavioral Scientist, 43*(3), 475–493.

Hemby, K. V. (1998). Predicting computer anxiety in the business communication classroom. *Journal of Business & Technical Communication, 12*(1), 89–109.

Holsendolph, E. (2001, September 2). A Georgia city decided to provide its residents with a year of free Internet access. But only half have signed on. Why LaGrange isn't more "wired." *Atlanta Journal Constitution,* Q1.

Horrigan, J. B., & Rainie, L. (2002). *Getting serious online: As Americans gain experience, they use the Web more at work, write emails with more significant content, perform more online transactions, and pursue more activities online.* Washington, DC: Pew Internet & American Life Project. Retrieved September 24, 2002, from http://www.pewinternet.org/

Kavanaugh, A. L., & Patterson, S. J. (2001). The impact of community computer networks on social capital and community involvement. *American Behavioral Scientist, 45*(3), 496–510.

Kiesler, S., Zdaniuk, B., Lundmark, V., & Kraut, R. (2000). Troubles with the Internet: The dynamics of help at home. *Human–Computer Interaction, 15*(4), 323–352.

Kuhlman, E., & Balderjahn, I. (1989). Information-seeking behavior in interactive videotex: Training effects in an experimental investigation. *Journal of Communication Policy, 11*, 185–207.

Kraut, R., Patterson, M., Lundmark, V., Kiesler, S., Mukophadhyay, T., & Scherlis, W. (1998). Internet paradox: A social technology that reduces social involvement and psychological well-being? *American Psychologist, 53*(9), 1017–1031.

Lee, B., & Lee, R. S. (1995). How and why people watch TV: Implications for the future of interactive television. *Journal of Advertising Research, 35*(6), 9.

Levy, P. (1997). *Collective intelligence: Mankind's emerging world in cyberspace.* New York: Plenum Trade.

Markus, L. M. (1990). Towards a "critical mass" theory of interactive media. In J. Fulk & C. Steinfield (Eds.), *Organizations and communication technology* (pp. 194–218). Newbury Park, CA: Sage Publications.

Margolis, M., & Resnick, D. (2000). *Politics as usual: The cyberspace "revolution."* Thousand Oaks, CA: Sage Publications.

Masi, C. G. (1997). Developing an interactive television system that works. *Research & Development, 39*(7), 54–58.

Miles, I. (1997). Cyberspace as product space. *Futures, 29*(9), 769–789.

Mitchell, W. J. (1995). *City of bits: Space, place, and the infobahn.* Cambridge, MA: MIT Press.

Nie, N. H. & Erbring, L. (2000). *Internet and society: A preliminary report.* San Francisco: Stanford Institute for the Quantitative Study of Society. Retrieved January 31, 2001 from http://www.Stanford.edu/group/siqss/Press_Release/Preliminary_Report.pdf

Norman, D. A. (1999). *The invisible computer: Why good products can fail, the personal computer is so complex, and information appliances are the solution.* Cambridge, MA: MIT Press.

NTIA (1995, July). *Falling through the Net: A survey of the "have nots" in rural and urban America.* National Telecommunication and Information Administration, U.S. Department of Commerce. Retrieved January 23, 2002, from http://www.ntia.doc.gov/ntiahome/fallingthru.html

NTIA (1998, July). *Falling through the Net II: New data on the digital divide.* National Telecommunication and Information Administration, U.S. Department of Commerce. Retrieved January 10, 2002, from http://www.ntia.doc.gov/ntiahome/net2/

NTIA (1999, July). *Falling through the Net: Defining the digital divide.* National Telecommunication and Information Administration, U.S. Department of Commerce. Retrieved August 7, 2000, from http://www.ntia.doc.gov/ntiahome/fttn99/contents.html

NTIA (2000, July). *Falling through the Net: Toward digital inclusion.* National Telecommunication and Information Administration, U.S. Department of Commerce. Retrieved March 12, 2002, from http://www.ntia.doc.gov/ntiahome/fttn00/contents00.html

NTIA (2002, July). *A nation online: How Americans are expanding their use of the Internet.* National Telecommunication and Information Administration, U.S. Department of Commerce. Retrieved March 21, 2003, from http://www.ntia.doc.gov/ntiahome/dn/index.html

Olander, F., & Sepstrup, P. (1987). The use of electronic media for advertising and selling: A consumer policy outline. *Journal of Consumer Policy, 10*(3), 283–306.

Pew Internet & American Life Project (2000). *Tracking online life: How women use the Internet to cultivate relationships with family and friends.* Pew Research Center: Washington, DC. Retrieved July 29, 2000, from www.pewinternet.org

Read, W., & Youtie, J. (1996). *Telecommunications strategy for economic development.* Westport, CT: Praeger.

Rheingold, H. (2000). *The virtual community: Homesteading on the electronic frontier* (rev. ed.). Cambridge, MA: MIT Press.

Riedel, E., Dresel, L., Wagoner, M., Sullivan, J., & Borgida, E. (1998). Electronic communities: Assessing equality of access in a rural Minnesota community. *Social Science Computer Review* [Special Issue: Equality and inequality in information societies], *16*(4), 370–390.

Russo, J. E. (1987). Toward Intelligent Product Information Systems for Consumers. *Journal of Consumer Policy, 10*(2), 109–149.

Schuler, D. (1996). *New community networks: Wired for change.* New York: Addison Wesley.

Schwartz, E. I. (1995). People are supposed to pay for this stuff? *Wired, 3*(7). Retrieved September 24, 2002, from http://www.wired.com/wired/archive/3.07/cable.html

Sepstrup, P., & Mayer, R. N. (1988). Mayer on French videotex: Some critical observations; response to Sepstrup. *Journal of Consumer Policy, 11*(3), 335–345.

Stoll, C. (1995). *Silicon snake oil.* New York: Doubleday.

Teilhard de Chardin, P. (1964). *The future of man.* New York: Harper & Row.

Youtie, J. (2000). Field of dreams revisited: Economic development and telecommunications in La-Grange, Georgia. *Economic Development Quarterly, 14*(2), 146–153.

# 8

# Home Internet Use in Low-Income Families: Is Access Enough to Eliminate the Digital Divide?

Linda A. Jackson
Gretchen Barbatsis
Frank A. Biocca
Alexander von Eye
Yong Zhao
Hiram E. Fitzgerald
*Michigan State University*

The 20th century closed with a flurry of activity surrounding the issue of the "digital divide." The term was first used by Lloyd Morrisett, former president of the Markle Foundation, to refer to the division between the information haves and have-nots—between those who have access to digital technologies and those who do not (Hoffman & Novak, 1999). From the moment the digital divide entered the public consciousness, countless resources, both human and monetary, have been poured into reducing it, primarily by increasing access to technology (Benton Foundation, 1998; Coley, Cradler, & Engel, 1997; Cooper & Kimmelman, 1999; Harmon, 1997; Keller, 1996; Roberts, 1997; Sheppard, 1997). These efforts were motivated in part by a recognition that digital technologies are increasingly important to educational and economic outcomes in the information age (Beaupre & Brand-Williams, 1997; Educational Testing Service, 1999; Morrisette, 1999; Rutkowski, 1998; Schon, Sanyal, & Mitchell, 1999), and in part by the assumption that the digital divide is fundamentally an economic divide (Hoffman & Novak, 1998; National

Telecommunications and Information Administration [NTIA], 1995, 1998, 1999, 2000, 2002). Thus, once access to digital technologies is assured, the divide will essentially "go away."

Mixed reports and inconsistent findings about the nature and extent of the digital divide led some to question the assumption that the divide is fundamentally economic. In an invited discussion at the turn of the century, Andy Carvin, Senior Associate at the Benton Foundation's Communications Policy Program in Washington, DC, suggested that issues of literacy, broadly defined, and issues of content relevance must be addressed before access to digital technologies will result in use of technologies that eliminate the digital divide (Carvin, 2000). Supporting this view, Hoffman and Novak's (1999) in-depth analysis of three national representative surveys led them to conclude that income and education cannot explain race differences in Internet use. African Americans earning less than $40,000 annually, and African Americans at all levels of education, use the Internet less than comparable Whites. Hoffman and Novak encouraged research to shed light on the basis for race differences in Internet use that are not explained by race differences in demographic characteristics (e.g., income, education).

HomeNetToo is a research project designed to examine the sociopsychological characteristics that influence Internet use in low-income families. Participants in the project were African Americans and European Americans who agreed to have their Internet use continuously recorded, to complete surveys at multiple points during the 15-month project, and to participate in home visits during which instruction on how to use the Internet was provided. In exchange, participants received a home computer, Internet access, technical support for their computer, and help using the Internet. We report here the results of the first 6 months of home Internet access, focusing on relationships between personality, attitudes about the Internet, and Internet use. The importance of these sociopsychological characteristics and the surprising unimportance of income, speak to the issue of whether access alone will be enough to eliminate the digital divide. Ethnographic accounts of participants' experiences using the Internet reinforce quantitative findings and their implications for the access solution to the digital divide problem.

## PARTICIPANTS IN THE HomeNetToo PROJECT

Participants in the HomeNetToo project were 117 adults residing in a low-income, medium-sized, urban community in the midwestern United States.[1] They were recruited at meetings held at their children's middle school and at the Black Child and Family Institute, Lansing, MI, USA. Invitations to attend the middle school meetings were extended to all parents whose children were currently eligible for the federally subsidized school lunch program. To participate, the family had to have home telephone service for at least the previous 6 months, consent to having their

TABLE 8.1
Demographic Characteristics of Adult Participants in the HomeNetToo
Project ($n = 117$)

| | | |
|---|---|---|
| *Age* | M: 38.57 years old | Range: 19 to 75 years old |
| *Sex* | Male: 20% | Female: 80% |
| *Race* | African American: 67% | European American: 33% |

*Income (annual household)*
Less than $10,000: 28%
$10,000–$14, 999: 21%
$15,000–$24.999: 26%
$25,000–$34.999: 17%
$35,000–$49, 999: 7%
$50,000–$75,000: 1%
Greater than $75,000: 0%

*Education*
8th grade or less: 4%
Some high school but did not graduate: 10%
High school graduate or Graduate Equivalency Degree: 24%
Some college: 49%
College graduate or above: 13%

*Marital Status*
Never married: 42%
Married, living with spouse: 25%
Other (divorced, separated, widowed): 33%

Internet use continuously recorded, and agree to complete surveys and participate in home visits.

Demographic characteristics of adult participants are presented in Table 8.1. Participants were primarily African American (67%), female (80%), never married (42%), and earning less than $15,000 annually (49%; net household income). The high percentage of females and African Americans in the sample is attributable to the high percentage of female-headed, single-parent families who attended recruiting meetings and met the requirements for participation (i.e., children eligible for the federally subsidized school lunch program). The majority of participants reported having some college education or earning a college degree (62%), indicating that the sample was better educated than is typical of low-income samples (e.g., Hoffman & Novak, 1999; NTIA, 1995, 1998, 1999, 2000, 2002). Average age of participants was 38.6 years old.

A subsample of 30 adults participated in 2-hour home interviews and observations while they were actively engaged in using the Internet. Interviews were conducted as a conversation between interviewer and participant during which they explored the Internet together (Dervin, 1989). Internet use was approached as a social practice that is codetermined by and integrated with other social practices in the home (e.g., television use). Interviews were recorded unobtrusively using a small digital recorder and transcribed for content analyses.

## INTERNET USE, PERSONALITY, AND
## ATTITUDE MEASURES

Eleven measures of Internet use were automatically and continuously recorded by the server: time online, number of Internet sessions (logins), number of unique domains visited, number of e-mails sent, number of e-mails received, number of listserv messages posted, number of listserv messages received, number of newsgroup postings, number of newsgroups read, number of chats visited, and total time in chats.[2] To detect changes in Internet use and its correlates over time, Internet use measures were divided into two time periods—Time 1: first three months; Time 2: second three months. In addition, participants' self-reports of the frequency with which they engaged in a variety of Internet activities were obtained 3 months into the project (e.g., e-mailing family).

Personality characteristics were assessed by the Big Five Personality Inventory (John, 1990), which measures the following dimensions: extraversion (e.g., sociable), neuroticism (e.g., moody), conscientiousness (e.g., dependable), agreeableness (e.g., affectionate), and openness to experience (e.g., wise).

Attitudes about the Internet were assessed at pretrial and again after 3 months of home Internet access. Participants indicated the extent to which they agreed with eight statements about the Internet, four worded favorably (e.g., Using the Internet helps children to do well in school.) and four worded unfavorably (e.g., Using the Internet takes time away from family and friends).

Demographic characteristics were obtained at pretrial. Participants indicated their gender, race, income, education, and marital status using the categories depicted in Table 8.1. Previous experience using the Internet was measured at pretrial by four questions (e.g., How would you rate the extent of your experience using the Internet? 1 = not much experience, 5 = a great deal of experience).

### Frequency and Nature of Internet Use

Frequency of Internet use during the first 6 months of home Internet access is summarized in Table 8.2. Not included in the table are measures of listserv, newsgroup, and chat activities, which were essentially zero. Participants initially spent an average of 41.51 minutes a day online, participating in one session and visiting nine domains. Time online did not change significantly between the first and second time periods. Sessions became somewhat fewer and the number of domains visited became somewhat greater, but these differences were not statistically significant.

E-mail activity during the first 6 months of home Internet access was infrequent. During both time periods, participants sent about three e-mails a week.

Evident from Table 8.2 is the high variability in Internet use among project participants. For example, 25% of participants spent essentially no time online, whereas another 25% spent over 36 minutes a day online. About half the participants never used e-mail.

TABLE 8.2
Internet Use

| | | Time Online (Minutes) | Number of Sessions | Number of Domains Visited | Number of e-mails Sent | Number of e-mails Received |
|---|---|---|---|---|---|---|
| | | | | Time 1: First three months | | |
| M | | 41.51 | 1.00 | 9.05 | .39 | 1.78 |
| sd | | 87.79 | 1.47 | 13.40 | 1.07 | 3.97 |
| Percentile | 25th | 2.45 | .09 | .66 | .00 | .12 |
| | 50th | 12.25 | .47 | 3.48 | .02 | .41 |
| | 75th | 36.47 | 1.31 | 11.14 | .22 | 1.22 |
| | | | | Time 2: Second three months | | |
| M | | 43.53 | .74 | 10.94 | .36 | 3.31 |
| sd | | 96.15 | 1.03 | 17.06 | 1.36 | 8.11 |
| Percentile | 25th | 1.21 | .04 | .50 | .00 | .14 |
| | 50th | 12.70 | .34 | 4.24 | .00 | .47 |
| | 75th | 46.25 | 0.98 | 13.24 | .22 | 2.14 |

Note: Values are means per day. All measures were automatically recorded at the server. $M$ = Mean. $sd$ = standard deviation.

Participants' self-reported Internet activities after 3 months of home Internet access were consistent with automatically recorded measures of Internet use insofar as none of the activities was reported as frequent. The five most frequent activities, engaged in "sometimes," were finding information about interests/hobbies, finding information about a product, e-mailing friends, playing games, and listening to music. Note, however, that the latter two activities may be computer activities rather than Internet activities. The least frequent activities were viewing pornography, creating a Web page, and obtaining job training. On average, participants reported never engaging in these activities.

## Is Internet Access Leading to Internet Use Among Low-Income Adults?

The frequency and nature of Internet use among HomeNetToo participants raise two questions. First, are participants using the Internet as frequently as the "average" Internet user? Second, are participants engaging in similar Internet activities as the "average" Internet user? Despite the plethora of research on home Internet use, comparable statistics on frequency of Internet use and engaging in specific Internet activities are difficult to find. With respect to frequency of Internet use, only one other study, which began in 1995, automatically recorded Internet use rather than relying on self-reports of use. The Carnegie Mellon University HomeNet project, which served as a model for the HomeNetToo project, found that in Study 1 (1995–1996; 48 families; Kraut, Scherlis, Mukhopadhyay, Manning, & Kiesler, 1996) participants used the Internet about 1 hour a week, participated in two sessions a week, visited two domains a week, and sent less than 1 e-mail a week. Listserv, newsgroup, and chat activities were negligible. Comparable data for Study 2 have yet to be reported (1998–1999; 216 families; Kraut et al., 2002). Thus, in comparison to one of the HomeNet studies, HomeNetToo participants appear to be using the Internet more frequently than the "average" user. However, a number of considerations caution against this conclusion.

First, changes in the Internet since 1995–1996, when the first HomeNet study was conducted, may explain the higher frequency of Internet use by HomeNetToo participants in 2000–2001. For example, the number of Web pages has increased exponentially since 1995–1996, and more content is now aimed at the "average" Internet user, rather than the professional (e.g., computer scientists; *Internet Trends,* n.d.). Second, the original HomeNet participants may not have been representative of the "average" Internet user, despite efforts by HomeNet researchers to obtain a diverse sample. By virtue of their willingness to participate in an Internet study in 1995, HomeNet participants were early adopters of this technology. They were also better educated and more affluent than the average U.S. citizen (U.S. Census Bureau, 1996–2000).

Turning next to the comparability of Internet activities, both similarities and differences emerge between HomeNet and HomeNetToo participants. Summarizing findings from the HomeNet studies, these researchers concluded that, "People use the Internet for pleasure: to communicate with family, friends, and strangers, to track sports and popular culture, to listen to music, to play games, and to pursue specialized interests. These pleasurable uses supplement and, for many people, are more important than the practical uses of the Internet for jobs, school, and shopping." (Kraut et al., 2002). HomeNetToo participants also used the Internet for both pleasure and practical purposes. However, this simple dichotomy obscures differences in the nature of Internet use by HomeNet and HomeNetToo participants.

Research from the perspective of the uses and gratifications model in communication sciences (Blumler & Katz, 1974; Weiser, 2002; Weiss, 1971) argues that all forms of communication media should be viewed as sources of need gratification. The rationale for this argument is that to understand the effects of media use on individuals requires understanding the needs that a particular medium is intended to satisfy. With respect to the Internet, the needs most often associated with use are information, communication, entertainment, and escape (Jansen, Spink, Baterman, & Saracevic, 1998; Katz & Aspden, 1997; Kraut et al., 2002; UCLA Center for Communication Policy, 2000, 2001). Our findings suggest that HomeNetToo participants used the Internet primarily for information and entertainment whereas HomeNet participants used it primarily for information and communication.

The lesser importance of communication among HomeNetToo than HomeNet participants is most evident in the former group's infrequent use of e-mail. More than half of the HomeNetToo participants never sent an e-mail during the first 6 months of home Internet access. In contrast, HomeNet participants used the communication tools of the Internet about as often as they used its information tools.

The frequency and nature of Internet use among HomeNetToo participants may also be compared to findings of two recent and much-publicized research projects. The Stanford University Internet project reported that approximately 66% of Internet users spent less than 5 hours a week online (Nie & Erbring, 2000). The most common use of the Internet was to find information (products, travel, hobbies, and general information; 100% of users), followed by e-mail (90%). Entertainment was a distant third (33%), followed by shopping (25%) and chat (20%).

Later in 2000, UCLA published its first Internet report. Findings indicated that people spent an average of 9.42 hours a week online, primarily surfing/browsing the Web (82%) and using e-mail (82%). The next most frequent activities were finding hobby information (57%), reading news (57%), finding entertainment information (54%), and buying online (52%). Less frequent activities were finding travel information (46%), instant messaging (40%), finding medical information (37%), and playing games (33%). The second UCLA report, released in November 2001, found an increase of 0.38 hours in time spent online (i.e., 9.8 hour a week). The most popular Internet activities were e-mail and instant messaging (88%), Web surfing/browsing (76%), buying online (49%), finding entertainment information (48%), and reading news (48%). However, it is important to note that both the Stanford and UCLA projects used self-report measures of Internet use, not automatically recorded measures as in the HomeNet and HomeNetToo projects. On the other hand, both former projects have the advantage of national probability samples that better represent the behavior of the "average" Internet user than do the HomeNet and HomeNetToo samples.

Overall, comparisons between HomeNetToo and other reports of frequency of Internet use suggest that during the first 6 months of home Internet access, HomeNetToo participants used the Internet *more* than does the average Internet user, but used e-mail much less. One obvious explanation for the infrequent use of e-mail is that our low-income participants simply had fewer family and friends who had access to the Internet at home. Implications of not being able to satisfy communication needs via the Internet for sustaining Internet use in low-income groups remain to be seen. It may be that reliance on other media to satisfy communication needs will undermine Internet use in low-income families. Alternatively, as more low-income families gain access, e-mail communication with family and friends may increase, possibly replacing the use of other communication media (e.g., telephone), and sustaining Internet use.

## Personality and Internet Use

The relationship between personality and Internet use has been a topic of much discussion but little systematic research. Two prior questions must be addressed in considering this relationship. First, should there be a relationship between personality and Internet use? Second, if so, what dimensions of personality should be related to what dimensions of Internet use?

Central to answering both questions are again the uses and gratifications associated with Internet use (Jansen et al., 1998; Katz & Aspden, 1997; Kraut et al., 2002; UCLA Center for Communication Policy, 2000, 2001). As discussed earlier, using the Internet serves information, communication, entertainment, and escape needs for its users. Thus, the question of whether there should be a relationship between personality and Internet use may be reframed as a question of whether there should be a relationship between personality and the needs typically satisfied by Internet use.

The first of the Carnegie Mellon University HomeNet studies considered relationships between two personality dimensions and Internet use: social extraversion and innovativeness. Neither personality dimension accounted for differences in Internet use after controlling for demographic characteristics or socioeconomic status (Kraut et al., 1996; Kraut et al., 1998). In the second HomeNet study (Kraut et al., 2002), the consequences of Internet use were different for extraverts and introverts. For extraverts, greater use was associated with greater community involvement, compared to using the Internet rarely. For introverts, greater use was associated with less community involvement, compared to using the Internet rarely. However, it is unclear from the report whether extraverts used the Internet more or less than did introverts, or whether they used it differently.

In the HomeNetToo project, we examined relationships between the Big Five personality factors and Internet use (John, 1990). Given evidence that the Internet is used to satisfy communication needs, we expected that extraverts would use the communication tools of the Internet more often than would introverts (i.e., e-mail). Less certain were predictions about relationships between other personality dimensions and other needs satisfied by the Internet. For example, it may be that individuals who are more open to experience will use the information tools of the Internet more than will individuals less open to experience (i.e., the Web). It may be that individuals who are more neurotic will use the Internet for escape more often than will less neurotic individuals (e.g., games). However, the rationale for these predictions is more tentative than the rational for predicting a relationship between extraversion and Internet use, specifically, e-mail use.

Pearson correlations between the Big Five personality dimensions and Internet use indicated that extraversion was related to time online ($r = .20$), number of sessions ($r = .19$), and number of e-mails sent ($r = .29$) during the first 3 months of home Internet access ($ps < .05$).[3] Neuroticism was negatively related to number of Internet sessions ($r = -.22$, $p < .05$). Thus, during the first 3 months of home Internet access, more-extraverted individuals used both the Web and e-mail more often than did less-extraverted individuals. Neurotic individuals used the Web less than did more-stable individuals. However, none of the personality dimensions was related to Internet use during the second 3 months. Thus, although personality was related to early Internet use, its influence was quickly overwhelmed by other factors that motivated and sustained Internet use after the novelty of having home Internet access had waned.

## Attitudes and Internet Use

Market and media researchers, public opinion pollsters, government agencies, and academic researchers have been tracking attitudes about the Internet since the mid-1990s (e.g., GVU Center, 1999; Kehoe & Pitkow, 1997; Neilsen Media Research, 1997a, 1997b, 1998; NTIA, 1995, 1998, 1999, 2000, 2002). For example, both the Stanford and UCLA Internet studies, discussed earlier, used multiple measures of Internet attitudes, including attitudes about how using the Internet affects everyday life (e.g., family relationships). However, missing from much of this research is the link between Internet attitudes and Internet use. Although it is reasonable to expect that favorable Internet attitudes would be related to greater Internet use, and that unfavorable Internet attitudes would be related to less Internet use, the link between attitudes and behavior has eluded researchers for decades (Eagly & Chaiken, 1993). Two recent studies that considered this link found that attitudes about the importance of Internet use to achieving personal goals were related to Internet use (Jackson, Ervin, Gardner, & Schmitt, 2001a, 2001b). However, participants in these studies were a self-selected sample of college students who reported their Internet use retrospectively.

In the HomeNetToo project, participants indicated the extent to which they agreed or disagreed with favorable and unfavorable attitudes about the Internet at pretrial, and again after 3 months of home Internet access. Mean ratings are presented in Table 8.3. At pretrial, participants' strongly believed that using the Internet

TABLE 8.3
Attitudes About the Internet

|  | Pretrial | | Three Months | |
| --- | --- | --- | --- | --- |
|  | M | sd | M | sd |
| Using the Internet helps children to do better in school. | 4.14 | 1.13 | 4.26 | 0.95 |
| Internet skills will be necessary for getting good jobs in the future. | 4.00 | 1.11 | 4.28 | 0.92 |
| There is no privacy on the Internet. | 2.95 | 1.10 | 2.92 | 1.06 |
| Children can come to harm if they use the Internet. | 2.82 | 1.30 | 2.79 | 1.20 |
| Most of the information on the Internet is true. | 2.69 | 0.95 | 2.73 | 0.93 |
| Using the Internet takes time away from family and friends. | 2.45 | 1.09 | 2.26 | 1.19 |
| Using the Internet can cause health problems. | 2.06 | 1.05 | 2.00 | 1.01 |
| No one can find out what you are doing on the Internet. | 1.91 | 1.08 | 1.81 | 1.04 |

Note: 1–5 rating scales were used: Higher values indicate stronger agreement with the attitude statement. M = mean. sd = standard deviation.

helps children to do better in school, and that Internet skills will be necessary to getting good jobs in the future. Participants were moderate in their beliefs that there is no privacy on the Internet, that children can come to harm if they use the Internet, and that most of the information on the Internet is true. Participants tended not to believe that using the Internet takes time away from family and friends, that Internet use can cause health problems, and that no one can find out what you are doing on the Internet (i.e., participants believed that others can find out what you are doing on the Internet). These attitudes did not change after 3 months of home Internet access.

Relationships between pretrial Internet attitudes and Internet use are presented in Table 8.4. Believing that using the Internet can cause health problems was negatively related to all four measures of Internet use. Believing that children can come to harm if they use Internet, and that using the Internet takes time away from family and friends, were negatively related to e-mail use. Interestingly, believing that most of the information on the Internet is true, and that no one can find out what you are doing on the Internet were *negatively* related to e-mail use during the first 3 months of home Internet access.

Attitudes about the Internet were also related to Internet use during the second 3 months of home access. Once again, believing that the Internet can cause health problems was negatively related to use, but these relationships were weaker than during the first 3 months, or were not significant. In contrast, believing that most of the information on the Internet is true and that no one can find out what you are doing on the Internet were still *negatively* related to e-mail use. In addition, believing that most of the information on the Internet is true was *negatively* related to number of Internet sessions and number of domains visited. Believing that there is no privacy on the Internet was *positively* related to all measures of Internet use except e-mail use.

## Making Sense of Relationships Between Personality, Attitudes, and Internet Use

Two personality dimensions were related to Internet use during the first 3 months of home Internet access. More-extraverted participants used e-mail more than did less-extraverted participants. More-neurotic participants used the Internet less than did more-stable participants. However, after 3 months of home Internet access, personality was no longer related to Internet use. These findings suggest that fundamental dispositional characteristics, like personality, may be important in the early stages of Internet use, and perhaps technology adoption in general, but their influence quickly fades as an individual becomes more familiar with the technology and as other factors become more important in determining use.

Attitudes were related to Internet use in a number of unexpected ways. Contrary to the expectation that favorable Internet attitudes would be related to greater Internet use, there were no such relationships. Thus, although participants strongly

TABLE 8.4
Relationships Between Internet Attitudes and Internet Use

| | Time Online (Minutes) | Number of Sessions | Number of Domains Visited | Number of e-mails Sent |
|---|---|---|---|---|
| *Time 1: First three months* | | | | |
| Using the Internet helps children to do better in school. | .14 | .13 | .09 | .04 |
| Internet skills will be necessary for getting good jobs in the future. | .10 | .06 | .05 | .12 |
| There is no privacy on the Internet. | .09 | .13 | .08 | −.17 |
| Children can come to harm if they use the Internet. | −.08 | −.10 | −.06 | −.37** |
| Most of the information on the Internet is true. | −.14 | −.15 | −.16 | −.36* |
| Using the Internet takes time away from family and friends. | .08 | .05 | .05 | −.21* |
| Using the Internet can cause health problems. | −.22* | −.23* | −.24* | −.39** |
| No one can find out what you are doing on the Internet. | −.15 | −.20* | −.11 | −.27* |
| *Time 2: Second three months* | | | | |
| Using the Internet helps children to do better in school. | .10 | .09 | .11 | −.06 |
| Internet skills will be necessary for getting good jobs in the future. | .12 | .13 | .08 | .02 |
| There is no privacy on the Internet. | .20* | .20* | .26* | .08 |
| Children can come to harm if they use the Internet. | .01 | −.04 | −.09 | −.04 |
| Most of the information on the Internet is true. | −.19† | −.24* | −.24* | −.41** |
| Using the Internet takes time away from family and friends. | .15 | .10 | .01 | .11 |
| Using the Internet can cause health problems. | −.16 | −.16 | −.22* | −.25* |
| No one can find out what you are doing on the Internet. | −.12 | −.19† | −.14 | −.34** |

*Note:* Correlations are Pearson correlations between attitude measures and log transformations of Internet use measures. Attitudes were measured on 5-point rating scales; higher values indicated stronger agreement with the attitude statement.

†$p < .10$,* $p < .05$,** $p < .01$.

believed that using the Internet helps children to do better in school, and that Internet skills will be necessary to getting good jobs in the future, these attitudes were not related to how frequently they used the Internet.

Unexpected were positive relationships between seemingly unfavorable attitudes about the Internet and Internet use. Believing that others can find out what you are doing on the Internet, and that there is no privacy on the Internet, and not believing that most of the information on the Internet is true were related to *more* rather than less Internet use. One explanation for these seemingly paradoxical findings is that what appear to be unfavorable, distrusting attitudes about the Internet are actually more informed attitudes based on previous experience with the Internet. Consistent with this explanation, more experienced Internet users are more concerned about privacy and confidentiality than are less experienced users (Rosenbloom, 2000; UCLA Center for Communication Policy, 2001). To test this explanation, we re-examined relationships between this set of Internet attitudes and Internet use after controlling for previous experience.

Four measures of previous experience using the Internet were combined (arithmetic average) to create a reliable index ($\alpha = .94$). Modal and median values for the composite measure were 1.00 and 1.75, respectively, indicating that participants had little or no experience with the Internet prior to participating in the project ($M = 1.92$, $sd = 1.00$). Correlations between the composite measure of previous experience and Internet use during the first 3 months were not significant for time online, number of sessions, and number of domains visited, but were significant for e-mail use ($r = .30$, $p < .05$). During the second 3 months, previous experience was related to time online ($r = .28$), number of sessions ($r = .22$), and number of domains visited ($r = .26$; $ps < .05$), but not to e-mail use ($r = .08$, $p > .1$).

Regression analyses were performed to examine the mediational role of previous experience in the relationship between Internet attitudes and Internet use. Demographic characteristics related to both attitudes and use (i.e., age, income, education), discussed later, were included in the analyses because they, too, like previous experience, may account for relationships between Internet attitudes and Internet use. Separate regression equations were estimated for each Internet use measure for each attitude related to it, with previous experience, age, income, and education entered first, followed by the Internet attitude. Results of the 18 analyses estimating 36 regression equations indicated that, without exception, beta coefficients for the prediction of Internet use from attitudes remained significant after controlling for previous experience and demographic characteristics. Thus, neither previous experience nor demographic characteristics can account for relationships between these Internet attitudes and Internet use.

## Demographic Characteristics and Internet Attitudes

Race, gender, age, income, education, and marital status differences in Internet attitudes were examined using one-way analyses of variance.[4] Significant effects were obtained for all characteristics except education.

Race effects indicated that African Americans were less likely to believe that Internet skills will be necessary to getting good jobs in the future ($M = 3.84$) than were European Americans ($M = 4.33$; $F(1, 108) = 5.02$, $p < .05$). Females were more likely than males to believe that Internet skills will be necessary to getting good jobs in the future (females, $M = 4.13$, males, $M = 3.40$; $F(1, 108) = 5.02$, $p < .05$).

Older participants (38 years old and older) were more likely to believe that children can come to harm if they use the Internet ($M = 3.05$) than were younger participants ($M = 2.55$; $F(1, 107) = 4.18$, $p < .05$). Income was related to the belief that most of the information on the Internet is true, $F(1, 106) = 3.30$, $p < .05$, and that there is no privacy on the Internet, $F(1, 106) = 3.61$, $p < .05$. Participants in the two lowest income levels were more likely to believe that most of the information on the Internet is true than were participants in the two highest income levels (under \$10, 000, $M = 2.96$; \$10, 000 − \$14, 999, $M = 2.91$; \$15, 000 − \$24, 999, $M = 2.54$; \$25,000 and above, $M = 2.30$). Participants in the lowest income level were least likely to believe that there is no privacy on the Internet ($M = 2.66$), whereas those in the next two income levels were most likely to believe this ($Ms = 3.57, 3.04$, respectively). These groups did not differ from the highest income group ($M = 2.79$).

Participants who were married and living with spouse were more likely to believe that using the Internet takes time away from family and friends ($M = 2.89$) than were never-married participants ($M = 2.29$), or participants in the "other" marital status category (i.e., divorced, separated, or widowed, $M = 2.29$; $F(2, 108) = 3.20$, $p < .05$).

## Demographic Characteristics and Internet Use

One-way analyses of variance were used to examine demographic group differences in Internet use. Relationships among demographic characteristics were also examined using chi-square analyses. There were no gender or income effects on Internet use.

Race differences in Internet use were obtained during the second 3 months of home Internet access. African Americans spent less time online ($M = 42.08$), participated in fewer Internet sessions ($M = 0.56$), and visited fewer domains ($M = 9.12$) than did European Americans ($Ms = 46.55, 1.10, 14.73$, respectively; $F(1, 103) = 6.48$, $p < .01$; $F(1, 103) = 9.70$, $p < .01$; $F(1, 103) = 5.44$, $p < .01$, respectively). There was no race difference in e-mail use.

Chi-square analyses revealed race differences in income, $\chi^2(3) = 12.95$, $p < .01$, but not in other demographic characteristics (i.e., age, education, marital status), or in previous experience using the Internet. African Americans had lower incomes than did European Americans. However, income was unrelated to Internet use and therefore cannot explain the relationship between race and use.

Older participants (age 38 and above) engaged in fewer Internet sessions ($M = 0.62$) and visited fewer domains ($M = 8.63$) than did younger participants during the second 3 months of home Internet access ($Ms = 0.88, 13.57$, respectively; $F(1, 103) = 3.86$, $p < .05$; $F(1, 103) = 6.00$, $p < .05$, respectively). Age was related to marital status, $\chi^2(2) = 10.86$, $p < .01$. Younger participants were more likely to be never married than were older participants, whereas older participants were more likely to be divorced, separated, or widowed than were younger participants. However, age differences in marital status did not account for age differences in Internet use in the regression analyses to predict Internet use from age, controlling for marital status.

Education was related to Internet use during the second 3 months of home Internet access. Participants who were college graduates or better spent more time online ($M = 57.66$) than participants with only some college education ($M = 41.54$) or participants with only a high school education or less ($M = 41.75$; $F(1, 103) = 4.44$, $p < .05$). College or better-educated participants also engaged in more Internet sessions ($M = 0.85$) than did participants with only some college education ($M = 0.75$) or participants with only a high school education or less ($M = 0.69$; $F(1, 103) = 4.81$, $p < .05$). Education was related to income, $\chi^2(6) = 14.96$, $p < .05$. More educated participants earned more than did less educated participants.

Marital status was related to Internet use during the first 3 months of home access, but not thereafter. Never-married participants spent less time online ($M = 26.27$) than participants who were married and living with spouse ($M = 57.00$), but not significantly less time than did participants in the "other" marital category (divorced, separated or widowed: $M = 31.61$; $F(1, 103) = 3.34$, $p < .05$).

Overall, as in previous research, race, age, and education were related to Internet use (e.g., Pew Internet & American Life Project, 2000a, 2000b, 2000c; UCLA Center for Communication Policy, 2000, 2001). African Americans, older participants, and less-educated participants used the Internet less than did European Americans, younger participants, and more-educated participants, respectively. The persistence of race, age and education effects after several months of home Internet access contradicts the conclusion of Stanford researchers (Nie & Erbring, 2000) that "Once people are connected to the Net they hardly differ in how much they use it and what they use it for, except for a drop off after age 65" (p.12). In fact, relationships between race, age, education and Internet use were stronger during the second 3 months of home Internet access than they were initially. These findings challenge the view that providing access to digital technology will be sufficient to overcome demographic barriers to Internet use.

Income was unrelated to Internet use, contrary to previous research (e.g., GVU Center, 1999; Nielsen Media Research, 1997a, 1997b, 1998; UCLA Center for Communication Policy, 2000, 2001). However, the absence of income effects may be attributable to characteristics of the HomeNetToo sample, which was relatively homogeneous with respect to (low) income, compared to samples used in previous research. Gender was unrelated to Internet use in our research. Previous findings for gender have been mixed, although more recent studies find no gender differences in frequency of Internet use, but differences in the nature of Internet use (Jackson et al., 2001b; Morahan-Martin, 1998; Pew Internet & American Life Project, 2000a, 2000b).

## ETHNOGRAPHIC ACCOUNTS OF PARTICIPANTS' EXPERIENCES WITH THE INTERNET

Content analysis of transcribed 2-hour interviews with 30 participants revealed four clusters of general subject matter categories (Holsti, 1969). The first cluster, Using the Internet, accounted for 46% of the conversational content and is the focus of this discussion.[5] Within this cluster, participants talked about how they used the Internet, concerns about the Internet, frustrations with using the Internet, and obstacles encountered while using the Internet.

### How Participants Used the Internet

Participants' talk about how they used the Internet accounted for 28% of the conversational content. Four categories were identified that encompassed how participants made sense of the Internet as a presence in their daily lives: interpersonal communication, parenting support, practical information, and another diverse category that included such uses as refuge and image source.

*Interpersonal Communication.* Communication was a primary strategy of understanding that emerged from participants' engagement with the Internet. Among those who used e-mail, the Internet made sense as a communication devise, often as an alternative to the expense of long distance phoning and the preparation necessary for letter writing. For some, it was meaningful for maintaining friendships:

> To me the e-mail has been the best part.

> We were able to communicate with each other, and caught up, and with the exception of catching each other's tears, we were able to communicate without a phone bill after all those years.

> I don't have to search the house for a phone book, I can go straight to the computer for it. I don't have to be running around looking for a typewriter. I can do it right here; it's all right here.

Participants also made sense of the Internet in ways that achieved different and sometimes novel approaches to their interpersonal communication practices. For one participant, writing rather than speaking served to stimulate the creative muse, and she good-naturedly warned:

> Anyone I have given my e-mail to, be prepared because you will get a novel. I can express myself better when I am writing or typing. I really like e-mail.

On the other hand, talking with strangers did not make sense to too many participants, particularly African American participants. Some expressed a purposeful nonuse of chat rooms. As one woman said:

> I don't like it . . . I don't talk to people I don't know. I have people I can talk to, so no, I don't go to the chat room.

In addition, the subject matter of many chat rooms was not meaningful to participants who had either heard about or visited them:

> I would definitely shut it right off if I thought the wrong question or anything came about. But see, why even put yourself in that situation if you think that might happen?

*Parenting Support.*   Participants readily made sense of the Internet as a parenting tool and, as such, its most significant meaning was access to resources so that homework could be completed at home rather than having to arrange library access. Freed from these constraints, parents felt they were better able to level the educational playing field for their children. As one parent said:

> If it weren't for this, that meant that I had to go in my car, go to the library, and if you get to go to the computer . . . because there's only so many there, you know. That was one thing that was really helpful. That worked a lot. That really helped.

Parents also attributed a basic sense of social literacy to the Internet:

> This is the future of our kids, this is what the world's going to; to survive our future is right here.

*Practical Information.*   Participants made sense of the Internet as a personalized source of practical information to meet specific, individualized needs:

> It's allowed us to access information we'd normally wouldn't have, we'd have to go out of our homes for, so that helps us; it's served a very good purpose.

> I can just sit here and you see how big it is, the inside; it's like all this is knowledge and I want this knowledge and there's so much in there and I just want to learn it.

*Other Sense-Making Uses of the Internet.*   Participants made sense of the Internet as a place of personal retreat. Some found this refuge meaningful as a way to fill time, relieve boredom, or transition from one activity to another:

> When somebody's on the computer whatever it is they're doing on that computer at that time, that's the world they're in . . . it's another world."

> I escape on the computer all the time . . . I like feeling 'connected to the world' and I can dream."

The most inclusive pattern, however, was the sense made of the Internet as a refuge from tension and as a means of stress relief. Typical are the words of one woman, who said:

> If I'm stressed out or depressed or the day is not going right, I just get on the computer and just start messing around and I come up with all sorts of things like "okay, wow!"

In addition to the Internet as refuge, some participants made sense of Internet access as an image enhancer. Just having it was meaningful:

> You get a lot of respect because you have a computer in your house. I just think it makes us look more progressive.

## Concerns About the Internet

Along with participants' meaningful embrace of the Internet's usefulness, there was also a sense of some very real dangers associated with it. Participants were distressed by a sense of the Internet as pernicious, and their primary focus was on their responsibilities as parents. Parenting concerns included talk about the "bad stuff out there," about pornographic and sexual predators, and about the unwanted temptation the Internet posed for their children.

*Predators.* In addition to specific concerns about pornography and about what goes on in chat rooms, some participants had a general sense of the Internet as a place "out there" that contained "bad stuff:"

> At first I thought it was like a danger zone, when they talk about the Internet. I thought it was a way of looking for trouble. Like steal your kid or some weirdo could come and kidnap you and kill you.

> I just tell them there are some things in the computers that are bad, that you have to be careful with ... you can find a lot of things on the computer, things you wouldn't think you could see, in the computer you can find it.

Participants were particularly outraged with their sense that predatory pornographers inhabited the Internet. As one father reported:

> The very first time we got this my daughter got on it and she went to White House dot com thinking she was going to the White House, but that's White House dot gov, but we didn't know this and it was a porno site. And I thought this was really outrageous, that they put it so close, knowing that children go there so much ... I was pretty ticked off about it. I think that was intentional on the people who made the site. They're dirty people. ... I thought it was pretty pathetic that they would do something like that ... that was low.

Participants also understood the chat room as a predatory space, both for themselves and their children:

> This word right here scares me ... "chat" ... because I like to know who I'm communicating with. But at the same time they can never find out who I am, but still ... Just watching the TV, things that have happened ... bad things. I don't see good things happen to them. I just rather for me and my family not to chat. Especially my girls.

> I have talked to them about chat lines and stuff, and you shouldn't get on to nothing like that because you don't know who you're talking to. Whether they sound friendly or not, you don't even know who you're talking to.

Even chatrooms that might have seemed safe were sometimes disappointing:

> This is kind of confusing because when you go to the Christian chat rooms they're doing the same thing as the regular chat rooms. Language-wise and trying-to-find-a-mate-wise, it's kind of the same. And you hear a lot of different things on it.

Some participants had a sense that the Internet created issues of parent–child trust. Although they recognized a need to set guidelines and monitor their children's Internet use, they also recognized the need to trust their children:

> Any time they're on the computer, I worry that they're seeing something they're not supposed to, but she'll tell me "mama, don't worry."

> You have to have some trust in your children, but then again you have to be a parent and realize that children are going to make mistakes, and they're going to do things, and they are easily influenced.

Parents sought various means of finding some sense that, as one parent said, "I can control this." As another reported:

> I know how to go into the computer and look up what's been looked up on the web site for the last three weeks ... I know how to go to the history and pull up a page ... I just, for my personal, I want to know what they're looking at. I like to monitor.

Others attempted to harness the technology to assist them, but were uniformly disappointed with the results. One user's words were common knowledge:

> We can control pornography on here, but then it limits what we can do.

> If I block them, they can't do their homework. I found that out. They can't get into what they really need to get into.

*Peril.* Some users, but particularly low-skill users, sensed a danger of addiction and isolation about the Internet. One person called it "hypnotic." Others commented that:

> The more you deal with the computer it seems like it clings to you and you want to get deeper into it, so actually I run from it because I could get stuck to it.

I heard of people having mental problems [when they] get on and don't know how to get off or cook dinner or go to work.

Participants also had a sense of the Internet as a risky place to reveal personal and private information, such as credit card, address, and telephone information. One participant questioned the validity of information available on the Internet:

The scary thing about the computer is anybody can put anything on the computer, and there is something in the written word. Hopefully my kids won't suffer from this, but there's something about putting things in writing that makes it believable to people.

*Frustrations with the Internet.* Although participants envisioned a place for the Internet in the practices of their daily lives, its actual as well as potential usefulness was frequently accompanied by a sense of its deficiencies. It failed to perform as expected. It failed to understand or help the user.

*Faulty performance.* Unlike their experiences with other media that were seamlessly integrated into daily life, there was a sense of obtrusiveness about the Internet. Whereas television, radio, and telephone responded instantaneously to their commands, the Internet made them wait:

I used to call my kids to ask them what's wrong, and they're like "Mom, you still have the hour glass there."

Some participants developed strategies for dealing with this performance deficiency:

It takes a while to move from site to site . . . and sometimes when I am waiting I'll get up and grab something to eat and drink . . . and I'll still be waiting.

Sometimes it freezes up and I can be in the middle of looking for something or playing a game or something or reading and I'll be "Oh, no, not now!" But I'll just have to wait until it passes, so I wait and then try again and sometimes right again.

I've learned to adapt, I'll sit back . . . I give myself more extra time.

Others simply vented their frustrations:

How frustrated I get when I go on the Internet and I get mad and I shut it off and about fifteen minutes I'll come back and get on again and get mad and shut it off . . . pouncing and stomping up the stairs.

*Inadequate Guidance.* Participants recognized that there was a learning curve associated with using the Internet. As participants said:

That gets frustrating because I don't know everything about the computer yet.

Like I said, my technology words aren't clear.

Nevertheless, they expected the computer itself to be more helpful in guiding them through its processes. They thought it should be a partner that would know and be responsive to their needs and understand their intentions. And they were uniformly disappointed:

> Computers are supposed to be pretty smart, they say. I feel like it's supposed to be showing me things that make sense. I don't know if it's just not loading, or the computer don't figure out what I put down.

> I don't know what the word is because I don't know the computer verbiage ... I get frustrated ... just give me the information!

> Sometimes I get this prompt that says "Save Mode." Everything would be different, you couldn't print, you couldn't access the Internet. I couldn't figure it out.

> I also don't like when it says "you have a debug error, do you want to fix it now?" And I hate that. No answer ... then it redials on you.

Some users found the instructions for using and fixing software applications inadequate. As one user explained:

> We've been having problems with this thing right here and it tells you what to do and how to test it and if you do what it tells you to do and it still doesn't work, you're stuck. I got stuck on that.

Another said:

> I tried to build my own web site ... it just frustrated me. I just couldn't do what I wanted, I just couldn't figure certain things out. I did everything it said to do and I still couldn't do it.

***Duplicit.*** Many participants had a sense that the Internet delivered less than was claimed or implied. Users found the commercialization of the Internet in conflict with its implied promise as a great information resource. For some, it was disappointing to discover that access to content might require payment. For others, it was a more general annoyance with the intrusiveness of advertisements.

> I was bummed out when I saw it. When it popped up I was excited but when I clicked on it and saw I had to pay $30. I was let down.

> I wish they didn't have these things here ... I don't want to go ... I know some people would like to, and look at a 2 percent credit card, but I'm not so.

***Obstacles to Internet Use.*** Many participants had a sense of the Internet as alien and enigmatic. Its logic did not make sense to them. It appeared to be working in a foreign language. Using the Internet generated apprehension about what one might do to "mess-up" the technology. For the most part, these obstacles were attributed to the limitations of the user rather than to the performance of the Internet. But some participants did blame the technology itself.

*Alien Logic.* The logic of the Internet was not intuitive for participants. Far from it:

> It just seems so, I don't know, convoluted or something.

> I know how to find what I need usually, but in this medium ... I don't really. It's less familiar, it's not comfortable.

> But I don't think I really understand the Internet. I feel there's some sort of secret behind using it.

The language system of the Internet seemed foreign to many participants. They had a sense that it consisted of jargon and codes that baffled the imagination and did not seem to be defined anywhere. Faced with this discontinuity, users said:

> I feel like I somehow don't have the right words, or that it's just too narrow.

> I always have to find out the way to abbreviate some of the ways you get in, like I needed to go back to school to get the correct stuff.

Formal instruction was not uniformly the answer to decoding the Internet. As one user lamented:

> I never cried here ... but in that class, it was like Chinese, and this was supposed to be an introduction ... and I didn't know how to click ... "On an icon?" An icon is something in church ... Mary and Jesus is what I saw growing up.

*Apprehension.* Using the Internet meant being afraid of making a "fatal" mistake.

> I was afraid to touch it. I guess what I was afraid of was getting on there and messing everything up, of deleting everything.

> I don't know, I don't know how to put it in words. It was like I wanted to get right to it, but then again I didn't want to do anything wrong and mess it up.

> I don't ever unplug it. I don't mess with it.

> I am not very comfortable with the technology itself ... I feel like I am going to break it. I am always afraid of doing something wrong.

*High-Maintenance Learning.* Participants who lacked computer experience were adrift in their early attempts to use the Internet. Relying on their children for instruction did not always work:

> My kids get tired of telling me. They just want to get me to where I want to go, do what I gotta do, and then say "get off so I can get to my instant chat." So they don't want to take me step by step, and I get frustrated, then I frustrate them, and then we'll both quit ... then I'm mad at the computer because I don't understand the computer ... I'll say "just forget it!"

Other participants reiterated this sense of wanting to use the Internet, but not having the tools they needed to bridge that gap:

> You know regular people like me, who want a computer, what would they do without support?

> I mean I'm trying to learn, but I don't know how.

At the same time, participants also recognized that learning how to use the Internet was time consuming. It required practice. It meant finding and devoting time to using it. One person's story is rather typical:

> A lot of times I'm real busy, and it was hard for me to get a turn on the computer too. My best chance of getting time on the computer is I get up at six am and the rest of the family gets up at seven. So if I finish my bath and get ready quickly I can get on before anyone else is up. And I can have an hour space to do whatever I want while they're sleeping and getting up and dressed themselves.

For others, there was just not enough time anywhere in the ongoing requirements of their daily lives for using the Internet. Several participants characterized this sense of discontinuity between their daily life activities and using the Internet:

> I feel like I don't have time . . . who has time to watch or play with these machines?

> Kids will just start clicking . . . but I don't have the patience or the time to get to clicking and clicking and clicking and clicking . . . or I may go through the first ten sites and then I say forget it. I don't have time . . . That's what I say, "I don't have time for this."

Overall, ethnographic accounts of participants' experiences with the Internet highlight the pleasures and problems they encountered in using it at home. The Internet was a pleasure in many ways. For some, it facilitated communication that would otherwise be costly or inconvenient. For all, it allowed more convenient access to information that their children needed for school, helping them to level the educational playing field. But participants encountered problems with the Internet: problems of inappropriate content (i.e., pornography), problems getting the Internet to behave as they expected, and problems finding the time to learn how to use the Internet and then use it.

The fact that participants used the Internet despite these problems may be attributable in part to the high level of technical and instructional support available through the project. In addition to regularly scheduled home visits, project staff made additional visits to address specific problems called in to the project help-line. Problems included accessing e-mail, installing and uninstalling software, and responding to inscrutable error messages. Many participants had no "mental model" of the computer and were unable to fix even the most minor problems on their own. Those who used the computer more frequently and engaged in more varied activities were also more likely to run into problems. Without technical and instructional support, it seems likely that at least some HomeNetToo participants would have used the Internet much less or given up using it altogether.

## SUMMARY AND IMPLICATIONS

Low-income adults given home Internet access make use of the technology, primarily as an information tool and to support parenting. Participants in the Home-NetToo project used the Internet about 42 minutes a day during the first 6 months of home Internet access. They participated in one session a day and visited about 10 domains a day. Internet activities focused on the information and entertainment functions of the Internet, and not on its function as a communication tool. On average, participants sent only three e-mails a week.

An explanation for the low level of e-mail use may lie in participants' self-reports of Internet activities. Participants reported that they seldom used e-mail to communicate with family members, in contrast to the "average" Internet user, who ranks e-mail communication with family as among the most frequent and satisfying uses of the Internet (Kraut et al., 1998; UCLA Center for Communication Policy, 2000, 2001). The low level of e-mail communication with family members among HomeNetToo participants may be attributable in part to the fact that few had family members who had home Internet access.

Mailing list, newsgroup, and chat activities were also infrequent among Home-NetToo participants. Ethnographic accounts of how participants made sense of the Internet provide one explanation for their infrequency. Communicating with strangers did not make sense to many participants. They questioned the value of spending time and effort in such pursuits. As several participants commented: "I don't have time . . . That's what I say, I don't have time for this." "There's so much more in life to do." "I don't talk to people I don't know. I have people I can talk to, so no, I don't go to the chat room." African American participants, in particular, were disinclined to communicate with strangers. For them, communication with strangers raised concerns about duplicity and the danger of sexual predators who might harm their children or themselves.

Another explanation for the infrequency of mailing list, newsgroup, and chat activities, and possibly of e-mail activity is that these activities required somewhat greater Internet skills than did Web activities. Many participants in the HomeNet-Too project had difficulty using the Internet. They were frustrated by its inscrutable logic, its inability to understand their intentions, its slow, plodding pace, and its unreliability: "It just seems so, I don't know, convoluted or something." "It's less familiar, it's not comfortable." "I feel there's some sort of secret behind using it." "Computers are supposed to be pretty smart, they say. I feel like it's supposed to be showing me things that make sense." The combination of user skill deficits and deficiencies in the Internet itself may have discouraged more ambitious and time-consuming activities such as newsgroups and chat.

Personality was related to Internet use during the first few months of home Internet access, but not thereafter. Extraverts initially used e-mail more than did introverts. More-neurotic individuals engaged in fewer Internet sessions than less-neurotic individuals. However, the initial effects of personality disappeared after 3 months of home Internet access. These findings are consistent with those of the HomeNet project, which reported no effects of social extraversion after 18 months of Internet use and after controlling for demographic characteristics (Kraut et al., 1996). They also suggest that fundamental dispositional characteristics, like personality, may be important in the early stage of Internet use, but less important as an individual becomes more familiar with the technology and as other factors, such as the ability of the Internet to satisfy important needs, become more important to use.

Attitudes about the Internet were related to Internet use in a number of unexpected ways. First, favorable attitudes, which were strongly held by our participants, were unrelated to Internet use. In particular, although participants strongly believed that using the Internet helps children to do better in school, and that Internet skills will be necessary to getting good jobs in the future, these beliefs were unrelated to how frequently they used the Internet. Second, unfavorable attitudes about the potential harm that could come to children who used the Internet, and about health risks associated with using the Internet, were related to less Internet use. However, these relationships were stronger initially than after 3 months of home Internet access. Moreover, these attitudes were not strongly held by participants.

Third, seemingly unfavorable attitudes about privacy and confidentially on the Internet were related to greater, not less Internet use. Specifically, believing that others can find out what you are doing on the Internet, and that there is no privacy on the Internet, and not believing that most of the information on the Internet is true, were related to more rather than less Internet use. Controlling for previous experience using the Internet, age, income, and education did not eliminate the effects of these attitudes on Internet use.

These surprising relationships between attitudes and Internet use are explicable if attitudes about privacy and the reliability of information on the Internet are viewed as informed attitudes, rather than unfavorable or distrusting attitudes. Consistent with this view, in national surveys more experienced Internet users express more concern about privacy and confidentiality than do novice users (e.g., UCLA Center for Communication Policy, 2001). These more informed attitudes are apparently not based on previous experience using the Internet. Few HomeNetToo participants had much experience using the Internet prior to participating in the project. Moreover, previous experience did not mediate relationships between attitudes about privacy and reliability of information and Internet use.

We suggest that other mass media, such as television or newspapers, may be the source of participants' attitudes about the Internet. It may be that heavy media users are more informed about the Internet, including information about privacy and information reliability, and are also more likely to use the Internet. Additional research is needed to identify the source of people's attitudes about the Internet and whether attitudes are causally related to Internet use. What is noteworthy about our findings is that informed attitudes about the Internet, even attitudes about its potential liabilities, were positively related to use. Thus, efforts to encourage use of the Internet should include the provision of information about both the liabilities and benefits of using it.

Demographic characteristics were related to Internet use in ways that raise concerns about whether access alone will be enough to eliminate the digital divide. African Americans used the Internet less than did European Americans a difference that increased with time (Pew Internet & American Life Project, 2000c). More educated participants used the Internet more than did the less educated participants, and this difference remained stable over time (GVU Center, 1999; Media Metrix, 2000; Nielsen Media Research, 1997a, 1997b, 1998; UCLA Center for Communication Policy, 2000, 2001). Older participants used the Internet less than did younger participants, and this difference increased with time. These findings contradict the conclusion of Stanford researchers (Nie & Erbring, 2000) that "Once people are connected to the Net they hardly differ in how much they use it and what they use it for, except for a drop off after age 65" (p.12).

Income and gender had no effect on frequency of Internet use (cf. Morahan-Martin, 1998; GVU Center, 1999). The absence of income effects may be attributable to characteristics of our sample, which was relatively homogeneous with respect to (low) income. Moreover, most studies demonstrating income effects have focused on Internet access rather than Internet use (e.g., GVU Center, 1999). Thus, our findings suggest caution in generalizing results from predominantly European American samples to other racial/ethnic groups, and drawing conclusions about Internet use based on research about Internet access.

Ethnographic accounts of participants' experiences with the Internet enrich and extend quantitative findings in important ways. They underscore the need for technology to better address the needs of the user. They also speak to the value of combining quantitative and qualitative measures in the same study.

Participants' talk about how the Internet fit into their everyday lives indicated that, despite an infrequent use of e-mail, some participants did embrace the Internet as a communication tool. As one participant said, ". . . with the exception of catching each other's tears, we were able to communicate without a phone bill after all those years." Had we collected only quantitative data, the importance of e-mail to at least some participants would have been lost.

All participants made sense of the Internet as an information tool, primarily to support parenting. Consistent with the quantitative results, participants talked about finding information on the Internet as one of their most frequent Internet activities. Extending the quantitative findings, they talked about the convenience of having this information resource in their homes, and about how having a home computer and Internet access helped to level the educational playing field for their children: "It's allowed us to access information we'd normally wouldn't have, we'd have to go out of our homes for, so that helps us. . . ." "This is the future of our kids, this is what the world's going to; to survive our future is right here."

For some participants, the Internet provided a welcome escape from the stresses of everyday life: "I escape on the computer all the time . . . I like feeling 'connected to the world' and I can dream." Still others derived status from having the technology in their homes: "You get a lot of respect because you have a computer in your house." These accounts of participants' subjective experiences with the Internet go beyond the quantitative finding that people use the Internet for pleasure (e.g., Kraut et al., 2002).

On the other hand, conversations with participants about how they made sense of the Internet in their homes also revealed a "dark side" to the Internet. For some participants, the Internet was potentially predatory and perilous, particularly for their children: "At first I thought it was like a danger zone, when they talk about the Internet. . . .like steal your kid or some weirdo could come and kidnap you and kill you." "I didn't know it [pornography] was that easy to access." Participants developed a variety of strategies for coping with these concerns. Some routinely monitored their children's Internet use. Others attempted to harness the technology designed for the task (i.e., filtering software), but were generally unsuccessful and disappointed. In contrast, quantitative results indicated that, participants did not endorse the belief that children can come to harm if they used the Internet, but rather were neutral with regard to this belief. Moreover, the extent to which they endorsed this statement was unrelated to their own Internet use. Taken together, the results suggest that parents found ways of coping with the potential dangers of the Internet for their children, ways that did not involve banning the technology from use in their homes.

Early findings from the HomeNetToo project reported here have implications for the design of technology if universal use of the Internet, not just universal access, is to be achieved. First, new technology is needed that is better able to assist the user through its processes. This new technology must go beyond more efficient ways to retrieve information to a better understanding of the mind of the user—his or her questions, intentions, and goals. Said another way, we need technology that can think like the user (Baecker, Grudin, Buxton, & Greenberg, 1996; Green, Davies, & Gilmore, 1996; Nickerson, 1995; Oviatt & Cohen, 2000; Rudsill, Lewis, Polson, & McKay, 1996).

Second, new technology is needed that allows parents to better control the content of the Internet that comes into their homes. Currently available filtering software is not up to the task. As our participants learned, this software blocks both desirable and undesirable content and renders the Internet more frustrating to use—slower, less reliable, and more confusing than it already is for many new users, and for some old ones as well.

At a more general level, findings from the HomeNetToo project highlight the need for user-oriented design, not just for Internet applications but for information and communications technology in general (Carroll, 1992; National Science &

Technology Council, 1999; Norman, 1988; Shneiderman, 1992). Both hardware and software design have thus far been driven by a limited set of users, namely, well-educated professionals, often in information technology fields. As the Internet and other digital technologies extend their reach to every point on the globe, the need to adapt design to user characteristics becomes all the more urgent. Now is a propitious time to begin an assessment of user characteristics, including cultural and sociopsychological characteristics important in using digital technology, and to develop guidelines for user-oriented design that will maximize the benefits of technology for all.

## ACKNOWLEDGMENT

This research was supported by a National Science Foundation-Information Technology Research Grant, #0085348, titled "HomeNetToo: Motivational, affective and cognitive factors and Internet use: Explaining the digital divide and the Internet paradox." September 1, 2000 to September 30, 2003.

## ENDNOTES

[1] Approximately 140 children of the 117 adult participants discussed in this report participated in the project. Automatically recorded measures of their Internet use, project survey measures at multiple points in time, and school performance measures have been obtained for these children.

[2] Although time online is generally considered a crude index of Internet use, it is an informative measure in this sample for two reasons. First, participants in the HomeNetToo project had only one telephone line. Second, other data, to be reported elsewhere, indicated that participants used the telephone a great deal. Thus, it seems unlikely that they would remain connected to the Internet if they were not using it.

[3] Because Internet use measures were highly skewed, log transformations were used in the analyses.

[4] For the analyses, age was categorized at two levels (under 38 years old and 38 years old and older), income was categorized at four levels (1 = under $10,000; 2 = $10,000 − $14,999; 3 = $15,000 − $24,999; 4 = $25,000 and above, gross annual household income), education was categorized at three levels (1 = high school education or less; 2 = some college; 3 = college graduate or above), and marital status was categorized at three levels (1 = never married, 2 = married, living with spouse; 3 = other—divorced, widowed).

[5] The remaining three clusters were friendliness of the Internet (familiarity, design preferences), integration of the Internet (location in the home, effect on family), and engagement with the Internet (processes of interaction, creative activity).

## REFERENCES

Baecker, R., Buxton, W., Greenberg, S., & Grudin, J. (1996). *Human–computer interaction: Towards the year 2000.* San Francisco: Morgan-Kaufman.

Beaupre, B., & Brand-Williams, C. (1997, February 8). Sociologists predict chasm between black middle-class, poor will grow. *The Detroit News*, B23.

Benton Foundation (1998). *What's going on? Losing ground bit by bit: Low-income communities in the Information Age*. Retrieved October 23, 1998, from http://www.benton.org/Library/Low-Income/

Blumler, J. G., & Katz, E. (1974). *The uses of mass communication*. Thousand Oaks, CA: Sage.

Carroll, J. M. (Ed.). (1991). *Designing interaction: Psychology at the human–computer interface*. Cambridge: Cambridge University Press.

Carvin, A. (2000, January/February). Mind the gap: The digital divide as the civil rights issue of the new millenium. *Multimedia Schools*. The Benton Foundation. Washington, DC. Retrieved November 10, 2001, from http://www.infotoday.com/mmschools/jan00/carvin.htm

Coley, R. J., Cradler, J., & Engel, P. K. (1997). *Computers and classrooms: The status of technology in U.S. schools*. Educational Testing Service Policy Information Report. ETS Policy Information Center, Princeton, NJ. Retrieved August 23, 2000, from www.eds.org/research/pic/compclass.html

Cooper, M., & Kimmelman, G. (1999, February). *The digital divide confronts the Telecommunications Act of 1996: Economic reality versus public policy*. The First Triennial Review, Consumers Union. Retrieved September 10, 2000, from http://www.consunion.org/other/telecom4-0299.htm

Dervin, B. (1989). Audience as listener and learner, teacher and confidante: The sense-making approach. In R. Rice & C. Atkin (Eds.), *Public communication campaigns* (2nd ed., pp. 67–86). Newberry Park, CA: Sage.

Eagly, A. H., & Chaiken, S. (1993). *The psychology of attitudes*. Orlando, FL: Harcourt, Brace, Jovanovich.

Educational Testing Service (1999). *The status of technology in U.S. schools*. Educational Testing Service Policy Information Report. ETS Policy Information Center, Princeton, NJ. Retrieved September 10, 2000, from http://www.ets.org/research/pic/compclass.html

Green, T. R. G., Davies, S. P., & Gilmore, D. J. (1996). Delivering cognitive psychology to HCI: The problems of common language and knowledge transfer. *Interacting with Computers, 8*, 89–111.

GVU Center. (1999). *GVU's 1$^{st}$–10$^{th}$ World Wide Web User Surveys*. Graphics, Visualization, & Usability Center. Georgia Institute of Technology, World Wide Web (WWW) User Survey Home Page. Retrieved August 23, 2000, from http://www.gvu.gatech.edu/user_surveys/

Harmon, A. (1997, October 25). Internet's value in U.S. schools still in question. *New York Times*, p. A1.

Hoffman, D. L., & Novak, T. P. (1998). Bridging the racial divide on the Internet. *Science, 280*, 390–391.

Hoffman, D. L., & Novak, T. P. (1999). *The evolution of the digital divide: Examining the relationship of race to Internet access and usage over time*. Paper presented at the "Understanding the digital economy: Data, tools and research" conference. U.S. Government Working Group on Electronic Commerce. Retrieved November 15, 2001, from http://www2000.ogsm.Vanderbilt.edu

Holsti, O. (1969). *Content analysis for the social sciences and humanities*. Reading, MA: Addison-Wesley.

*Internet Trends—August '99*. (n.d.) Retrieved December 6, 2000, from http://www.ngi.org/trends.htm

Jackson, L. A., Ervin, K. S., Gardner, P. D., & Schmitt, N. (2001a). The racial digital divide: Motivational, affective, and cognitive correlates of Internet use. *Journal of Applied Social Psychology, 31*, 2019–2046.

Jackson, L. A., Ervin, K. S., Gardner, P. D., & Schmitt, N. (2001b). Gender and the Internet: Women communicating and men searching. *Sex Roles, 44*, 363–380.

Jansen, B. J., Spink, A., Baterman, D., & Saracevic, T. (1998, November). *Searchers, the subjects they search, and sufficiency: A study of a large sample of Excite searches*. Proceedings of WebNet98—World Conference of the WWW, Internet & Intranet (p. 52), Orlando, FL.

John, O. P. (1990). The "Big Five" factor taxonomy: Dimensions of personality in the natural language and in questionnaires. In L. Pervin (Ed.), *Handbook of personality theory and research* (pp. 261–275). New York: Guilford.

Katz, J. E., & Aspden, P. (1997). Motivations for and barriers to Internet usage: Results of a national public opinion survey. *Internet Research: Electronic Networking Applications and Policy, 7*(3), 170–188.

Kehoe, C. M., & Pitkow, J. E. (1997). Surveying the territory: GVU's five WWW user surveys. *The World Wide Web Journal, 1*, 15–21.

Keller, J. (1996). Public access issues: An introduction. In B. Kahin & J. Keller (Eds.), *Public access to the Internet* (pp. 34–45). Cambridge, MA: MIT Press.

Kraut, R., Kiesler, S., Boneva, B., Cummings, J., Helgeson, V., & Crawford, A. (2002). Internet paradox revisited. *Journal of Social Issues, 58*(1), 49–74.

Kraut, R., Patterson, M., Lundmark, V., Kiesler, S., Mukopadhyay, T., & Scherlis, W. (1998). Internet paradox: A social technology that reduces social involvement and psychological well-being? *American Psychologist, 53*, 1017–1031.

Kraut, R., Scherlis, W., Mukhopadhyay, T., Manning, J., & Kiesler, S. (1996). The HomeNet field trial of residential Internet services. *Communications of the ACM, 39*, 55–66.

Media Metrix (2000, August). *The dollar divide: Demographic segmentation and Web usage patterns by household income.* Retrieved September 23, 2000, from http://www.mediametrix.com/press/releases/20000821.jsp

Morahan-Martin, J. (1998). Males, females, and the Internet. In J. Gackenbach (Ed.), *Psychology and the Internet* (pp. 169–198). San Diego, CA: Academic Press.

Morrisette, S. (1999, January). Consumer's digital decade. *Forrester Research Reports, 2(2)*, 32–35.

National Science and Technology Council. (1999). *Networked computing for the 21st century.* Subcommittee on Computing, Information Technology and Communications Research & Development. Washington, DC: National Research Council.

Nickerson, R. S. (Ed.). (1995). *Emerging needs and opportunities for human factors research.* Washington, DC: National Academy Press.

Nie, N. H., & Erbring, L. (2000). *Internet and society: A preliminary report.* Stanford Institute for the Quantitative Study of Society. Stanford University, Stanford, CA. Retrieved September 10, 2001, from http://www.stanford.edu/group/siqss/Press_Release/Preliminary_Report.pdf

Nielsen Media Research. (1997a). *The spring '97 CommerceNet/Nielsen Media Internet demographic survey* (Full Report). Northbrook, IL: A. C. Nielsen Co.

Nielsen Media Research. (1997b). *The fall '97 CommerceNet/Nielsen Media Internet demographic survey* (Full Report). Northbrook, IL: A. C. Nielsen Co.

Nielsen Media Research. (1998). *The spring '98 CommerceNet/Nielsen Media Internet demographic survey* (Full Report). Northbrook, IL: A. C. Nielsen Co.

Norman, D. A. (1988). *The design of everyday things.* Hillsdale, NJ: Lawrence Erlbaum Associates.

NTIA. (1995, July). *Falling through the Net: A survey of the "have nots" in rural and urban America.* National Telecommunication and Information Administration, U.S. Department of Commerce. Retrieved January 23, 2002, from http://www.ntia.doc.gov/ntiahome/fallingthru.html

NTIA. (1998, July). *Falling through the Net II: New data on the digital divide.* National Telecommunication and Information Administration, U.S. Department of Commerce. Retrieved January 10, 2002, from http://www.ntia.doc.gov/ntiahome/net2/

NTIA. (1999, July). *Falling through the net: Defining the digital divide.* National Telecommunication and Information Administration, U.S. Department of Commerce. Retrieved August 7, 2000, from http://www.ntia.doc.gov/ntiahome/fttn99/contents.html

NTIA. (2000, October). *Falling through the Net: Toward digital inclusion.* National Telecommunication and Information Administration, U.S. Department of Commerce. Retrieved March 12, 2002, from http://www.ntia.doc.gov/ntiahome/fttn00/contents00.html

NTIA. (2002, February). *A nation online: How Americans are expanding their use of the Internet.* National Telecommunication and Information Administration, U.S. Department of Commerce. Retrieved March 21, from http://www.ntia.doc.gov/ntiahome/dn/index.html

Oviatt, S., & Cohen, P. (2000). Multimodal interfaces that process what comes naturally. *Communications of the ACM, 43*, 45–53.

Pew Internet & American Life Project. (2000a). *Tracking online life: How women use the Internet to cultivate relationships with family and friends.* Washington, DC: Pew Foundation. Retrieved September 4, 2001, from http://www.pewinternet.org/

Pew Internet & American Life Project. (2000b). *African-Americans and the Internet.* Washington, DC: Pew Foundation. Retrieved September 4, 2001, from http://www.pewinternet.org/

Pew Internet & American Life Project. (2000c). *Trust and privacy online: Why Americans want to rewrite the rules.* Washington, DC: Pew Foundation. Retrieved September 5, 2001, from http://www.pewinternet.org/

Roberts, R. M. (1997, June 19). Program lowers costs of going online: Families can get break on equipment. *The Atlanta Journal and Constitution,* K3.

Rosenbloom, A. (2000). Trusting technology. *Communications of the ACM, 43,* 31–32.

Rudsill, M., Lewis, C., Polson, P., & McKay, T. (1996). *Human–computer interface design.* San Francisco: Morgan Kaufman.

Rutkowski, A. M. (1998). *Internet trends.* Washington, DC: Center for Next Generation Internet. Retrieved July 15, 1999, from http://www.ngi.org/trends.htm

Schon, D. A., Sanyal, B., & Mitchell, W. J. (Eds.). (1999). *High technology and low income communities: Prospects for the positive use of advanced information technology.* Cambridge, MA: MIT Press.

Sheppard, N. (1997, April 30). Free-Nets reach out to communities' needs. *The Ethnic News Watch,* p. 27.

Shneiderman, B. (1992). *Designing the user interface.* Reading, MA: Addison-Wesley.

UCLA Center for Communication Policy (2000, October 25). *Internet Report: Surveying the digital future.* Retrieved January 17, 2001, from http://www.ccp.ucla.edu

UCLA Center for Communication Policy (2001, November 29). *Internet Report: Surveying the digital future: Year 2.* Retrieved November 15, 2001, from http://ccp.ucla.edu

U.S. Census Bureau (1996–2000). Resident population of the United States, 1996–2000. Retrieved March 12, 2001, from http://www.census.gov:80/population/projections/nation/nsrh/nprh9600.txt

Weiser, E. B. (2001). The functions of Internet use and their social and psychological consequences. *Cyberpsychology and Behavior, 4*(6), 723–743.

Weiss, W. (1971). Mass communication. *Annual Review of Psychology, 22,* 309–336.

# Media Access to the Public Sphere

# 9

# Conceptual Elasticity of the Public Sphere: Tracking Media and Psychological Determinants of Access

JOHNETTE HAWKINS MCCRERY
*Louisiana State University, Shreveport*

JOHN E. NEWHAGEN
*University of Maryland, College Park*

The concept of access to a public sphere is central to any notion of a democratic society. In a real sense, the very notion of access to the public sphere defines the texture of a society's political fabric. It can be argued that such a sphere exists even in the most repressive regimes, where ideas deemed acceptable by the authorities are debated and discussed openly—and illicit ones whispered. The concept of a public sphere has, however, been the object of considerable slippage and elasticity in use as political, social, and technological circumstances have changed over time. The terrorist events of September 11, 2001, although effective in cultivating a sense of civic pride and patriotism unknown before the attacks, only underlined a trend that had been occurring in the United States for some time, namely, the contraction of the public sphere as a physical place and the resultant exclusion of important members of the citizenry from it.[1] Since the attacks, the meaning of strident political criticism, not to mention the security atmosphere at large public venues, has changed. And as the meaning of the public sphere continues to shift, so does the idea of access to it.

The instant the hijacked jetliners crashed into the two icons to the American political and economic system, the public sphere simultaneously contracted and expanded. In the days and weeks following the catastrophic event, the public sphere immediately contracted as a physical space, with travelers refusing to fly on airplanes or attend events with large numbers of people, fearing terrorists would once again target large public spaces. Even after conditions stabilized, it became clear that the simple cost of increased security would permanently alter the previously casual access to public places that had, to a large extent, epitomized American society. But in another sense, the public sphere has expanded, as concerned citizens spend more hours reading and viewing media and discussing the events with others than they had in generations—all in an attempt to understand what had taken place around them and their resulting feelings toward it. But even during periods of historically high civic participation, such as the weeks following the September 11 terrorist attacks, not all Americans participate in public life to the same extent. Over the past several decades, a growing number of citizens have elected to not take part in the public life of their nation or community (Putnam, 2000).

This study examines the idea that the public sphere is more than a single place. The conceptualization treats the public sphere as multiple spheres and explains how different arenas of political activity vary in the extent to which citizens, comprised primarily of nonelites, have access. Some political spaces are largely open to citizens, whereas others have highly defined requirements for participation and are thus difficult to penetrate. Communication technologies have always been a key factor in determining access to the public sphere, and the rise of new media formats such as political talk radio and online chat offers highly efficacious citizens the opportunity to participate in a mediated public sphere to which they have unfettered access (see Bucy & Gregson, 2001; chapter 10, this volume).

The analysis uses survey data gathered from a probability sample of likely voters in a middle-sized southern city and compares it to data taken from the same instrument administered to members of the U.S. Congress, their staff, and lobbyists. This comparison serves to test the idea that access to the public sphere as a physical location is becoming more and more difficult even for citizens who may have the social capital and cognitive skills, but not the right credentials. The analysis further considers the psychological construct of self-efficacy to determine what role it plays in influencing participation in the various public spheres. The notion that there are citizens who feel they can cope with the political process, but do not have access to it, is investigated. Finally, because communication technologies play an important role in the different public spheres, the analysis looks at media usage patterns among elites and nonelites to see whether there are systematic differences between the two groups that can be discerned.

## EVOLUTION OF THE CONCEPT OF THE PUBLIC SPHERE

Habermas (1962/1989) most prominently explicated the idea of the public sphere in his work on the topic beginning in the 1960s. Habermas conceptualized the public sphere as a process of public conversation and deliberation that took place in the coffeehouses and salons of 18th-century Europe, where the burgeoning middle class came to meet and discuss issues of economic and political importance. These centers of discourse were linked by newspapers into a network that spread throughout Europe. According to Habermas, these centers of discourse shared four characteristics. First, they were places where differences in status were ignored or at least downplayed so that ideas were judged simply on their merit. Second, within the public sphere, the argument that prevailed was the one considered most rational. Third, the topics discussed had formerly been controlled by church and state, and fourth, the spheres were open to anyone meeting the criteria and having access to cultural materials (Calhoun, 1992).

Eisenstein (1979) saw the incipient public sphere forming about 100 years earlier than Habermas, and in print shops more than coffeehouses and salons. In addition, she distinguished between the literate merchant and the free-floating bourgeois intellectual, known as a "philosophe," who she described as the ideologist of the growing middle class (p.146).

In either case, the idea of the public sphere hinges on the concept that political power was centralized among elites, the royals, and church hierarchy of the time, and that a combination of circumstances, including a nascent mass media system and an Enlightenment ethos that promoted public deliberation, gave rise to the formation of public opinion by an incipient bourgeois middle class. Perhaps more than any other reason, the public sphere came into being because an important segment of society—literate printers, merchants, and other financially self-sufficient mercantilists—was denied access to political power. Royals and church leaders appeared in public mainly through ceremonial display rather than as part of a meaningful and rational political discourse with the citizenry.

An important shift took place in the role of the public sphere in the 18th century as it applied to the American political system. De Tocqueville (1835/1956) detailed how citizen involvement increased in nascent American democracy as "voluntary associations" of men where political decision making actually took place. These associations, which began to appear around 1793, were organized to debate public questions, criticize government, and influence public policy (Schudson, 1998). Some were even formed for highly specific purposes, to address distinct problems such as public safety, commerce, industry, and morality, as well as religious concerns. This shift was due largely to the fact that the insurgent middle class of Europe came to take the reins of power in the United States, displacing traditional elites from the political arena. Putnam (2000, p. 384) described how "civic inventiveness reached a crescendo unmatched in American history" between the years 1870 and 1920 in terms of the range and durability of newly founded voluntary associations. Indeed, "most major, broad-gauged civic institutions of American life today were founded in several decades of exceptional social creativity around the turn of the twentieth century" (Putnam, 2000, pp. 384–385).

The idea of the public sphere as a physical place where public opinion is formed and political power exercised lives on in political discourse today. Contemporary critiques, however, depict the American political process as being increasingly isolated from public opinion (see Bucy & Gregson, 2001). Decision making is done by a new bureaucratic and professional elite while the ordinary citizen is increasingly marginalized from the process. And although many citizens are content to have others address issues of public concern, there are some who long for a voice and opportunity to participate and are frustrated by their lack of access. This dilemma suggests it may be time to reexamine the concept of the public sphere anew.

## THE PROCESS AND OPINION SPHERES

Lippmann (1922), in the early 20th century, wrote of the complexities of modern society and the difficulties these complexities present in a democracy where common people without special expertise are expected to be informed and participate in the affairs of government. He was concerned that society was becoming so vast and complex that a specialized group of technocratic elites was necessary to steer national policy, sharing with the citizenry only what they felt necessary in an effort to shape public opinion. Lippmann's concerns appear to have materialized, as citizens with little expertise in public affairs have become increasingly removed from the political process. The exclusion of nonelites from material influence over policymaking and governmental expenditures (see Bucy & Gregson, 2001) means that contemporary explications of the public sphere must take into account how the complexity of society has changed the policymaking process, resulting in the formation of multiple public spheres.

One way to think about the problem is to consider two spheres, one for opinion and one for process. The *opinion sphere* serves as a forum for discussion among citizens seeking to understand and be heard. The opinion sphere is also the place where policy positions may be born and mature. But it is the *process sphere* that encompasses the policymaking arena where the levers of political power are pulled. Government officials are key players in the process sphere, as are others vested with the authority to implement policy decisions.

This conceptualization of the public sphere resonates with Bucy and Gregson's (2001) discussion of material versus symbolic influence over political power, where opinion formation by the masses and policymaking by elites are both conducted to a greater or lesser extent through mass media but remain discrete processes. Within this context, it can be argued that there is currently a disjuncture between the two spheres of influence. Members of the bourgeois middle class, once excluded from political power, now comprise the policymaking elite. But as various social movements such as women's suffrage, the student movement, and civil rights causes have created new insurgent groups wanting to take advantage of their newfound access, activists have frequently been frustrated as they discover their access is largely limited to the opinion sphere.

## THE PUBLIC SPHERE AS BOTH PHYSICAL AND VIRTUAL SPACE

Reconceptualizing the public sphere must further take into account how new technologies have enabled the public sphere to evolve from the limits of a physical space. When Habermas (1962/1989) first described the public sphere, it was a place where propertied, educated men gathered for a face-to-face discussion of public affairs. Habermas's insistence that discourse be oral is understandable if viewed from within the context of interpersonal communication. That view holds face-to-face discourse to be the highest or purest form of interactive communication. But it is clear that interactive discourse can occur through media as well.

Mass media generally do not rank well in terms of their potential for interactivity; both radio and television score low on their capacity to sustain interactive communication, and newspapers fare even worse (Newhagen, 1997). But some types of radio and television programs, such as talk shows, at least appear to be interactive (Newhagen, 1994), and for some core elites with access to op-ed pages, even the newspaper can be interactive.

Although all interactive media likely serve at least a minor role in both the process and opinion spheres, there are probably some differences. To begin with, the membership of the process sphere is quite small, limited to an elite group armed with the necessary knowledge and authority to make policy decisions. This group is small for several reasons: There are few who have the necessary resources to participate, small membership helps facilitate and maintain consensus, and the framers of the U.S. Constitution designed the American political system, on which state and local governments are modeled, in such a way as to require little direct participation from the masses. Although the framers believed civic input and participation were key to limiting power of government and ensuring that the rights of citizens were protected, they also believed Americans lacked the civic judgment, expertise, and virtue to make sound decisions in the public interest (Delli Carpini & Keeter, 1996). Initially, voters only directly elected members of the U.S. House of Representatives; the framers vested elites with the responsibility to select members of the Senate, Supreme Court, and president.

Although this lack of trust in the ability of citizens to wisely choose elected leaders and make other sound civic choices has waned over time, and the U.S. Constitution has been amended to enhance rights and participation opportunities for all Americans, participation is still optional and the process sphere remains difficult to penetrate in as much as the core of the political system was designed to exclude direct citizen participation. Because the process sphere is relatively small, it works well in a physical space. For example, although new technologies could allow lawmakers to vote from their home districts and have committee hearings via teleconferencing, they still privilege face-to-face communication to such a great extent that they continue to gather in a physical space, their respective capitol buildings, for committee meetings and official votes.

The physical delineation of the process sphere further limits the access of citizens. In the chambers of deliberative bodies, there are always limits on who is allowed in the room, and there is the burden of having to travel to the physical place, typically the seat of government. Over the last two decades, citizens have been able watch the workings of the U.S. government on the C-SPAN cable network, providing visual and verbal proximity to elites, as well as open-mike access to a wide audience (although small by television standards). Still, even active callers are not full participants engaged in the process sphere. What this *media participation* does have the potential for is changing the opinion climate and enhancing the political efficacy of citizens (Bucy & Gregson, 2001), a theme revisited later.

The opinion sphere, on the other hand, is often quite large and thus works well as a virtual sphere. New media formats, including talk radio, call-in television programs, and online chat rooms, are capable of supporting debate in the opinion sphere. These media provide even more than simple interactivity—they allow for discussions that are more like real-time conversations. Newspapers also are capable of sustaining interactivity, but they cannot do so in real time or with large groups. One should not assume, though, that the opinion sphere has ceased to be a physical space. Citizens still gather in public places to discuss public issues. However, through media participation, some now enter the opinion sphere via information or communication technologies, such as the Internet, to acquire information for future in-person conversations or to take part in political discussions that never go beyond cyberspace.

## MEDIA AND THE PUBLIC SPHERES

Although the process sphere is often a physical space, there is still a role for mass media in facilitating discussion and shaping policy within the process sphere, especially on the national level. For example, research suggests that members of Congress routinely use newspapers to communicate with one another. In 1960, political scientist Donald Matthews observed that, "It is ironic but still true that the members of so small a legislative body should find it necessary to communicate with each other via public print, but they often do" (cited in Cook, 1998, p.126). Newspapers have long been dependent on elites, especially those in official positions, as sources of information, so it is not surprising that members of Congress, who have easy entry into the pages of newspapers, would use the print medium to communicate with one another.[2]

Elected officials also find newspapers preferable to broadcast media as a tool for public sphere communication because newspapers are information dense, with detailed textual information about public affairs. And because the details can be critical in a discussion among policymakers, newspapers (whether online or offline) may be the only mass medium capable of facilitating discussion within the process sphere.

Newspapers are probably a poor medium, however, for facilitating discussion within the opinion sphere. Newspapers are generally not interactive for large audiences, and nonelites are less likely to be quoted or even have their ideas included. A media format more conducive for the opinion sphere is political talk programs (see chapter 10, this volume), which have grown considerably in number and popularity since the 1980s, with 20% of adult radio listeners now listening to political talk radio more than once a week (Heath, 1998; Rubin & Step, 2000). There is a sense among political observers that political talk shows, especially those on talk radio, play an important role in shaping listeners' political views and behavior (Hofstetter & Gianos, 1997; Page & Tannenbaum, 1996), much the way debate in an opinion sphere would shape political views. Oravec (2000) wrote that political talk shows create a kind of community that is "successful in mobilizing support for various causes and political candidates, linking audience members into action networks that can focus on addressing specific problems" (p. 58). Others have even gone so far as to call the community of talk show listeners and participants a *public sphere* in its own right (Livingstone & Lunt, 1994; Wyatt, Katz, & Kim, 2000). In one study, political talk radio surpassed newspapers in contributing to knowledge of public affairs (Stamm, Johnson, & Martin, 1997), suggesting that discussions on talk radio can serve as a rich source of information.

## POLITICAL EFFICACY AND PARTICIPATION IN THE PUBLIC SPHERE

Participation in the public sphere requires more than a knowledge base, however; it also requires the belief that one can be an effective participant in the political arena, what experimental psychologists and political scientists call *self-efficacy*. Self-efficacy is defined as "a belief in one's capabilities to organize and execute the courses of action required to produce given attainments" (Bandura, 1997, p. 3). Self-efficacy has been called the "key factor of human agency," meaning it is the chief determinant of whether someone tries something new or difficult (Bandura, 1997, p. 3). When self-efficacy is applied to the political arena, it is referred to as *perceived political efficacy*, which Bandura (1997) defined as "people's beliefs that they can influence the political system" (p. 483). Political efficacy has proven to be a key determinant as well in whether one participates in politics (Bandura, 1997; Finkel, 1985; Gamson, 1968; Zimmerman & Rappaport, 1988). Citizens with high political efficacy can be found in all strata of society (Newhagen, 1994), but persons of high socioeconomic status are more likely to have a high sense of political efficacy, especially if they have strong ties to their communities (Bandura, 1997).

Empirical evidence suggests that citizens with high political efficacy are likely to participate in the public sphere and have found their voice in the opinion sphere. Listeners and callers of talk radio, for instance, tend to be more educated (Avery & Ellis, 1979), have higher socioeconomic status (Hofstetter & Gianos, 1997), and report higher levels of self-efficacy (Hofstetter & Gianos, 1997; Newhagen, 1994) than the media audience overall.

This study explores whether there are two types of public spheres, one process and one opinion, accessed by different groups and enabled by different mass media. Members of the *process sphere* are operationally defined as members of the U.S. Congress, their staff, and lobbyists. All three of these groups have a direct role in the political process at a national level. Differences may exist, however, in these groups' access to power and their claim to legitimacy. Members of Congress can claim that their legitimacy in the process sphere is drawn from electoral mandate and their ability to vote directly on issues of importance in the public sphere. Both staff and lobbyists work closely with members of Congress but derive their legitimacy somewhat less directly. Staff members are appointed by elected representatives, whereas lobbyists are hired by special interest groups for their expertise or political influence. Regardless of their claim to legitimacy, all three groups are members of a small elite capable of dealing directly with the machinery of political decision making.

Membership in the *opinion sphere* is operationally defined as survey respondents who belong to a pool of what pollsters qualify as "likely voters." Importantly, not all survey respondents who qualify as likely voters are necessarily active in the opinion sphere. As suggested earlier, other variables—especially political efficacy—may influence active participation in this sphere.

This reconceptualization of the public sphere into process and opinion domains raises several questions about how elite and nonelite groups participate in the public sphere and the different mass media they use to access issues and events in public life. Another area of interest centers around differences in political efficacy, or beliefs that individuals can influence the political system. Accordingly, this study poses the following research questions:

*RQ1*: Is membership in the process and opinion spheres associated with varying levels of political efficacy?

*RQ2*: What forms of mass media do members of the process and opinion spheres most rely on?

*RQ3*: What forms of political participation do members of the process and opinion spheres engage in?

The analysis proceeds with the expectation that members of the process sphere—members of Congress, congressional staff, and lobbyists—will score high on political efficacy as well as items measuring involvement in the policymaking arena. Moreover, participants in the process sphere are expected to prefer newspapers to other media, in as much as newspapers have proven interactive for elites and carry detailed messages. Participants in the opinion sphere are expected to favor talk programs, which more easily provide opportunities for political expression among those highly efficacious (but not highly influential) individuals wanting to share their views.

## METHOD

This study combined survey and field experimental methodologies. The first part of the study used a cross-sectional survey of registered, likely voters in Louisiana's 4th Congressional District to assess media use and political efficacy.[3] This portion of the study was administered by a professional political polling firm. The second part of the study utilized a similar questionnaire but was administered to members of the U.S. House of Representatives, congressional staff, and registered lobbyists.

### Likely Voter Survey

Public Opinion Strategies, a national political and public affairs research firm, used random-digit dialing to telephone households in Louisiana's 4th Congressional District.[4] The households were selected from a sample of 4,000 names. The sample was stratified by using filter questions along with quotas for gender, geography, and race to ensure the sample demographics mirrored the 4th congressional district population demographics. Ten percent of the sample of 4,000 households completed the survey ($N = 400$). The margin of error was 4.9% with a confidence interval of 95%. The survey was a standard political survey containing 31 questions measuring voter attitudes, media use, candidate preference, and political behavior.[5]

### Public Policy Participant Questionnaire

The second stage of data collection was intended to gather similar information on participants directly involved in the public policy arena, or process sphere. Consequently, a questionnaire similar to the survey administered to likely voters was administered to members of Congress, congressional staff, and registered lobbyists. A total of 106 questionnaires were completed and returned (members of Congress, $n = 39$; congressional staff, $n = 38$; lobbyists, $n = 29$). Convenience sampling was used along with an individually tailored process of questionnaire distribution and return for each process sphere group.

The instrument used in this wave of the study was a questionnaire containing 24 items, most of which were identical to questions used in the survey administered to likely voters. For each of the process sphere groups, this questionnaire was self-administered, and the participants remained anonymous. The data from each survey administration were scored similarly so an analysis could be conducted comparing responses between likely voters and participants in the process sphere.

## RESULTS

Factor analysis generated three indexes used as dependent variables. The first analysis led to the creation of indexes grouping respondents into process and opinion spheres. Another analysis led to the creation of an index reflecting respondent political efficacy.[6] Analysis of variance showed a relationship between public sphere group and efficacy index scores, $F(3, 476) = 36.30$, $p < .001$. The public sphere group with the highest political efficacy was members of Congress ($M = 1.20$, $SD = .12$), followed by lobbyists ($M = .80$, $SD = .44$), congressional staff ($M = .70$, $SD = .42$), and citizens ($M = .25$, $SD = .66$).

### Citizen Efficacy

Variance for the citizens' group was substantially greater than the other three public sphere groups and warranted closer examination. Figure 9.1 shows the distribution of political efficacy scores to be skewed toward high scores. The skewed area of the distribution accounted for approximately 19% of the citizens' group. Based on those results, a new group was constructed, dividing the citizens' group into high and low efficacy groups. This resulted in an expanded public sphere group membership variable, now containing categories for members of Congress, congressional staff, lobbyists, high efficacy citizens, and low efficacy citizens.

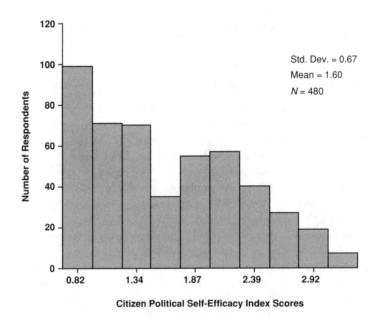

FIG 9.1.   Citizen political self-efficacy index distribution.

TABLE 9.1
Factor Analysis of Public Sphere Participation Variables

| Variable | Factor Loading[1] | |
|---|---|---|
| | Process Sphere | Opinion Sphere |
| Good understanding of issues | — | .653 |
| Good job in public | .799 | — |
| Good understanding of issues | — | .653 |
| Qualified to participate in politics | .702 | — |
| Keep up to participate | .614 | — |
| Highest elected office held | .473 | — |
| Eigenvalue | 2.79 | .92 |
| Percent Variance Explained | 46.5 | 15.3 |

[1] Factor loadings .60 and above are reported.

## Process and Opinion Sphere Indexes

Table 9.1 shows two factors indicating public sphere membership. The first factor, named *process sphere*, explained 46.5% of the variance and had an eigenvalue of 2.79. The variables with loadings greater than .60 were: "I feel I could do a good job in public office;" "I consider myself well-qualified to participate in politics;" "What is the highest elected office you have held?" and "I could express my views about important political issues on TV or in the newspapers as well as most people the media actually quote." The second factor, called *opinion sphere*, accounted for 15.3% of the variance and had an eigenvalue of .92. This factor was determined by political efficacy questions tapping knowledge or cognition of issues. The two variables associated with this factor with loadings greater than .60 included: "I feel that I have a pretty good understanding of the important issues facing this country" and "How important is it to you to keep up with the news to participate in politics?"

## Political Efficacy Index

Factor analysis of political self-efficacy variables generated one factor (see Table 9.2). The factor, labeled *political efficacy*, explained 59.1% of the variance and had an eigenvalue of 2.36. Table 9.2 shows all four efficacy questions with factor loadings greater than .60. An index for political efficacy was created from these questions.

## Public Sphere Membership and Process Sphere Index Scores

Analysis of variance showed a relationship between public sphere group and process sphere index scores, $F(4, 478) = 189.82$, $p < 001$. As Figure 9.2 illustrates, members of Congress scored highest ($M = 1.0$, $SD = .01$), followed by high efficacy citizens ($M = .51$, $SD = .19$), lobbyists ($M = .27$, $SD = .31$), congressional staff ($M = .16$, $SD = .27$), and low efficacy citizens ($M = -.29$, $SD = .39$). The

TABLE 9.2
Factor Analysis of Political Efficacy Questions

| Variable | Factor Loading[1] |
|---|---|
| | Political Efficacy |
| Good understanding of issues | .689 |
| Good job in office | .788 |
| Qualified to take part in politics | .848 |
| Express views well | .744 |
| Eigenvalue | 2.36 |
| Percent Variance Explained | 59.1 |

[1] Factor loadings .60 and above are reported.

fact that members of Congress scored the highest of all groups on the process sphere index, and low efficacy citizens score the lowest, confirms expectations. However, the relatively high score for high efficacy citizens, ranking above both lobbyists and congressional staff, is somewhat surprising.

## Public Sphere Group and Newspaper Use

Analysis of variance showed a relationship between public sphere group and frequency of newspaper readership $F(4, 481) = 8.04$, $p < .001$.[7] Figure 9.3 shows

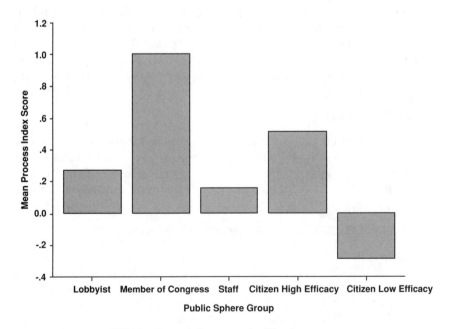

FIG 9.2.   Process index score and public sphere group.

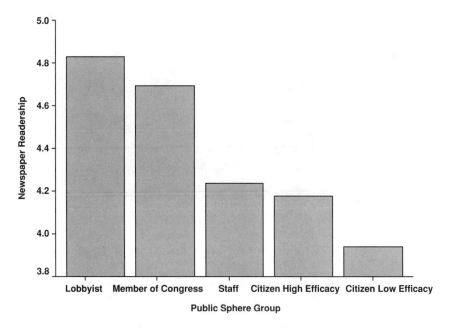

FIG 9.3.   Newspaper readership and public sphere membership group.

lobbyists reported using newspapers the most ($M = 4.83$, $SD = .47$), followed by members of Congress ($M = 4.69$, $SD = .52$), congressional staff ($M = 4.24$, $SD = .85$), high efficacy citizens ($M = 4.17$, $SD = 1.22$), and low efficacy citizens ($M = 3.92$, $SD = 1.2$). These scores reinforce the idea that newspapers serve elites as an important information source, with both members of Congress and lobbyists showing high readership. Congressional staff might have been expected to also be heavy users, but show readership levels similar to high efficacy citizens. The fact that low efficacy citizens indicated the lowest level of newspaper readership is not surprising.

### Public Sphere Membership and Opinion Sphere Index Scores

Analysis of variance showed a relationship between public sphere group and opinion sphere index scores $F(4, 481) = 24.23$, $p < .0001$. High efficacy citizens scored the highest ($M = .41$, $SD = .26$), but they are only slightly ahead of members of Congress ($M = .36$, $SD = .26$), followed by congressional staff ($M = .19, SD = .44$), lobbyists ($M = .07, SD = .53$), and then low efficacy citizens ($M = -.16$, $SD = .62$; see Fig. 9.4). The finding that high efficacy citizens and members of Congress were associated with the highest opinion sphere index scores was not surprising; neither was the fact that low efficacy citizens were associated with the lowest opinion sphere index scores of all groups.

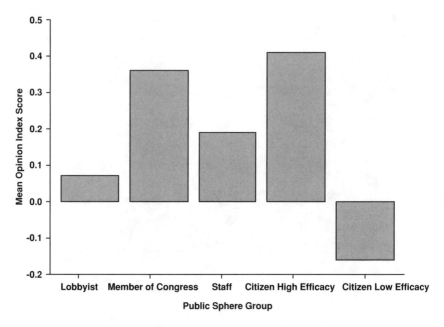

FIG 9.4.    Opinion sphere index score by public sphere group.

## Public Sphere Membership and Talk Show Use

Figure 9.5 shows a relationship between public sphere group and frequency of listening to talk shows $F(4, 480) = 8.88$, $p < .0001$.[8] Lobbyists reported listening to talk shows the most ($M = 3.59$, $SD = 1.02$), followed by high efficacy citizens ($M = 3.03$, $SD = 1.50$), congressional staff ($M = 2.95$, $SD = 1.39$), members of Congress ($M = 2.77$, $SD = .81$), and then low efficacy citizens ($M = 2.42$, $SD = 1.23$). Levels of talk show listening for members of Congress, staff, and high efficacy citizens were similar, but the high level of talk show listening by lobbyists was somewhat surprising. Low efficacy citizens again scored very low on this index.

## Public Sphere Membership and Political Participation

Finally, the relationship between public sphere group and political participation, measured as the highest office the respondent reported holding and the number of times the respondent reported being quoted in a newspaper or appearing on television, were examined. Figure 9.6 shows a relationship between public sphere group and the highest public office the respondent reported holding $F(4, 485) = 150.10$, $p < .0001$.[9] As expected, members of Congress all reported holding elected office within national government ($M = 5.0$, $SD = .01$). All other groups reported means corresponding to not having held *any* public office—even in a civic group in

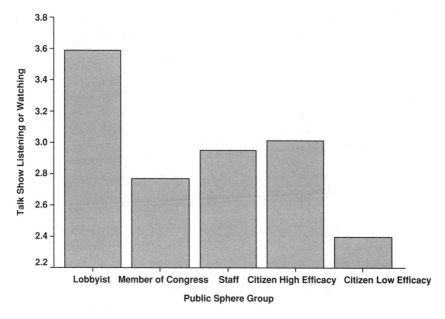

FIG 9.5.    Talk show listening or watching and public sphere group.

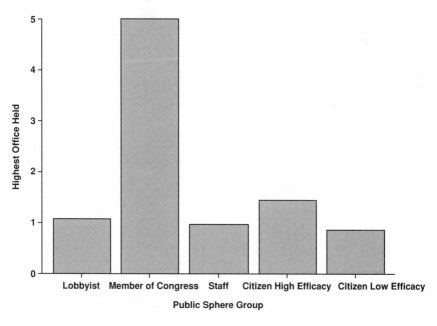

FIG 9.6.    Highest office held and public sphere group.

high school or college. High efficacy citizens ($M = 1.44$, $SD = 1.21$) scored only slightly higher than lobbyists ($M = 1.07$, $SD = 1.02$), congressional staff ($M = .97$, $SD = .75$), and low efficacy citizens ($M = .86$, $SD = 1.01$).

In addition, there was a relationship between public sphere group membership and number of times the respondent reported being quoted in a newspaper or appearing on television, $F(4, 485) = 111.80$, $p < .0001$. All members of Congress (100%) reported being quoted. Lobbyists (37.9%), congressional staff (36.8%), and high efficacy citizens (40.5%) all reported being quoted at about the same rate. Low efficacy citizens (17.6%) lagged behind all other groups.

## DISCUSSION

This study attempts to provide insight into how the modern public sphere is organized, what media facilitate discussion within it, and who has access to it. The results support the proposition that there are at least two types of public spheres: a process sphere and an opinion sphere. Although different groups dominate the two spheres, membership may overlap in interesting ways. Figure 9.7 illustrates one way of conceptualizing the relationship between the two spheres. The process and opinion spheres are presented as two separate but intersecting orbs, with a shared portion representing the region of overlap between the different civic domains. The opinion sphere is notably larger than the process sphere, reflecting the large number of citizens compared to the small number of politically influential members of society.

Notably, the results showed that elected officials are the primary participants in the process sphere and high efficacy citizens are the primary participants in the opinion sphere. The prominence of different groups in the two spheres further supports the theory that they have different roles in society. It could be argued that a strong process sphere is necessary to ensure that the wheels of government and

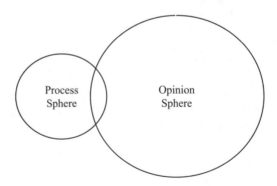

FIG 9.7.   Intersection of the process and opinion spheres.

society keep turning, and a strong opinion sphere is necessary in an open society to ensure that those wheels turn the way citizens desire. It should be noted, however, that the region of overlap between the two spheres serves to index how responsive the process sphere is to the opinion sphere, where a larger shared area means a more responsive polity.

Results show that a notable segment of the opinion sphere does share certain attributes with members of the process sphere, such as high political efficacy and media access. As might be expected, members of Congress stand out from other groups, including nonelected political professionals working in Washington, DC. One of the more interesting findings is how high efficacy citizens, about 20% of the likely voters surveyed, stand out along with members of Congress in high scores on opinion sphere activity. On the other hand, lobbyists and members of Congress stand out as newspaper readers. For these key players, newspapers are an interactive medium that facilitates discussion when the participants are not all in the same room. However, members of Congress listen or view political talk programs less than all other groups except low efficacy citizens. High efficacy citizens may take part in political talk shows not to influence policy so much as to reap various civic rewards such as proximity to elites, increased political efficacy, and a heightened sense of social status (Bucy & Gregson, 2001). Such activity may at least provide the perception of interactive civic involvement, whereas newspapers fail to offer even highly efficacious citizens any meaningful input. Lobbyists and congressional staff, in turn, may be tuning in to talk radio to monitor what these efficacious callers have to say.

In application, the concept of the public sphere has considerable theoretical elasticity. It was first described as a place where those excluded from political power could form and sustain public opinion; however, the idea has come to symbolize the arena of policymaking activity in which the administration of power actually takes place.

This study provides evidence that the concept of the public sphere has subsumed both arenas. The term *public sphere* is used to describe the physical seat of power occupied by elected officials and their associates, and to describe a virtual meeting place where high efficacy citizens can go to discuss public affairs. Democratic theory implies there must be sufficient interaction between these two spheres to keep the system responsive and viable. Yet, poll after poll indicates that citizens have decreasing trust and confidence in those with their hands on the levers of political power. This problem may be best understood by reflecting on the size of the overlapping area between the two spheres shown in Fig. 9.7 because it represents the region of true interaction between qualified citizens and their leaders. If the overlap is small or does not exist at all, the system may be perceived as exclusionary and dysfunctional; as the overlap grows in size, public discourse should become correspondingly vibrant.

The events of September 11, 2001 underscored the longstanding trend of the contraction of the public sphere as a physical place and the resulting exclusion of important members of the citizenry from it. Critics such as Putnam (2000) bemoan the lack of civic engagement and argue that mass media, especially television, have been an important factor in that trend. Habermas (1962/1989) himself expressed the belief that the public sphere has been contracting for most of the 20th century. One thing that seems certain is that the United States will never enjoy the laissez faire attitude about public association it had in the past. In a real sense, evoking a psychological state of terror among large numbers of people by using television as a vehicle has proved to be highly successful as a political weapon, if the goal is to make people slightly more suspicious of one another, increase internal policing of citizens, and, at least in the short run, intimidate participation in secular democracy. The challenge for the political system to counter this threat is to adjust the boundaries of the process sphere to include a larger virtual component, enabling increasing access to it by qualified members in the opinion sphere.

The challenge for the media system is to sustain a virtual space where citizens have access to a place where they can engage in meaningful dialogue—both among themselves and with members of the process sphere. It is interesting to note the persistent appeal of political talk shows to high efficacy citizens in studies such as this (see Hollander, 1995–1996; Newhagen, 1994). Some critics regarded the talk show phenomenon as an important political instrument of the Clinton years but expected its appeal to fade as time went on. That, however, does not appear to be the case; political talk media continue to show up in polling data as an important venue for political discourse. Another medium that has to be considered as a vehicle for political communication is the World Wide Web. Here, reviews have been mixed, with early optimism about the Web's capacity to revitalize American democracy being followed by more pessimistic assessments of its actual use (see Grossman, 1995; Margolis & Resnick, 2000).

In any case, pitting optimistic and pessimistic accounts of old and new media against one another may only obscure more important underlying issues that deal with the nature of the public sphere and access to it. Meaningful access to the public sphere is an absolute prerequisite for the kind of citizen involvement necessary to sustain participatory democracy. The social and political fabric of the world has and surely will continue to change very rapidly, making the kinds of institutional adjustments and corrections necessary to create such a climate even more difficult. Under an increased state of global security that open societies now find themselves in, one thing is for sure—the stakes will remain very high.

## ENDNOTES

[1] Areas designated as public spaces have been contracting for some time. Loeffler (1998), for instance, documented how the bunker-like architecture of recently built embassies reflects a siege mentality within the U.S. State Department. She argued that although the new buildings may be more secure, both their design and location inhibits free public access to them. This same trend can be seen throughout public space, domestic as well as foreign.

[2] In addition, since 1801 members of Congress have been allowed to use government funds to purchase newspaper subscriptions for their offices.

[3] The U.S. Representative from Louisiana's 4th Congressional District is Jim McCrery, the first author's spouse.

[4] Questions in this survey were funded by the 2000 McCrery for Congress campaign, Johnette McCrery, and the Philip Merrill College of Journalism at the University of Maryland, College Park.

[5] A copy of the questionnaire is available from the first author.

[6] See (Craig, Niemi, & Silver, 1990) for a discussion of the efficacy items used in this study.

[7] The newspaper question used in the tests asked the respondent, "How often do you read a newspaper?" The response choices to the question included never, rarely, sometimes, frequently, and all of the time.

[8] The talk show question used in the tests asked the respondent, "How often last week did you listen to talk programs on the radio or television where people call in to talk about political issues?" The response choices to the question included never, rarely, sometimes, frequently, and all of the time.

[9] The highest office held question asked respondents if they had: not held office; held office in high school or college; held office in a civic group; held office in a local government; held office in a state government; held office in national government.

# REFERENCES

Avery, R. K., & Ellis, D. G. (1979). Talk radio as an interpersonal phenomenon. In G. Gumpert & C. Cathcart (Eds.), *Inter/Media: Interpersonal Communication in a Media World* (pp. 108–115). New York: Oxford University Press.

Bandura, A. (1997). *Self-efficacy: The exercise of control.* New York: W. H. Freeman and Company.

Bucy, E. P., & Gregson, K. S. (2001). Media participation: A legitimizing mechanism of mass democracy. *New Media & Society, 3*(3), 359–382.

Calhoun, C. (1992). *Habermas and the public sphere.* Cambridge: MIT Press.

Cook, T. E. (1998). *Governing with the news.* Chicago: University of Chicago Press.

Craig, S. C., Niemi, R. G., & Silver, G. E. (1990). Political efficacy and trust: A report on the NES pilot study items. *Political Behavior, 12*(3), 289–314.

Delli Carpini, M. X., & Keeter, S. (1996). *What Americans know about politics and why it matters.* New Haven: Yale University Press.

Eisenstein, E. (1979). *The printing press as an agent of change: Communications and cultural transformations in early-modern Europe.* Cambridge: Cambridge University Press.

Finkel, S. E. (1985). Reciprocal effects of participation and political efficacy: A panel analysis. *American Journal of Political Science, 29*(4), 891–913.

Gamson, W. A. (1968). *Power and discontent.* Homewood, IL: Dorsey.

Grossman, L. K. (1995). *The electronic republic: Reshaping democracy in the information age.* New York: Viking.

Habermas, J. (1989). *The structural transformation of the public sphere.* (T. Burger & F. Lawrence, Trans.). Cambridge, MA: MIT Press. (Original work published 1962)

Heath, R. P. (1998). Tuning in to talk. *American Demographics, 20*(2), 48–53.

Hofstetter, C. R., & Gianos, C. L. (1997). Political talk radio: Actions speak louder than words. *Journal of Broadcasting & Electronic Media, 41*(4), 501–515.

Hollander, B. A. (1995–1996). The influence of talk radio on political efficacy and participation. *Journal of Radio Studies, 3,* 23–31.

Loeffler, J. C. (1998). *The architecture of diplomacy: Building America's embassies.* New York: Princeton Architectural Press.

Lippmann, W. (1922). *Public opinion.* New York: Simon & Schuster.

Livingstone, S., & Lunt, P. (1994). *Talk on television: Audience participation and public debate.* London: Routledge.

Margolis, M., & Resnick, D. (2000). *Politics as usual: The cyberspace "revolution."* Thousand Oaks, CA: Sage.

Newhagen, J. E. (1994). Self-efficacy and call-in political television show use. *Communication Research, 21*(3), 366–379.

Newhagen, J. E. (1997). The role of feedback in the assessment of news. *Information Processing and Management, 33*(5), 583–594.

Oravec, J. A. (2000). A community of iconoclasts: Art Bell, talk radio, and the Internet. *Journal of Radio Studies, 7*(1), 52–69.

Page, B. I., & Tannenbaum, J. (1996). Populistic deliberation and talk radio. *Journal of Communication, 46*(2), 33–54.

Putnam, R. D. (2000). *Bowling alone: The collapse and revival of American community.* New York: Simon & Schuster.

Rubin, A. M., & Step, M. M. (2000). Impact of motivation, attraction, and parasocial interaction on talk radio listening. *Journal of Broadcasting & Electronic Media, 44*(4), 635–654.

Schudson, M. (1998). *The good citizen: A history of American civic life.* New York: The Free Press.

Stamm, K., Johnson, M., & Martin, B. (1997). Differences among newspapers, television, and radio in their contribution to knowledge of the Contract with America. *Journalism and Mass Communication Quarterly, 74*(4), 687–702.

Tocqueville, A. de (1956). *Democracy in America.* New York: Penguin. (Original work published 1835)

Wyatt, R.O., Katz, E., & Kim, J. (2000). Bridging the spheres: Political and personal conversation in public and private places. *Journal of Communication, 50*(1), 71–92.

Zimmerman, M. A., & Rappaport, J. (1988). Citizen participation, perceived control, and psychological empowerment. *American Journal of Community Psychology,16*(5), 725–750.

# The Skills and Motivations of Interactive Media Participants: The Case of Political Talk Radio

C. RICHARD HOFSTETTER
*San Diego State University*

Access to political talk radio can mean many things involving the way the medium is used by audiences: opportunities for highly passive exposure to the medium, exposure accompanied by a modicum of attention to portions of what is being said (Crittenden, 1971), close attention to and psychological engagement with what is being said (Hofstetter, Smith, Zari, & Hofstetter, 1999) and attention to discussions about public affairs with callers in the broadcasts, personal discussions with other persons about topics discussed in programs (Bennett, 1998; Hofstetter, 1998), intellectual stimulation (Hollander, 1995b; Hofstetter, Barker, Smith, Zari, & Ingrassia, 1999), contributions to the development of a public sphere of discourse (Herbst, 1995), or influencing the manifest content of public discussion (Avery, 1990; Page & Tannenbaum, 1996; Squires, 2000), just to mention some possibilities. The burgeoning body of research about political talk radio and its implications for a democratic polity has touched on all of these topics during the last several decades.

It is nearly a cliché to note that the fabled "hypodermic needle model" of an inert public that is injected with information is an inadequate view of mass communications studies. Rather, audiences are conceptualized as active participants in a communication process in which readers, viewers, and listeners process information. Audiences usually contribute to the flow of information before, during, or after their use of mass media as mediators themselves in personal interaction with others. Use of mass media is best perceived as an "N-way structure of interaction" in which information is processed, interpreted, passed forth and back, and meanings are constructed. The motivational structures, skills required, and implications vary considerably for each of these types of access. Whatever form access takes, some level and type of motivation is required, and the implications of political talk radio depend on the kinds of skills listeners apply to what they hear.

Perceived interactivity may be the most discriminating aspect of political talk as an instance of a medium (Newhagen, 1996), and may drive audience motivation concerning the medium because linkages to others are crucial in the construction of self-definition, perceptions of reality, and public discourse. Interaction is simply a two-way flow or exchange of communications usually assumed to occur in real time. The public sphere is constructed from such interactions with others (McCarthy, 1978). In an electronic age, the bulk of these interactions are mediated and often vicarious. Print media supply an important type of information useful to the maintenance of the public sphere but do not provide two-way interaction between the medium and the public aside from an extremely limited set of letters to the editor. Television and radio news generally offer no greater possibility for two-way interaction except in the vicarious sense of imagined parasocial interaction (Levy, 1979). Call-in talk programming on television and radio are different. Members of the public can actually contact a host and guests, make comments or raise questions or objections, and contribute to what is broadcast and to what listeners hear— apparently in real time. Although all programs screen callers, some to an extreme degree, the impression that audiences usually receive is that of a spontaneous series of exchanges.

Many studies have reported limited observations on the motives linked to political talk radio. With the exception of Newhagen (1994, 1996), few studies have attempted to relate motives directly to the interactivity of electronic talk programming or to the possible effects of perceived interactivity on correlates of the medium in a systematic way. The perception of interactivity, of two-way communication in real time, may be key to understanding the appeal of political talk radio and its role, and also key to understanding attractions of other new interactive media technologies of communication such as the World Wide Web. The purpose of this chapter is to investigate the implications of motives audiences harbor in using call-in political talk programs, paying particular attention to the perceived interactivity of the medium, and to discuss briefly the kinds of skills involved in processing information from political talk. The guiding hypothesis is that perceived interactivity constitutes a general motive of engagement that explains many aspects of the political talk experience among audiences.

Observations that are reported here are drawn from data collected by a random-digit-dial sample survey of adults conducted in San Diego, California, by telephone during 1997, in large part stimulated by the innovative thinking of John Newhagen. Although not strictly representative of the larger domain of political talk radio in America, the findings from numerous studies conducted in other locales and nationally during the 1990s generally concurred with findings in San Diego. Further details concerning the survey are available from the author.


## BACKGROUND

Radio is an easily accessible and nearly universal medium. It can be experienced passively, does not require print literacy to use, is inexpensive, and is capable of linking diverse mass publics and social, economic, and political elites in a variety of ways. Radio can be an especially effective medium of mass communication and political mobilization in societies characterized by low rates of literacy. Political activists from Roosevelt to Reagan, from Caughlin to Clinton, from Hitler to Castro, democrats, demagogues, and others, have demonstrated the efficacy of radio to mobilize citizens for a multitude of social and political ends. In societies that lack other forms of mass communication, radio may play a key role in the evolution of political life.

Political uses of radio are common in contemporary America, and radio has been a medium of politics almost since its inception. As Davis (1997) indicated, political activists have used radio to tout a variety of causes. Numerous studies suggest that some activists have had a degree of success in attracting and mobilizing listeners.

Political talk radio is an instance of the "new media," a medium that has the properties of traditional radio but also involves interaction between hosts, specific members of the audience, and the entire listening audience through the use of recently available technologies (Davis & Owen, 1998; Hollander, 1997). Hollander (1995a, pp. 1–2) argued that this medium, an instance of what he termed "new news," is characterized by "direct, unmediated communication between leaders and the public, interaction between hosts and listeners/viewers, 'many-to-many' communication as opposed to the 'few-to-many' model in the mainstream press." He also described political talk programming in the context of the 1992 presidential election as emphasizing entertainment over information, easy questioning of guests by hosts, direct call-in access to guests and hosts by individuals, and public–candidate interaction (1995b, pp. 786–787).

Political talk (or call-in) radio, radio programming that includes a host who may talk with guests about political topics and appears to chat directly with anonymous audience members who call the program, has been present for a number of years. Audience access to hosts and guests soon followed the development of the talk format in small, local markets. Reforms in communication policy (especially the repeal of the fairness doctrine in 1985), technological developments (particularly market needs for programming AM stations to facilitate competition with FM stations), transmission by satellite to ease problems of national syndication, and the development of an inexpensive 800 national telephone system, all converged to make national political talk radio possible (Cappella, Turow, & Jamieson, 1996, pp. 6–7).

Audiences burgeoned during the early 1990s. Correspondingly, the nature of the political talk radio audience changed about that time (Bennett, 1998; Hofstetter, 1998). These changes had strong implications for the role of the medium in American society. Prior to the 1990s, political talk audiences were relatively small, listening primarily to local hosts and to programming emphasizing both local and sometimes national concerns. There was no meaningful national political talk audience that listened to a single national host. Later, as talk audiences became massive, and highly skilled, flamboyant national hosts such as Rush Limbaugh dominated ratings for the medium. Audiences became less provincial, less marginalized economically, socially, and politically, and more like the larger attentive public in the nation.

## Conceptualizing Political Talk Radio as a New Technology

Conceptualizing political talk primarily as a force to manipulate its audiences, as one-way communication, overly narrows the roles of the medium in society. Political talk radio has become a part of the national public sphere (Herbst, 1995; Williams & Delli Carpini, 2001) and has been a part of local public spheres for a longer time (Crittenden, 1971; Squires, 2000). Successful political talk is perceived as highly interactive, even when callers are kept on a tight leash and rigidly screened for the sake of audience share and ratings.

Conceptualizing political talk radio as journalism, viewed in the "objective" traditional roles some associate with that profession earlier in the 20th century, is no more appropriate than conceptualizing the talk medium purely as entertainment or diversion without political ramifications (Williams & Delli Carpini, 2001). Not only has the style and content of electronic news programming and other forms of programming linked in one way or another to public affairs converged with the development of the new media that include audience participation, discussion, and call-in shows, but the simple fact is that all entertainment programming conveys political values, preferences, and information. Listeners learn about political and social life from all media of communication. Politics is a great American spectator sport that many find enjoyable, and electronic media provide easily accessible, entertaining ways to engage in the sport at minimal cost.

Call-in political talk radio employs a more interactive format than most mass communication media, a format in which hosts, listeners, and guests appear to engage in exchanges. The medium has been conceptualized as a form of interpersonal communication (Armstrong & Rubin, 1989; Bierig & Dimmick, 1979) and parasocial interaction (Houlberg, 1984; Rubin & Step, 2000). Newhagen (1996) forcefully argued that both the interactive and perceived interactive character of the medium have strong implications for information processing. Interactivity may make political talk more effective in diffusing information and impressions among the mass public than other electronic media because of its capacity to engage its audience psychologically (Hofstetter, 1998).

Audiences participate in the construction of discourse in programs vicariously by listening to "arguing, reasoning, and discussing" occurring on the shows. Some call in and participate directly, but skilled hosts convey the impression that all are participating. Such participation, especially the intellectual and emotional engagement, may also encourage audience members to "fill in" details, draw conclusions, and filter and organize cognitions in ways not present explicitly in the manifest content of programs (Hofstetter, Barker et al., 1999). Talk provides a venue for "horizontal" exchanges among audiences, often linking hosts, other audience members, public officials, and other notables within the constraints of particular programming practices (Pan & Kosicki, 1997). The active engagement of audiences in programming may make the medium highly effective in forming, shaping, maintaining, and changing views.

Political talk may be a particularly influential medium because it optimizes the circumstances for effects to occur. Talk radio usually presents "clear, consistent, and repetitious" messages, listeners attribute relatively high credibility to the host, message legitimization is bolstered by reactions of callers and others in broadcasts, and message content is often loaded with strong persuasive content (Barker, 1998, 1999). Listeners are more likely to "receive the messages" from programming (Zaller, 1996, pp. 18–21), to attribute credibility to the messages, and to be influenced by the messages. Political talk also includes some of the characteristics that Graber (1993) considered to be "user friendly" aspects of news media: Content is attractive to the audience; it provides the analysis the audience wants; messages are framed in a manner listeners find comfortable; and it supplies information for use by the public. She concluded that political talk "made people feel like insiders, able to articulate concerns of their choice framed in their own way, and able to listen to other ordinary people doing the same" (p. 333).

The medium may also be more effective than other media in creating and sustaining communities of political interest (Crittenden,1971), and in mobilizing people to participate in public decision making (Hofstetter, 1998). Page and Tannenbaum (1996, pp. 51–52) presented evidence that political talk shows can provide a venue for a public that feels ignored, isolated, alienated, and powerless to channel their anger concerning legal and ethical standards related to actions by political elites, in this instance Zoe Baird's 1993 nomination to Attorney General. U.S. During the confirmation process, it came to light that Baird had what has come to be known as a "nanny problem," in which she had evaded paying her share of income tax and social security benefits for a day-care worker she employed. The issue was one that many people viewed as a breach of ethical conduct and much more important than officials and conventional news media reports reflected about the issue. Talk radio enhanced awareness of Baird's transgressions and provided a channel through which people could become active in discussions concerning the issue. Engaged segments of the public spoke by exercising influence through messages to members of Congress, the press, and other political influentials.

A burgeoning literature suggests that exposure to political talk has been associated with many "effects," and has been differentially viewed by scholars as either enhancing or undermining democratic processes. Correlates of political talk have included increased political efficacy, political interest, and political involvement (Bennett, 1998; Hofstetter, 1998; Hofstetter et al., 1994; Newhagen, 1994; Squires, 2000; Traugott et al., 1996), increases in both political information and misinformation (Hofstetter, Barker et al., 1999), perceived and actual information (Hollander, 1995b), negative and positive images of government and public institutions (Pfau et al., 1998), and support or opposition for specific policies and personalities (Barker, 1998, 1999; Barker & Knight, 2000). It appears that those most involved with the political talk medium (those who talk about what they hear, take actions based on programming, or try to call in) are more likely than the less involved to be more participatory, interested in politics, better informed, efficacious, attentive to politics in other media, less culturally estranged, more likely to attribute greater credibility to media, and more likely to listen to political talk to gain information (Hofstetter, Smith et al., 1999). Barker and Knight (2000) linked support for specific issue positions to specific foci Limbaugh emphasized in contemporaneous programming, and Kennedy and Hofstetter (2001) found that exposure to Limbaugh was associated with antifeminist-misogynist attitudes after statistically controlling for a number of possibly confounding variables.

Not all political talk radio is national, nor do all stations fit a common mold in style or content of broadcasts. Local programming may be more important to individuals' political lives than national programming, especially when mainstream media fail to provide programming that is relevant, appropriate, trusted, and perceived as useful for citizens (Crittenden, 1971). Squires (2000) argued that African Americans in Chicago regard political talk on WVON-AM, an African American owned and operated station, as an important part of the Black public sphere in the city. Listeners use talk programming as a forum, a place to discuss a broad variety of public concerns. Station ownership and willingness of hosts to play effective moderator roles in discourse contribute to listener trust and attribution of credibility. Having overcome some initial skepticism, Crittenden (1971) concluded that a local talk radio program also served at least partially as a community forum in Terre Haute, Indiana, in one of the first systematic studies of the medium.

## MOTIVATION TO USE POLITICAL TALK RADIO

### Conceptualization

The nature of a medium, such as political talk radio, is closely linked to the motivation to use it. Motivation is one key to understanding the role of the medium because information processing is directly linked to the experience (Armstrong & Rubin, 1989; Rubin & Step, 2000). Thus, whereas communication technologies set limits on the use of any communication medium, the social and political significance of a communication medium is in large part contingent on the way people use it, and these uses depend on what the user brings to a situation. The broader meaning of a technology in society is shaped by the uses to which it is put by citizens. Communication media are particularly important sources of information in helping citizens to understand the world and their place in it (Dervin, 1989). Political talk radio may be particularly important not only because of message characteristics but because listeners find programming to be engaging psychologically and to serve needs to "make sense" of political and social environments. It is not only what you hear but what you do with what you hear that is important (Hofstetter & Gianos, 1997).

Political talk radio is distinct from more orthodox sources of public affairs information on radio and other media (Davis, 1997). It is primarily commercial in nature, driven by the imperatives of audience share and demographics. Talk radio appears to have prospered by emphasizing populist themes and giving nonelite listeners a chance to state their views before a large audience. The medium uses a series of mechanisms to provide gratifications beyond simple acquisition of information. These include personalization of current events, emphasizing personalities, controversies, scandals, and the bizarre, making inflammatory statements, employing shock talk (e.g., making outrageous, conventionally improper statements that are designed to produce emotive responses from the audience), and a host of other tactics to engage audiences emotionally (Davis, 1997, pp. 324–326).

Political talk radio is also a medium that permits discussion concerning pressing events of the day. It gives some citizens the ability to speak their minds in a public forum, under the guise of anonymity, and to appear to contribute to a national discourse in a meaningful way. It makes participation in the public sphere possible for those who penetrate producer screening, and it may give all the impression that they are participating in an ongoing dialogue.

A number of studies of the motives to listen to and/or call talk radio programming were conducted prior to the explosion of audiences for the medium during the early 1990s. Not all focused on political talk, but they nonetheless provide useful hypotheses about how the audience relates to the medium. Armstrong and Rubin (1989, p. 89) conducted one of the early comprehensive studies of motivation to use (not necessarily political) talk radio by comparing differences in motives for listening between callers and those who listened only. Sampling talk radio callers and probable listeners, Armstrong and Rubin reported that measures of relaxation, exciting entertainment, convenience, escape, and information seeking were intercorrelated. Those variables, in turn, were correlated with affinity to the medium. They also found that social and communication variables were negatively related to exposure to talk radio. In particular, people who listened more were less likely to communicate socially. Armstrong and Rubin also reported that callers, more than listeners who did not call, were more likely to avoid personal communication, were less mobile, listened to talk radio more, felt talk radio was more important in their lives, and were more strongly motivated to listen. They concluded that listeners' affinity to the medium may involve the ability to listen to two-way conversations without getting involved directly and without their self-esteem being threatened by direct participation.

Many of the earlier studies of talk radio stressed the motivational strength of desire to avoid isolation from others as a reason for listening and/or calling talk programs. Avery (1990, p. 93) reported that both calling and listening fulfill a need for interpersonal interaction, possibly promoted by the anonymity of the caller, the host, and the audience. Others (Bierig & Dimmick, 1979; Tramer & Jeffres, 1983; Turow, 1974) reported that a strong need for interpersonal communication motivated callers who were more likely to be socially isolated than others. In contrast, Surlin (1986) reported that information seeking (surveillance) was a dominant motive for listening to talk radio in Jamaica, and that companionship was less sought from programming. Crittenden (1971) related similar findings among his Terre Haute sample.

Hofstetter and Gianos (1997) argued that political talk radio was particularly attractive to persons who engaged in more active communication about an issue. These were people who were aware of particular political problems, who felt that the problems made a difference to them personally, and who felt they might be able to do something about the problems. People who were actively oriented to political problems in that sense were more likely to use political talk shows and to be engaged with them by talking about program content, taking actions due to program content, and calling a show.

## Measurement

Motivation to use a medium has been measured in several ways. The most common procedures involve asking respondents to rate the importance of reasons for using various media. Armstrong and Rubin (1989) and Hofstetter et al., (1994) measured motivation to listen to talk radio, including both political and nonpolitical shows. The majority of listeners in the latter research mentioned specific political programs when asked and those who mentioned other programming were omitted. Rubin and Step (2000) measured motivation to listen to public affairs call-in talk radio. In their study, Hofstetter et al., (1994, p. 473) reported that the dominant self-reported motivation for listening to political talk radio was information seeking (48.6% of listeners). Another 19.3% reported listening for entertainment, 11.9% for personal interest, 10.7% to pass time, and the rest for a variety of other reasons. Beyond these, few quantitative data have been reported on specific reasons for listening to political talk radio.

Very similar results were found in a more recent survey of adults in San Diego conducted in 1997 in the responses to an open-ended question asked of those who reported having listened to distinctively political talk programming. Although diversion and entertainment were mentioned by some in the political talk audience, the dominant motivation for listening was information. About 55.4% of political talk listeners reported that information seeking (finding out information about politics and political issues or learning about events and personalities) was "the most important reason" for listening to "the most recent (political talk) show." Passing time or diversion was mentioned by 22.3%, and entertainment or fun by 21.5%.

Respondents who reported having listened to political talk radio at least once during the prior month were also asked to agree or disagree with a series of statements reflecting information seeking, entertainment, and diversion reasons for listening to political talk. Distributions reported in Table 10.1 indicate the predominance of information seeking.

TABLE 10.1

Motivation: Importance of Selected Reasons for Listening to Political Talk Radio[a]

| Item | Not Important | Not Very Important | Important | Very Important | N |
|---|---|---|---|---|---|
| a. To get information about government and political issues? | 8.1% | 20.8% | 49.4% | 21.8% | 308 |
| b. To listen to government and political issues being discussed in an entertaining way? | 12.4% | 26.4% | 48.5% | 12.7% | 307 |
| c. To get away from the stress and tedium of daily events in my life? | 37.0% | 33.1% | 22.7% | 7.1% | 308 |
| d. To learn about government and political issues? | 8.8% | 17.6% | 51.0% | 22.5% | 306 |
| e. To obtain information about government and political issues that I can talk to friends about? | 16.4% | 25.6% | 47.2% | 10.8% | 305 |
| f. To pass time so that I have something to occupy myself? | 31.1% | 35.4% | 28.2% | 5.2% | 305 |
| g. To find out how to vote on issues and candidates? | 14.9% | 26.3% | 43.2% | 15.6% | 308 |
| h. To find out what I should think about important national events and controversies? | 19.1% | 27.0% | 42.1% | 11.8% | 304 |
| i. To find out what other people think about government and political issues? | 13.0% | 23.1% | 49.0% | 14.9% | 308 |
| j. To learn the real truth about important national events and controversies that I cannot learn from news media? | 22.7% | 26.3% | 36.8% | 14.1% | 304 |

[a]Respondents were asked: "Some people tell us that listing to talk radio programs helps them to in their daily lives, others say that talk radio is simply enjoyable, and others say that talk radio has no impact on their lives. As I read each of the following things that people have told us, just tell me whether political talk radio is very important, important, not very important, or not at all important for you personally."

The modal location of listening among San Diegans was driving to and from work (67.3% of listeners). Fewer, 48.9%, reported listening at home, and 28.9% reported listening at work and 20% at other places. Motivation was not strongly related to where one listened to political talk radio. The only location related to motivation was listening at home. Home listeners were more likely to be characterized by information seeking (55.7%) than diversion (38.6%) or entertainment (39.3%). The relationship is statistically significant ($\chi^2 = 7.05$, $p = .03$).

Distinctions among the motives for following political talk have some but not other consequences when one-way ANOVAs are computed using "most important reason to listen to PTR" as a predictor. Exposure to political talk programming is higher among those who report that the most important reason for listening is to seek information than it is among those listening for entertainment, and least among those who report listening for diversion ($F_{(2,218)} = 8.64$), $p < .001$. Involvement with the medium also follows a similar pattern when measured by an index of political talk radio activity, a behaviorally oriented indicator of engagement with the medium (Hofstetter, 1998; Hofstetter, Smith et al., 1999). Political talk activity was measured by a cumulative index of activities (talking about something on a broadcast, taking an action because of a program, calling the show) associated with listening. Information seekers were more involved with political talk than were those using the medium for entertainment. Those who report diversion as the most important reason for listening were least involved ($F_{(2,255)} = 9.46$, $p < .001$). Those motivated by information seeking were more likely to pay attention to talk radio when listening ($F_{(2,246)} = 7.06$, $p < .001$), find programming credible ($F_{(2,222)} = 4.01$, $p = .019$), find political talk to be useful for getting information about politics ($F_{(2,250)} = 15.16$, $p < .001$), and trust political talk radio the most ($F_{(2,240)} = 4.37$, $p = .014$). The latter findings contrast to some extent with the arguments advanced by Jackson and colleagues (chapter 8, this volume), although the nature and use of the medium contrasts sharply with the Internet.

On the other hand, the most important reason for listening to political talk in San Diego was not statistically significantly related to a measure of conventional political information (Hofstetter, Barker et al., 1999) or to self-ratings of "perceived information" (Newhagen, 1996). Paradoxically, the most important reason for listening was related ($p < .05$) to a measure of "misinformation," a summed index of agreement with counterfactual policy positions for which correct answers were clear and well-defined information was publicly available at the time of the survey (Hofstetter, Barker et al., 1999). Those seeking information from political talk actually scored higher on an objective index of misinformation, those seeking diversion were somewhat lower, and those seeking entertainment were lowest on the misinformation index. Some sought information and processed misinformation; some sought entertainment or diversion and gained information.

The motivational items in Table 10.1 were factor analyzed and rotated to simple structure using varimax procedures in order to assess the number of dimensions required to structure the data. Results of the analysis are presented in Table 10.2.

TABLE 10.2
Motivation Associated With Political Talk Radio[a]

| *Some people tell us that listing to talk radio programs helps them to in their daily lives, others say that talk radio is simply enjoyable, and others say that talk radio has no impact on their lives. As I read each of the following things that people have told us, just tell me whether political talk radio is very important, important, not very important, or not at all important for you personally:* | *Information Seeking* | *Entertainment* | $h^2$ |
|---|---|---|---|
| a. To get information about government and political issues? | .805 | .005 | .64 |
| d. To learn about government and political issues? | .803 | −.010 | .64 |
| h. To find out what I should think about important national events and controversies? | .735 | .155 | .56 |
| j. To learn the real truth about important national events and controversies that I cannot learn from news media? | .717 | .134 | .53 |
| g. To find out how to vote on issues and candidates? | .697 | .137 | .50 |
| i. To find out what other people think about government and political issues? | .673 | .166 | .48 |
| e. To obtain information about government and political issues that I can talk to friends about? | .666 | .187 | .47 |
| b. To listen to government and political issues being discussed in an entertaining way? | .459 | .438 | .40 |
| f. To pass time so that I have something to occupy myself? | .074 | .843 | .71 |
| c. To get away from the stress and tedium of daily events in my life? | .076 | .822 | .68 |
| Percent of total variance explained | 39.6% | 17.0 | 56.6 |

[a]Coefficients are factor loadings rotated to simple structure by varimax procedures and item communalities ($h^2$).

Two theoretically interpretable dimensions that bear on information seeking and entertainment or diversion emerged from the analysis. Items stressing companionship, loneliness, and parasocial interaction (Levy, 1979; Rubin & Step, 2000) were not included in the questions put to respondents so that the dimensionality of the data was constrained in this respect. However, the information-seeking dimension explained nearly 40% of the variance among items. Two indices were formed by computing the means of the items loading most highly on each of the factors. Both measures attained acceptable levels of reliability with Cronbach's alpha = .87 for the information-seeking scale and .65 for the entertainment scale.

Measures of partial association indicate that the two motivation scales have implications for behaviors relating to political talk radio as reported in Table 10.3. Each of the variables in Table 10.3 was regressed on the information and entertainment

TABLE 10.3

Regression of Political Talk Radio Motivation on Selected Variables Controlling for Total Exposure to Political Talk Radio Exposure, Partisanship, Ideology, Political Interest, Age, Education, and Gender[a]

| Dependent Variables | Information Seeking | | Entertainment | |
|---|---|---|---|---|
| | Beta | p | Beta | p |
| Q8a. Would you say you agreed with the talk show host nearly all the time, most of the time, some of the time, or very little of the time? | .14 | .026 | -.02 | .345 |
| Q8c. Do you pay close attention, some attention, or not much attention to what people are saying when you listen to talk radio? | .36 | .001 | -.15 | .006 |
| Q8d. Have you ever talked to someone else because of something you heard on a political talk show? | .06 | .127 | -.00 | .233 |
| Q8f. Have you ever taken an action because of something you heard on a political talk show? | .02 | .373 | -.04 | .059 |
| Q8h. Have you ever called a political radio talk show? | -.00 | .071 | .08 | .113 |
| Q9. Generally, do you feel that people who call in to political talk radio shows are like you: A lot, somewhat like you, neither like you nor different than you, somewhat different than you, a lot different than you? | -.22 | .001 | -.04 | .268 |
| Q10. Would you say that the people who call in to the shows know what they are talking about: Never, rarely, sometimes, usually, all the time? | .23 | .001 | -.03 | .240 |
| Q11. When you listen to the shows, do you get new ideas or learn about issues: never, rarely, sometimes, usually, all the time? | .35 | .001 | -.08 | .096 |
| Q15a. Is it very true, true, untrue, or very untrue that most political talk radio is factual? | -.30 | .001 | -.00 | .497 |
| Q15b. Can be trusted? | -.30 | .001 | -.01 | .438 |
| Q15c. Is fair? | -.29 | .001 | .03 | .245 |
| Q15d. Tells the whole story? | -.24 | .001 | .02 | .403 |
| Q15f. Hosts separate facts from opinions? | -.32 | .001 | .03 | .314 |
| Q15h. Concerned about the community's well being? | -.19 | .005 | .03 | .302 |
| Q15i. Concerned mainly about the public interest? | -.12 | .034 | .05 | .224 |
| Q15l. Watches out after your interests? | -.18 | .003 | .01 | .465 |
| Q15p. Does not care what the audience thinks? | .02 | .360 | .03 | .303 |

| Item | | | | |
|---|---|---|---|---|
| Q25c. How would you grade the radio news program you are most familiar with? | .26 | .001 | −.09 | .073 |
| Q25f. How would you grade most journalists who report news about government and politics on radio? | .31 | .001 | −.05 | .222 |
| Q28e. People can trust radio talk programs to tell the truth about government and politics more than the major news media. | .22 | .001 | −.02 | .374 |
| Q28g. If the major news media and the radio talk show I listen to the most reported conflicting views about government and politics, I would believe the radio talk show. | .31 | .001 | −.21 | .001 |
| Q32d. When you are listening to the radio something is said about politics and public affairs how much attention do you pay to it? | .21 | .001 | −.07 | .112 |
| Q35g. Now, consider a longer period of time, say one month. How many days would you say you talk to others about something you have heard on a radio program during an average month? | .06 | .187 | −.11 | .046 |
| Q36c. Would you say you find each of the following very useful, useful, not very useful, or not at all useful for getting information about government and politics? Political talk radio programs. | −.44 | .001 | .13 | .019 |
| Perceived information index. | .08 | .088 | −.00 | .495 |
| Conventional information index. | −.09 | .069 | −.01 | .467 |
| Misinformation index. | .00 | .498 | −.15 | .010 |
| Exposure to radio news. | .19 | .002 | −.06 | .186 |
| Exposure to discussion public affairs. | −.01 | .444 | −.04 | .254 |
| Exposure to newspapers public affairs. | −.04 | .247 | −.08 | .112 |
| Exposure to nonnews TV. | .01 | .460 | .06 | .187 |
| Exposure to TV news. | −.06 | .144 | −.05 | .235 |
| Exposure to news magazines. | −.08 | .125 | .04 | .267 |

[a]Numbers in cells are standardized regression coefficients produced by regressing each item on level of interactivity characterizing political talk radio (reported by respondents when total exposure to political talk radio exposure, partisanship, ideology, political interest, age, education, and gender are controlled), associated one-sided probabilities, and zero-order correlations.

scales along with total exposure to political talk programming, political interest, partisanship, ideological identification, age, education, and gender. Standardized regression coefficients, reported in Table 10.3 along with associated probabilities, show the extent to which each variable in the rows of the table is associated with the information-seeking and entertainment motives after the other variables have been controlled.

After controlling for possibly confounding variables, information seeking was related to agreement with talk show hosts, paying close attention to talk programming, perception that callers are just like the respondent, the view that callers know what they are talking about, and reporting being stimulated with ideas from the shows. Information seeking was also related to beliefs that the programs are factual, can be trusted, are fair, and tell the whole story, and that hosts separate fact from opinion, are concerned about the community's well-being, are concerned about the public interest, and watch out for "your interests."

Information seekers also tended to grade radio news programs and most journalists who report on radio favorably, and believe that people can trust radio talk to tell the truth. They also attributed high levels of credibility to radio talk if it gave interpretations to events that conflicted with major news media, and felt that political talk radio is very useful for getting information about government and politics. Although information seeking was related to total exposure to political talk programming and to radio news, information seeking was unrelated to measures of information, misinformation, and perceived information.

In sharp contrast, entertainment motivation was unrelated to most measures in Table 10.3 after controlling for possibly confounding variables. Those motivated by seeking entertainment were less likely to pay attention to what was being said on political talk programs, to attribute credibility to the medium, and to find political talk very useful in getting information about politics and government. Again, information seeking was unrelated to any of the measures of information/misinformation, perceived or behavioral, whereas entertainment motivation was associated with a decrease in misinformation.

### Interactivity

Talk radio is characterized by greater interactivity than other mass media. A survey of 764 adults residing in San Diego, California, was conducted by telephone during the spring and early summer of 1997 by students in the author's graduate and undergraduate political behavior classes. Respondents were asked to rate the interactivity of a series of communication media (very interactive, somewhat interactive, not very interactive, not interactive).

Findings from the survey, reported in Table 10.4, indicate that 27.7% reported that political talk radio was very interactive, 50.1% somewhat interactive, 13.9% not very interactive, and 8.3% not interactive. Nearly four in five respondents perceived that political talk was very or somewhat interactive. Among the 764

TABLE 10.4
Rated Interactivity by Medium[a]

"How would you rate the interactivity of the following? Would you say that each of the following is very interactive, somewhat interactive, not very interactive, or not at all interactive?"

| Medium | Very Interactive | Somewhat Interactive | Not Very Interactive | Not Interactive | N |
|---|---|---|---|---|---|
| a. Telephone | 70.4% | 23.0% | 3.7% | 2.9% | 734 |
| b. Newspapers | 12.8% | 28.0% | 35.5% | 23.7% | 729 |
| c. Network TV News | 13.9% | 26.7% | 30.6% | 28.8% | 733 |
| d. Political Talk Radio | 27.7% | 50.1% | 13.9% | 8.3% | 617 |
| e. The Internet | 56.0% | 31.0% | 8.2% | 4.7% | 571 |

[a] Percentages are of those rating interactivity of each medium, total $N$ sampled $= 764$.

who completed interviews in the survey, 19.2% could not rate the interactivity of political talk, doubtlessly due to unfamiliarity with radio talk programming by a substantial proportion of subjects. Only telephones and the Internet were viewed as more interactive than political talk, although 25.3% of all interviewed could not evaluate the interactivity of the Internet probably also due to unfamiliarity with the medium. Newspapers and network TV news, the traditional mass media, were evaluated to be much less interactive, as one would presume.

Interactivity was related to use while driving and at work but not at home or in other places. About 72% who viewed political talk as highly interactive used the medium while driving, in comparison to 48.6% of those who viewed the medium as low in interactivity and 69.8% who viewed the medium as medium in interactivity. About 40.2% who said political talk is highly interactive used the medium at work, whereas 28.2% used it there among those who said it was medium in interactivity and 13.9% among those who said it was low in interactivity.

Perceived interactivity was also related to motivations to listen to political talk ($\chi^2 = 9.90$, $df = 4$, $p < .05$) among those who reported listening. Those who reported that seeking information or entertainment was their most important motive for listening to political talk radio (35% and 36.4%, respectively) were more likely than those using the medium for diversion (18.2%) to perceive it as highly interactive. Those who mentioned diversion were more likely to perceive political talk as not interactive or not very interactive (21.8% vs. 8.8% and 10.9% for information seeking and entertainment, respectively). Each of the motivational groups reported seeing political talk as somewhat interactive at about the same rate.

Perceptions of interactivity were assumed to influence the use of political talk radio, especially the level of psychological involvement with programming. We would expect that reported agreement with the host, paying attention to program content, talking to others, taking actions because of something heard on the programs, and calling a program are all associated with degree of involvement with political talk shows. Respondents in the San Diego survey who reported listening to any political talk radio were asked whether they agreed with the talk show host (they listened to the most) nearly all the time, most of the time, some of the time, or very little of the time, whether they pay close attention, some attention, or not much attention to what people are saying on the shows, whether they ever talked to someone else because of something (they) heard on a political talk show, ever took an action because of something (they) heard on a political talk show, and whether they had ever called a political radio talk show.

The zero-order correlations between perceived interactivity and agreement was .22 ($p < .001$), paying attention .21 ($p < .001$), talking to others .14 ($p < .01$), taking an action .11 ($p < .05$), and calling a show .09 ($p < .05$). In order to test whether the correlations between perceived interactivity and each of the variables was spurious, each item was first regressed on total exposure to political talk programming, political interest, partisanship, ideological identification, age, education, and gender. Zero-order and standardized regression coefficients are presented in Table 10.5. Pairwise deletion of missing data was used. Perceived interactivity was then added to the equation to determine if the variable increased $R^2$ significantly once the others had been controlled. The partial association between interactivity and agreement with the host, paying attention, and talking to others remained significant ($p < .05$), although interactivity was no longer related significantly to taking an action or calling a show once the other variables had been controlled.

Listeners were also asked about the perceived public sphere, the character of other participants in the talk radio experience. The assumption was that perceived interactivity is related to more favorable views of participants in as much as an electronically constructed community engaged in discussion of public affairs is formed through the programming. Listeners were asked whether they felt that people who call in to political talk radio shows "are like you . . . a lot, somewhat like you, neither like you nor different than you, somewhat different than you, (or) a lot different than you," "know what they are talking about, never, rarely, sometimes, usually, all the time," and when one listens to the programming "do you get new ideas or learn about issues, never, rarely, sometimes, usually, all the time."

Each of the items was correlated with perceived interactivity in the hypothesized direction ($p < .01$). After controlling for total exposure to political talk programming, political interest, partisanship, ideological identification, age, education, and gender using multiple regression, interactivity continued to be associated with perception that callers are like oneself, know what they are talking about, and the perception that one gets new ideas about issues ($p < .01$).

Perceptions of interactivity were assumed also to influence views of political talk programming and hosts. Respondents were asked to indicate whether each of a series of characteristics is very true, true untrue, or very untrue that political talk radio is: "factual," "can be trusted," "is fair," "tells the whole story," "hosts separate facts from opinions," "are concerned about the community's well-being," "are concerned mainly about the public interest," "watches out after your interests," "and does not care what the audience thinks."

## TABLE 10.5
### Regression of Political Talk Radio Perceived Interactivity on Selected Variables Controlling for Total Exposure to Political Talk Radio Exposure, Partisanship, Ideology, Political Interest, Age, Education, and Gender[a]

| Dependent Variables | Beta | p | r |
|---|---|---|---|
| Q8a.. Would you say you agreed with the talk show host nearly all the time, most of the time, some of the time, or very little of the time? | .20 | .001 | .22*** |
| Q8c. Do you pay close attention, some attention, or not much attention to what people are saying when you listen to talk radio? | .16 | .007 | .21*** |
| Q8d. Have you ever talked to someone else because of something you heard on a political talk show? | .11 | .078 | .14** |
| Q8f. Have you ever taken an action because of something you heard on a political talk show? | .05 | .384 | .11* |
| Q8h. Have you ever called a political radio talk show? | .06 | .360 | .09* |
| Q9. Generally, do you feel that people who call in to political talk radio shows are like you: A lot, somewhat like you, neither like you nor different than you, somewhat different than you, a lot different than you? | .12 | .068 | .14** |
| Q10. Would you say that the people who call in to the shows know what they are talking about: Never, rarely, sometimes, usually, all the time? | .16 | .008 | .20** |
| Q11. When you listen to the shows, do you get new ideas or learn about issues: never, rarely, sometimes, usually, all the time? | .11 | .074 | .15** |
| Q15a. Is it very true, true, untrue or very untrue that most political talk radio is factual? | .14 | .023 | .18*** |
| Q15b. Can be trusted? | .28 | .000 | .32*** |
| Q15c. Is fair? | .22 | .000 | .25*** |
| Q15d. Tells the whole story? | .20 | .002 | .24*** |
| Q15f. Hosts separate facts from opinions? | .09 | .150 | .12* |
| Q15h. Concerned about the community's well being? | .05 | .403 | .10* |
| Q15i. Concerned mainly about the public interest? | .08 | .211 | .12* |
| Q15l. Watches out after your interests? | .11 | .057 | .17* |
| Q15p. Does not care what the audience thinks? | .11 | .100 | .12* |
| Q25c. How would you grade the radio news program you are most familiar with? | .18 | .004 | .20** |

(continues)

TABLE 10.5  (Continued)

| Dependent Variables | Beta | p | r |
|---|---|---|---|
| Q36c. Would you say you find each of the following very useful, useful, not very useful, or not at all useful for getting information about government and politics? Political talk radio programs. | .23 | .000 | .28*** |
| Q25f. How would you grade most journalists who report news about government and politics on radio? | .08 | .192 | .09* |
| Q28e. People can trust radio talk programs to tell the truth about government and politics more than the major news media. | .10 | .115 | .14* |
| Q28g. If the major news media and the radio talk show I listen to the most reported conflicting views about government and politics, I would believe the radio talk show. | .08 | .184 | .13* |
| Q32d. When you are listening to the radio and something is said about politics and public affairs, how much attention do you pay to it? | .08 | .172 | .14** |
| Q35g. Now, consider a longer period of time, say one month. How many days would you say you talk to others about something you have heard on a radio program during an average month? | .09 | .148 | .13* |
| Perceived information index. | .16 | .004 | .23*** |
| Conventional information index. | .07 | .191 | .11* |
| Misinformation index. | −.09 | .153 | −.09* |
| Exposure to radio news. | .16 | .007 | .20** |
| Exposure to discussion public affairs. | .05 | .428 | .10* |
| Exposure to newspapers public affairs. | .03 | .573 | .06 |
| Exposure to nonnews TV. | −.04 | .565 | −.02 |
| Exposure to TV news. | −.02 | .778 | −.02 |
| Exposure to news magazines. | .01 | .840 | .04 |
| Information seeking motivation. | .12 | .024 | .15** |
| Entertainment motivation. | .04 | .245 | .06 |

[a] Numbers in cells are standardized regression coefficients produced by regressing each item on level of interactivity characterizing political talk radio (reported by respondents when total exposure to political talk radio exposure, partisanship, ideology; political interest, age, education, and gender are controlled), associated one-sided probabilities, and zero-order correlations. Statistical significance of zero-order correlations is designated as * $p < .05$, ** $p < .01$, and *** $p < .001$.

Interactivity was associated with traditionally desirable characteristics of media journalism. The greater the perceived interactivity, the more listeners attributed dimensions of credibility to political talk radio, the more they saw the medium as being factual, trustworthy, fair, and as telling the whole story ($p < .001$). Interactivity was also associated with reports of hosts separating facts from opinions, being concerned about the community's well-being and about the public interest, watching out for the respondent's personal interests, and not caring about what the audience thinks ($p < .05$).

After controls for total exposure to political talk programming, political interest, partisanship, ideological identification, age, education, and gender using multiple regression, all relationships remained statistically significant ($p < .05$) except for perceptions concerning the host: The host's ability to separate facts and opinions, and the host's concern for the community's well-being and for the public interest ($p > .05$) were unrelated to interactivity once statistical controls were applied. Thus, although listeners who see political talk as being highly interactive are impressed with traits characterizing the objective journalism of the early 20th century, they hold no systematic opinion concerning the host's ability to be objective and the host's level of concern for the broader collective good, for the host's "public regardingness." Perhaps audiences assume that hosts are politicized and view them as hewing to a political line that, as entertaining and engaging as the line may be, is far from objective and disinterested in many respects. Most observers regard this conclusion to be accurate for most commercial radio political talk hosts. Can it be that political talk radio is the end point of the merging of journalism and entertainment in electronic media?

Two additional characteristics of political radio are important in the way people relate to the medium: Evaluations of radio news and perceived utility of political talk programming and exposure to radio journalists and general exposure to political talk radio were measured separately to obtain independent evaluations of the two types of programs. Respondents apparently failed to distinguish the two types of programs clearly with respect to interactivity. Those who perceived talk programming to be highly interactive gave high grades to radio news programs and also agreed that political talk radio is highly "useful for getting information about government and politics ($p < .001$)." The relationships are statistically significant ($p < .001$) after application of control variables.

An additional question remains: Is the relationship between perception of political talk interactivity and the preceding variables confounded with involvement and exposure to other media of communication or is the relationship narrowly a function of the political talk medium? To answer that question, perception of political talk radio interactivity was correlated with amounts of exposure to radio news programming, discussion of public affairs with other people, exposure to public affairs in newspapers, TV news programs, other TV programs, and news magazines. It appears that the role of perception of political talk interactivity discriminates by type of medium if not by specific content. The zero-order correlation between perceived interactivity and exposure to radio news was statistically significant ($p < .001$), and the results were replicated when controls using multiple regression were applied ($p < .05$). Exposure to none of the other media was related to perceived political talk interactivity once the set of controls were applied. As Newhagen (2002, personal communication) pointed out, perhaps these findings represent a shift to using radio as a source of information, a way to seek information about social and political life that is driven not only by commuting but also as "an efficient and credible source for 'real news.'"

That interpretation of the relationship between interactivity and perceived traits of political talk radio was reinforced when scores from more reliable scales based on 15 items reflecting how respondents characterized the medium were computed and then correlated with perceived interactivity. Three theoretically meaningful orthogonal dimensions, explaining 50.3% of the total variance among the items, were isolated by factor analysis rotated to simple structure using varimax procedures. The rotated loadings appeared to group items by talk credibility, endorsement of traditional values, and talk radio irresponsibility. Statistics and item wording for the factor analysis are presented in Table 10.6. Scales for the dimensions were formed by computing means of items loading most highly on each factor. Two

TABLE 10.6
Characteristics of Political Talk Radio[a]

| "People have told us a number of things they believe about political talk radio. Regardless of how much you listen to it, just tell me whether you think that each of the following is very true of most political talk radio, true, untrue, or very untrue of most political talk radio?" | Credibility | Values | Irresponsibility | $h^2$ |
|---|---|---|---|---|
| a.  Most political talk radio can be trusted .......... | .795 | .222 | −.051 | .68 |
| b.  Is fair ........................................ | .751 | .229 | .142 | .63 |
| c.  Tells the whole story ......................... | .693 | .244 | −.074 | .54 |
| d.  Is factual ..................................... | .684 | .279 | −.022 | .54 |
| e.  Hosts separate facts from opinions ............. | .660 | .207 | −.019 | .47 |
| f.  Unbiased ..................................... | .516 | .169 | −.131 | .31 |
| g.  Patriotic ..................................... | .147 | .684 | −.220 | .53 |
| h.  Moral ........................................ | .322 | .674 | −.097 | .56 |
| i.  Watches out after your interests ................ | .246 | .649 | .017 | .48 |
| j.  Concerned about the community's well being.... | .250 | .645 | .347 | .59 |
| k.  Concerned mainly about the public interest ..... | .206 | .616 | .322 | .52 |
| l.  Respects peoples' privacy ..................... | .228 | .568 | −.389 | .52 |
| m.  Talk hosts are well trained .................... | .258 | .346 | −.012 | .18 |
| n.  Sensationalizes .............................. | −.225 | −.031 | .698 | .53 |
| o.  Does not care what the audience thinks ........ | .075 | .006 | .593 | .35 |
| Percent of total variance explained | 22.1% | 19.3 | 8.8 | 50.3 |

[a]Coefficients are factor loadings rotated to simple structure by varimax procedures and item communalities ($h^2$).

of the scales, credibility and values, reached satisfactory levels of internal consistency (Cronbach's alpha = .83 and alpha = .79, respectively), although the two-item scale labeled "irresponsibility" failed to attain a minimal level of reliability and was dropped from the analysis.

Political talk credibility and endorsement of traditional values were both correlated with perception of interactivity ($p < .01$ and $p < .05$, respectively). The results were replicated after controlling for the set of possibly confounding variables outlined earlier, which included partisanship and self-identified ideological stance.

The role of talk interactivity is strictly related to the medium as well as to political talk. It is quite likely that listeners do not discriminate precisely between call-in talk and news venues on most AM radio (Hofstetter et al., 1994, p. 470) so that the perception associated with talk programming generalizes to the radio news programming format, or listeners perceive political talk as news, or both. It is likely that parasocial interaction plays a relatively greater role in the process when no interactivity is involved, as in news programming (Rubin & Step, 2000).

## DISCUSSION

Drawing from his own and much of the research cited here, Bennett (1998) concluded that political talk radio listeners are more knowledgeable and more politically active than nonlisteners and therefore the medium may enhance democratic citizenship.

Two views of the relationship between mass media exposure and democratic citizenship, an optimistic and a pessimistic view, have been presented. The optimistic view, propounded by Graber (1988, 2001) with some reservations, argues that citizens are capable of distilling useful information from news media and that the news media frequently, if not always, include useful information for citizenship. The pessimistic view, propounded by Entman (1989), is that news media are unlikely to provide systematically useful and extensive information to help produce widespread informed citizenship due to a complex set of market, social, and political forces in the news creation and dissemination processes, and due to the public's prevailing news preferences. One might suppose that the trend for both electronic and printed "news" presentations to present in more entertaining formats might support the more pessimistic view.

Speculating a bit, one might consider the relative level of information citizens hold. If large segments of the American public are devoid or nearly devoid of information and even larger segments of the public operate on very minimal information (Converse, 1964), then it is entirely possible that more entertaining and engaging media might attract persons and provide a modicum of political information for those who otherwise would receive no politically relevant information at all. Successful political talk radio hosts are characterized by their flamboyance, their ability to attract and engage audiences in ways other media do less effectively. Coupled with information-seeking motivation, the perceived interactive character of political talk radio is strongly engaging for mass audiences, as demonstrated in this chapter. Even if the quality of political commentary in political talk programming is sadly lacking by objective criteria in comparison to more orthodox news media, there may still be a net gain in information levels in society as a whole. Once attracted, many in the audience may become interested in politics and use other, more "objective" media and thereby enhance their stock of information and sophistication in analyzing their knowledge base of politics even more.

Many studies conducted during the last decade documented that the use of political talk radio is associated with information and participation, with the use of other media of communication, including news media, and with a variety of other activities and characteristics associated with citizenship such as political involvement, interest, political efficacy, and discussion. The partial associations between exposure to political talk and information and participation reported in these studies are not large, but remain robust even after many alternative explanations have been taken into account through statistical controls. We also know that many political talk programs include content that is hardly objective, balanced, or correct in implication.

Lest we become too enamored with political talk, it is vital to indicate that many of the studies also show that use of political talk radio is associated with misinformation, limited skepticism of host credibility, serious doubts about the vitality and value of fundamental American institutions, and a tendency to attribute knowledge and homophily to participants in programming. It is by no means clear that political talk generally enhances reasoned debate and discussion among citizens and, in many instances, anecdotal if not systematic evidence has been presented that associates exposure to political talk with a variety of forms of political and social mischief. One would be hard pressed to find much reasoned debate in the programming of the more popular national hosts.

On the other hand, instances can be cited in which particular, usually local, programming has contributed to the development of the public sphere in ways that encourage knowledgeable popular participation. Data here and elsewhere suggest that the medium may lead to a spiral of citizenship: Political talk is intrinsically engaging, audiences are further motivated to use political talk for information-seeking reasons, and political talk may provide an impetus for increased interest in politics among politically marginal citizens that also leads to the increasing use of alternative, more orthodox news media and to greater levels of political participation and knowledge. Talk hosts such as Limbaugh employ some if not most of the tools of modern propagandists (Swain, 1999, p. 38), many of which resemble typical advertising techniques. Talk-show hosts do not present themselves as neutral observers on issues discussed in programs nor do they make a pretense of being other than advocates. Some even claim to present "the truth" about public issues.

Using the medium in seeking information for popular participation requires many skills involved in gleaning political information from news media. The skills are generally those that good journalists and social scientists employ. They include the capacity to collect and compare information from political talk shows with information collected from a variety of other, more conventional, news sources. Judgments are made based on evidence, theories about events and personalities constructed, and conclusions reached inductively. Effective use of media requires an independent information base that is derived largely from other media. The broader the base of independent sources, the better. To the extent that political talk programs promote interest in politics and information-seeking behaviors from a variety of sources, they contribute to the broadening of the public information base and to an enrichment of the public sphere.

Effective use of political talk radio also requires that citizens hone their skills in separating conclusions based on reasoned analysis from demagogic appeals designed to enhance ratings rather than convey politically useful information. Not just analysis, but skeptical analysis, is required to evaluate and disentangle the multitude of images and impressions that impassioned commentators are so good at conveying in distilling valid arguments concerning the public sphere. Little evidence exists that bears on the capacity of political talk audiences to employ such reasoned analyses to issues of public policy.

## REFERENCES

Armstrong, C. B., & Rubin, A. M. (1989). Talk radio as interpersonal communication. *Journal of Communication, 39*(2), 84–94.

Avery, R. K. (1990). Talk radio: The private–public catharsis. In G. Gumpart & S. L. Fish (Eds.), *Talking to strangers: Mediated therapeutic communication* (pp. 87–97). Norwood, NJ: Ablex.

Barker, D. C. (1998). Rush to action: Political talk radio and health care (un) reform. *Political Communication, 15*(1), 83–98.

Barker, D. C. (1999). Rushed decisions: Political talk radio and vote choice, 1994–1996. *Journal of Politics, 61*(2), 527–539.

Barker, D. C., & Knight, K. (2000). Political talk radio and public opinion. *Public Opinion Quarterly, 64*(2), 149–170.

Bierig, J., & Dimmick, J. (1979). The late night radio show as interpersonal communication. *Journalism Quarterly, 56*, 92–96.

Bennett, S. E. (1998). Political talk radio's relationships with democratic citizenship. *American Review of Politics, 19*, 17–29.

Cappella, J. N., Turow, J., & Jamieson, K. H. (1996). *Call-in political talk radio: Background, content, audiences, portrayal in mainstream media.* Philadelphia, PA: University of Pennsylvania.

Converse, P. E. (1964). The nature of belief systems in mass publics. In D. Apter (Ed.), *Ideology and discontent* (pp. 206–261). New York: The Free Press.

Crittenden, J. (1971). Democratic functions of the open mike radio forum. *Public Opinion Quarterly, 35*(2), 200–210.

Davis, R. (1997). Understanding broadcast political talk. *Political Communication, 14*(3), 323–332.

Davis, R., & Owen, D. (1998). *New media and American politics.* Oxford: Oxford University Press.

Dervin, B. (1989). Audience as listener and learner, teacher and confidante: The sense-making approach. In R. Rice & C. Atkin (Eds.), *Public communication campaigns* (2nd ed., pp. 67–86). Newbury Park, CA: Sage.

Entman, R. M. (1989). *Democracy without citizens: Media and the decay of American politics.* New York: Oxford University Press.

Graber, D. A. (1988). *Processing the news: How people tame the information tide.* Chicago: Longman.

Graber, D. A. (1993). Making campaign news user friendly. *American Behavioral Scientist, 37*(2), 328–336.

Graber, D. A. (2001). *Processing politics: Learning from television in the Internet age.* Chicago: University of Chicago Press.

Herbst, S. (1995). On electronic public space: Talk shows in theoretical perspective. *Political Communication, 12*(3), 263–274.

Hofstetter, C. R. (1998). Political talk radio, situational involvement and political mobilization. *Social Science Quarterly, 79*(2), 273–286.

Hofstetter, C. R., Barker, D. C., with Smith, J. T., Zari, G. M., & Ingrassia, T. A. (1999). Information, misinformation, and political talk radio. *Political Research Quarterly, 52*(2), 353–369.

Hofstetter, C. R., Donovan, M. C., Klauber, M. R., Cole, A., Huie, C. J., & Yuasa, T. (1994). Political talk radio: A stereotype reconsidered. *Political Research Quarterly, 47*, 467–479.

Hofstetter, C. R., & Gianos, C. L. (1997). Political talk radio: Actions speak louder than words. *Journal of Broadcasting & Electronic Media, 41*, 501–515.

Hofstetter, C. R., with Smith, J. T., Zari, G. M., & Hofstetter, C. H. (1999). The political talk radio experience: A community study. *American Review of Politics, 19*, 217–237.

Hollander, B. A. (1995a, November). *Talk radio, the new news, and the old news.* Paper presented at the annual meeting of the Southern Political Science Association, Tampa, FL.

Hollander, B. A. (1995b). The new news and the 1992 presidential campaign: Perceived vs. actual political knowledge. *Journalism & Mass Communication Quarterly, 72*(4), 786–798.

Hollander, B. A. (1997). Fuel to the fire: Talk radio and the Gamson hypothesis. *Political Communication, 14*(3), 355–369.

Houlberg, R. (1984). Local television news audience and parasocial interaction. *Journal of Broadcasting, 28*, 423–429.

Kennedy, C., & Hofstetter, C. R. (2001). *Does Rush Limbaugh cause anti-feminist views? Feminism, misogyny and political talk radio in a community study.* Paper presented at the annual meeting of the Western Political Science Association, Las Vegas, NV.

Levy, M. R. (1979). Watching TV news as parasocial interaction. *Journal of Broadcasting, 23*, 69–80.

McCarthy, T. (1978). *The critical theory of Jurgen Habermas.* Cambridge: MIT Press.

Newhagen, J. E. (1994). Self-efficacy and call-in political television show use. *Communication Research, 21*(3), 366–379.

Newhagen, J. E. (1996). *Interactivity as a factor in the assessment of political call-in programs.* Presented at the annual meeting of the International Society of Political Psychology, Vancouver, BC, Canada.

Page, B. I., & Tannenbaum, J. (1996). Populistic deliberation and talk radio. *Journal of Communication, 46*(2), 33–54.

Pan, Z., & Kosicki, G. M. (1997). Talk show exposure as an opinion activity. *Political Communication, 14*(3), 371–388.

Pfau, M., Moy, P., Holbert, R. L., Szabo, E. A., Lin, W., & Zhang, W. (1998). The influence of political talk radio on confidence in democratic institutions. *Journalism & Mass Communication Quarterly, 75*(4), 730–746.

Rubin, A. M., & Step, M. M. (2000). Impact of motivation, attraction, and parasocial interaction on talk radio listening. *Journal of Broadcasting & Electronic Media, 44*(4), 635–654.

Squires, C. R. (2000). Black talk radio: Defining community needs and identity. *Harvard International Journal of Press/Politics, 5*(2), 73–95.

Surlin, S. J. (1986). Uses of Jamaican talk radio. *Journal of Broadcasting & Electronic Media, 30*, 459–466.

Swain, W. N. (1999). Propaganda and Rush Limbaugh: Is the label the last word? *Journal of Radio Studies, 6*(1), 27–40.

Tramer, H., & Jeffres, L. W. (1983). Talk radio—forum and companion. *Journal of Broadcasting, 27*(3), 297–300.

Traugott, M., Berinsky, A., Cramer, K., Howard, M., Mayer, R., Schuckman, H. P., Tewksbury, D., & Young, M. (1996, April). *The impact of talk radio on its audience.* Paper presented at the annual meeting of the Midwest Political Science Association, Chicago, IL.

Turow, J. (1974). Talk show radio as interpersonal communication. *Journal of Broadcasting, 18,* 171–179.

Williams, B. A., & Delli Carpini, M. X. (2001, August). *Political relevance in the new media environment.* Paper presented at the annual meeting of the American Political Science Association, San Francisco, CA.

Zaller, J. (1996). The myth of massive media impact revived: New support for a discredited idea. In D. C. Mutz, P. M. Sniderman, & R. A. Brody (Eds.), *Political persuasion and attitude change* (pp. 17–78). Ann Arbor: University of Michigan Press.

# 11

# Divides in Succession: Possession, Skills, and Use of New Media for Societal Participation

JAN VAN DIJK

*University of Twente*

## A DYNAMIC MODEL OF NEW MEDIA ACCESS

This chapter develops a dynamic view of using the new media for the participation in society. Most everyday notions and many scientific analyses of the so-called "digital divide" are *static* views of social inclusion and participation. It is presumed that problems of new media access are solved when everyone has a computer and a network connection and is able to work with them. This is seen as a single event in history after the technical and commercial introduction of a particular kind of technology, in this case the personal computer and the Internet. In doing this, one also reveals a *technical* view of new media access: a hardware and software orientation. Access is a matter of having and being able to operate a computer and an Internet connection. How they are used, and for what purposes, receives much less attention. Finally, one tries to explain the differences observed in new media access by the usual, in this respect rather shallow, *demographic* variables of income, education, age, gender, ethnicity, and urban or rural background. In this way, one misses the opportunity of going deeper in the analysis. Perhaps new (in)equalities emerge in the information society and in new media access not fitting these classical distinctions. Anyway, these distinctions are hiding the deeper social, psychological, and cultural roots of media access, the central perspective of this book.

To start with, I present a dynamic model of new media access in four successive stages. This serves as the backbone of this chapter. Subsequently, this model is filled with further conceptual distinctions and the latest empirical data of new media access in the United States and Europe, in particular the Netherlands, the author's native country and the source of a large-scale survey with multiple regression models of factors behind the demographic variables just mentioned. In the third section I return to the interpretations in public opinion of the inequalities of new media access described. This means further criticism of the static, technical, and superficial demographic views. Then I deal with scientific explanations on the basis of empirical multivariate analyses and theoretical elaborations of concepts like social and cultural capital and the primary and positional goods of information and communication in an information and network society. The whole analysis in this chapter is directed to societal participation in the public sphere. This means economic participation in the labor market, political participation in a democracy, social participation in a community, and cultural participation in public expression. No assumption is taken for granted. For example, is old media access really necessary for social participation or is old media access (still) sufficient? Finally, a number of general policy perspectives fitting the four successive types of new media access are proposed.

The first obstacle in all research and discussion on information and communication inequality is the multifaceted concept of access. It is used freely in everyday discussions without notification that there are many divergent meanings in play. Possessing a computer and a network connection is the most common meaning in the context of digital technology. However, according to my analysis, this only refers to the second of the four successive kinds of access I have distinguished (van Dijk, 1999):

- Lack of *elementary digital experience* caused by lack of interest, computer anxiety, and unattractiveness of the new technology (mental access);
- No *possession of computers and network connections* (material access);
- Lack of *digital skills* caused by insufficient user-friendliness and inadequate education or social support (skills access); and,
- Lack of significant *usage opportunities* (usage access).

Clearly, public opinion and public policy are strongly preoccupied with the second kind of access. Many people think that the problem of information inequality regarding digital technology is solved as soon as everyone has a computer and a connection to the Internet. The first kind of access problem, the mental barrier, is neglected or viewed as a temporary phenomenon touching only elderly people, some categories of housewives, illiterates, and unemployed. The problem of inadequate digital skills is reduced to the skills of operation, managing hardware and software. Sometimes this is also viewed as a temporary phenomenon to be solved shortly after the purchase of a computer and a network connection. Differential usage of computers and network connections is also a neglected phenomenon. Because differential usage is presumed to be the free choice of citizens and consumers in a differentiating postmodern society, it has not been viewed as important to social and educational policies.

I have argued before that access problems of digital technology gradually shift from the first two kinds of access to the last two kinds (van Dijk, 1999). When the problems of mental and material access have been solved, wholly or partly, the problems of structurally different skills and uses become more operative. I define digital skills not only as (a) the skill to operate computers and network connections, but also as (b) the skill to search, select, process, and apply information from a superabundance of sources and (c) the ability to strategically use this information to improve one's position in society. They are called instrumental, informational, and strategic skills respectively. This distinction is further explained later. In earlier publications I projected the appearance of a *usage gap* between parts of the population systematically using and benefiting from advanced digital technology and the more difficult applications for work and education, and other parts using only basic digital technologies for simple applications, largely entertainment (van Dijk, 1997, 1999). Arguing for this projection, I had to stress that computers are more multifunctional than any medium in history before, enabling them to be used in extremely divergent ways.

Figure 11.1 contains the model of new media access that is the backbone of this chapter.

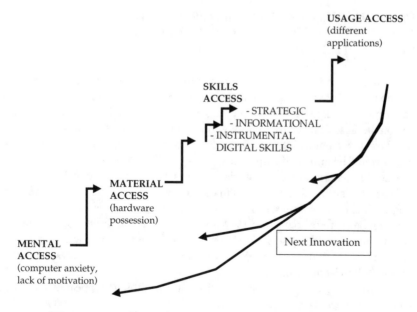

FIG 11.1.   A cumulative and recursive model of types of access to new media.

The background assumptions of this model are explained as follows:

1. The stages are *successive:* The priority of the kinds of access for the adoption of media shifts from the first to the last.

2. The stages are *cumulative:* The first is a condition of the latter. In this case, new media adoption starts with sufficient attractiveness of the innovation and motivation for adoption; as soon as it is purchased, skills to use it have to be mastered, starting with operational skills and followed by skills of using it. Finally, it is differently used in all kinds of practices.

3. The stages are *recursive:* With every new innovation—the problem is to separate an innovation from the next or another one—the process starts anew with one of the previous stages, not necessarily the first one. For example, right now we can observe the diffusion of broadband digital connections undergoing the same processes of differential adoption as the innovation of narrowband Internet and the PC before, with people having a higher income and education coming first (see following data). However, this time there is no problem of mental access, but of material access (income) and usage access (relevant applications).

4. The stages are assumed to be *general* for both old and new media access; however, every new medium or innovation requires the stages to be filled in differently, like the skills in this model of new media access.

## DATA ANALYSIS OF MENTAL, MATERIAL, SKILLS AND USAGE ACCESS OF THE NEW MEDIA IN THE UNITED STATES AND EUROPE

Unfortunately, most survey data about computer and Internet penetration or use are too unreliable and invalid to draw definite conclusions about the existence and development of digital divides. In particular, Internet statistics are notoriously unreliable because of defective sampling, the nonresponse and bad quality of much (marketing) telephone interviewing, and the novelty of affairs to be observed. Research would be improved with large surveys that have sufficient representation or with census material and other official statistics. Furthermore, to make statements and to test hypotheses about trends in computer or Internet penetration and use, longitudinal data or time series are required. These are rather rare, but they are beginning to appear now. From 1994 until 1999 we could use the biannual GVU surveys among Internet users (GVU Center, 1994–1999). Time series could be constructed from their data. However, a major problem with these surveys is that they involve (self)selective sampling.

Census material and other official statistics are beginning to appear in the United States and Europe. The trends of the 1980s and 1990s, with 1998 and 2000 as the last years of measurement, can be derived from them. We prefer to base our conclusions on these data: the U.S. Census Bureau data of 1984, 1989, 1993, 1997, and 2000;

the partly overlapping NTIA data about telephone and computer penetration of 1994, 1997, and 2000; and the annual Eurobarometer (European Union) and Dutch official statistics (by the SCP) of 1985, 1990, 1995, and 1998.

## Elementary Digital Experience

Few data are available—particularly in official statistics—concerning the first experiences of potential users of digital technology. Mental barriers of access are neglected in the discussion about the digital divide. It is known that large segments of (even) the developed countries marked by high technology still have very little digital experience. Measuring the resulting digital skills (the ability to operate digital media and to search for information in them), one finds that even in one of the nations in Europe most equipped for digital communication, the Netherlands, 36% of the 1998 population had no or very little digital skills. Among people 65 and older, this figure reached 67% and among people with low education, 69%. The average of women with no skills was 45%, and among people with low middle education, it was 49% (see Table 11.1).

In another Dutch survey for digital skills, subjective and emotional factors appeared to be responsible for this lack of skills to a large degree (Doets & Huisman, 1997). These factors entail experiences of personal shortcoming (leading

TABLE 11.1
Digital Skills of Dutch Computer Users, 1998

|  | No or Very Few Skills Index Score 1.0–2.0 | Reasonable Skills Index Score 2.1–3.5 | Good Skills Index Score 3.6–5.0 |
|---|---|---|---|
| Percent total Dutch population of computer users | 36 | 52 | 12 |
| AGE |  |  |  |
| 18–34 years | 27 | 56 | 17 |
| 35–49 years | 37 | 54 | 9 |
| 50–64 years | 48 | 46 | 6 |
| 65+ years | 67 | 31 | 2 |
| GENDER |  |  |  |
| Male | 28 | 55 | 17 |
| Female | 45 | 49 | 6 |
| EDUCATION |  |  |  |
| Low eductation | 69 | 25 | 6 |
| Low middle | 49 | 46 | 5 |
| High middle | 30 | 58 | 12 |
| High education | 27 | 55 | 18 |

Note: Percentages of the population of computer users in the Netherlands in 1998, 18 years and older, with a particular score of digital skills in using 10 applications on a 1–5 scale: Windows, word processing in DOS and Windows, spreadsheets, drawing/graphics, working with key boards, e-mail, Internet, programming, and statistical programmes. (Source: representative "GNC-Survey" reported in SCP, 2000).

to insecurity), being excluded, and negative attitudes toward this technology—factors leading to so-called "computer anxiety."

Such mental access problems become more important when it is claimed that there are not only information have-nots, but also information *want*-nots. So there also are important motivational problems. In 1999, a couple of European surveys were published revealing that about half of the population that was not connected to the Internet also did not want such a connection. One of these surveys was the German Online Non-users Survey (ARD/ZDF, 1999a). Among the 501 nonusers in this representative sample for Germany, 234 (54%) declared that they would not connect to the Internet for a variety of reasons such as "I don't need it," "I do not know any home use," "I haven't got the time for it," "I don't like it," "I can't buy it," and "I can't handle it." Similar reasons were provided by households in the United States having a computer or Web TV in the year 2000, but never using it to access the Internet (NTIA, 2000): don't want (31%), too expensive (17%), can use it elsewhere (10%) and no time (9%). Presumably, there are differences in motivations for using computers and the Internet among the populations of (even) high-tech countries. Older people, those with low education, a large proportion of women, and (functional) illiterates are strongly over-represented among the less motivated (ARD/ZDF, 1999a; NTIA, 2000). Further research concerning the ingredients of the mixture of reasons observed here (anxiety, negative attitude, lack of motivation) is needed.

## Possession of Computers and Network Connections

Current discussions about the digital divide are dominated by the (lack of) universal availability of the hardware. Increasingly, longitudinal data in official statistics are being supplied. These data constitute strong evidence of gaps in the possession of computer and network connections among a number of social categories during the 1980s and 1990s: income, education, occupation, age, gender, ethnicity, and geographic location. By constructing time series from these data, it can be shown that most of these gaps of possession have *increased* during the 1980s and 1990s. Figure 11.2 shows this for the variables of income, education, and age in both the United States (see U.S. Census Bureau, 1984, 1989, 1993, 1997, 2000; Kominski & Newburger, 1999) and the Netherlands (see SCP, 2000). Ethnicity is added as a category for the United States data. Gender is not included because both sets of official statistics employed households as the unit of data collection. Gender differences related to possession of equipment are not sufficiently articulated in this type of research. They did appear significant in the biannual GVU surveys among individual web-users (GVU Center, 1994–1999). However, it appears that the original gender gap in actually using PCs and the Internet *decreased* during the 1990s. In the year 2000, the gender difference in the possession of computers and the Internet and in the time using them had been equalized in the United States (see NTIA, 2000). In the European Union (EU), women are still catching up (see the annual Eurobarometer survey's of the EU). However, it is important to

**Income** Gap, USA, 1984-2000
Household Possession of Computers

**Income** Gap, The Netherlands, 1985-1998
Household Possession of Computers

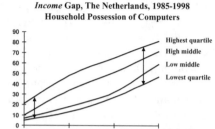

**Education** Gap (Head of Household), USA, 1984-2000
Household Possession of Computers

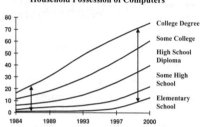

**Education** Gap, The Netherlands, 1985-1998
Household Possession of Computers

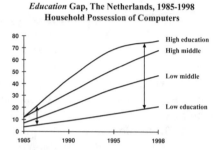

**Age** Gap (Head of Household), USA, 1984-1998
Household Possession of Computers

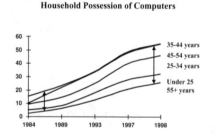

**Age** Gap, The Netherlands, 1985-1998
Household Possession of Computers

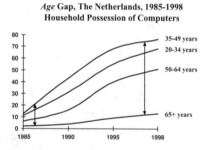

**Ethnicity** Gap (Head of Household), USA, 1984-2000
Household Possession of Computers

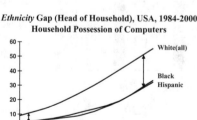

FIG 11.2.   Gaps of income, education, age and ethniciy, USA 1984–2000. Source: Computed from U.S. census bureau data 1984, 1989, 1993, 1997, 1998, 2000, data also contained in NTIA, *Falling Through the Net* Studies (1999, 2000). Gaps of income, education, employment and age, The Netherlands 1985–1998. Source: SCP, 2000.

emphasize that a gender gap concerning different skills and kinds of usage remains (see Tables 11.1, 11.2, 11.3, and Pew Internet & American Life Project, 2000).

The big question concerning the widening gaps is whether these trends will continue. From a statistical point of view, it is evident that they will not. *Saturation* of computer and network possession among the "higher" categories will set in, and presumably has already begun in countries like the United States and the Netherlands. For the "lower" categories, there is much more room for catching up. Therefore, the question becomes how much current gaps will close in the first two decades of the 21st century. More importantly, we need to ask what *kind of* computers and network connections people will possess. I return to this crucial issue later.

Other important questions deal with the most important factors or variables among the familiar set of background variables. Evidently, income, education, and employment are strongly associated. Holding the other factors constant, it can be shown in the American and Dutch statistics that they keep an independent effect. The Dutch SCP study, however, employed elaborate multiple regression analyses for the weight of the most important variables in the possession, skills, and use of information and communication technology (ICT). The results, summarized in Fig. 11.3, are informative.

The most important conclusion from the 1998 Dutch SCP study is that household income is the most important factor explaining differences in the possession

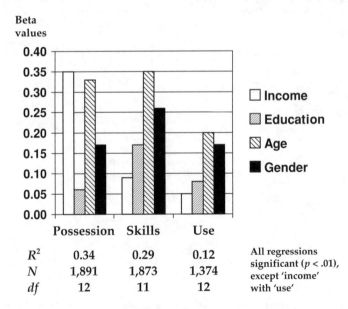

| | Possession | Skills | Use |
|---|---|---|---|
| $R^2$ | 0.34 | 0.29 | 0.12 |
| $N$ | 1,891 | 1,873 | 1,374 |
| $df$ | 12 | 11 | 12 |

All regressions significant ($p < .01$), except 'income' with 'use'

FIG 11.3.  A multiple regression comparing the relative significance of the variables of income, education, age, and gender in the possession, skills, and use the ICTs in the Netherlands in 1998. (Source: Representative GNC-Survey, 1998; SCP, 2000).

of ICTs, first of all PCs, and that income diminishes or even disappears in the explanation of differences in digital skills and ICT usage. Surprisingly high, perhaps, is the relative weight of age and gender. As for age the distribution is curved: First possession increases with age (with a top at age 30 to 40), then it decreases. Women have significantly lower possession (in the EU, not in the United States), skills, and use of ICTs. Next I explain why the possession of ICT is not only a matter of material resources but also of the attractiveness of this technology and the necessary skills to use it among people of different age and gender.

## Digital Skills

PCs and computer networks were renowned for their user-unfriendliness until well into the 1990s. Major improvements were made with the introduction of graphical and audiovisual interfaces. However, the situation is still far from satisfactory if we look once again at Table 11.1, presenting differences of digital skills among social categories in the Netherlands. Gaps of digital skills are shown to exist. The most common definition of digital skills is *instrumental* skills: the ability to operate hardware and software. In the Dutch study, digital skills were operationalized using an index called *informacy*, measuring both skills of operating digital equipment and skills of searching information using digital hardware and software. This means that so-called *informational* skills are added to the definition. I recommend adding a third type of digital skills to the operational and informational ones: the *strategic* skills of using information for one's own purpose and position. Figure 11.3 reveals the (perhaps) surprising result that digital skills (instrumental and informational, together called *informacy* here) are not primarily related to educational levels but to age and gender. It may be that this means that real practice and motivation are more important in acquiring digital skills than formal education. Indeed, many studies reveal that having computer experience at work, having particular hobbies, and having a family with schoolchildren are decisive factors in the acquisition of digital skills by adults.

## Different Uses

In this chapter and in other publications (van Dijk, 1997, 1999, 2000), it is predicted that different uses of ICT will bring about the most important digital and information inequalities in society. Presently, the differences observed in this kind of access are not as large as those in differential possession and skill.

Unfortunately, data about differential usage are still scarce and only a few years old. They are available for computer use and Internet use, both in the U.S. Census material and the Dutch SCP investigation. According to my view, only computer use has had enough time to crystallize; Internet use only appeared as a mass phenomenon at the turn of the century. We must wait for longitudinal data to construct the time series we need for testing our prediction: the rise of a *usage gap*. The state of

TABLE 11.2
Usage of PC at home, USA, 1997

| | Word Processing | Games | E-mail | Internet | Book-keeping | Work at Home | Spread-sheets | Data-bases |
|---|---|---|---|---|---|---|---|---|
| Total using PC at home | 70.5 | 53.6 | 44.5 | 44.2 | 43.6 | 34.3 | 28.7 | 26.1 |
| AGE | | | | | | | | |
| 18–24 years | 69.7 | 61.4 | 42.8 | 44.3 | 19.5 | 14.0 | 18.7 | 17.1 |
| 25–49 years | 70.3 | 55.0 | 45.8 | 45.9 | 46.9 | 38.5 | 30.9 | 27.3 |
| 50 years + | 71.4 | 44.7 | 41.4 | 39.3 | 48.6 | 34.4 | 28.3 | 28.1 |
| GENDER | | | | | | | | |
| Male | 66.3 | 57.6 | 48.1 | 49.4 | 46.3 | 38.0 | 32.5 | 29.4 |
| Female | 74.7 | 49.6 | 40.7 | 38.9 | 40.8 | 30.6 | 24.7 | 22.7 |
| FAMILY INCOME | | | | | | | | |
| <$25.000 | 69.1 | 57.2 | 40.6 | 38.9 | 35.5 | 22.7 | 22.3 | 20.9 |
| $25–49,900 | 66.2 | 58.4 | 39.7 | 39.8 | 43.7 | 29.2 | 25.3 | 23.9 |
| $50–74,900 | 71.2 | 55.4 | 44.9 | 45.1 | 43.9 | 35.5 | 29.7 | 26.7 |
| >$75.000 | 75.8 | 47.6 | 52.1 | 52.3 | 47.3 | 44.8 | 34.7 | 31.1 |

*Note.*  Source: U.S. Census Bureau.

affairs concerning computer use in the United States in the year 1997 is summarized in Table 11.2.

Here we can see substantial differences in the use of PC applications among people with different levels of age, gender, and income. With age, fairly large differences appear in using games, spreadsheets, databases, and bookkeeping. With gender, we see that females use all applications significantly less than males, except word processing. Higher income—unfortunately, control for education was not available for these data—means more use of e-mail, Internet, bookkeeping, work at home, spreadsheets, and databases.

A recent *Falling Through the Net* study (NTIA, 2000) revealed important differences of Internet usage by income, education, ethnicity, and other variables, but unfortunately only informational, educational, and work-related types of Internet use were reported. It appears that with rising educational levels, the Internet applications of information searching, doing job-related tasks, searching for jobs, and, to a lesser extent, using e-mail increase significantly (see Table 11.3).

On the other hand, people with lower education use the Internet relatively more to take courses. When we examine income, these differences are less pronounced (see NTIA, 2000, Fig. A47), supporting the SCP conclusion that income is less important than education considering usage (Fig. 11.3). Taking courses and searching for jobs on the Internet was practiced more by Americans with low incomes than with high incomes in the year 2000. The same goes for unemployed Americans as compared to the employed (see NTIA, 2000, Fig. A50). This reveals the importance of usage access and skills access compared to their necessary condition, material access. Having a computer and Internet connection and also having the skills to use them are becoming increasingly important resources on the labor market.

TABLE 11.3
Internet Use by Level of Education, USA in 1997.

| | Elementary | Some High School | High School Diploma or GED | Some College | B.A. or more |
|---|---|---|---|---|---|
| E-mail | 80.1 | 84.2 | 84.7 | 87.6 | 90.1 |
| Info search | 36.4 | 45.5 | 53.5 | 63.1 | 72.6 |
| Take courses | 38.3 | 59.7 | 17.8 | 26.7 | 24.0 |
| Do job-related tasks | 5.8 | 6.8 | 19.6 | 28.0 | 48.2 |
| Job search | 8.9 | 8.7 | 15.4 | 19.9 | 22.7 |

*Note.* Source: NTIA and U.S. Department of Commerce using August, 2000 U.S. Bureau of Census Current Population Survey Supplement.

## INTERPRETATIONS OF THE DIGITAL DIVIDE IN PUBLIC OPINION

Social and political opinion has developed four positions with an interpretation of the current state of affairs:

• Denial of the existence of a digital divide.

• Acceptance of some present divides, claiming that they will soon disappear.

• Emphasis of digital divides that are supposed to grow and come on top of old inequalities of income, education, age, gender, ethnicity, and geographical location.

• Differentiation: some divides are decreasing while others grow.

A number of market research institutions, other corporate interests, and conservative think tanks deny or trivialize the existence of digital divides. Basically, their arguments are threefold (see United States Internet Council, 1999, based on Forrester research; Thierer, 2000):

1. The adoption rate of computers and the Internet and the growth rates of their use are faster than any medium before, perhaps with the exception of (color) TV.

2. The distribution among the population approaches normality: The averages of income, education, ethnicity, and gender rapidly parallel society as a whole.

3. Computers and Internet connections are becoming cheaper by the day, cheaper than a color TV system adopted by almost every Western household. The market is doing its work and solves all problems.

Indeed, growth rates are enormous. However, there are some basic problems with the S-curve of adoption of innovations that usually is the basis of this argument.[1] One of them is the demarcation problem of the media supposed to be entering an S-curve: A computer and an Internet connection now are very different from a computer and Internet connection 10 years ago. The new computer and Internet technologies are easier to use, but they have varying levels of complexity and options in hardware and software.

It goes without saying that a medium that is increasingly adopted into society is approaching average parts of the population. However, in my view, digital divides are about *relative* differences between categories of people. In the 1980s and 1990s, most of these divides concerning possession of computers and Internet connections increased, as was convincingly demonstrated by the American and Dutch official statistics supplied earlier. One is free to predict that these divides will close rapidly, an argument to be dealt with later, but their existence in the present and recent past cannot be denied. The argument about cheaper hardware is correct, but only partly so. It neglects many facts like: (a) The new media add to the older mass media that do not disappear: One still needs a TV, radio, VCR, telephone, and perhaps a newspaper; low income households continually have to weigh every new purchase (with the newspaper beginning to lose); (b) computers are outdated much faster than any other medium and continually new peripheral equipment and software has to be purchased; and (c) "free" Internet access or computer hardware is not really free, of course. There are nominal monthly fees, long-term service agreements, privacy selling, and low-quality service, for instance.

However, the most important problem of this interpretation, and the next one, is their hardware orientation. Perhaps the most common social and political opinion is that the problem of the digital divide is solved as soon as every citizen or inhabitant has the ability to obtain a personal computer and an Internet connection. In contrast, my analysis suggests that the biggest problems of information and communication inequality just start with the general diffusion of computers and network connections.

The second interpretation might accept that there are, or have been, gaps but that they will soon disappear, perhaps to be succeeded by other inequalities. It is simply a question of some having the technology now and others having it later. The early adopters pay for the innovation and make the adoption cheaper for the late adopters. There is a strong faith in the trend of the S-curve of adoption and in the extension of access by market forces alone. This interpretation comes from the authors of the Dutch SCP-Survey (SCP, 2000), among others. From a statistical point of view, their position will be backed by future data automatically. The saturation of possession by the "higher" social categories sets in, and has already started in some Western countries, as one can see in the bending end of the curves in Fig. 11.2. This argument looks like a dynamic one because it accounts for trends into the future, but in fact it is static on several grounds. It reasons from present technologies and their uses. The questions are what relative differences will remain in 10 to 20 years and what kind of computers and Internet will be possessed. How will they be used? What skills will be needed? In the meantime, the next round of innovation in digital technology has already appeared: broadband or high-speed Internet access. It is striking to observe that the same divides in the possession of this technology among people with different income and education reappear, albeit in a mitigated form (see NTIA, 2000, Figs. A18 and A19). This means that the differences between people with broadband and narrowband access are smaller than those between people with and without any access to computers and the Internet. Still, it is reasonable to say that all these differences work in accumulation and that the relative differences in hardware possession between people with different income and education are increasing.

Another argument of the disappearing gaps position is that there is no digital divide in the sense of a structural gap or a two-tiered society: The differences are of a gradual nature (see SCP, 2000). This qualification has some basis: The two-tiered position is too simple. The digital divide is a simplifying metaphor. In fact, we see the stretching of a whole spectrum of differentiating positions in (post)modern society, not two classes of people (van Dijk, 1997, 2000). From a substantial point of view, this qualification might also be right concerning the *basic possession* of computers and Internet connections, although the SCP survey's own conclusion is that household income is the most important factor explaining it. Anyway, I am not so sure that structural divides will disappear concerning digital *skills and usage*, the core of my argument.

A third set of interpretations does emphasize the persistence and growth of a digital divide. It is supported by left-wing political forces, social democrats, socialists, progressive NGOs, etc. They stress the rise of social and economic inequality in Western society and on a world-scale in general during the last two decades. They claim information inequality only adds another layer to increasing old inequalities of income, education, occupation or social class, ethnicity, and gender (see among others Schiller, 1996). They hold that the claim of cheaper ICT products is a corporate trick. After the relatively cheap supply of hardware access, the selling of expensive service and content starts. There may be large elements of truth in this interpretation: General inequality has increased both nationally and internationally (see United Nations Development Programme, 1998), and old inequalities do not disappear with the advent of an information or knowledge society. However, this position underestimates the import and complexity of changes that are occurring. Increasing differences in the skill and usage of the new information technologies might lead to new inequalities of a nature not known before and to be contested, if one chooses to do so, with other means than the traditional ones. Moreover, less expensive hardware with more capacity and free Internet access as a public service are very real and important phenomena. The new technologies offer new opportunities for citizen participation and consumer interest.

The last set of interpretations stresses current differentiation in society in general and the use of ICTs in particular. Theoretical work on the information society or the network society sheds another light on social inequality (see Castells, 1996, 1998; van Dijk, 1991, 1999, 2000). Others even claim that the information or knowledge society will discard old inequalities and bring completely new ones based on differential knowledge and education. My analysis indicates that there also is continuity, as it is elaborated in the next section. Concerning the different divides discussed here, these interpretations stress that some current divides or gaps may (partly) disappear, while others stay or increase.

## SCIENTIFIC EXPLANATIONS OF THE DIGITAL DIVIDE

The differences of possession, skill, and use of ICTs usually lack scientific explanation. Even multivariate analyses trying to weigh determining factors are rare. An exception is made by the Dutch SCP-Survey (SCP, 2000) constructing regression models to explain these differences by unequal possession of resources by individuals or households. This is a classical sociological approach in empirical research. Three kinds of resources were distinguished: material, social, and cognitive resources. In this survey, a very narrow definition of material resources appeared to explain more (in the regression models) than the usual variable in this respect: income. The variable constructed is narrow because it is only composed by questions about the possession of all kinds of *equipment* by households, not only digital equipment. Social resources are made operational in a number of questions about having a social *network* also possessing and using digital technology, and having social *support* in managing it. Cognitive resources are threefold: *literacy, numeracy, and informacy*. Literacy is the skill of reading and of searching information in texts; numeracy is the ability to handle numbers, figures, and tables and to compute; informacy is equal to digital skills in this survey. It is made operational in two ways: operating digital equipment and searching for information in digital sources. The cognitive resources taken together appear to explain more than the variable of education.

The results of the regression model based on these resources are very interesting. Striking differences of the importance of these resources are found at the possession, skill, and use of ICTs respectively (see Fig. 11.4).

Possession of ICTs is explained more by informacy (instrumental and informational digital skills) than by material resources. Skills are explained by literacy and social resources (having a social network and support). A remarkable result is that literacy is far more important for the explanation of digital skills than numeracy. Apparently, people with the ability to process textual information are more likely to develop digital skills defined in this way than people who are good in numbers and computing. Clearly, computers are no longer only number-crunching machines these days. Usage is overwhelmingly determined by informacy or digital skills.

The general conclusion of the SCP research team is that differences of skill and use are smaller than differences of possession. After the threshold of having a computer and network connection has been passed, material and social resources play a relatively minor role. Sociocultural differences of age, gender, literacy, and informacy come forward. Present differences and even divides are observed—see figures and tables in this chapter—but according to the SCP team, they are old inequalities that are reproduced, rather than new inequalities like the ones often

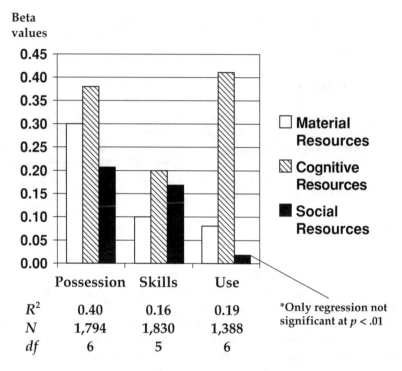

| | Possession | Skills | Use |
|---|---|---|---|
| $R^2$ | 0.40 | 0.16 | 0.19 |
| $N$ | 1,794 | 1,830 | 1,388 |
| $df$ | 6 | 5 | 6 |

*Only regression not significant at $p < .01$

FIG 11.4. A multiple regression comparing the relative significance of material, cognitive, and social resources in the possession, skills, and use the ICTs in the Netherlands in 1998. (Source: Representative GNC-Survey, 1998; SCP, 2000).

related to a knowledge or information society. The team claims that there is no unbridgeable digital divide and government intervention is not needed.

It is likely that these far-reaching political conclusions are drawn prematurely. They are based on a rather static and superficial sociological analysis of the present situation. Constructing rather arbitrary background variables of *individual* resources at a single point in time does not make a theory that is able to relate to social and technological development, that is to say, the level of *society and technology*. Technology is changing rapidly: Very advanced and very simple applications are appearing side by side. And according to many scientists and other observers, society is evolving into an information society and a network society where social (in)equality will partly be different from old modern societies.

In an information society, information is known as a primary good. Everybody needs it to function in society. However, people also need cultural capital (Bourdieu, 1986) and social capital (Mansell & Wehn, 1998) to use information in appropriate ways: that is, the skill to select and process information and being able to use it in one's social position and network. These kinds of capital are distributed very unequally in society. Moreover, information is a positional good. This means that it becomes increasingly important to get the information *first* in economic, social, and cultural competition. This is why it is so important to look at the *relative* differences in all inequalities observed.

The importance of cultural and social capital for the ability to extract relevant information from innumerable sources and to use it for the benefit of one's position is even stronger in the network society, a typification in the line of the information society. A network society consists of social and media networks shaping the prime mode of organization and most important structures of modern society (van Dijk, 1999). Here the position inside and outside networks becomes vital. This position defines one's opportunities and power in society. Remaining outside networks means total exclusion. Being inside might mean partial exclusion when the position occupied is a marginal one. The position acquired at work, at school, at home, and in the local community also determines the chances to acquire elementary digital experience, to develop further digital experience, and to use particular applications. Therefore, I want to add a third type of digital skills to the instrumental and information skills described above: *strategic* skills, the ability to use digital means to improve one's position in society and in work, education, and cultural practices. This means taking one's own initiatives in searching, selecting, valuing, and applying information from all sources. Here the new sources of computer media add to the old sources of print and audiovisual media. For all these sources, instrumental, informational, and strategic skills can be developed. All sources and skills are summarized in Table 11.4.

Strategic digital skills are closely related to the possession of social capital or social resources as previously defined, and they are the direct basis of usage access. In

TABLE 11.4
Kinds of skills to be developed in using print, audiovisual, and computer media.

|  | Instrumental Skills | Informational Skills | Strategic Skills |
|---|---|---|---|
| PRINT MEDIA | Read and write texts Understand and count numbers | Search, select and process information from texts and numbers (e.g. statistical information) | Taking own initiatives in searching, selecting, |
| AUDIOVISUAL MEDIA | View, listen and make audiovisual programs | Search, select and process information from images, sounds and narratives | integrating, valuing and applying information |
| COMPUTER MEDIA | Operate computers and programs | Search, select and process information from computer and network files | from all sources as a means to improve ones position in society |

*Note.* Digital skills are skills for computer media (narrow definition) or for all media in convergence (broad definition). Table inspired by Steyaert (2000).

measuring social capital and resources, it is insufficient to observe only whether one is employed or not, and how big one's household is. The precise positions at work (occupation, function, task), at school, in the family, and in the community have to be recorded and related to the possession, skill, and use of ICTs. Unfortunately, these data are scarce. We have seen that measuring skills and usage is a fairly recent research activity, particularly in relationship to the Internet. Thus, we are not able to look for such clear "gap pictures" as they are available on the field of the possession of computers and network connections. The evidence is only fragmentary, like the tables of usage we supplied earlier, or it is too recent to construct time series, like the 1993 and 1997 U.S. Census Bureau statistics of the precise occupations and industries using particular applications of ICT (see U.S. Bureau of the Census, 1993, 1997).

Further research for the different kinds of digital skills and for usage is urgently required. This will allow us to investigate whether more or less structural inequalities in skills and usage appear between social classes and people of different age, gender, ethnicity, and geographical location. This is the hypothesis of simple versus advanced, businesslike versus entertainment applications adopted relatively more by particular classes of people, a suggestion made earlier.

## DIGITAL DIVIDES AND SOCIETAL PARTICIPATION

What do these different kinds of access or divide mean for societal participation? We should be aware of easy thinking answering this question. Is new media access really necessary for full or satisfactory societal participation, or is old media access still sufficient? Strong arguments against the drive to provide everyone with a computer and Internet connection as soon as possible are the accusations of technological determinism and of patronizing attitudes held by people with higher professions and education imposing their style of living, working, learning, and entertaining on others with lower professions and education. The superiority of digital technology as compared to old technologies should not be taken for granted. It is not an easy job to prove that particular applications of the new media are really vital for social inclusion. I deal with these (self) critical observations passing the four kinds of new media access presented here.

Considering mental access, I referred to the mass of "information want-nots" in (even) high-tech societies. They clearly indicate that they at least think they are able to live in their societies without any access to digital technology. In fact, there are still a lot of jobs, households, cultural practices, and local communities that do not need this technology at all. For voting and other venues of citizen participation, the new media are not vital, either. However, precisely the people with no digital skills, a lack of motivation in this respect, and suffering computer anxiety feel most insecure about this state of affairs. The Doets and Huisman (1997) survey revealed that these people called their lack of digital technology and skill a personal shortcoming and that they were afraid of becoming excluded from future society. Moreover, at the end of the 1990s, we observed the pressing need of the older generations to buy a computer, get access to the Internet, and take computer courses in a conspicuous recovery operation with the prime motivation to participate in a development they expect to be inevitable (Doets & Huisman, 1997, and many other surveys). Perhaps this instinctive reaction is an indication of real exclusion to be expected.

With regard to material access, it becomes increasingly clear that the possession of a computer and Internet connection does not decide about social participation in an absolute sense, but in a relative way. The old media still offer basic entries, but those who possess particular new media tend to come first on the labor market, in political competitions, and in social and cultural affairs. Still, the result will be not less absolute: one is in or one is out. Most likely, the information want-nots will be persuaded in a rather negative way: flights will be booked, performances be sold out, jobs be given away, and sexual dates be granted in electronic channels only for those having access to them. Evidently, communication capacities of the new media like speed, reach, selectivity, and interactivity are very effective on these occasions (see van Dijk, 1999).

Relative advantage becomes even more important for societal participation if we look at differential digital skills and usage opportunities. Here the really decisive differences are made. Let me give an example from the field of economic participation: investing in stocks and shares on the Internet. This medium has provided amateur investors with splendid sources of information about shares and companies that were only available to banks until recently. But what are their skills of mastering these new opportunities and are they in a better condition to make profit out of them than before? In the meantime, professional investors have increased their lead on the amateurs by even more advanced applications of ICTs for financial information and investment. They have the skills to use these complex applications and they possess the social, cultural, and economic capital of using their social networks, visiting business meetings and parties, and looking for loans and all kinds of complex new financial sources to invest. Most likely, the difference between amateur and professional investors will become larger, not smaller, in using ICTs. Comparable examples can be given for political participation (van Dijk, 2000), social participation (Mansell & Wehn, 1998), and cultural participation (Pew Internet & American Life Project, 2000).

## CONCLUSIONS AND POLICY PERSPECTIVES

Following the line of the argument in this chapter, the complexity of the picture of the so-called digital divide comes to mind. A number of significant gaps have been observed and supported by relatively reliable official statistics and surveys. However, there is no question of an *absolute,* yawning, and unbridgeable gap between two classes of people. Talk about "technological segregation" and "classical apartheid" is exaggerated and misses the point. The point is that the gaps observed show, first of all, *relative* and gradual differences. This makes them no less important. In the information and network society, relative differences in getting information and lines of communication become decisive for one's position in society, more than in any society in history before. Giving everybody a computer and a network connection, banning the cutting lines of "segregation" in this way, will not remove them. Much deeper and clear-cut differences in skill and usage will appear as both technology and society increasingly differentiate. The fundamental task of future society will be to prevent *structural* inequalities in the skill and usage of ICTs from becoming more intense. Inequalities become structural when they "solidify," that is, when positions people occupy in society, in social networks, and in media networks, or other media, become lasting and determine to a large degree whether they have any influence on decisions made in several fields of society.

Another reason for the complexity of the digital divide is that there are, in fact, several divides. Some are widening while others are closing. Time series of official statistics have demonstrated that during the 1980s and 1990s, gaps of income, employment, education, age, and ethnicity in the possession of computers and hardware have grown, at least in the United States and the Netherlands. Clearly, the people at the "better side" of these gaps have increased their lead during these decades. Although these gaps of possession will (at least partially) close in the next decades, if only for the statistical reason of saturation effects, it is very unlikely that those having acquired a big advantage will stop and lean backwards. Technology is advancing, splitting in simple and highly evolved applications, spreading into society and sticking to old and new social differences.

In the course of the 1990s, the gender gap in the possession of ICTs started to close. However, gender gaps in skill and usage remain or mature, although they are much smaller for girls and boys than for adults (see ARD/ZDF, 1999b; GVU Center, 1994–1999; Pew Internet & American Life Project, 2000; SCP, 2000).

Large differences in digital skill and usage have been observed recently. Here gaps might grow in the future, although this cannot be proven at this moment for a lack of time series data.

These conclusions have highlighted the dynamic nature of every digital divide. One should not stop at a particular point in time and say that a particular technology or application will be available to everybody within a couple of years or any projected date in the future. Information and communication technology will differentiate considerably in the first decades of the 21st century. Computers will be available in the simplest (palmtop and other) forms and very advanced types of desktops, laptops, and servers. The Internet will be accessible via televisions, mobile phones, and other small information appliances next to fast broadband connections. An important policy question will be whether palmtop computers and mobile phones or all kinds of narrowband access will be sufficient to be called the basic connection every citizen needs. Moreover, what does basic access to the Internet mean: both at home and at work or school, or is one of them sufficient, or perhaps even a connection in a public utility?

An important characteristic of ICT in this respect is its extended multifunctionality. Printed media, radio, television, and telephone have all been used differently by people with high and low education in particular. However, their difference in functionality is small compared to computers and the Internet. In the meantime, society is also differentiating at an unprecedented scale. Together they may create a usage gap that is somewhat similar to the *knowledge gap* described by Tichenor, Donohue, and Olien (1970) three decades ago in relation to mass media. Although the evidence in favor of the thesis of knowledge gap has not been conclusive (Gaziano, 1987), it might get another chance in the information or network society where information is a positional good. I propose to relate this gap to a *usage gap*, not primarily based on differential derived knowledge or information but on differential practical use and positions in society.

The policy perspectives to be linked to this analysis clearly depend on one's central objectives concerning information inequality and one's political position. Central objectives might be twofold. The most basic one is *social inclusion*. A step further is made in the objective of an *equal distribution* of resources or life chances. The first objective is backed by a coalition of forces in advanced high-tech societies. Corporations look for a large electronic market place. Politicians want extended reach for political persuasion and a grip on new channels of political communication bypassing traditional mass media. Military people and security agencies want everybody to be connected for purposes of control and surveillance, as the offliners of the future will create unknown risks. Educators are concerned about universal and public access to all learning resources. Community builders want every citizen to be involved in online communications linked to offline local activities.

The second objective is more traditional and it is supported more strongly in Europe than in the United States, for instance. The minimum is an equal distribution of *chances* to every individual, an objective also having broad support. Filling in what this means for actual material, social, and cognitive resources reveals the differences of political position.

Policy perspectives should be linked to the four kinds of access that have been distinguished. Accordingly, governments, civil societies, and markets all have important roles to play in the support of these kinds of access. Elementary digital experience is, first of all, a question of the market developing and offering ICTs that really are user-friendly and that offer such a clear surplus value as compared to old applications that the information want-nots will be convinced. Even then, many elderly and low educated people and some categories of housewives will stay behind. This will be the most important mission of adult education to be offered by governments, community centers and corporate training.

Concerning the general possession of computers and networks, markets have done a good job of lowering prices for technologies with higher capacities. However, this has not prevented the growth of digital divides in the possession of hardware, at least until very recently. Household income is still the most important factor here. So, tax and income policies of governments certainly do make sense. However, general tax credits or subsidies are not effective. They have to be *focused* on the groups clearly staying behind, all of them in the lowest quarter of the income distribution. A second qualification is the need of public or private *service and guidance*. Simply offering cheap boxes with computers and Internet connections makes little sense in this situation.

Learning digital skills will be a strategic objective for educational institutions at all levels. The official American and Dutch surveys cited in this chapter indicate that present digital skills are learned more at work than at schools or at home. In general, formal education runs behind because means are lacking and teachers are not sufficiently trained or motivated. Filling in this strategic objective, it will become evident that digital skills do not only mean abilities to operate the hardware and software (instrumental skills). Increasingly, it will mean the ability to search, select, process, and apply information from digital sources (informational skills) and to strategically use them to improve one's position in society (strategic skills). At least instrumental and informational skills have to be learned at schools.

Improving usage opportunities for all means making them more attractive to some people in the first place. We have observed the surprisingly high independent effects of age, gender, and ethnicity (in the United States) for the actual use of ICTs. Applications should be made more attractive to many old people, women, and ethnic minorities. This is a matter of design, culture, language, and identity being included and addressed in the applications concerned. Producers, designers, and representatives of citizens and consumers have a job here.

## ACKNOWLEDGMENT

This chapter has been adapted from Jan van Dijk and Kenneth Hacker (in press), The digital divide as a complex and dynamic phenomenon. *The Information Society*. An earlier version of this chapter also was presented at *The 50ᵗʰ Annual Conference of the International Communication Association, Acapulco, Mexico, June, 2000*.

## ENDNOTE

[1] The S-curve of the adoption of innovations presupposes that the medium in question is easy to identify and to mark from others. This might be true for older mass media like a radio, a TV, or a VCR but not for computers and network connections. They fall apart in extremely different types, strongly complicating the construction of any valid time series of adoption. The second questionable proposition is the maximum population of potential adoption. The classical S-curve presupposes whole populations. However, some new computer and network media are too advanced, complicated, and expensive to be ever adopted by 100% of the population.

# REFERENCES

ARD/ZDF-Arbeitsgruppe Multimedia (1999a, August). ARD/ZDF online studie 1999. *Media Perspektiven*, 388–409.

ARD/ZDF-Arbeitsgruppe Multimedia (1999b, August). Internet—(k)eine männerdomäne. *Media Perspektiven*, 423–429.

Bourdieu, P. (1986). The forms of capital. In J. G. Richardson (Ed.), *Handbook of theory and research for the sociology of education*. New York: Greenwood Press.

Castells, M. (1996). *The Information Age: Economy, society and culture, Vol. I: The rise of the network society*. Oxford, UK: Blackwell Publishers.

Castells, M. (1998). *The Information Age: Economy, society and culture, Vol. III: End of millennium*. Oxford, UK: Blackwell Publishers.

Doets, C., & Huisman, T. (1997). *Digital skills: The state of the art in the Netherlands*. Hertogenbosch: CINOP. Retrieved online, from http://www.cinop.nl (English summary).

Gaziano, C. (1987). The knowledge gap: An analytical review of media effects. *Communication Research, 10*, 447–486.

GVU Center (1994–1999). *GVU's 1st–10th World Wide Web User Surveys*. Graphic, Visualization, & Usability Center, Georgia Institute of Technology. Retrieved online from http://www.gvu.gatech.edu/user_surveys/

Kominski, R., & Newburger, E. (1999, August). *Access denied: Changes in computer ownership and use: 1984–1997*. Paper presented at the meeting of the American Sociological Association, Chicago, IL.

Mansell, R., & Wehn, U. (Eds.). (1998). *Knowledge societies: Information technology for sustainable development*. Oxford: Oxford University Press.

NTIA, (2000, October). *Falling through the Net: Toward digital inclusion*. National Telecommunication and Information Administration, United States Department of Commerce. Retrieved December, 1, 2000, from http://www.ntia.doc.gov/ntiahome/fttn00/contents00.html

Pew Internet & American Life Project (2000). *Tracking online life: How women use the Internet to cultivate relationships with family and friends*. Retrieved December 1, 2000, from http://www.pewinternet.org

SCP (Sociaal-Cultureel Planbureau), van Dijk, L., de Haan, J., & Rijken, S. (2000). *Digitalisering van de leefwereld, Een onderzoek naar informatie en communicatietechnologie en sociale ongelijkheid* [summary in English]. Rijswijk, The Netherlands: SCP.

Schiller, H. (1996). *Information inequality: The deepening social crisis in America*. New York: Routledge.

Tichenor, P. J., Donohue, G., & Olien, C. N. (1970). Mass media flow and differential growth in knowledge. *Public Opinion Quarterly, 34*, 159–170.

Thierer, A. (2000, April 20). How free computers are filling the digital divide. *The Heritage Foundation Backgrounder, No 1361*. Retrieved August 15, 2000, from http://www.heritage.org

United Nations Development Programme. (1998). *Human development report 1998*. New York: Oxford University Press.

U.S. Census Bureau. (1984, 1989, 1993, 1994, 1997, 1998, 2000). *Current Population Surveys*. Washington, DC: Author.

United States Internet Council (1999). *State of the Internet: USIC's report on use and threats in 1999*. Retrieved December 1, 2000, from htpp://www.usic.org/usic_state_of_net99.htm

van Dijk, J. (1991). *De netwerkmaatschappij: Sociale aspecten van nieuwe media* [The Network Society, Social aspects of the new media]. Houten, Zaventem: Bohn Stafleu van Loghum.

van Dijk, J. (1997). *Universal service from the perspective of consumers and citizens* (Report to the Information Society Forum). Brussels: European Commission/ISPO.

van Dijk, J. (1999). *The network society: Social aspects of new media*. London: Sage.

van Dijk, J. (2000). Widening information gaps and policies of prevention. In K. Hacker & J. van Dijk (Eds.), *Digital democracy: Issues of theory and practice* (pp. 166–183). London: Sage.

van Dijk, J., & Hacker, K. (in press). The digital divide as a complex and dynamic phenomenon. *The Information Society*.

# 12

# Universal Usability: Pushing Human–Computer Interaction Research to Empower Every Citizen

BEN SHNEIDERMAN

*University of Maryland, College Park*

*I feel... an ardent desire to see knowledge so disseminated through the mass of mankind that it may... reach even the extremes of society: beggars and kings.*

—Thomas Jefferson
Reply to the American Philosophical Society, 1808

*In a fair society, all individuals would have equal opportunity to participate in, or benefit from, the use of computer resources regardless of race, sex, religion, age, disability, national origin or other such similar factors.*

—ACM Code of Ethics

The goal of universal access to information and communications services is compelling. Enthusiastic networking innovators, business leaders, and government policymakers see opportunities and benefits from widespread usage. But even if they succeed and the economies of scale bring low costs, computing researchers still have much work to do. They have to deal with the difficult question: How can information and communications services be made usable for every citizen? Designing for experienced frequent users is difficult enough, but designing for a broad audience of unskilled users is a far greater challenge. Scaling up from a listserv for 100 software engineers to 100,000 schoolteachers to 100,000,000 registered voters will require both inspiration and perspiration.

Designers of older technologies such as postal services, telephones, and television have reached the goal of universal usability, but computing technology is still too difficult to use for many people (Shneiderman, 1998). One survey of 6,000 computer users found an average of 5.1 hours per week wasted trying to use computers. More time is wasted in front of computers than on highways. The frustration and anxiety of users is growing, and the number of nonusers is still high. Low-cost hardware, software, and networking will bring in many new users, but interface and information design breakthroughs are necessary to achieve higher levels of success.

Universal usability can be defined as having more than 90% of all households as successful users of information and communications services at least once a week. A 1998 survey of U.S. households showed that 42% had computers and 26% used Internet-based e-mail or other services (NTIA, 1999). The French Minitel reaches 21% of residences, but the percentage of ICT users declines in poorer and less educated areas within the United States and in many countries around the world. Cost is an issue for many, but hardware limitations, perceived difficulty level, and lack of utility discourages others. If countries are to meet the goal of universal usability, then researchers must aggressively address usability issues.

This chapter presents a research agenda based on three challenges in attaining universal usability for Web-based and other services:

- **Technology variety:** Supporting a broad range of hardware, software, and network access.

- **User diversity:** Accommodating users with different skills, knowledge, age, gender, disabilities, disabling conditions (mobility, sunlight, noise), literacy, culture, income, and so forth.

- **Gaps in user knowledge:** Bridging the gap between what users know and what they need to know.

This list may not be complete, but it addresses important issues that are insufficiently funded by current initiatives. Research devoted to these challenges will have a broad range of benefits for first-time, intermittent, and frequent users.

The term *universal access* is usually linked to the U.S. Communications Act of 1934 covering telephone, telegraph, and radio services. It sought to ensure "adequate facilities at reasonable charges," especially in rural areas, and to prevent "discrimination on the basis of race, color, religion, national origin, or sex." The term universal access has been applied to computing services, but the greater complexity of computing services means that access is not sufficient to ensure successful usage. Therefore *universal usability* has emerged as an important issue and a topic for computing research. The complexity emerges, in part, from the high degree of interactivity that is necessary for information exploration, commercial applications, and creative activities. The Internet is compelling because of its support for interpersonal communications and decentralized initiatives:

Entrepreneurs can open businesses, journalists can start publications, and citizens can organize political movements.

The increased pressure for universal access and usability is a happy by-product of the growth of the Internet. Because services such as e-commerce, communication, education, health care, finance, and travel are expanding and users are becoming dependent on them, there is a strong push to ensure that the widest possible audience can participate. Another strong argument for universal usability comes from those who provide access to government information (such as the U.S. Library of Congress' THOMAS system that provides full texts of bills before the Congress) and the movement toward citizen services at federal, state, and local levels. These services include tax information and filing, social security benefits, passports, voting, licensing, recreation and parks, police and fire departments. Another circle of support includes employment agencies, training centers, parent-teacher associations, public interest groups, community services, and charitable organizations.

Critics of information technology abound, but they often focus on the creation of an information-poor minority—or worse—Internet apartheid. Although the gap in Internet usage has been declining between men and women, and between old and young, the gap is growing between rich and poor (see Fig. 12.1) and

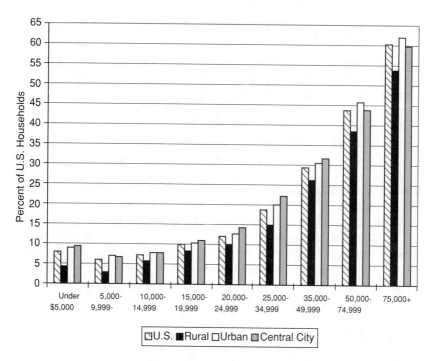

FIG 12.1.  Internet Use by Income—1998: Percent of U.S. households using the Internet is extremely low for low-income citizens, and rises dramtically for high-income citizens (NTIA, 1999).

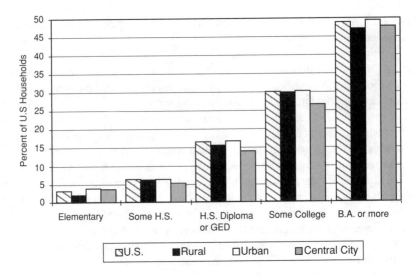

FIG 12.2.  Internet Use by Education—1998: Percent of U.S. households using the Internet is extremely low for poorly educated citizens, and rises dramtically for well-educated citizens (NTIA, 1999).

between well and poorly educated (see Fig. 12.2; Anderson, Bikson, Law, & Mitchell, 1995; NTIA, 1999). Less well documented is the continuing separation between cultural and racial groups and the low rates of usage by disadvantaged users whose unemployment, homelessness, poor health, or cognitive limitations raise further barriers (Silver, 1999; see also chapter 1, this volume).

There are other criticisms of information and communications systems that should be heard by technology promoters. These include concerns about break-down of community social systems, alienation of individuals that leads to crime and violence, loss of privacy, expansion of bureaucracies, and inadequate attention to potential failures (such as loss of power/data). Open public discussion of these issues by way of participatory design strategies and social impact statements might reduce negative and unanticipated side effects.

Technology enthusiasts can be proud of what has been accomplished and by the number of successful Internet users, but deeper insights will come from un-derstanding the problems of frustrated users and of those who have stayed away. Each step to broaden participation and reach these forgotten users by providing useful and usable services will bring credit to the field. A necessary first step is to formulate a research agenda.

## PREVIOUS RESEARCH AGENDAS

Growing attention has been paid to computing research issues related to univer-sal access and usability. The thoughtful and focused Rand Corporation report on universal access to e-mail (Anderson, Bikson, Law, & Mitchell, 1995) made it clear that better understanding of the capabilities and limitations of current user–computer interfaces is needed. Similarly, when the National Academy of Science/National Research Council convened a panel on "every-citizen" interfaces, it recommended an aggressive research program, funded by government and private sources, to examine both the human performance side of interfaces and the interface technologies, current and potential (CSTB, 1997).

During a well-financed but controversial study of 48 Pittsburgh-area homes, 133 participants received computers, free network connections, training, and assistance with problems. Even in such optimal conditions, a central limitation was the difficulties that users experienced with the services (Kraut, Scherlis, Mukhopadhyay, Manning, & Kiesler, 1996). The researchers wrote that even the easiest-to-use computers and applications pose significant barriers to the use of online services; even with help and our simplified procedure, HomeNet participants had trouble connecting to the Internet (for an update, see chapter 8, this volume).

As attention to the issue of universal access and usability grew, frameworks for analyzing problems appeared. Clement and Shade (1999) suggested seven layers of analysis: carriage facilities, devices, software tools, content services, service/access provision, literacy/social facilitation, and governance. They see usability as a problem, especially for users with disabilities, and encourage consideration of the wide range of users and needs. Universal usability is sometimes tied to meeting the needs of users who are disabled or work in disabling conditions. This important research direction is likely to benefit all users. The adaptability needed for users with diverse physical, visual, auditory, or cognitive disabilities is likely to benefit users with differing preferences, tasks, hardware, and so forth (Laux, McNally, Paciello, & Vanderheiden, 1996). Plasticity of the interface and presentation independence of the contents both contribute to universal usability.

## A UNIVERSAL USABILITY RESEARCH AGENDA

The research agenda presented here focuses on three universal usability challenges: technology variety, user diversity, and gaps in user knowledge. Skeptics caution that accommodating low-end technology, low-ability citizens, and low-skilled users will result in a lowest common denominator system that will be less useful to most users. This dark scenario, called *dumbing down*, is a reasonable fear, but my experience supports a brighter outcome.

I believe that accommodating a broader spectrum of usage situations forces researchers to consider a wider range of designs and often leads to innovations that benefit all users. For example, Web browsers, unlike word processors, reformat text to match the width of the window. This accommodates users with small displays (narrower than 640 pixels), and benefits users with larger displays (wider than 1,024 pixels), who can view more of a Web page with less scrolling. Accommodating narrower (less than 400 pixels) or wider (more than 1,200 pixels) displays presents the kind of challenge that may push designers to develop new ideas. For example, they could consider reducing font and image sizes for small displays, moving to a multicolumn format for large displays, exploring paging strategies (instead of scrolling), and developing overviews.

A second skeptics' caution, called the *innovation restriction scenario*, is that attempts to accommodate the low end (technology, ability, or skill) will constrain innovations for the high end. This is again a reasonable caution, but if designers are aware of this concern, the dangers seem avoidable. A basic HTML Web page accommodates low-end users, and sophisticated user interfaces using Java applets or Shockwave plug-ins can be added for users with advanced hardware and software, plus fast network connections. New technologies can often be provided as an add-on or plug-in, rather than a replacement. As new technologies become perfected and widely accepted, they become the new standard. Layered approaches have been successful in the past and they are compelling for accommodating a wide range of users. They are easy to implement when planned in advance, but often difficult to retrofit.

Advocates who promote accommodation of disabled users often cite the curb-cut—a scooped-out piece of sidewalk that allows wheelchair users to cross streets. Adding curb-cuts after the curbs have been built is expensive, but building them in advance reduces costs because less material is needed. The benefits extend to baby carriage pushers, delivery service workers, bicyclists, and travelers with roller bags. Computer-related accommodations that benefit many users are power switches in the front of computers, adjustable keyboards, and user control over audio volume, screen brightness, and monitor position.

Automobile designers have long understood the benefits of accommodating a wide range of users. They feature adjustable seats, steering wheels, mirrors, and lighting levels as standard equipment and offer optional equipment for those who need additional flexibility.

Reaching a broad audience is more than a democratic ideal; it makes good business sense. The case for network externalities, the concept that all users benefit from expanded participation, has been made repeatedly. Facilitating access and improving usability expands markets and increases participation of diverse users whose contributions may be valuable to many. Broadening participation is not only an issue of reducing costs for new equipment. As the number of users grows, the capacity to rapidly replace a majority of equipment declines, so strategies that accommodate a wide range of equipment will become even more in demand. With these concerns in mind, a three-part research agenda for universal usability may provoke innovations for all users.

## Technological Variety

Technological variety requires supporting a broad range of hardware, software, and network access. The first challenge (see Fig. 12.3) is to deal with the pace of

# Technology variety: Support broad range of hardware, software, and network access

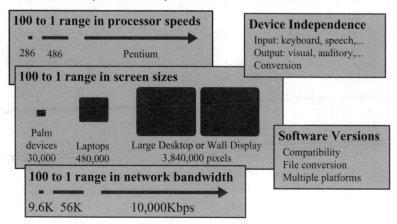

FIG 12.3. The first challenge is to cope with the technology variety by supporting the 100-to-1 range of hardware, software, and network access speeds.

technology change and the variety of equipment that users employ. The stabilizing forces of standard hardware, operating systems, network protocols, file formats, and user interfaces are undermined by the rapid pace of technological change. The technological innovators delight in novelty and improved features. They see competitive advantage to advanced designs, but these changes disrupt efforts to broaden audiences and markets. Because limiting progress is usually an unsatisfactory solution, an appealing strategy is to make information content, online services, entertainment, and user interfaces more malleable or adaptable.

The range of processor speeds in use varies by a factor of 1,000 or more. Moore's Law, which states that processor speeds double every 18 months, means that after 10 years, the speed of the newest processors are 100 times faster. Designers who wish to take advantage of new technologies risk excluding users with older machines. Similar changes for RAM and hard-disk space also inhibit current designers who wish to reach a wide audience. Other hardware improvements such as increased screen size and improved input devices also threaten to limit access. Research on accommodating varying processor speed, RAM, hard disk, screen size, and input devices could help cope with this challenge. How could users run the same calendar program on a handheld device, a laptop, and a wall-sized display?

Another research topic is software to convert interfaces and information across media or devices. For users who wish to get Web-page contents read to them over the telephone or for blind users, there are already some services (www.conversa.com), but improvements are needed to speed delivery and extract information appropriately (Thomas, Basson, & Gardner-Bonneau, 1999). Accommodating assorted input devices by a universal bus would allow third-party developers to create specialized and innovative devices for users with disabilities or special needs (Perry, Macken, Scott, & McKinley, 1997).

Software changes are a second concern. As applications programs mature and operating systems evolve, users of current software may find their programs become obsolete because newer versions fail to preserve file format compatibility. Some changes are necessary to support new features, but research is needed on modular designs that promote evolution while ensuring compatibility and bidirectional file conversion. The Java movement is a step in the right direction, in as much as it proposes to support platform independence, but its struggles indicate the difficulty of the problems.

Network access variety is a third problem. Some users will continue to use slower speed (14.4Kbps) dialup modems while others will use 10Mbps cable modems. This 100-fold speedup requires careful planning to accommodate. Because many Web pages contain large graphics, providing user control of byte counts would be advantageous. Most browsers allow users to inhibit graphics, but more flexible strategies are needed. Users should be able to select information-bearing graphics only or reduced byte count graphics, and invoke procedures on the server to compress the image from 300K to 80K or to 20K.

### User Diversity

User diversity involves accommodating users with different skills, knowledge, age, gender, disabilities, disabling conditions (mobility, sunlight, noise), literacy, culture, income, and so forth. A second challenge (see Fig. 12.4) to broadening

## User diversity: Accommodate different users

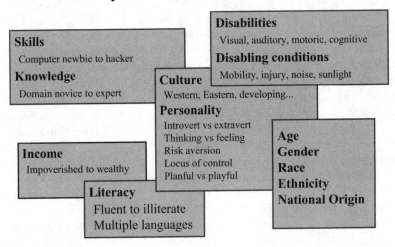

FIG 12.4.   The second challenge is to accommodate the enormous diversity of users.

participation is the diversity of users (Kobsa & Stephanidis, 1998). Because skill levels with computing vary greatly, search engines provide a basic and advanced dialogue box for query formulation. Since knowledge levels in an application domain vary greatly, some sites provide two or more versions. For example, the National Cancer Institute provides introductory cancer information for patients and details for physicians. Children differ from adults in their needs, so NASA provides a children's section on its space mission pages. Universities often segment their sites for applicants, current students, or alumni, but then provide links to shared resources of mutual interest. Segmentation creation and management tools would help developers wishing to pursue this strategy.

Similar segmenting strategies can be employed to accommodate users with poor reading skills or users who require other natural languages. Although there are some services to automatically convert Web pages to multiple languages (www.altavista.com and www.scn.org/spanish.html, for example), the quality of human translations is much better. Research on tools to facilitate preparation and updating of Web sites in multiple languages would be helpful. For example, if an e-commerce site maintained multiple language versions of a product catalog, then it would be useful to have a tool that facilitated simultaneous changes to a product price (possibly in different currencies), name (possibly in different character sets), or description (possibly tuned to regional variations). A more difficult problem comes in trying to accommodate users with a wide range of incomes, cultures, or religions. Imagine trying to prepare multiple music, food, or clothing catalogs that were tuned to local needs by emphasizing highly desired products and eliminating offensive items. E-commerce sites that are successful in these strategies are likely to be more widely used.

Another set of issues deals with the wide range of disabilities, or differential capabilities of users. Many systems allow partially sighted users, especially elderly users, to increase the font size or contrast in documents, but they rarely allow users to improve readability in control panels, help messages, or dialogue boxes. Blind users will be more active users of information and communications services if they can receive documents by speech generation or in Braille, and provide input by voice or their customized interfaces. Physically disabled users will eagerly use services if they can connect their customized interfaces to standard graphical user interfaces, even though they may work at a much slower pace. Cognitively impaired users with mild learning disabilities, dyslexia, poor memory, and other special needs could also be accommodated with modest changes to improve layouts, control vocabulary, and limit short-term memory demands.

Expert and frequent users also have special needs. Enabling customization that benefits high-volume users, macros to support repeated operations, and inclusion of special-purpose devices could benefit many. Research on high-end users could improve interfaces for all users.

Finally, appropriate services for a broader range of users need to be developed, tested, and refined. Corporate knowledge workers are the primary audience for many contemporary software projects, so the interface and information needs of the unemployed, homemakers, disabled, or migrant workers usually get less attention. This has been an appropriate business decision until now, but as the market broadens and key societal services are provided electronically, the forgotten users must be accommodated. For example, Microsoft Word provides templates for marketing plans and corporate reports, but every-citizen interfaces might help with job applications, babysitting cooperatives, or letters to city hall. And what about first aid, 911 emergency services, crime reporting, or poison control on the Web?

The growth of online support communities, medical first-aid guides, neighborhood-improvement councils, and parent-teacher associations will be accelerated as improved interface and information designs are developed. Community-oriented plans for preventing drug or alcohol abuse, domestic violence, or crime could also benefit from research on interface and information design. Such research is especially important for government Web sites, as their designers are moving toward providing basic services such as driver registration, business licenses, municipal services, tax filing, and eventually voting. Respect for the differing needs of users will do much to attract them to advanced technologies.

## Gaps in User Knowledge

Gaps in user knowledge addresses bridging the gap between what users know and what they need to know. A third challenge (see Fig. 12.5) is to bridge that gap. Many users do not know how to begin, what to select in dialogue boxes, how to handle system crashes, or what to do about viruses. Strategies include fade-able scaffolding, training wheels, and just-in-time training. Competing theories include minimalism, constructivism, and social construction, but their efficacy needs study.

Users approach new software tools with diverse skills and multiple intelligences. Some users need only a few minutes of orientation to understand the novelties and begin to use new tools successfully. Others need more time to acquire knowledge about the objects and actions in the application domain and the user interface. Research goals include validated guidance on lucid instructions, error prevention, graphical overviews, effective tutorials for novices, constructive help for intermittent users, and compact presentations for experts. Other researchable topics are easily reversible actions and detailed history keeping for review and consultation with peers and mentors. Reliable evidence from systematic logging of usage and observations of users would help greatly. Research on software tools and architectures would enable developers to provide higher quality universal interfaces.

A fundamental interface and information design research problem is how to support evolutionary learning. Proposals for layered designs, progressive disclosure, and comprehensible user-controlled options need to be implemented and tested. Could users begin with an interface that contained only basic features (say 5% of the full system) and become experts at this level within a few minutes? Game designers have created clever introductions that gracefully present new features as users acquire skill. Could similar techniques apply to the numerous features in

# Gaps in User Knowledge: Bridge the gap between what users know and what they need to know

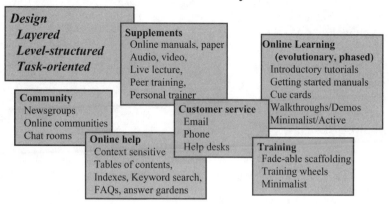

**Design**
**Layered**
**Level-structured**
**Task-oriented**

**Supplements**
Online manuals, paper
Audio, video,
Live lecture,
Peer training,
Personal trainer

**Online Learning**
(evolutionary, phased)
Introductory tutorials
Getting started manuals
Cue cards
Walkthroughs/Demos
Minimalist/Active

**Community**
Newsgroups
Online communities
Chat rooms

**Customer service**
Email
Phone
Help desks

**Online help**
Context sensitive
Tables of contents,
Indexes, Keyword search,
FAQs, answer gardens

**Training**
Fade-able scaffolding
Training wheels
Minimalist

FIG 12.5. The third challenge is to bridge the gap between what users know and what they need to know. Many strategies have been proposed but there are few evaluations and validated guidelines.

modern word processors, e-mail handlers, and Web browsers? A good beginning has been made with concepts such as layered implementations and the minimal manual (van der Meij & Carroll, 1995), but scaling up and broader application require further research.

Finally, the provision of online help by way of e-mail, telephone, video conferencing, and shared screens needs further research and design improvements. There is appealing evidence that social mechanisms among peers such as newsgroups, online communities, and FAQs are helpful, but there is little research that distinguishes among the best and worst of these. Best practices, validated analyses, guidelines, and theories could all be improved through extensive research.

## CONCLUSION

Attaining the benefits of universal access to Web-based and other information, communications, entertainment, and government services will require a more intense commitment to lowering costs, coupled with human-computer interaction research and usability engineering. A starting point for research would be a program that addressed at least the universal usability challenges of technology variety, user diversity, and gaps in user knowledge.

Research could pave the way for broad citizen participation in quality online services and novel social, economic, and political programs. America Online claims its service is "so easy to use, no wonder it's number one." They recognize the centrality of its service is usability, and have done well to make their services usable by many. Their success is admirable in reaching a fraction of the potential audience, but much work remains to achieve the goal of universal usability.

## ACKNOWLEDGMENT

This chapter is reprinted with permission from *Communications of the ACM*, May 2000, Vol. 43(5), 84–91.

## REFERENCES

Anderson, R. H., Bikson, T. K., Law, S. A., & Mitchell, B. M. (1995). *Universal access to e-mail: Feasibility and societal implications.* Santa Monica, CA: The Rand Corporation. Retrieved from www.rand.org/publications/MR/MR650/

Clement, A., & Shade, L.R. (1999). The access rainbow: Conceptualizing universal access to the information/communications infrastructure. In M. Gurstein (Ed.), *Community informatics: Enabling communities with information and communications technologies* (pp. 32–51). Hershey, PA: Idea Publishing.

Computer Science and Telecommunications Board (CSTB), National Research Council (1997). *More than screen deep: Toward an every citizen interface to the nation's information infrastructure.* Washington, DC: National Academy Press.

Kobsa, A., & Stephanidis, C. (1998). Adaptable and adaptive information access for all users, including disabled and elderly people. In *Proceedings of the Second Workshop on Adaptive Hypertext and Hypermedia,* ACM HYPERTEXT'98. Retrieved from wwwis.win.tue.nl/ah98/Kobsa.html

Kraut, R., Scherlis, W., Mukhopadhyay, T., Manning, J., & Kiesler, S. (1996). The HomeNet field trial of residential Internet services. *Communications of the ACM, 39*(12), 55–63.

Laux, L. F., McNally, P. R., Paciello, M. G., & Vanderheiden, G. C. (1996). Designing the World Wide Web for people with disabilities: A user-centered design approach. In *Proceedings of the Assets '96 Conference on Assistive Technologies* (pp. 94–101). New York: Association for Computing Machinery.

NTIA (1999, July). *Falling through the Net: Defining the digital divide.* National Telecommunication and Information Administration, U.S. Department of Commerce. Retrieved from http://www.ntia.doc.gov/ntiahome/fttn99/contents.html

Perry, J., Macken, E., Scott, N., & McKinley, L. (1997). Disability, inability, and cyberspace. In B. Friedman (Ed.), *Human values and the design of technology* (pp. 65–89). Cambridge, UK: CSLI Publications and Cambridge University Press.

Shneiderman, B. (1998). *Designing the user interface: Strategies for effective human–computer interaction* (3rd ed.).Reading, MA: Addison Wesley.

Silver, D. (1999). Margins in the wires: Looking for race, gender, and sexuality in the Blacksburg Electronic Village. In B. Kolko, L. Nakamura, & G. Rodman (Eds.), *Race in cyberspace: Politics, identity, and cyberspace* (pp. 133–150). London: Routledge.

Thomas, J. C., Basson, S., & Gardner-Bonneau, D. (1999). Universal design and assistive technology. In D. Gardner-Bonneau (Ed.), *Human factors and voice interactive systems* (pp. 135–146). Boston: Kluwer Academic Publishers.

van der Meij, H., & Carroll, J. M. (1995). Principles and heuristics in designing minimalist instruction. *Technical Communication, 42*(2), 243–261.

# Conclusions and Connections

# 13

# Integrating the Research on Media Access: A Critical Overview

Leah A. Lievrouw

*University of California, Los Angeles*

What is *media access?* The chapters in this volume attempt to formulate an answer to this question through analyses of the social and psychological factors that may affect it. To their credit, the contributors have attempted to breathe some life into a term that has become overused and flattened out, an easy, almost value-free placeholder for a complex of resources, actions, expectations, and institutional forms and arrangements that affect the distribution and uses of media in society.

Yet "access," as it relates to information and communication technologies (ICTs), is seldom explicitly defined, even by experts. We tend to use the word as though we all know what we are talking about, or that we know it when we see it (just as we frequently do with such commonly used terms as *information, technology,* or *communication,* for that matter). Alternatively, we use it to mean different things: sometimes the existence of certain technologies or services, sometimes the policies that encourage technology adoption, sometimes technology use itself, sometimes the cognitive abilities to make sense of content. We are casual with definitions despite the fact that the ones that survive, either by design or default, shape the ways that important social, cultural, cognitive, economic, and political problems are framed and studied. So the definitional purpose of this book is not a trivial exercise.

I appreciate this opportunity to comment on the phenomenon of media access in general, and to the contributions to this book in particular. In this final chapter, I summarize some of the basic premises and findings that are presented and point out themes or frames that seem to me to run through the whole work. Second,

I return to the definitional question and propose a framework for synthesizing the various premises and themes that places the notion of "access" in a larger conceptual context.

## THEMES IN MEDIA ACCESS RESEARCH

One of the main strengths of the preceding chapters is that they question some enduring assumptions in the research on ICTs and access. Principal among these is the traditional idea (widely held by policy researchers) that "access" is reducible to the availability of a service: the equivalent of telephone dial tone, over-the-air broadcasts, or the open doors of a library. It is achieved when a given technology or service is made available, whether or not it is relevant to the community involved, useful to its members, or, in fact, used at all. In the United States, as contributor Ben Shneiderman points out, the concept has its roots in the universal service policy for telephony, the brainchild of AT&T President Theodore Vail, which was integrated into the U.S. Communications Act of 1934. Vail understood that "universal service at affordable prices," based on a system of cross-subsidies for different levels of service, could serve as a strategic *quid pro quo* in exchange for monopoly protection. It would allow AT&T to eliminate or absorb its competitors and expand its system nationwide. Furthermore, AT&T's universal service obligations were strictly limited to the provision of service itself (i.e., "dial tone"); the firm would have no control over or responsibility for the messages or other information carried by the system (Brooks, 1975; Fischer, 1992; Mueller, 1993; Pool, 1977).

When "access" is conceived this way—that is, strictly in terms of technological infrastructure—the technology tends to be treated as a given. The analytic focus shifts to the demographic characteristics (e.g., income, education, gender, age, ethnicity) of the individuals who use the service versus those who do not. Data is collected about the distribution of these traits among users and nonusers, and inferences are drawn about the extent to which the traits influence or drive access. The bias toward a focus on technological availability (sometimes referred to as the *conduit* metaphor; Day, 2000; Lievrouw, 2000) has persisted in media and information policy to the present day. However, many policy experts now contend that the mere availability of an information or communication system is not a sufficient condition for real media access (for example, see the recent special issue of *The Information Society* on changing notions of universal service; Sawhney, 2000). Some have suggested that the term *universal access* should replace *universal service* because access must take into account the abilities of users and the availability of relevant and useful content as well as the provision of an information technology system or service.

The contributors here would certainly agree. If there is a single premise that knits these chapters together, it is that neither the availability of technology infrastructure or services, nor the demographics of ICT users, is enough to explain, let alone predict, whether or how those technologies will be used in everyday life. Yet, as many of the authors assembled here note, most of the recent "digital divide" studies have been framed in just this way. Although such studies lay some important groundwork and suggest interesting problems for further research, in the end they do not say much about media access *per se* or how it works.

In a recent volume of the *Annual Review of Information Science and Technology*, Sharon Farb and I have argued that most research on the digital divide, like other traditional studies of access to information, take what we call a *vertical* perspective on equity. Investigators often (implicitly) equate demographic advantages (greater wealth, higher education levels, youth, "whiteness," and so on) with greater access to, and more effective use of, better quality information resources across the board. Yet a moment's reflection suggests that access to ICTs, like access to information, is likely to vary even within groups that are demographically homogeneous, to the extent that those individuals' interests, experiences, roles, and skills differ. Such within-group differences have rarely been studied in media access research, and they require what we call a *horizontal* analytical perspective to complement the conventional vertical view (Lievrouw & Farb, 2003).

That said, there seems to be ample, if implicit, appreciation for the horizontal perspective throughout the chapters of *Media Access*. The studies presented here consistently focus on the abilities or readiness of people to use and benefit from ICTs, and on the nature of available media content. The book is organized by discipline; the more psychologically (or social-psychologically) inclined authors tend to think about user abilities in terms of individual differences in cognitive information processing, attitudes, motivations, self-efficacy, personality, and so on. Those who lean toward sociological accounts emphasize users' (and nonusers') social networks, family ties, gender and ethnic roles, technical and job skills, cultural capital, institutional resources, and the like. On the political side, several contributors examine the effects of differing levels of political participation, efficacy, and power, along with the willingness and ability of citizens to express opinions and debate issues.

Clearly, a complex and interacting set of factors comes into play when users engage with any type of media system. Influences at both the individual and social levels help shape the kind and quality of content that people seek and share through those systems. However, I suggest that there may be no stable inventory of factors or "determinants" implicated in every instance of media access. Instead, it may be useful to think about the relevant factors in terms of what the economist and philosopher Amartya Sen called *capabilities*. Sen doubted that complete equality in the distribution of any ability, resource, or outcome is ever achievable and famously posed the question, "Equality of what?" (Sen, 1973, 1992). Rather than viewing resources, skills, and other individual-level characteristics as ends in themselves, and attempt to equalize or remediate them, he argued, they are more properly seen as means to an end. The ability to effectually utilize various resources, technologies, or skills varies from person to person, group to group, situation to situation.

Therefore, Sen argued, our main concern should be in creating and maintaining the individual's *agency*, that is, his or her achievement of well being (not just the state of well-being itself). Agency is fostered by cultivating one's *functionings* and *capabilities*. "Functionings," Garnham (1999, p. 117) noted, "are what a person does or is. Capabilities are the set of alternative functionings a person has (his or her real opportunities)." Therefore, to promote access, we should think more generally in terms of the fair distribution of opportunities that allow people to achieve whatever they may value doing or being, the individual's "freedom to lead one type of life or another" (Sen, 1992, p. 40). Put another way, an effectual approach to enhancing media access would promote the fair distribution of capabilities.

A third thread that runs through these chapters is that many of the authors see media access through the prism of *barriers*. They are often as interested in what *prevents* media access as what *promotes* it. Bucy's notion of the "interactivity paradox"—that the increased skills required of and cognitive demands imposed on users of interactive systems can lead to cognitive overload, confusion, uncertainty, and to less effective access—is a prime example, as is the focus by Bessiere et al. on the frustrations that users of ICTs (specifically, computers) experience in the face of system breakdowns. Several authors examine demographic and cultural barriers to media access. Grabe and Kamhawi, for instance, find that education level is an important factor influencing media users' ability to encode information. Rojas et al. conclude that the cultural "habitus" of underserved ethnic groups can discourage computer use. Other contributors find that personality traits, self-efficacy, motivations, and uneven technical skills are potential barriers as well.

## THE DEFINITIONAL QUESTION

But let us return to the original question: What exactly *is* media access? Although this discussion has unearthed some clues about what can promote or prevent it, we have not yet arrived at a clear definition of media access itself. The title of this volume and several of the chapters (e.g., Rojas et al., Youtie et al., Jackson et al.) seem to equate access with ICT use. Other authors seem to be more concerned with whether individuals have the abilities or psychological resources to benefit from use (e.g., Newhagen & Bucy, Grabe & Kamhawi, Finn & Korukonda, McCrery & Newhagen, van Dijk). The availability of meaningful and relevant content is frequently cited as an essential factor.

Yet "media access," even in a book dedicated to explicating it, still seems to be a moving target. Perhaps the difficulty lies not with the term itself, nor with the authors' attempts to nail it down. Rather, it may be that we are asking the term to do too much, theoretically. I argue that access is just one element—perhaps not even the major element—in a complex process of information generation, circulation, sharing, and use that is supported by media technologies.

Elsewhere (Lievrouw, 2000, 2001), I proposed a model of the *information environment* that includes access as one element among many in a cycle of "informing." Ultimately, people who engage with ICTs exist in a complex life-world where "access" is just one step in an ongoing process of sense-making and action-taking. Individuals, groups, and societies inhabit different information environments at different times and places. Indeed, most of us move among several environments at once, and for some people, new media technologies have made this complex topography much easier to navigate.

In a sense, the editors have handed me the "data" (in the form of the preceding chapters) that comprise a sort of natural experiment or test of the model. Figure 13.1 summarizes the main features of the information environment model. Interested readers may wish to consult the more extensive discussion in the article that appeared in *New Media & Society* (Lievrouw, 2001). For the present discussion, I focus on two components of the model that are reflected in the chapters here: *capacity* (the central two-headed arrow) and the *cycle of informing* (the circular dotted arrow). Both elements span the boundary between the institutional and personal/relational domains or aspects of the model. That is, both capacity and informing are phenomena that are affected by the larger social, cultural, and institutional setting or milieu on one hand, and by people's individual actions and relationships on the other.

*Capacity* is defined as one's state of knowledge or ability to act individually or collectively. People exercise their capacity through face-to-face and mediated communication. Knowledge implies an understanding (tacitly, in many cases) of the circumstances and relationships within an individual's social world. I have suggested that capacity includes *personal factors*, such as literacy, innovativeness, technical or communicative competence, motivation, social intelligence, or social capital (see Coleman, 1988; Cronin & Davenport, 1993; Putnam, 2000). The evidence presented in this book suggests that several of these factors, including innovativeness, motivation, and social capital, play an important role in the cycle of informing. Studies gathered here specifically explain how cognitive abilities, emotions, attitudes, personality characteristics, and self-efficacy affect access to the information environment.

Capacity also includes *situational factors* that are more external to the actors involved: geographic location, community norms and beliefs, social network structures, time, economic means, and the like. The findings from several other chapters testify to the influential role that situational factors, notably social networks, cultural capital, and habitus (especially the normative expectations of the social group), play in determining access. Other situational factors suggested in this book include public sphere participation and the range of technologies and infrastructures available to users. Overall, then, the contributors have demonstrated that a complex set of interrelated factors, which might be characterized collectively as *capacity*, are involved in media access and use.

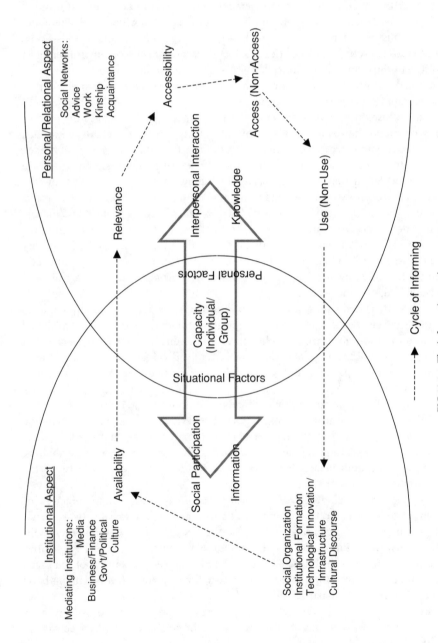

FIG 13.1. The information environment.

In the end, however, capacity is a state. The challenge is to relate that state to action, specifically, to "access." This brings in the second element of the model, informing.[1] Informing is fundamentally social and interactive; it is never complete but is a perpetual structuration-type process of organization, disorganization, and reorganization of knowledge and information[2] that occurs recursively. People in an information environment share what they know; they create and use information via various information and communication technologies. And in their interpersonal relations they express, break down, and change their shared understanding(s). Through this process, individuals share a sense of understanding the same things and, therefore, that they belong together, or share an information environment. When this understanding is lost or shifts, the information environment changes and can break down.

There is no beginning or ending point of informing. But to follow the dotted arrow in Fig. 13.1, we can begin in the institutional domain with *availability.* This is the presence and circulation of information in the environment via interpersonal interaction as well as through the use of ICTs. Individuals, groups, organizations, or institutions can create and distribute information, that is, make it available. The availability of information, in turn, can affect the character or sensibility of the environment. However, just because information is available does not insure that potential users will necessarily know about it or share it. For information to be appropriated and used, we move to the personal/relational domain, where users must first recognize the *relevance* of the information that is available, often through interaction with others.[3] That is, they must decide whether the information is interesting or useful to them personally or to people they know. So the presence or availability of information is distinct from its relevance in a particular social or cultural context.

When information is both available and relevant, the next step is assessing its *accessibility,* that is, whether it can in fact be obtained, either from other people or via media channels. All of us have experienced situations in which we learn that information is available and relevant to our interests but may not be accessible due to technical, economic, or cultural barriers. Agada (2002) gave the example of people in certain West African nations who have accessibility problems with the Internet because, of all the content that is available online and relevant to them, perhaps only a handful of pages are in their local language.

## DEFINING MEDIA ACCESS

So in the context of the present discussion, what is media access? I argue that it is the act of employing ICTs to obtain or retrieve information, or to communicate with others, in personally meaningful ways. This seems to be the definition that most of the contributors to this book share, although not explicitly in these terms. Indeed, users of information and communication technologies must first recognize what media (both channels and content) are available to them, and then determine their relevance to their interests or purposes. If perceived as relevant, these technologies must be understandable, usable, affordable, and local (i.e., accessible) if they are going to be employed in meaningful ways. If information is indeed accessible, one must then choose whether to actually *access*, capture, or retrieve it.

Importantly, access to information can be an end in itself. The research experience, in which articles downloaded or photocopied for potential use are not always cited or even consulted, provides a familiar example. Upon retrieval of a particular citation that sounds interesting, we may read the article and use ideas or findings from it in our next paper, book, or conference presentation. Or we may simply add the copy to one of a half-dozen project stacks where it may sit until, and if, we decide to even read it![4] In this respect, *media* access is more complex than *information* access—the act of obtaining information that is available, relevant, and accessible, from whatever source—because with media access, it is necessary to distinguish between access to, and use of, a particular channel. In the typology employed by Newhagen and Bucy in the introduction to this book, *access to* a media channel constitutes technological access, while *use of* a particular media channel constitutes content access. If we include both channel and content considerations in our definition, as the editors and contributors advocate, it seems clear that barriers to media access may indeed occur on multiple levels.

When they argue that appropriate, relevant, and understandable content should be made available via ICTs, a number of the authors represented here seem to be describing elements of the informing process diagrammed in Fig. 13.1. When Rojas et al., for example, propose that the cultural habitus of Hispanic teens in East Austin prevents or discourages them from using computers, they are talking about relevance and accessibility. When Bucy says that interactive technologies demand so much cognitive effort that users become overloaded and confused, or Bessiere et al. document the frustration of computer users, they are telling stories about what makes ICTs accessible. When McCrery and Newhagen find that people with high levels of political efficacy attend to or "consume" more media and engage in more political participation, they are discussing not just media access but the uses of media in the process of social and institutional change. In his provocative and insightful chapter, van Dijk even unpacks "access" into four progressive stages— mental, material, skills, and usage—that, from my perspective, resemble relevance, accessibility, access, and use in the cycle of informing. There are a half-dozen more examples in the preceding pages.

To conclude this brief commentary, I believe that the authors have done an outstanding job of trying to shift the media access research agenda in a new direction. Many of their theoretical constructs and empirical findings can be knitted together into a more comprehensive descriptive framework, which itself may suggest new categories of research questions or hypotheses. Media access is a multifaceted and rich phenomenon, and this book sets a new criterion for future work in the area.

# ENDNOTES

[1] The notion of informing is derived from definitions of information that emphasize its organized, represented, formal nature. That is, information is created when an actor gives shape or imposes structure on experience, sense perceptions, or otherwise less-organized data or stimuli—the actor "in-forms" their perception of the world. See Machlup (1983) and Pratt (1977).

[2] In Lievrouw (2001, p. 13) I proposed the following definitions: "*Knowledge* is the state of the 'knower,' the 'capacity for social action' which 'enables an actor . . . to set something in motion' (Stehr, 1994, p. 95). *Information* is a consequence or product of knowledge in the form of artifacts or expressions (such as documents, conversations, artworks, or cultural practices). *Communication*—coordinated action that achieves understanding or shares meaning (Rogers & Kincaid, 1981)—is the bridge between knowledge and information."

[3] Relevance is a key concept in information seeking and retrieval research. For overviews, see Harter (1992); Saracevic (1975); and Schamber (1994).

[4] Our use or nonuse sends us back into the institutional domain of the information environment model, as it affects such factors as social organization, institutional forms, cultural discourse, and content production. These factors, in turn, determine what information is subsequently available.

# REFERENCES

Agada, J. (2002, November). *Bridging the digital divide as capacity building for the information economy.* Presentation to the annual conference of the American Society for Information Science and Technology, Philadelphia, PA.

Brooks, J. (1975). *Telephone: The first hundred years.* New York: Harper & Row.

Coleman, J. S. (1988). Social capital in the creation of human capital. *American Journal of Sociology, 94,* S95–S120.

Cronin, B., & Davenport, E. (1993). Social intelligence. *Annual Review of Information Science and Technology, 28,* 3–44.

Day, R. E. (2000). The "conduit metaphor" and the nature and politics of information studies. *Journal of the American Society for Information Science, 51,* 805–811.

Fischer, C. (1992). *America calling: A social history of the telephone to 1940.* Berkeley: University of California Press.

Garnham, N. (1999). Amartya Sen's "capabilities" approach to the evaluation of welfare: Its application in communications. In A. Calabrese & J.-C. Burgelman (Eds.), *Communication, citizenship and social policy: Rethinking the limits of the welfare state* (pp. 113–124). Lanham, MD: Rowman & Littlefield.

Harter, S. (1992). Psychological relevance and information science. *Journal of the American Society for Information Science, 43*(9), 602–615.

Lievrouw, L. A. (2000). The information environment and universal service. *The Information Society, 16*(2), 155–159.

Lievrouw, L. A. (2001). New media and the "pluralization of life-worlds": A role for information in social differentiation. *New Media & Society, 3*(1), 7–28.

Lievrouw, L. A., & Farb, S.E. (2003). Information and equity. *Annual Review of Information Science and Technology, 37,* 499–540.

Machlup, F. (1983). Semantic quirks in studies of information. In F. Machlup & U. Mansfield (Eds.), *The study of information: Interdisciplinary messages* (pp. 641–671). New York: John Wiley & Sons.

Mueller, M. (1993). Universal service in telephone history: A reconstruction. *Telecommunications Policy, 17*(5), 352–369.

Pool, I. de S. (Ed.). (1977). *The social impact of the telephone.* Cambridge, MA: MIT Press.

Pratt, A. D. (1977). The information of the image: A model of the communications process. *Libri, 27*(3), 204–220.

Putnam, R. D. (2000). *Bowling alone: The collapse and revival of American community.* New York: Simon & Schuster.

Rogers, E. M., & Kincaid, D. L. (1981). *Communication networks: Toward a new paradigm for research.* New York: The Free Press.

Saracevic, T. (1975). Relevance: A review of a framework for thinking on the notion of information science. *Journal of the American Society for Information Science, 26,* 321–343.

Sawhney, H. (2000). Universal service: Separating the grain of truth from the proverbial chaff. *The Information Society, 16*(2), 161–164.

Schamber, L. (1994). Relevance and information behavior. *Annual Review of Information Science and Technology, 29,* 3–48.

Sen, A. (1973). *On economic inequality.* Oxford: Clarendon Press.

Sen, A. (1992). *Inequality reexamined.* Cambridge, MA: Harvard University Press, for the Russell Sage Foundation of New York.

Stehr, N. (1994). *Knowledge societies.* London: Sage.

# About the Contributors

**Gretchen Barbatsis** is a professor in the Department of Telecommunication at Michigan State University. Her primary research interests are the use of mass media for empowering the global community, participant-voiced design, and the construction of culturally sensitive media for education in developing countries. She is the author of numerous media material and journal articles and has led several major media projects in Africa.

**Katherine Bessière** is a PhD student in the Human–Computer Interaction Institute at Carnegie Mellon University. Her interests lie in the social impact of information and communications technology, the Internet as a social medium, and user frustration.

**Frank Biocca** is the Ameritech Chair of Telecommunication Technology and Information Services and professor of cognitive science at Michigan State University. Biocca studies how mind and media interfaces can be coupled to extend human cognition and enhance human performance. He directs the networked Media Interface and Network Design (M.I.N.D.) Lab. The M.I.N.D. Lab is an international, multiuniversity human–computer interaction and communication research lab (http://www.mindlab.org).

**Erik P. Bucy** is an assistant professor in the Department of Telecommunications and adjunct assistant professor in the School of Informatics at Indiana University, Bloomington. His research focuses on the social impact of information technology, the effects of compelling images in the news, and normative theories of media and democracy. Bucy is the editor of *Living in the Information Age: A New Media Reader* (Wadsworth, 2002). His research has recently been published in the *Journal of Communication, New Media & Society, Communication Research, Press/Politics, JASIS,* and *Journalism & Mass Communication Quarterly.*

**Irina Ceaparu** is a graduate student in the Department of Computer Science at the University of Maryland, College Park. She is currently working in the Human–Computer Interaction Laboratory, under the guidance of Ben Shneiderman.

**Seth Finn** is a professor of Communications and Information Systems at Robert Morris University in Pittsburgh. Since his days as a television news producer at KRON-TV, San Francisco, he has been interested in the nature of information, human motivations for processing it, and the impact of personality on media and computer use. His research, addressing issues in uses and gratifications and information theory, has been published primarily in *Communication Research, Written Communication,* and *Journalism & Mass Communication Quarterly.*

**Hiram E. Fitzgerald** is University Distinguished Professor of Psychology at Michigan State University. His research interests include methods for connecting universities and their knowledge base to the community by way of programs for children, youth, and families, the consequences of parental alcoholism for child development, and the health care and policy issues for children of color. Recent publications include a three-volume series (with Barry M. Lester and Barry S. Zuckerman): *Children of Addiction* (RoutledgeFalmer, 2000), *Children of Color* (Garland, 1999), and *Children of Poverty* (Garland, 1995). He is author of over 150 professional publications and is currently serving as Assistant Provost University Outreach.

**Maria Elizabeth Grabe** is an associate professor in the Ernie Pyle School of Journalism at Indiana University, Bloomington. Prior to earning her PhD from Temple University, she was a television news producer for the South African Broadcasting Corporation and documentary news producer for KCTF public television in Waco, Texas. Her research focuses on the content and effects of electronic media. She has recently published work in *Communication Research, Journalism & Mass Communication Quarterly, Journal of Broadcasting & Electronic Media,* and *Critical Studies in Media Communication.*

**C. Richard Hofstetter** is a professor in the Department of Political Science and adjunct professor in the Graduate School of Public Health at San Diego State University. Areas of research and teaching include political communication, research methods, statistics, public health (health promotion), and computer applications. He has published numerous articles in political science, communication, and public health and medicine. He has also published a series of articles about political talk radio.

**Linda A. Jackson** is a professor in the Department of Psychology at Michigan State University. Her areas of research interest include the motivational, affective, and cognitive antecedents and consequences of technology use (e.g., Internet), the sociopsychological bases for the racial digital divide, cultural influences on cognition that impact learning in information technology environments, and race/ethnicity and gender differences in values that influence the choice of IT careers. She is author of over 100 professional publications, including two books and five book chapters, and principal investigator on a grant from the National Science Foundation to study Internet use in low-income families.

**Rasha Kamhawi** is a lecturer at Ain Shams University in Cairo, Egypt and a doctoral candidate in the Ernie Pyle School of Journalism at Indiana University, Bloomington. Her research interests include visual communication and information processing of television messages. Her work has appeared in *Journalism & Mass Communication Quarterly.*

**Appa Rao Korukonda** is a professor of Computer Information Systems in the College of Business at Bloomsburg University of Pennsylvania. Korukonda has published in such journals as *Interfaces, Journal of Organization Change Management, Group & Organization Studies, International Journal of Quality and Reliability Management, OR/MS Today, International Journal of Production Economics, IBS Computing Quarterly, SAM Advanced Management Journal,* and *International Journal of Production Research.* His current research interests include management information systems, organization theory, business ethics, philosophy of science, and artificial intelligence.

**Greg Laudeman** is a community technology specialist in the Economic Development Institute at the Georgia Institute of Technology in Atlanta, Georgia. He conducts training and provides technical assistance on information technology and telecommunications issues to state and local governments and economic development organizations. His work has appeared in *Municipal Telecom* and he has been a featured speaker at the Directions and Implications of Advanced Computing Symposium as well as the Telecommunications Policy Research Conference (TPRC).

**Jonathan Lazar** is an assistant professor in the Department of Computer and Information Sciences at Towson University and affiliate professor in Towson University's Center for Applied Information Technology. He is the author of *User-Centered Web Development* (Jones and Bartlett, 2001) and editor of *Managing IT/Community Partnerships in the 21st Century* (Idea Group Publishing, 2002). Lazar's current research focuses on user frustration, errors, Web usability, Web accessibility, and online trust.

**Leah A. Lievrouw** is a professor in the Department of Information Studies at the University of California, Los Angeles. She is also affiliated with UCLA's Communication Studies program. Her research and writing focus on the social and cultural changes associated with information and communication technologies and the relationship between new technologies and knowledge. She is co-editor of *The Handbook of New Media: Social Shaping and Consequences of ICTs* (with Sonia Livingstone; Sage, 2002); *Mediation, Information and Communication: Information and Behavior, Vol. 3* (with Brent Ruben; Transaction, 1990); and *Competing Visions, Complex Realities: Social Aspects of the Information Society* (with Jorge Reina Schement; Ablex, 1987). She also serves as an editor of the journal *New Media & Society,* published by Sage.

**Johnette Hawkins McCrery** is an assistant professor of communications at Louisiana State University at Shreveport. Her research focuses on political efficacy and public sphere participation, and her teaching interests include print and broadcast journalism and public relations.

**John E. Newhagen** is an associate professor in the Philip Merrill College of Journalism, University of Maryland, College Park. He worked as a foreign correspondent in Central America and the Caribbean for nearly 10 years and served as bureau chief in San Salvador, regional correspondent in Mexico City, and foreign editor in Washington, DC for United Press International during the 1980s. Newhagen's research on the effects of emotion in television and on the Internet have been published widely in a number of leading academic journals. He has also written about the effects of new media on journalism and is currently looking at the role of emotion in socially desirable responses to Web-based surveys.

**John Robinson** is a professor in the Department of Sociology at the University of Maryland, College Park. His areas of specialization include time use; societal trends and social change; the impact of the mass media and Internet on society; and social science methodology. He is the author of *Time for Life: The Surprising Ways Americans Spend Time* (Penn State Press, 1997), *Measures of Political Attitudes* (Academic Press, 1999), and *Measures of Personality and Social Psychological Attitudes* (Academic Press, 1991).

**Viviana Rojas** is an assistant professor at the University of Texas, San Antonio. She teaches intercultural communication and communication theory. Her research focuses on Latinos and media, Latina feminist studies, minorities and the digital divide, gender studies, intercultural communication, cultural and critical studies, and qualitative methodologies. Her dissertation, completed at the University of Texas, Austin, was a study of Latinos' image on Spanish-language television.

**Philip Shapira** is a professor in the School of Public Policy at the Georgia Institute of Technology in Atlanta, Georgia, and visiting researcher, Fraunhofer Institute for Systems and Innovation Research (ISI) in Karlsruhe, Germany. He teaches and conducts research on industrial competitiveness, innovation, and technology, as well as economic and regional development. Among other titles, Shapira is co-editor of *Learning from Science and Technology Policy Evaluation* (Edward Elgar, 2003).

**Ben Shneiderman** is a professor in the Department of Computer Science, founding director (1983–2000) of the Human–Computer Interaction Laboratory (HCIL), and member of the Institutes for Advanced Computer Studies and Systems Research, all at the University of Maryland, College Park. He is the author of *Designing the User Interface: Strategies for Effective Human–Computer Interaction* (3rd ed., Addison-Wesley, 1998). His most recent book is *Leonardo's Laptop: Human Needs and the New Computing Technologies* (MIT Press, 2002).

**Joseph D. Straubhaar** is Amon G. Carter Professor of Communication in the Radio-TV-Film Department at the University of Texas, Austin and director of the Brazil Center within the Lozano Long Institute of Latin American Studies. He previously taught at Brigham Young University and Michigan State University. Prior to earning his PhD in International Communication from the Fletcher School of Law and Diplomacy, Tufts University, he worked as a foreign service officer in Brazil and Washington. He has published extensively on international media studies, new information technologies, and the digital divide.

**Jan A.G.M. van Dijk** is chair of the Sociology of the Information Society and professor of applied communication science in the Department of Communication at the University of Twente, the Netherlands. He has been investigating the social aspects of information and communication technology since 1984. His research specializes in social, cultural, and political/policy issues. Recent books in English include *The Network Society: Social Aspects of New Media* (Sage, 1999) and *Digital Democracy: Issues of Theory & Practice* (co-edited with Kenneth L. Hacker; Sage, 2000).

**Alexander von Eye** earned his PhD in 1976 from the University of Trier, Germany. He is a professor in the Department of Psychology at Michigan State University. His main research interests include methods of analyzing categorical data, longitudinal data, computational statistics, and modeling. He has authored or edited 16 books, mostly on topics concerning statistical methods and their application in social science research.

**Jan Youtie** is a principal research associate in the Economic Development Institute and an adjunct associate professor in the School of Public Policy at the Georgia Institute of Technology in Atlanta, Georgia. Her research areas are in technology-based economic development, telecommunications policy, and manufacturing modernization. Her work has appeared in *Economic Development Quarterly, Evaluation and Program Planning,* and the *Journal of Technology Transfer.* She is co-author of *Telecommunications Strategy for Economic Development* (with William H. Read; Praeger, 1996).

**Yong Zhao** is an associate professor of Educational Psychology and Technology in the College of Education at Michigan State University. His research areas include innovation diffusion in educational settings, online learning communities, and teacher adoption of technology. He has recently published in *Teachers College Record, Journal of Computers and Human Behavior,* and *Journal of Education Computing Research.*

# Author Index

# Subject Index